SENECA

VIII

TRAGEDIES

LCL 62

SENECA

HERCULES · TROJAN WOMEN
PHOENICIAN WOMEN
MEDEA · PHAEDRA

EDITED AND TRANSLATED BY

JOHN G. FITCH

HARVARD UNIVERSITY PRESS
CAMBRIDGE, MASSACHUSETTS
LONDON, ENGLAND
2002

First published 2002

LOEB CLASSICAL LIBRARY® is a registered trademark
of the President and Fellows of Harvard College

Library of Congress Control Number 2002-190202
CIP data available from the Library of Congress

ISBN 978-0-674-99602-1

*Composed in ZephGreek and ZephText by
Technologies 'N Typography, Merrimac, Massachusetts.
Printed on acid-free paper and bound by
The Maple-Vail Book Manufacturing Group*

CONTENTS

For Linda

comes comis

ACKNOWLEDGMENTS

For many turns of translation that could not be improved, I am indebted to Frank Justus Miller, my predecessor as Loeb translator, and to others including Frederick Ahl, A. J. Boyle, Elaine Fantham, H. M. Hine, Douglass Parker, and E. F. Watling. In perplexities I have been helped by the commentaries now available on individual plays, above all those of R. J. Tarrant (*Agamemnon, Thyestes*). My University of Victoria colleague C. J. Littlewood read my translation of *Trojan Women* at an early stage and improved it substantially. This work is dedicated to my wife, Linda, who has read aloud every word of these translations, and has offered companionship throughout my Senecan studies.

J.G.F.

Senecan Plays:

Ag = Agamemnon
Herc = Hercules
Med = Medea
Oed = Oedipus

Pha = Phaedra
Phoen = Phoenician Women
Thy = Thyestes
Tro = Trojan Women

Probably Not By Seneca:

HO = Hercules on Oeta   Oct = Octavia

GENERAL INTRODUCTION

Rhetoric

Senecan drama is a drama of the word. Its speeches are eloquent, forceful, delighting in the language and in the poetic medium. Their fluency reflects the rhetorical training which Seneca received, and which had become established as the standard form of higher education at Rome in the second half of the first century B.C.—so much so that all Roman writers from Ovid on reflect its influence in varied ways. Seneca's interest in powerful utterance does not, of course, exclude an interest in other things, in action and character, but they are mediated through the rhetoric. He is a master of pace and diction: a master at contrasting long, flowing sentences with brief pithy ones, and at varying high-flown poetic language with simple direct speech. Such verbal energy is highly theatrical, in all senses; it invites comparison immediately with the verve of blank verse in the hands of Marlowe or Shakespeare. Often, too, Senecan rhetoric, like that of the Elizabethan dramatists, makes a virtue of excess, in the sense that its excesses match excesses of emotion and attitude in the *dramatis personae*. Above all, the script of Seneca's dramas demands performance, as much as a musical score does. At the very least, the reader needs to imagine this poetry spoken on the living voice, in order to gain some sense of its intoxicating richness.

The flow of Seneca's rhetoric carries one soon to a list or catalogue. Such lists were a constituent of eloquence long before the systematisation of rhetoric (witness Clytemnestra's account of the beacon relay in Aeschylus' *Agamemnon*), but in Seneca they become an important resource in *inventio*, the development of material. He gives us memorable lists of constellations in the night sky (*Herc* 6–18), of kingdoms in Asia Minor (*Phoen* 602–13), of places in the countryside of Attica (*Pha* 1–30), of the far-ranging exploits of Bacchus (*Oed* 413–505). One deployment of a list is to give definition first by multiple negations and then by affirmation: not A, not B, not C, but D. So the famous passage in *Thyestes* on gaining kingship declares that one does not need to use horses, nor weapons, nor arrows such as those shot by the Parthians, nor siege engines: true kingship is self-bestowed (381–89). Just the same pattern appears in Hamlet's eloquent distinction between outward and inward grief:

> 'Tis not alone my inky cloak, good mother,
> Nor customary suits of solemn black,
> Nor windy suspiration of forc'd breath,
> No, nor the fruitful river in the eye,
> Nor the dejected 'haviour of the visage,
> Together with all forms, modes, shows of grief,
> That can denote me truly; these indeed seem,
> For they are actions that a man might play;
> But I have that within which passeth show.
>
> (I.2.77–85)

The Senecan list in *Thyestes* gains Roman colouring from its reference to ballistae, and from its allusion to Parthians, Rome's longstanding enemy on the eastern border. In fact Seneca has just earlier mentioned the nomadic Dahae, and peoples on the coast of the Indian Ocean, and others to the south and east of the Black Sea, and dwellers by the Danube, and the Chinese (369–79). Such imaginative ranging across far-flung places and peoples is characteristic of Senecan drama, a rhetorical expansiveness inseparable from the geopolitical expansiveness of the Roman empire.

Another rhetorical aspect of the dramas is their delight in pointed, epigrammatic statement. Seneca's interest in epigram was so great that his father, himself a keen amateur of rhetoric, gathered examples which he remembered hearing from leading rhetoricians at Rome, and published them for his sons' use in a handbook which is our chief source for the rhetorical training of the period.[1] What appealed to Seneca about the epigram was no doubt that it displays the mind at the moment of capturing verbally some unusual or paradoxical aspect of a situation: "if they call him uncle, he is their father"; "for such suffering, we need Thyestes sober" (*Thy* 329, 900). Paradox in particular is a verbal register of the dark vision of these plays, in which so much is awry in human nature and the nature of the world. King Priam lacks a pyre though Troy is burning; humans are never wretched except by comparison; the Greeks weep for the crime they have committed (*Tro* 55, 1023, 1119).

[1] *The Elder Seneca: Declamations*, transl. M. Winterbottom (Loeb Classical Library), 2 vols.

Closely allied to epigrams are *sententiae* or brief general statements, such as were eagerly collected in countless Renaissance commonplace books (including no doubt Hamlet's). "In desperate times the headlong way is best." "Where only honest deeds to kings are free, / It is no empire, but a beggary." "Who would not fall with all the world around him?" These are Elizabethan dramatists' adaptations of Senecan originals.[2] Seneca uses epigrams and *sententiae* to punctuate and point the longer speeches, by rounding off each movement of thought with a flourish (e.g. *Ag* 4, 11, 27, 36, 43, 52, 56). In dialogue there is verbal point of many kinds, as the characters compete in turning each others' words against them. Here the challenge for the reader, as in a coded conversation in a Jane Austen novel, is to appreciate both the verbal brilliance and the reality of emotion, motive, and situation which it expresses or masks. (These realities would be more evident to an audience, who would have the speaker's tone of voice for guidance.) The prophet Cassandra's responses to Agamemnon at *Ag* 791–99 are not simply repartee, but reflect her deeper insight into past and future. Pyrrhus' *sententia* "Often a compassionate man will grant death rather than life" (*Tro* 329) sounds humane but is unmasked by the context as a hypocritical pretext for sacrificing a young woman's life.

Rhetorical training, especially for the lawcourts, involved arguing from the known facts of a case by inference and extension—often, too, by exaggeration. This practice

---

[2] Respectively *Ag* 154 in Thomas Hughes, *The Misfortunes of Arthur*; *Thy* 214–15 in John Marston, *Antonio and Mellida Part II*; *Thy* 886–87 in Ben Jonson, *Catiline*.

is reflected in Seneca's dramas in the frequency with which characters make inferences from previous events concerning themselves or their families or other mythical figures; the past is constantly invoked as a paradigm for the present and future. "What I am demanding is now custom and practice," claims Pyrrhus (*Tro* 249), arguing that Agamemnon's earlier sacrifice of Iphigenia justifies his present intention to sacrifice Polyxena. Medea calibrates the scale of her revenge by a desire to match her former crimes or even to outdo them (49–54). Particularly when their social identities collapse, Seneca's characters understand and define themselves in terms of their childhood or family history. Medea, set aside as Jason's wife, reverts to her earlier identity as a "barbarian" princess. Phaedra, abandoned by Theseus, sees herself as cursed to repeat the self-destructive behaviour of her mother Pasiphae, though her nurse argues vigorously that reason and willpower offer freedom from the past. The Oedipus of the first part of *Phoenician Women*, his kingship lost, insists on identifying with the evil of his conception and birth, though his daughter Antigone holds out to him another kind of self-understanding based on his innocence of intention. In such fixation with the past, rhetoric becomes inseparable from the psychology of the self.

The Self and the World

In comparison with the Greek tragedies of the fifth century B.C., Seneca's dramas have a greater inwardness, a greater focus on the individual and the psychology of the self. Many of the longer speeches, particularly in the earlier Acts of individual plays, depict the characters thinking

5

aloud, proceeding by association of idea, scolding or cajoling themselves, discarding one possibility and seizing
on another (e.g. *Herc* 1–124, *Pha* 85–128, *Thy* 176–204,
cf. *Hamlet* II.2.550–604 beginning "O, what a rogue and
peasant slave am I!"). Inner thoughts are revealed through
dramatic techniques rarely found in fifth-century drama
but developed thereafter, the aside, the soliloquy, and the
entrance monologue, in which an entering character
voices his thoughts before interacting with others (e.g.
Med 431–46). Together with this increased introspection
comes an increased isolation of the individual. Not only is
the amount of dialogue reduced in comparison with fifth-
century drama, but the pointed quality of the dialogue in
Seneca lessens the sense of real interaction between the
characters. Furthermore the convention that the chorus
represents a community has largely disappeared, so that
individuals are as distanced from society at large as from
each other.

Within these isolated individuals we watch the development of obsessive emotions, emotions so powerful that
they can only be called passions. There may be a single
overriding passion (anger in Atreus) or an interaction between passions (love and anger in Medea, guilt and fear
in Oedipus), or a conflict between two emotional forces
(desire and modesty in Phaedra). The characters, lacking a
secure sense of self, ally themselves with their passions
and find identity in them. Atreus calls himself *iratus
Atreus*, "an angry Atreus" (*Thy* 180), implying that his
name, which is indeed almost an anagram of *iratus*, casts
him as a man of anger. Phaedra "recognises" her mother's
perverse passion in herself (*Pha* 113), and simultaneously
recognises herself (or rather, a version of herself) in that

supposed resemblance to her mother. Hence the eagerness with which the passion figures drive themselves on
even when the emotional tide of their passion ebbs (e.g.
Med 895ff., 988ff.).

Pervasive insecurity about the self in Senecan drama is
reflected in fierce but desperate assertions of selfhood.
Hercules refers to himself by name twelve times in *Hercules*, as if reminding himself of his identity as "Hercules the
mighty conqueror." Inevitably this version of himself dis-
places other aspects of a fuller identity, for example as a father. Even after the murder of his family, his chief concern
is what action is appropriate to his heroic persona. Other
figures, as we have seen, identify with passion, or with precedents from the past of themselves or their families. Such
identifications are always misidentifications because they
represent only one aspect or version of the self; the full self
is fragmented in this way. Medea reifies two versions of
herself, "wife" and "mother," and is torn between them
(*Med* 928).

These insecure individuals need to assert power over
others to assure themselves of their selfhood. Almost every
dialogue in these dramas can be read as a power struggle:
the debate in Act 2 of *Trojan Women*, supposedly about
principles, comes down to the question who has the stronger will, who will blink first. Even Phaedra's supposed love
for Hippolytus comes to look, in light of her imagery of
hunting, more like a desire to capture and dominate him.
For Lycus might is right, and for Atreus supreme power is
amoral by nature, exempt from "private" virtues such as
loyalty (*Herc* 400–01, *Thy* 217–18). Successful revenge is
an ultimate assertion of power over others, convincing
Atreus that he is "king of kings," and deluding Medea that

she has recovered her royal sceptre (*Thy* 912, *Med* 982).
When Polynices asks his brother whether he would sacrifice country, housegods, and wife for the sake of power, Eteocles responds, "Power is well purchased at any price" (*Phoen* 664). This power lust finds a deep resonance in Elizabethan drama: in addition to the passages cited in the footnote on *Phoenician Women* 664, compare the words of Marlowe's Tamburlaine:

> A God is not as glorious as a King:
> I think the pleasure they enjoy in heaven
> Cannot compare with kingly joys on earth
> (*1 Tamburlaine* II.5.57–59)

—a passage which, despite its blasphemy, is less stark and chilling than Eteocles' words.

Power is asserted not only over other humans but also over the natural world. Cosmic imagery is familiar in poetry ("Thou that art now the world's fresh ornament / And only herald to the gaudy spring"), but in Seneca such language goes beyond imagery, for his characters claim, and sometimes possess, actual dominance over the physical world. Seneca's Hercules is like Lady Macbeth in believing that his bloody hands will stain the whole ocean; but his belief that the whole world shuns his guilt has a deeper resonance just because he is a world conqueror: "By being known everywhere, I have forfeited a place for exile" (*Herc* 1323–31). Oedipus' guilt similarly pollutes the whole of Thebes. Those lists so characteristic of Senecan rhetoric extend the individual's power over the world. Hippolytus is able to organise a hunt covering all of Attica. Medea can command destructive forces from all over the world, even from the heavens; not only that, but she seems to embody in herself the destructive forces of sea and fire. Such a world picture has analogues in Greek myth, where Agamemnon's actions can bring plague on the army, and the actions of Atreus can turn back the sun in his course. But it also has an unmistakable resonance with the Roman world of Seneca's day, in which the actions of one man, the emperor, could indeed affect the known world. The global perspective in Seneca's catalogues of far-flung places implies a world that has become globalised, a world such as that described in the second choral ode of *Medea* (364–74), where one can speak in one breath of Indians and Persians, of the Araxes and the Rhine.

Human power over the world appears all the greater because the gods (if they exist) seem supine or powerless. Gods never intervene in these plays to prevent an atrocity or to correct one. Neptune acts in a mechanical way to carry out Theseus' curse on his son, but he will not act to reddress matters, as Theseus pointedly notes (*Pha* 1242–43). The chorus of that play contrasts Jove's ordering of the heavens with his indifference to moral chaos on earth (959–88). Juno in *Hercules* paints a picture of moral chaos in the heavens as well, as she descends to earth with the purpose of destroying the source of law and order there. Atreus claims, with apparent justification, to have frightened the gods from the heavens; *he* is the most exalted of gods, peer of the stars (*Thy* 885, 911).

The self-assertiveness of the Senecan figures derives ultimately from that of the old Homeric heroes such as Achilles and Ajax. Ajax displays it in his competitive desire to inherit Achilles' prestigious weapons, in his mad rage when they are denied him, in his brusque rejection of others' concern in Sophocles' play, in his assertion of

9

an unyielding selfhood through suicide. The old heroic-aggressive persona was adopted by the dynasts of the Hellenistic period, Alexander the Great and his successors, and in turn by the potentates of the Roman world, many of whom identified themselves with the conquering Hercules through the imagery of statuary and coinage. In Seneca we see an extreme form of such self-assertion, amplified by the loss of a sense of geopolitical and religious limits, and made more desperate by the loss of a sense of community.

In this world of extremes, the only apparent alternative to radical self-assertion is equally radical renunciation of ambition. Several passages praise a simple retired life, far from the dangerous passions of cities and palaces (e.g. *Herc* 192–201, *Thy* 391–403). But such a life seems to serve as a notional contrast to the ambitious life, rather than a realisable possibility. Its two representatives in the plays are seriously flawed: in Hippolytus rejection of social ambition is based on an instinctive shunning of society and particularly women; in Thyestes it is so feeble as to be easily overborn by his sons.

Date

Ten tragedies survive under the name of Seneca. Of these, two are now considered to have been written by imitators after his lifetime: see the separate introductions to *Hercules on Oeta* and *Octavia*. We have no firm dates for the composition or performance of the eight Senecan plays, and therefore cannot make any secure connections between them and his political or philosophical activities. Born between 4 and 1 B.C., Seneca received a standard education at Rome in grammar, literature, and rhetoric, and showed a particular interest in philosophy. Thereafter his career falls into five phases, whose astonishing vicissitudes match those dramatised in the plays.

1. Sometime in the 30's A.D. he entered public life through election to the quaestorship and so to the Roman Senate. He then rose quickly to prominence; according to an anecdote his brilliance as an orator aroused the unbalanced envy of the emperor Gaius (Caligula), and nearly cost him his life.

2. Within a year of Claudius' accession in 41, Seneca was exiled to the island of Corsica. The real cause may have been enmity on the part of Claudius' wife Messallina, though the overt charge was one of adultery with one of Gaius' sisters. The exile was to last eight years.

3. The return to Rome in 49 came at a heavy price, since it was arranged though the influence of Agrippina, Claudius' new wife: part of the deal was that Seneca should become tutor in rhetoric to her son Nero, then 12. Agrippina's purpose was no doubt to make use of the growing prestige of Seneca as a man of letters in her quest for supreme power through her son.

4. In 54, on Nero's accession, Seneca became the new emperor's chief adviser, writing his major public speeches and guiding affairs as best he could from behind the throne. His essay *On Clemency*, published in 55 or 56, was intended to suggest the tone of the new administration. Seneca and Burrus, the prefect of the praetorian guard, were jointly responsible for a period of good government in the first years of Nero's reign. Their influence began to wane after Nero's murder of his mother Agrippina in 59, as

the emperor became increasingly aware of his unlimited power.

5. Following the death of Burrus in 62, Seneca withdrew from public life. In 65, like his nephew the poet Lucan, he was accused of complicity in the Pisonian conspiracy, and ordered by the emperor to commit suicide.

The two small indications that do exist concerning the date of some of the plays point to period 3. First, a passing reference in Quintilian (8.3.31) can be interpreted to mean that Seneca presented one or more plays (titles unspecified) through public recitation in the early 50's. Second, the fact that passages from *Hercules* are echoed in *Apocolocyntosis*, a satire by Seneca on Claudius' official deification, suggests that that play may have been written shortly before 54. But clearly these indications do not exclude the possibility that some of the tragedies belong to earlier or later periods.

Beyond these indications we have to rely on internal evidence of stylistic development, which suggests relative but not absolute dates. Variations in the freedom with which enjambment is used would divide the plays into three groups:

1. a relatively early group, consisting of *Agamemnon*, *Oedipus*, and *Phaedra*;
2. a middle group, consisting of *Hercules, Medea*, and *Trojan Women*;
3. a later group, consisting of *Thyestes* and *Phoenician Women*.

This grouping correlates well with groupings suggested by independent metrical features. For example, the highly experimental polymetric odes are found only in *Agamem-*

non and *Oedipus*, and the metrical handling of anapaests is looser in those two plays and *Phaedra* than in the other plays. Again, the metrical treatment of words ending in *-o* suggests that *Thyestes* is significantly later than the other plays, and *Phoenician Women* later still. If an absolute date shortly before 54 is accepted for *Hercules* and combined with the evidence for relative dating, it seems likely that *Thyestes* and *Phoenician Women* were written in Nero's reign.

While the settings and the plots of the plays are Greek, their atmosphere is unmistakably that of Seneca's Rome. Such pictures as the early-morning *salutatio*, the stentorian lawyer in the forum (*Herc* 164–74), the gilded roof-beams and massed columns of a magnate's mansion (*Pha* 496–98), the palace louring over a sullen city populace (*Thy* 641–45), are not only Roman in themselves but evoke well-known passages of Horace and Vergil as if to underline their Romanness. The plays' geopolitical sense, too, is that of the Roman empire, as we have seen, with its awareness of exotic peoples and places to west and east, north and south, on the borders of the empire. Above all, the gigantic passions stalking the courts of these plays are akin to the passions of the imperial court: the lust of a Messallina, the ambition of an Agrippina, the madness of a Gaius. And running through other passions, in the plays as in Rome's court, is the lust for power over other individuals, and for the ultimate prize of supreme power. These were the realities of Seneca's experience. This is not to suggest that the tragedies sprang directly out of his experience, or that we should expect a one-to-one correspondence between the events of the dramas and the events of the court, but rather that the oppressive atmosphere of the plays is redolent of that which often prevailed at the centre of Roman power. Latter-day critics have sometimes considered the gigantic passions of the plays unrealistically exaggerated. We are unlikely to be so confident in the century following that of Hitler and Stalin. It is worth remembering that "Seneca himself lived through and witnessed, in his own person or in the persons of those near him, almost every evil and horror that is the theme of his writings, prose and verse. Exile, murder, incest, the threat of poverty and a hideous death, and all the savagery of fortune were of the very texture of his career" (Herington 1966, 430).

The Dramatic Tradition

The fact that half a millennium of theatre history lies between the tragedies of fifth-century Athens and those of Seneca, and that drama continued to evolve over that vast span of time, is obscured for us by the loss of every single tragedy written in that interval. Athens continued to be the centre for tragic drama in the fourth century B.C., and Alexandria became so in the third century. At Rome, the tragedies of the republican period were chiefly adaptations of Greek originals. They had a rough-hewn quality, and a metrical and musical exuberance in the episodes; these characteristics are also evident in the surviving comedies of Plautus and Terence. Tragedies written in the Augustan age aimed to be original compositions rather than adaptations. They also returned to the classic fifth-century practice of using the iambic trimeter as the regular metre between the odes. In both these respects, imperial writers including Seneca followed Augustan practice.

Accius (170–86 B.C.) was the last writer to devote his career largely to tragedy. Thereafter tragedy, though still widely written, became the province of gentlemen litterateurs, and the occasional activity of writers working chiefly in other genres. Instances in the first category include single tragedies by Julius Caesar, by the emperor Augustus, and by Mamercus Aemilius Scaurus; in the second category, by Varius Rufus (*Thyestes*) and Ovid (*Medea*).[3] Seneca's production of eight tragedies is in notable contrast. A possible hypothesis is that Seneca's initial interest was likewise that of a poetaster, as the nature of *Agamemnon* and *Oedipus* suggests, and that the genre then claimed his fuller powers as he realised its imaginative possibilities. The fact that he produced a substantial body of drama, in combination with his reputation as a philosopher and his historical importance, was no doubt what ensured that his tragedies survived when those of so many others were lost.

Because of the skewed historical perspective caused by the loss of almost all post-Euripidean tragedy, critics often assumed that Seneca worked directly from fifth-century models, and that changes in dramaturgy were largely his own. R. J. Tarrant (1978) corrected that view by showing how much Seneca inherited from the intervening centuries. In Seneca's *Agamemnon*, for instance, there is no evidence of direct influence from Aeschylus, and positive evidence, in the presence of a defiant Electra, of influence from a non-Aeschylean dramatic tradition.[4] Other plays

---

[3] A useful list with references is provided by H. M. Hine (see *Medea* bibliography), 7–8.

[4] Details in Tarrant's edition (see *Agamemnon* bibliography), 10–14.

sometimes offer evidence, in wording and plot, of direct
Euripidean influence, but not of substantial or continuous
imitation of Euripides by Seneca. We must bear in mind
that there had been countless retellings, dramatic, narrative, and pictorial, of the mythical events in the centuries
after Euripides. The case of *Medea* is indicative. There
were at least a dozen plays dealing with that myth between
Euripides and Seneca, including one by Ovid which must
have contributed much to Seneca's play; in addition, the
Senecan play shows the influence of poetry in other genres
by the three great Augustans, Vergil, Horace, and Ovid.
For Seneca the Greek tragedies were part of the "given,"
part of a rich dramatic and literary inheritance. His practice seems to have been close to his theory of composition,
which was to absorb influences from many sources, and to
blend them into a new creation (see his *Letter* 84).

Dramatic Technique
Features of Seneca's dramaturgy which reflect the inheritance of post-fifth-century tragedy include the standard
five-act structure, passed on to the Renaissance, and the
use of techniques that directly reveal a character's thinking, namely the aside and the entrance monologue. Another is a general loosening of the dramatic structure,
manifested in a greater emphasis on the individual speech
or scene, and a corresponding lack of interest in smooth
consistency of characterisation and plot. A striking instance is the disproportion with which Seneca develops
descriptive scenes at the expense of more traditional
dramaturgy: such scenes include Tiresias' animal sacrifice
and necromancy, Medea's gathering of magical resources,
and Theseus' description of the world of death (respec-

tively *Oed* Acts 2–3, *Med* Act 4, *Herc* Act 3). Such development of a descriptive element in overt disproportion to the whole work is characteristic of Alexandrian poetry and its influence on Roman literature. It is important to note, however, that such descriptions in Seneca, even if only loosely connected to plot structure, have a strong *thematic* relevance. The focus on death's dominion in Theseus' narrative, for example, casts a shadow over Hercules' claim to have conquered that realm. And in *Oedipus* the very disproportion of the necromancy scene, as well as its content, reflects the play's sense of a dissonance in the world at large.

Two features of dramaturgy are particularly characteristic of Seneca, though not without precedent. One is the use of the prologue not so much to provide background information, as to establish an atmosphere of dark foreboding and emotional intensity, which prepares the audience for the unfolding of the tragedy in the following acts. The other characteristic feature is a scene in which someone, usually an inferior, attempts to restrain the passion of one of the leading characters. The classic examples of such passion-restraint scenes are Act 1 of *Phaedra* and Act 2 of *Medea*, *Agamemnon*, and *Thyestes*. This type scene is also recognisable, though varied, in the first part of *Phoenician Women* and in Act 2 of *Trojan Women* (Agamemnon-Pyrrhus), and again, though more distantly, in Acts 2 and 5 of *Hercules* (Megara-Amphitryon, Hercules-Amphitryon).

Senecan dramaturgy has a somewhat distorted reputation for violence. Anyone coming to these plays, especially from Elizabethan drama, in expectation of rivers of blood, will be disappointed: there are as many deaths (four) onstage in the final scene of *Hamlet* as in all of Seneca's eight plays (two in *Medea*, one each in *Phaedra* and *Oedipus*). The sanguinary reputation is in part an accidental result of the fact that Seneca's *Thyestes* is the only play on this unavoidably gruesome subject to survive out of many composed in antiquity.[5] Nor will anyone who remembers Euripides' description of the physical dismemberment of Creusa and her father in *Medea* (absent from Seneca's *Medea*), or of Pentheus in *Bacchae*, think that Seneca has a corner on the horrific in antiquity. True, Seneca sometimes emphasises the grotesque aspect of violence, in part for shock value and in keeping with the taste of his age. But even as the grotesquery thrusts the physicality of violence in our faces, it also underlines its human meaning. The detailed descriptions of murder in *Hercules*, recalling so many gory descriptions in Homeric battle scenes, remind us that Hercules has a long-honed expertise in killing, now turned against his own family. And the mad precision of the human sacrifices in *Thyestes* illustrates how completely the power-crazed Atreus devalues humans to the level of beasts.

Chorus

In fifth-century drama the chorus generally refers in its first ode to its reason for appearing on the scene, and the continuous presence of its members thereafter as witnesses of the play's action can be assumed. But the chorus' involvement in the dramatic action lessened during the fifth century, and continued to lessen in the following centuries. A late stage of that development is found in

[5] Conveniently listed by Tarrant (see *Thyestes* bibliography), 40.

Senecan drama. Here the first ode of a play is never explicitly an entrance ode, and to speak of the chorus' "presence" or "absence" between odes would have little meaning; the chorus simply falls into dramatic abeyance during the Acts, except for those moments when the chorus leader is employed in dialogue in the absence of any other interlocutor. Correspondingly, the chorus' awareness of dramatic events is only such as the dramatist assigns to it at any given moment; we cannot assume that the chorus knows what has happened in any preceding scene through witnessing it. This separation of the chorus from the dramatic action should not, however, be assumed to mean that the choral odes in Seneca lack *thematic* relevance. Admittedly a few odes in the putatively early plays provide little more than a decorative contrast to the mood of the surrounding scenes (*Ag* 808–66, *Oed* 404–508). But elsewhere the odes make a substantial contribution to thematic richness and complexity. In *Medea*, for example, the two central "Argonautic odes" (301–79, 579–669) enlarge on the theme of human violation of natural boundaries, and strengthen the play's alignment of Medea herself with nature's forces.

Performance

Nineteenth-century critics first put forward the thesis that Seneca's plays were not intended for stage performance. Their arguments were based in part on the postclassical features of dramaturgy noted above, in the mistaken belief that since these features are foreign to fifth-century tragedy, they must be foreign to performed drama at any period.[6] With that assumption discarded, however, the thesis

---

[6] The settings of Seneca's plays are sometimes fluid and indefinite: see the introduction to *Medea*. This feature is one aspect

still deserves consideration, since we know that some ancient playwrights composed plays to be read aloud rather than performed. Furthermore we have no performance record from antiquity of a Senecan play, while Quintilian's passing reference (8.3.31) points to presentation through recital rather than performance.

The Senecan dramas are generally written within the conventions of ancient performance drama: *inter alia* they envisage using the roof of the stage building as an acting area (*Med* 973), and "wheeling out" an indoor scene on a movable platform (*Herc* Act 5, *Pha* 863, *Thy* 901–02), for both of which there are parallels in fifth-century drama. However, use of performance conventions need not imply expectation of performance. Critics have often claimed that individual scenes in the plays would be impracticable in performance, but when examined these claims usually turn out to be based on narrow or anachronistic ideas of what can be staged. The strongest suspicions of this sort concern Act 2 of *Oedipus*, where cattle are sacrificed and later rise to attack the priests; the scene seems better suited to recitation, where the audience could imagine the events from the verbal description in the text, rather than to live performance. But whatever conclusion is reached about *Oedipus* need not apply to the whole corpus, if *Oedipus* is regarded as an early and experimental play.

Indeed, certain scenes in the other plays seem almost to demand performance. Phaedra's initial faint when approaching Hippolytus, her throwing of herself at his feet,

of the "loosening of dramatic structure" noted above. But fluidity and vagueness of scene are not incompatible with stage drama, as the plays of Aristophanes and Shakespeare illustrate.

the tussle over his sword (*Pha* 585, 703–14)—all this would surely work more effectively in performance than in recitation, which is not to exclude the use of recitation to *introduce* a play to the public. Even more indicative is a passage such as that in which Medea kills the first of her children. That action is not specifically verbalised in the text, so that someone reading or listening to the text alone could not be sure, until some four lines further on (975), that the action had actually occurred. Here, in fact, action is primary, and the words of the text allude to it. While such a scene could presumably have been managed somehow in recitation, the primacy of action leaves little doubt that Seneca is envisaging stage performance as he composes.

What opportunities for performance existed in Seneca's day? Full-scale productions in public theatres were still given during the festivals: one of Pomponius' plays was offered in A.D. 47, not with resounding success. There were also more frequent performances in theatres, with props and costumes, of *extracts* from tragedies; particularly intense scenes such as Act 2 of *Phaedra*, Act 4 of *Hercules,* and Act 5 of *Medea* and *Thyestes* would have been suitable to such occasions. It is also likely, in view of the popularity of literary and dramatic entertainment in social settings among the Roman upper classes, that excerpts or full texts of Seneca's plays were performed in private mansions, and even in the imperial palace.

Stoicism and Tragedy

From the time of the exile or earlier, with increasing prolificacy right up to the time of his death, Seneca published on Stoic philosophy. These writings are mostly literary treatments of philosophical issues, rather than technical treatises. Belonging to the branch of Stoicism concerned with ethics, they set themselves the practical purpose of curing humans of emotional turmoil. Attempts have been made, naturally enough, to use these philosophical works as a key to understanding the dramas. But such attempts have invariably led to distorted readings of the plays, by reason of the very different nature of the two genres: moral philosophy in antiquity is optimistic, which tragedy is not; philosophy of a particular school takes a single systematic view of the world, which poetry does not. Certainly there are resonances between Seneca's philosophica and the dramas, but they need to be defined with caution. They lie chiefly in the presentation of the self and of two great threats to the self, the passions and death.

A deep concern with the *passions* links the dramas with the philosophica, which include a lengthy essay *On Anger*, the very passion that drives Medea and Clytemnestra and Atreus. Yet the dramas do not read like negative exemplars designed to warn of the dangers of passion. The psychological complexity with which Seneca depicts Phaedra, the sheer exuberance of language and imagery with which he depicts Atreus and Medea, suggest an imaginative involvement rather than the distance of moral condemnation. The complete absence of positive moral exemplars among Seneca's characters also tells against a didactic purpose. An interest in portraying the passions had long been central to Roman poetry at Rome, as seen in Vergil's *Aeneid*, and in Ovid's many passionate heroines. True, Vergil's depictions of gigantic passions in Dido and Turnus themselves have a Stoic colouring; yet they are generally seen as imaginative rather than didactic creations. Similarly the Senecan dramas are coloured but not controlled by Stoic thinking.

Attitudes to *death* form perhaps the strongest link between the dramas and the prose works. As philosopher, Seneca takes an agnostic view of the nature of death, which could be either an entrance into an afterlife, or simply a cessation of existence; in the tragedies, each of these possibilities is envisaged separately by the chorus of *Trojan Women*. As philosopher, he teaches repeatedly that death is not to be feared, whatever its nature, and often dwells on suicide as an ultimate guarantee of freedom; in the tragedies, death is often seen as a welcome release. But there are distinctions of tone, context, and genre. The welcoming of death in the dramas is tragic rather than philosophical in character, based on the tragic perception of life as so unbearable that death is preferred. The courage of a boy and a girl, Astyanax and Polyxena, in face of death has more to do with instinctive emotional defiance than with philosophical reasoning; such courageous acceptance or welcoming of death has a long pedigree in tragedy reaching well back beyond Stoicism to the fifth century B.C. And the vehement death wish of Oedipus in *Phoenician Women* is founded entirely on passion, not reason. One could argue further that the constant engagement with death in Seneca's prose works shows the issue as having a personal urgency for him, and that it comes close to a tragic vision when he speaks of death as release. "The welcome given to death as liberation answered an emotional need of Seneca himself, living under arbitrary autocracy" (Fantham's edition of *Tro* p. 81).

Stoicism preaches a radical *self-sufficiency*. Nothing

23

external to the self—wealth, position, friendship, even health—has value in itself, but only in our opinion of it. Consequently we can endure and be happy even under cirumstances that would conventionally be considered disastrous. The Stoic self is heroic, victorious over all blows from outside (personified as Dame Fortune) and over the internal fears, desires, and other passions that challenge the control of reason. In Senecan Stoicism it appears that this heroic self almost needs calamities, adversities, torments so that it can prove itself victorious over them. The dramas contain clear analogues. There we have seen how much energy goes into self-assertion, self-fashioning, self-dramatisation. Hercules is defined by everyone, including himself, as an all-conquering hero; he delights in a steady supply of foes against whom he can repeatedly assert his valour. Medea believes herself equal to all external forces, and envisages facing not just one foe but two together, or more than two (*Med* 166–67, 517–28). These can be seen as reverse images of Stoic selfhood, since self-fashioning in the dramas is based on passion not reason, and seeks dominance over others, not over the self.

Yet historically the reversal is in the opposite direction. The heroic self-assertiveness of the dramas is the older tradition, found already in the intransigence of the Homeric heroes, as we saw above in "The Self and the World." It was Stoicism that inverted this dominant tradition by turning it inwards, towards metaphorical conquest of the external world through spiritual conquest of the self. The selfhood of Seneca's dramas, then, descends from the older tradition of myth, epic, and tragedy. Yet it is also coloured by, or at least resonates with, Seneca's Stoicism in its constant sense of the self as under threat and needing to prove itself. Seneca sometimes goes out of his way to underline the similarities between the passionate and the Stoic self, perhaps even to deconstruct the difference between them, when he has passionate characters use Stoic language. "I have always risen above Fortune in every form," says Medea (520); "I abandoned the kingship gladly, but I keep the kingship over myself," says Oedipus (*Phoen* 104–05), meaning control not over his passions but over his death.

Despite the overt optimism of the philosophical works, their emphasis on the extremes of experience, on adversity, torture, violent death, gives them at times a darkness of timbre comparable to the tragedies. As for the governance of the world, however, the picture given by the philosophical works is completely at variance with that of the dramas. In the dramas, as we have seen, the gods are absent, fickle, or malign, unconcerned or unable to prevent or correct moral outrages; order is lacking, or is seen only in the distant heavens (*Pha* 959–88)—and even there order is imperilled by an Atreus. But as a Stoic Seneca confidently affirms that the cosmos is guided by divine Providence, which is synonymous with Reason and Nature.

Why, then, does Senecan drama depict a world of passion and moral chaos, so bleakly at variance with the determined optimism of his philosophical works? The answer must lie in the nature of tragedy, which as a genre is properly concerned with the forces, inner and outer, that destroy humans. (A Stoic tragedy would be a contradiction in terms.) The view given by tragedy is not a God's-eye view of reality but a partial and situated view, one situated in a specific genre. Nevertheless it is true that Seneca's drama is unusually bleak, even by the standards of tragic drama. We can only guess at the reasons, but they surely include the dark experience of his times, at least for those near the centre of power, where the weight of the entire Roman empire bore down on a few individuals and turned some of them into monsters. It is a fascinating thought that *Thyestes* may have been written by Seneca while he was immersed in the grim realities of supreme power at Nero's court.

Yet so dark a vision as that of Seneca's dramas does not seem out of keeping with the nature of tragedy. It should not be assumed, from the examples of certain Greek and Shakespearian tragedies, that tragedy necessarily ends with a movement towards correction or redemption; indeed one could argue that Senecan drama, where there is almost never such a movement,[7] represents a purer form of the genre. It asks us to lend ourselves to the rhetoric of a certain view of the world, to enter the heart of darkness. Yet it is not nihilistic, not reduced to minimalism; the vigour of its rhetoric, wordplay, and poetry asserts human creativity even in confronting disasters.

The terms "mannerist" and "baroque" have been used as tools to the understanding of Senecan drama (so, for example, J.-A. Shelton on *Medea* and Charles Segal on *Phaedra*). These terms usefully suggest connections be-

[7] Exceptions might be claimed for *Agamemnon* and *Hercules*. But Electra's rescue of Orestes in *Agamemnon* is handled in a perfunctory manner, while the prospect of Hercules' redemption is remote, envisaged only in the last line of *Hercules*; though forced by Amphitryon to renounce suicide, he remains consumed by guilt.

tween a variety of phenomena in the plays. In addition they suggest enlightening parallels with art and architecture in Seneca's era, and with art and literature in the sixteenth and seventeenth centuries. But aspects of Seneca's dramas also have a direct appeal to the modern era, and resonate in various ways with such movements as expressionism, symbolism, surrealism, and postmodernism. No doubt these plays will continue to find new resonances as the world unfolds two millennia after their creation.

Text and Translation

Text

The text of these dramas, like most ancient texts, underwent a substantial degree of corruption during the centuries of copying by hand—corruption which has been only partially removed by the painstaking work of scholars. Readers should not be misled by the apparent reliability of a modern printed text into supposing that the author's original words are securely known. Already in antiquity Seneca's tragedies suffered both accidental corruption and deliberate interpolation, the latter intended chiefly to clarify or amplify the text. Thereafter the transmission of the dramas divided into two manuscript branches, known as E and A. Each branch sustained further accidental corruption, but A also suffered a systematic revamping designed to purge unusual words and expressions.

The text presented here has been newly edited. Though any editor relies on the rich tradition of classical scholarship going back to the Renaissance, I have also tried to exercise independence of judgment, sometimes retaining transmitted readings that had been unjustifiably altered (e.g. *Tro* 197, *Phoen* 552, *Med* 53, 680, *Pha* 1099, *Oed* 832), and occasionally rejecting a phrase that had been passed over (e.g. *Phoen* 358, *Oed* 1052). As it turns out, my text steers a middle course between the boldness of Otto Zwierlein's Oxford Classical Text and the conservatism of Giardina and other editors—a course that is not, however, the result of a preconceived policy, but simply the outcome of decisions made on each issue in turn.

The following conventions are used in both text and translation: square brackets ([ ]) enclose material considered to be an interpolation; angle brackets (< >) enclose a modern supplement designed to indicate the gist of what is lost.

Places where E and A differ, or where the text has been corrected by conjecture, are listed succinctly in Zwierlein's edition, and more fully in that of Giardina. My apparatus criticus notes only those places where there is disagreement among modern editors about the original reading, and where the disagreement affects the translation. The following conventions are used: an asterisk (*) indicates that a spelling found in the manuscript(s) has been modernised; superscript ᵃᶜ indicates the reading of the manuscript before scribal alteration (*ante correctionem*); superscript ᵖᶜ indicates the manuscript's reading after scribal alteration (*post correctionem*).

Individual manuscripts are cited in the apparatus by their standard designations, e.g. T, C, Σ; the name of a scholar, e.g. Leo, Axelson, indicates the author of a conjecture. Information about the manuscripts and their affiliations will be found in Zwierlein's edition, which also indicates where conjectures were originally published. Brief accounts of the transmission of the text are given in most modern editions of individual plays; fuller accounts are found in Tarrant's edition of *Agamemnon* and in Zwierlein (1984).

Translation

In keeping with the character of the Loeb Classical Library, this translation stays close to the wording of the original. It is not, however, a crib. Seneca is nothing if not stylish, and it would be misleading to translate him unstylishly. In particular I have attempted, at George Goold's urging, to preserve Seneca's characteristic conciseness of phrasing, resisting the temptation to expand or explain rather than translate. For the most part I have translated his verse into prose, though conscious of the great loss involved. Where he uses metres other than the iambic trimeter of dialogue, however, I have translated line for line, chiefly in order to respect the lyric character of the choral odes. The metrical variety of the dramas is enormous, ranging from the lengthy trochaic tetrameters, akin to English fourteeners, down to the brief iambic dimeters, which fell naturally into three-stress lines. Most intermediate measures are represented here by a four-stress line, occasionally modified to three or five stresses by the needs of translation (and with two stresses for the monometers of the anapaests); readers might keep in mind that there are stronger differences in metrical character between one ode and another in the Latin.

Stage Directions

The texts of ancient drama do not contain stage directions: stage action must therefore be inferred from the words of the characters. While some indications of action are overt, for example Phaedra's faint at *Phaedra* 585, others are slighter, for example Medea's "I thank you" (*gratum est*) at *Medea* 553 indicating that Jason has silently nodded assent. Senecan drama allows the reader or producer considerable freedom in deciding when entrances and exits occur. Should Jocasta enter at the beginning of *Oedipus*, or just before she addresses Oedipus at line 81? Should Andromache stay onstage in *Trojan Women* during the choral ode beginning at 814, or exit at the end of Act 3 and return with Hecuba at the beginning of Act 4? Because this freedom is inherent in the text, I preferred to preserve it in my translation, rather than insert stage directions which would appear more authoritative than they are. I have therefore inserted stage directions only when they are both certain and necessary to prevent confusion in reading.

Footnotes and Index

The Index (in the second volume of this edition) is intended to serve not only as a regular index but also as a glossary of names. Seneca frequently makes allusions to the people, places, and events of myth, allusions which would have been more transparent to the original audience than today. To avoid peppering the translation with footnotes, I have placed explanatory material in the Index. Footnotes are used chiefly when the allusion in the Latin does not include a proper name. Adjectival forms of names are not indexed separately: for instance the entry "Cadmus" covers the adjective "Cadmean" also.

BIBLIOGRAPHY

Abbreviations are those of *The Oxford Classical Dictionary*, 3rd edn. (Oxford, 1996), xxix–liv.

Textual Editions of All Plays

G. C. Giardina (2 vols., Bologna 1966).
O. Zwierlein (Oxford, 1986, reprinted with corrections 1993).

Textual Criticism

J. G. Fitch, *Annaeana Tragica: Notes on the Text of Seneca's Tragedies* (*Mnemosyne* Supplement 256) (Leiden, 2004).
R. J. Tarrant (ed.), *Seneca: Agamemnon* (Cambridge, 1976), 23–101.
O. Zwierlein, *Prolegomena zu einer kritischen Ausgabe der Tragödien Senecas* (Wiesbaden, 1984).
——— *Kritischer Kommentar zu den Tragödien Senecas* (Stuttgart, 1986).

Translations

F. Ahl, *Seneca, Three Tragedies: Trojan Women, Medea, Phaedra* (Ithaca and London, 1986).
E. F. Watling, *Seneca: Four Tragedies and Octavia* [*Thy, Pha, Tro, Oed, Oct*] (Harmondsworth, 1966).

Date

J. G. Fitch, "Sense-Pauses and Relative Dating in Seneca, Sophocles and Shakespeare," *AJPhil* 102 (1981), 289–307.

INTRODUCTION

Performance

G. W. M. Harrison (ed.), *Seneca in Performance* (London, 2000).

D. F. Sutton, *Seneca on the Stage* (Leiden, 1986).

Criticism

A. J. Boyle, *Tragic Seneca: An Essay in the Theatrical Tradition* (London, 1997).

—— (ed.) *Seneca Tragicus: Ramus Essays on Senecan Drama* (Victoria, Australia, 1983).

W. M. Calder III, "Seneca: Tragedian of Imperial Rome," *CJ* 72 (1976), 1–11.

J. G. Fitch, "Character in Senecan Tragedy" (Dissertation, Cornell University, 1974).

—— and S. McElduff, "Construction of the Self in Senecan Drama," *Mnemos.* 55 (2002), 18–40.

D. and E. Henry, *The Mask of Power: Seneca's Tragedies and Imperial Rome* (Warminster, 1985).

C. J. Herington, "Senecan Tragedy," *Arion* 5 (1966), 422–471.

—— "The Younger Seneca," in E. J. Kenney (ed.), *The Cambridge History of Classical Literature* vol. 2 (Cambridge, 1982), 511–532.

E. Lefèvre (ed.), *Senecas Tragödien* (Darmstadt, 1972).

C. A. J. Littlewood, *Self-Representation and Illusion in Senecan Tragedy* (Oxford, 2004).

W. H. Owen, "Commonplace and Dramatic Symbol in Seneca's Tragedies," *TAPA* 99 (1968), 291–313.

T. G. Rosenmeyer, *Senecan Drama and Stoic Cosmology* (Berkeley, 1989).

INTRODUCTION

Influence and Reception

G. Braden, *Renaissance Tragedy and the Senecan Tradition* (New Haven and London, 1985).

B. J. Cohon, "Seneca's Tragedies in Florilegia and Elizabethan Drama" (Dissertation, Columbia University, 1960).

J. Cunliffe, *The Influence of Seneca on Elizabethan Tragedy* (London, 1893).

T. S. Eliot, "Seneca in Elizabethan Translation," and "Shakespeare and the Stoicism of Seneca," in *Selected Essays* (London, 1951), 65–105, 126–40.

G. K. Hunter, "Seneca and English Tragedy," in C. D. N. Costa (ed.), *Seneca* (London and Boston, 1974), 166–204.

D. Share (ed.), *Seneca in English* (London, 1998).

HERCULES

INTRODUCTION

Background

The goddess Juno, sister and jealous wife of Jupiter, has long persecuted her bastard stepson Hercules, whom Jupiter fathered on Alcmene, wife of Amphitryon. She has imposed on him a series of daunting labours, the most recent of which was to fetch the hound Cerberus from the world of the dead. Hercules' home, which he rarely sees, is in Thebes, where he has married Megara, daughter of King Creon. During Hercules' absence in the underworld, an upstart named Lycus has killed Creon and usurped the throne; Hercules' wife, his three sons, and his foster father Amphitryon are all in imminent danger.

Summary

Act 1

Appearing alone and at night, Juno expresses anger over the presence in heaven of so many of her husband's bastard children. Now her most hated stepson, Hercules, has triumphantly succeeded in the last task she set him; the next step will be his deification, as promised by Jupiter. Since he has proved superior to every external foe, she realises that the only hope of destroying him is to turn him against himself in madness.

Ode 1. As dawn breaks, the chorus describes the human and animal activities that it initiates in the world of nature, contrasting these with the frenetic, anxiety-ridden human activities of the city. In view of life's brevity, we should calmly appreciate each passing day, not rush towards death as Hercules has done literally by descending to the underworld.

Act 2

Amphitryon and Megara speak of Hercules' former heroic achievements and the possibility that he will return to save them. A marriage offer from Lycus, intended to legitimise his own position, is scornfully rejected by Megara. After sardonically questioning Hercules' heroic qualities, Lycus departs, ordering his attendants to annihilate the whole family. At the very end of the Act, sounds heralding Hercules' return are heard.

Ode 2. The chorus deplores Hercules' life of toil and danger, which took him to Scythia's frozen seas and now to the equally lifeless waters of the underworld. It hopes for his successful return, on the basis of his earlier defeat of Dis, and of Orpheus' partial success in recovering Eurydice.

Act 3

Hercules enters with Theseus, whom he has rescued from imprisonment in the underworld. After challenging Juno to set him any remaining tasks, Hercules learns of the situation in Thebes, and leaves immediately to dispatch Lycus. At Amphitryon's request, Theseus gives a detailed account of the nature of the underworld, and of how Hercules quelled Charon, Cerberus, and Dis and brought the hound into the upper world.

Ode 3. The chorus dwells on the descent to the under-world which must be faced eventually by all mortals. It celebrates Hercules' success, interpreting it as a pacification of the terrors of the underworld.

Act 4

Hercules reappears fresh from the killing of Lycus, and prepares to sacrifice to the gods in thanksgiving. As he prays for peace and order throughout the cosmos, the onset of madness announces itself through his vision of darkness and disorder in the sky, and his plan to lead a violent attack on the heavens. Mistaking his children for those of Lycus, and his wife for Juno, he kills them one by one. He then collapses in a coma.

Ode 4. The chorus calls on the cosmos to mourn, and on Sleep to heal Hercules' madness. It anticipates the cosmic scale of Hercules' own mourning, and laments his sons' unrealised promise.

Act 5

Hercules awakes, restored to sanity; he sees his slaughtered family, and deduces from his bloodstained hands that he himself was the killer. With vehement insistence he prepares to punish himself by suicide. Finally Amphitryon deters him by threatening to die simultaneously with him. Theseus promises to take Hercules to Athens for purification from bloodguilt.

Comment

The allied themes of darkness versus light, death versus life run through this text. The play begins at night, and Juno, more like a nightmarish demon than a goddess, summons powers from the world of darkness and death to aid her revenge. The first ode heralds dawn and the resumption of life's activities, and Hercules' return from the underworld is a metaphorical dawn of hope for his family and Thebes. But the narrative which fills most of Act 3, and the second and third choral odes that frame it, dwell once again on images of the lifeless world below. Hercules, descending into madness and murder, sees darkness reappearing at noon.

Indeed the power of death is evident in the everyday fabric of life. Sleep is Death's brother, our falling asleep a daily preparation for the "long night" of death (1066–77). The day's swift passing reminds us of our immersion in time's current (179–82). Dawn and birdsong recall ancient sorrows; life's fragility is evident in each small activity (134–58). The crowds on earth thronging to some great celebration are a reminder of the crowds always thronging into the underworld, elderly and young alike (838–57).

In this context of the tragic frailty of life, Hercules' claim to have conquered death (609–12) seems unrealistic and indeed hubristic. *Morte contempta redî*: "I flouted death, and returned." These are the words of an overreacher, one who does not understand the limits of his power. Though he claims victory over death, he is shortly to become death's agent for his family.

It may seem unfair to level such criticism at Hercules, since he was after all commanded by Juno to remove Cerberus from the underworld. But clearly he has undertaken this and other Labours with alacrity, and has moulded himself into the role of the all-conquering hero. Indeed he has undertaken to destroy not only monstrous beasts but also tyrants and all that threatens peace in the world, casting

39

himself as enforcer of universal law and order. In his obsession with peace and order he prays for an end to natural threats, to storms, floods, poisonous plants (931–36)—a noble vision, perhaps, but one that fails to understand the nature of the world. He is also obsessed with action, since there is always some new threat to be overcome; hence Amphitryon's complaint that he never has the opportunity to enjoy his son's presence and company (1252–57). Violence has become part of his way of life, so that he resorts to it instinctively in the task of fetching Cerberus: significantly Seneca does not follow some earlier versions which made Hercules rely less heavily on violence and intimidation in this exploit. It is surely no coincidence that Seneca portrays him, shortly before the onset of madness, as careless of cleansing blood from his hands before he sacrifices, and as longing to pour human blood as an offering to the gods (918–24). By a familiar corruption, the man of action has become a man of blood.

The ambivalence of Hercules' heroism can be traced through the term most often applied to it by Hercules himself and others, namely *virtus*. *Virtus* is the quality of a *vir*, a man, so "manliness, valour." It is normally used of valour employed in some good cause, as its connection with English "virtue" suggests, but its root is in self-assertion, not self-abnegation or adherence to external standards. Juno sardonically empties it of moral content in using it of Hercules' fighting qualities employed against his own family: "I have found the day on which Hercules' hated *virtus* can be an asset to me" (115). Indeed it can be a euphemism for successful crime, as Amphitryon notes (252). When we hear Lycus describing his own amoral self-assertion as *virtus* (340), we see in a distorting mirror, so to speak, how the fair-sounding *virtus* can disguise less fair qualities in Hercules himself, namely ambition and violent self-assertion.

The greatness of this Hercules, then, is a greatness not far removed from madness; he is already close to insanity in his daily *modus vitae*. On his return from the underworld, when he has reached a high point of megalomania, his mind topples over into madness. The obsessions that emerge in that madness are distorted forms of his "sane" obsessions: the danger that previously conquered forces may rebel, the ambition to reach heaven, the need for violent retribution.

Since Juno vows at the outset to make Hercules mad, how can his madness be seen as arising from his own attitudes and way of life? The answer is that divine and human causations for mental events are often not mutually exclusive in Greek and Roman literature. At the end of Book 1 of Vergil's *Aeneid*, for example, Queen Dido of Carthage falls in love with Aeneas; her growing passion is described as fostered by Cupid, yet it is hardly incomprehensible in human terms. Such "double motivation," though paradoxical at first sight, provides a vivid means of depicting mental events that occur without conscious human volition and with seemingly uncontrollable power. Juno is certainly "real" within the mythical framework of the plot, yet her prologue is somewhat separate from the main action of the play. As Hercules descends into madness in Act 4, it is the continuity of his own behaviour, from "sanity" to "insanity," that we observe.

Though the madness is connected with Hercules' way of life, it would diminish the play to see it only as a study of personal psychology. This mighty Hercules would hardly fit on the psychologist's couch. He is a figure of superhuman stature and force, comparable in some respects to Medea among the Senecan protagonists, and this force represents a danger to those near him and to himself. As the greatest exemplar of old-fashioned, intransigent heroism, he represents the power and the perils inherent in such heroism. Heroes like this live on the edge; Achilles goes beserk on the battlefield, and Ajax is maddened by a slight from the Greek leadership. Yet for centuries after Homer, the ancient world remained fixated on the image of the conquering hero. Vergil's portrait of Aeneas modifies that image by showing heroism reoriented towards the service of family and community. Stoicism attempts to modify it in another direction by commending a spiritual, not physical, conquest of the external world and of the irrational forces of the self. In the context of tragedy, however, Seneca explores the heroic ideal in its fundamental form, with its unstable mixture of self-regard and altruism, and reveals its tragic potential.

Critics have sometimes found a restorative transformation of Hercules in his final decision not to commit suicide. Such a development would be most untypical of Senecan drama, and more akin to patterns found in some Greek and Shakespearian tragedies. Seneca's Hercules after the madness is a continuation of Hercules before the madness, obsessed with self-image and with violent punishment of the transgressor, even when it turns out to have been himself. He is diverted from suicide only by extreme emotional blackmail on Amphitryon's part. Up to his very last speech in the play, he remains centred on himself and his punishment. Senecan tragedy denies any easy response, any sense of recuperation from loss and destruction, any meaningful softening of intransigent attitudes.

This denial of a straightforward response in Seneca, combined with the inherent ambivalence of a hero such as Hercules, perceived in antiquity from Homer on, has led to a wide divergence in the interpretation of this play. In complete variance with the reading of the *Hercules* sketched above, some critics have read the play as an affirmation of the positive qualities of Hercules' heroism, with a movement towards redemption of that heroism at the end of the play represented by his decision against suicide: see particularly Lawall and Mader in the bibliography below.

Sources

The procedure of using borrowed materials to create a new whole, recommended in ancient literary theory, is well illustrated in Ode 1. The idyllic opening images of countryside activities at dawn, drawn from Euripides' *Phaethon* with colouring from Ovid, are contrasted with images of restless human ambition, drawn partly from Horace's first ode and from the end of Vergil's *Georgics* 2; this seemingly innocuous contrast gently leads the audience into perceiving the disadvantages in Hercules' life of ambitious activity.

In outline Seneca's play is similar to Euripides' *Heracles*, and indeed recurrent similarities of phrasing and thought suggest a closer relationship to Euripides than that seen, for example, in Seneca's *Medea*. Nevertheless there is always a sense of independence and fresh development, and Seneca's play has several major differences from Euripides', including the following.

1. Juno's appearance at the outset of the play: in Euripides she does not appear, but her agents, Iris and Madness, appear at a later point, immediately before Hercules' madness. Seneca's distancing of the deity from the madness allows the continuity between the "sane" and "insane" Hercules to become evident. Her speech in Seneca recalls several speeches of the angry Juno in Vergil's *Aeneid* and Ovid's *Metamorphoses*.

2. Lycus' attempt to coerce Megara into marriage: this may be modelled on wooing attempts by tyrants in other myths or dramas, but the details escape us.

3. Theseus' description of the underworld and of Hercules' exploit, strongly reminiscent of Book 6 of Vergil's *Aeneid*. The Senecan narrative illustrates both the dominion of death and Hercules' tendency to resort to violence (in contrast to Aeneas' demeanour in the underworld).

4. The dramatisation of Hercules' murder of his family: this probably derives from an unidentified post-Euripidean drama on Hercules' madness. In Euripides the killings occur entirely within the palace, and are recounted to the audience later in a messenger speech.

The leading difference between the two plays, however, lies in the conception of the protagonist. Euripides' Hercules is a humane, philanthropic hero on whom madness falls with tragic injustice; he survives it in part through the loving friendship of Theseus, and finds a new exercise of his heroism in enduring the almost intolerable anguish of his loss. Seneca's Hercules is a figure of superhuman power who is betrayed by that very characteristic, by the grandiose nature of his thinking and his *modus vitae*; his complete failure to engage with a human mode of life is dramatised symbolically in his killing of his family.

Title

While E calls the play simply *Hercules*, the A manuscripts call it *Hercules Furens*, i.e. *Hercules Mad*. The word *Furens* was no doubt added in A to distinguish this play from the post-Senecan *Hercules on Oeta*, when that play was added to the corpus.

BIBLIOGRAPHY

Commentaries

M. Billerbeck, *Seneca, Hercules Furens: Einleitung, Übersetzung und Kommentar* (Leiden etc., 1999).

J. G. Fitch, *Seneca's Hercules Furens: A Critical Text with Introduction and Commentary* (Ithaca and London, 1987).

Criticism

J. D. Bishop, "Seneca's *Hercules Furens*: Tragedy from *modus vitae*," *C&M* 27 (1969), 216–224.

J. G. Fitch, "*Pectus o nimium ferum*: Act V of Seneca's *Hercules Furens*," *Hermes* 107 (1979), 240–248.

G. K. Galinsky, *The Herakles Theme* (Oxford, 1972).

G. Lawall, "Virtus and Pietas in Seneca's Hercules Furens," in Boyle (1983), 6–26.

G. Mader, "Form and Meaning in Seneca's 'Dawn Song' (*H.F.* 125–201)," *Acta Classica* 33 (1990), 1–32.

J.-A. Shelton, *Seneca's Hercules Furens: Theme, Structure and Style* (Göttingen, 1978).

E. M. Waith, *The Herculean Hero* (New York and London, 1962).

C. Zintzen, "*Alte virtus animosa cadit.* Gedanken zur Darstellung des Tragischen in Senecas *Hercules Furens*," in Lefèvre (1972), 149–209.

DRAMATIS PERSONAE

JUNO, *sister and wife of Jupiter, and queen of the gods*

AMPHITRYON, *husband of Alcmene and foster father of Hercules*

MEGARA, *wife of Hercules and daughter of the former King Creon*

LYCUS, *tyrant of Thebes, who usurped the throne of Creon*

HERCULES, *son of Jupiter and a mortal mother, Alcmene; mightiest hero of Greece*

THESEUS, *king of Athens and friend of Hercules*

CHORUS

Scene

The scene is set in front of the royal palace at Thebes. The stage setting includes an altar and associated shrine. The play begins at night.

HERCULES

IUNO

Soror Tonantis—hoc enim solum mihi
nomen relictum est—semper alienum Iovem
ac templa summi vidua deserui aetheris,
locumque caelo pulsa paelicibus dedi;
5   tellus colenda est, paelices caelum tenent.
hinc Arctos alta parte glacialis poli
sublime classes sidus Argolicas agit;
hinc, qua recenti vere laxatur dies,
Tyriae per undas vector Europae nitet;
10   illinc timendum ratibus ac ponto gregem
passim vagantes exerunt Atlantides.
ferro minax hinc terret Orion deos
suasque Perseus aureus stellas habet;
hinc clara gemini signa Tyndaridae micant
15   quibusque natis mobilis tellus stetit.
nec ipse tantum Bacchus aut Bacchi parens
adiere superos: ne qua pars probro vacet,

---

1 Juno begins to point out in the night sky various commemorations of Jupiter's infidelities and his bastards. The Bear (Ursa Major) is Callisto, mother by Jupiter of Arcas; the bearer of Europa is the Bull, Taurus; Atlas' daughters are the Pleiades, three of whom lay with Jupiter and bore him sons.

2 A tradition purporting to explain Orion's name said he was

HERCULES

ACT 1

JUNO

Sister of the Thunder God: this is the only title left me.
Wife no more, I have abandoned ever-unfaithful Jove and
the precincts of high heaven; driven from the skies, I have
given up my place to his whores. I must dwell on earth;
whores inhabit the skies. Over here is the Bear,[1] that lofty
constellation high in the frozen North, a lodestar for Greek
fleets. Here, where the daylight waxes in early spring,
shines the one that carried Tyrian Europa across the
waves. Over there rise the far-ranging daughters of Atlas,
feared by ships and the sea. Here Orion menaces the gods
with his sword, and golden Perseus has *his* constellation.[2]
Here glitters the brilliant sign of the twin Tyndarids, and
those at whose birth the drifting land stood still.[3] And not
only Bacchus himself and Bacchus' mother joined the gods
above: so that no quarter should be free of scandal, the

born without a mother from the *urine* of Jupiter and other gods.
Perseus was Jupiter's son by Danae.

[3] The latter twins are Apollo and Diana (sun and moon), borne
by Latona on the wandering isle of Delos; the former are Castor
and Pollux (Gemini), sons of Leda, whose cuckolded husband was
Tyndareus.

mundus puellae serta Cnosiacae gerit.
  Sed sero querimur; una me dira ac fera
20 Thebana tellus matribus sparsa impiis
quotiens novercam fecit! escendat licet
meumque victrix teneat Alcmene locum,
pariterque natus astra promissa occupet,
in cuius ortus mundus impendit diem
25 tardusque Eoo Phoebus effulsit mari
retinere mersum iussus Oceano iubar,
non sic abibunt odia: vivaces aget
violentus iras animus, et saevus dolor
aeterna bella pace sublata geret.
30   Quae bella? quidquid horridum tellus creat
inimica, quidquid pontus aut aer tulit
terribile dirum pestilens atrox ferum,
fractum atque domitum est. superat et crescit malis
iraque nostra fruitur; in laudes suas
35 mea vertit odia; dum nimis saeva impero,
patrem probavi, gloriae feci locum.
qua Sol reducens quaque deponens diem
binos propinqua tinguit Aethiopas face,
indomita virtus colitur et toto deus
40 narratur orbe. monstra iam desunt mihi,
minorque labor est Herculi iussa exequi
quam mihi iubere; laetus imperia excipit.

19 *EA have* sed vetera sero querimur: *Leo omits* vetera.
20 matribus *Axelson*: nuribus *EA*

heavens wear the garland of the girl from Cnossus.[4]

But these are old grievances. How often has this one land, this wild and monstrous land of Thebes, with its crop of impious mothers,[5] made me a stepmother! It may be that Alcmene will ascend to heaven and victoriously hold my place, and that her son likewise will gain the stars that were promised him—this son for whose begetting the whole world lost a day, when Phoebus, with orders to keep the sunlight immersed in Ocean, shone forth late from the Eastern seas. Even so, my hatred will not just evaporate. My mind will aggressively pursue undying anger, and my fierce resentment will abolish peace and wage eternal warfare.

What warfare? Any fearful thing the hostile earth produced, or sea or air brought forth, however frightening, monstrous, poisonous, dreadful, savage, has been broken and tamed. *He* prevails and grows greater through hardships, thrives on my anger, turns my hatred to his own glory. By imposing such cruel commands, I have proved his parentage and given scope to his reputation. Where the Sun restores the day and relinquishes it, blackening both Ethiop tribes with the closeness of its torch, *his* indomitable valour is revered, and throughout the whole world he is storied as a god. Now there are no monsters left me, and it is less of a labour for Hercules to fulfil my commands, than for me to give them; he receives my orders cheerfully!

[4] The mother is Semele; the girl is Ariadne, whose garland became the constellation Corona.

[5] I.e. women made pregnant by Jupiter (Semele, Alcmene, Antiope mother of Amphion and Zethus), called "impious" by Juno as representing an insult to her godhead.

quae fera tyranni iura violento queant
nocere iuveni? nempe pro telis gerit
45 quae timuit et quae fudit: armatus venit
leone et hydra.
                    Nec satis terrae patent:
effregit ecce limen inferni Iovis
et opima victi regis ad superos refert.
50 vidi ipsa, vidi nocte discussa inferum
et Dite domito spolia iactantem patri
fraterna. cur non vinctum et oppressum trahit
ipsum catenis paria sortitum Iovi
Ereboque capto potitur et retegit Styga?
49 parum est reverti, foedus umbrarum perît:
55 patefacta ab imis manibus retro via est
et sacra dirae Mortis in aperto iacent.
at ille, rupto carcere umbrarum ferox,
de me triumphat et superbifica manu
atrum per urbes ducit Argolicas canem.
60 viso labantem Cerbero vidi diem
pavidumque Solem; me quoque invasit tremor,
et terna monstri colla devicti intuens
timui imperasse.
                    Levia sed nimium queror:
caelo timendum est, regna ne summa occupet
65 qui vicit ima; sceptra praeripiet patri!
nec in astra lenta veniet ut Bacchus via:

43 iura *Fac*M: iussa *A,E*pc   54 potitur et *EA*: potitur?
en *Baden*   49 *placed after 54 by Leo*

---

6 Hercules is subject to the tyrant Eurystheus, through whom
Juno's commands have been imposed.

What cruel tyrant's authority[6] could harm this aggressive warrior? Why, he carries as weapons what he faced and felled: he comes armed with lion and hydra.[7]

Even the earth is not room enough. See, he has broken through the gates of nether Jove,[8] and brings spoils of triumph over that conquered king back to the upper world. With my own eyes I watched him, after he had shattered the gloom of the underworld and subdued Dis, as he showed off to his father spoils won from that father's brother. Why not drag off Dis himself, bound and loaded with chains—the god who drew a lot equal to Jove's? Why not rule over captured Erebus, and unroof the Stygian world? It is not enough to return: the terms governing the shades have been breached, a way back to earth has been opened from the deep underworld, and the sanctities of dread death lie in plain view. But he, in his arrogance at having smashed the prison of the ghostly dead, is celebrating his triumph over me, and highhandedly parading the black hound through Argive cities. I saw the daylight faltering at the sight of Cerberus, and the Sun afraid; I too was seized with trembling, and as I gazed at the triple necks of the defeated monster, I shuddered at what I had ordered.

But these complaints are too trivial. It is heaven we must fear for—that after conquering the lowest realm he may seize the highest. He will usurp his father's sceptre! And he will not reach the stars by a gradual approach, like

---

[7] The pelt of the Nemean Lion, which he uses as a shield, and the poison of the Hydra, with which he tips his arrows.

[8] I.e. Dis (also called Pluto and Hades), whose power in the underworld is equal to Jove's in the upper world.

iter ruina quaeret et vacuo volet
regnare mundo. robore experto tumet,
et posse caelum viribus vinci suis
70 didicit ferendo; subdidit mundo caput
nec flexit umeros molis immensae labor
meliusque collo sedit Herculeo polus.
immota cervix sidera et caelum tulit
et me prementem: quaerit ad superos viam.
75   Perge, ira, perge et magna meditantem opprime,
congredere, manibus ipsa dilacera tuis;
quid tanta mandas odia? discedant ferae,
ipse imperando fessus Eurystheus vacet.
Titanas ausos rumpere imperium Iovis
80 emitte, Siculi verticis laxa specum,
tellus Gigante Doris excusso tremens
supposita monstri colla terrifici levet.
[sublimis alias Luna concipiat feras]
     Sed vicit ista. quaeris Alcidae parem?
85 nemo est nisi ipse; bella iam secum gerat.
adsint ab imo Tartari fundo excitae
Eumenides, ignem flammeae spargant comae,
viperea saevae verbera incutiant manus.
i nunc, superbe, caelitum sedes pete,
90 humana temne! iam Styga et manes feros
fugisse credis? hic tibi ostendam inferos.
revocabo in alta conditam caligine,

72 meliusque *E*: mediusque *A*   83 *deleted by Leo*
90 feros Σ: ferox *A,Epc*

9 Typhoeus (also called Typhon), imprisoned under Mt Etna
in "Dorian" Sicily. Line 83 (deleted): "let the moon on high con-

Bacchus: he will forge a path by destruction, and he will want to rule in an empty sky. Swollen with confidence in his well-tested might, he has learnt through bearing the heavens that his strength can conquer them. When he bent his head to support the sky, the toil of that immense weight did not bow his shoulders; no, the firmament rested more securely on Hercules' neck. Without budging, his back supported the stars and heavens—and my pressure. Yes, he is seeking a path to the gods.

Onward, my anger, onward! Crush this overreacher! Grapple with him, tear him apart with your own hands. Why delegate such hatred? Let the wild beasts go, let Eurystheus too rest, weary with giving commands. Release the Titans who dared disrupt Jove's sway; open the cavern in the Sicilian peak, and let the Dorian land, which trembles whenever the giant struggles, free the pinioned neck of that horrific monster.[9]

But he has defeated these! Do you need a match for Alcides?[10] There is none but himself. Now he must war with himself. The Eumenides must be summoned here from the lowest depths of Tartarus, their burning hair must scatter fire, their cruel hands brandish snaky whips. Go ahead, proud man, aspire to the gods' abodes, despise human status! You think you have now escaped the Stygian world and its merciless spirits? *Here* I will show you infernal powers. I shall call up one buried in deep darkness,

ceive other wild beasts." ("Other" than the Nemean Lion, sometimes said to have come from the moon.)

[10] A frequently used synonym for Hercules, meaning "grandson of Alcaeus."

ultra nocentum exilia, discordem deam,
quam munit ingens montis oppositi latus;
95   educam et imo Ditis e regno extraham
quidquid relictum est: veniet invisum Scelus
suumque lambens sanguinem Impietas ferox
Errorque et in se semper armatus Furor—
hoc hoc ministro noster utatur dolor.
100   Incipite, famulae Ditis, ardentem incitae
concutite pinum, et agmen horrendum anguibus
Megaera ducat atque luctifica manu
vastam rogo flagrante corripiat trabem.
hoc agite, poenas petite vitiatae Stygis.
105   concutite pectus, acrior mentem excoquat
quam qui caminis ignis Aetnaeis furit;
ut possit animum captus Alcides agi,
magno furore percitus, vobis prius
insaniendum est.—Iuno, cur nondum furis?
110   me me, sorores, mente deiectam mea
versate primam, facere si quicquam apparo
dignum noverca. vota mutentur mea:
natos reversus videat incolumes precor
manuque fortis redeat. inveni diem,
115   invisa quo nos Herculis virtus iuvet.
me vicit? et se vincat, et cupiat mori
ab inferis reversus. hic prosit mihi
Iove esse genitum. stabo et, ut certo exeant
emissa nervo tela, librabo manu,
120   regam furentis arma, pugnanti Herculi
tandem favebo. scelere perfecto licet

94 latus *Bentley*: specus *EA*
104 vitiatae* *E*: violatae* *A*

beyond the sinners' banishment, the goddess Discord, immured by the vast flank of a mountain blocking her escape. I shall bring forth all that remain, and fetch them from the depths of Dis' kingdom: hateful Crime shall come, and savage Disloyalty, lapping its own blood, and Confusion, and mad Rage, always armed against itself—yes, *this* must be the agent of my resentment.

Begin, handmaids of Dis,[11] brandish the blazing pine torch violently. Let Megaera lead your troop, fearsome with snakes, and snatch a huge beam from a blazing pyre in her baleful hand. To your work: avenge the desecration of the underworld! Rouse your hearts, scorch your minds with fiercer fire than that raging in Etna's furnaces. So that Hercules can be hounded, deranged and enraged, you must first feel madness. —Juno, why are *you* not yet raging? Harry *me*, sisters, overthrow *my* mind first, if I plan to take some action worthy of a stepmother. I must change my prayer: may he return and find his sons safe, I pray, and may he come back strong of hand. I have found the day on which Hercules' hated valour can be an asset to me. Has he conquered me? Then let him conquer himself too, and let him long to die, though returned from the dead. This once let it serve my purpose that he is Jove's son. I shall stand beside him and aim his arrows with my hand, so they fly unerring from the bowstring; I shall guide the madman's weapons, and at last take Hercules' side in the fight. Once

11 The Furies.

108 vobis *EA*: nobis *recc.*
119 manu *E*: manum *A*

admittat illas genitor in caelum manus.
    Movenda iam sunt bella: clarescit dies
ortuque Titan lucidus croceo subit.

CHORUS

125	Iam rara micant
	sidera prono languida mundo;
	nox victa vagos contrahit ignes
	luce renata;
	cogit nitidum Phosphoros agmen;
	signum celsi glaciale poli
130	septem stellis Arcados Ursa
	lucem verso temone vocat.
	iam caeruleis evectus equis
	Titan summa prospicit Oeta;
	iam Cadmeis inclita Bacchis
135	aspersa die dumeta rubent,
136	Phoebique fugit reditura soror.
146	pendet summo stridula ramo
	pinnasque novo tradere soli
	gestit querulos inter nidos
	Thracia paelex,
150	turbaque circa confusa sonat
151	murmure mixto testata diem.
137	Labor exoritur durus et omnes

130 Ursa *Fitch*: ursae *E* (*A omits* 124-61)
132 equis *E*: aquis *recc.*
146–51 *placed after* 136 *by Zwierlein*

12 A Bacchic festival was held on the wooded slopes of Mt
Cithaeron. There Cadmus' daughters, including Agave, had torn
Pentheus apart in Bacchic frenzy.

58

the crime is completed, his father may admit those hands
to heaven!

Now let warfare begin: the daylight grows stronger, and
radiant Titan rises in saffron-coloured dawn.

CHORUS

Now scattered and weak
are the stars shining in the sinking heavens.
Vanquished night gathers her straggling fires
now the light is reborn;
the Dawnstar shepherds the glittering throng.
The icy constellation by the high Pole,
Arcas' Bear with its seven stars,
has turned its wain and summons the light.
Now, carried aloft by cerulean steeds,
the Titan looks out from the heights of Oeta;
now the thickets made famous by Cadmean
     Bacchants[12]
grow red, spattered with daylight,
and Phoebus' sister flees to return once more.
The Thracian paramour[13]
perches shrill-voiced on the topmost bough,
and amidst her plaintive nestlings she eagerly
presents her wings to the new sun;
and all around a mingled throng gives voice,
proclaiming the day with a medley of sounds.[14]
     Hard Toil arises, bestirs

[13] Philomela, raped by her sister's husband Tereus in Thrace,
and later metamorphosed into the nightingale.
[14] Cf. the close of Robert Bridges, "Nightingales": "while the
innumerable choir of day / Welcome the dawn."

agitat curas aperitque domos.
pastor gelida cana pruina
140 grege dimisso pabula carpit;
ludit prato liber aperto
nondum rupta fronte iuvencus;
vacuae reparant ubera matres;
errat cursu levis incerto
145 molli petulans haedus in herba.
152 carbasa ventis
credit dubius navita vitae,
laxos aura complente sinus.
155 hic exesis pendens scopulis
aut deceptos instruit hamos
aut suspensus
spectat pressa praemia dextra;
sentit tremulum linea piscem.

Haec, innocuae quibus est vitae
160 tranquilla quies
et laeta suo parvoque domus.
spes immanes urbibus errant
trepidique metus.
ille superbos aditus regum
165 durasque fores expers somni
colit; hic nullo fine beatas
componit opes,
gazis inhians
et congesto pauper in auro;
illum populi favor attonitum
170 fluctuque magis mobile vulgus
aura tumidum tollit inani;
hic clamosi rabiosa fori

every care and opens every home.
A herdsman turns his flock loose
and gathers fodder whitened by hoarfrost;
a calf, its brow not yet broken by horns,
plays freely on the open meadow;
dams replenish their empty udders;
a boisterous kid wanders lightly
on a meandering course in the soft grass.
A sailor, risking life, entrusts
his canvas to the winds,
as a breeze fills the loose folds.
One fellow, perched on eroded rocks,
either prepares his concealed hooks
or tensely
watches the prize with his hand kept firm;
the line senses the quivering fish.

Such are the guiltless lives of those
who have quiet peace
and a home that delights in its own small means.
But in cities giant ambitions roam
and trembling fears.
One man forgoes sleep to cultivate
the proud portals and hard doorways
of the mighty. Another endlessly hoards
rich resources,
gaping at his treasures
and poor amidst piled-up gold.
One is dazed by popular acclaim;
the mob, more shifting than seawaves,
hoists him as he swells with an empty breeze.
Another traffics in the frenzied disputes

iurgia vendens
improbus iras et verba locat.
175   Novit paucos secura quies,
qui velocis memores aevi
tempora numquam reditura tenent.
dum fata sinunt, vivite laeti.
properat cursu vita citato,
180 volucrique die
rota praecipitis vertitur anni;
durae peragunt pensa sorores
nec sua retro fila revolvunt.
at gens hominum fertur rapidis
obvia fatis incerta sui;
185 Stygias ultro quaerimus undas.
nimium, Alcide, pectore forti
properas maestos visere manes.
certo veniunt tempore Parcae.
nulli iusso cessare licet,
190 nulli scriptum proferre diem;
recipit populos urna citatos.
    Alium multis Gloria terris
tradat et omnes
Fama per urbes garrula laudet,
195 caeloque parem tollat et astris;
alius curru sublimis eat:
me mea tellus
lare secreto tutoque tegat.
venit ad pigros cana senectus,
humilique loco sed certa sedet
200 sordida parvae fortuna domus;

188 tempore Σ: ordine *A,Epc*

62

of the clamorous forum,
and shamelessly hires out indignation and words.
    Few are familiar with untroubled peace.
They, conscious of fleeting time,
hold fast the moments that will never return.
While fate allows, live gladly!
Life hurries apace,
and with each winged day
the wheel of the headlong year turns forward.
The relentless sisters[15] complete each day's spinning,
and do not unwind the threads again.
But humans, unsure of their own good,
walk into the path of hurrying fate;
of ourselves we head for the Stygian waves.
You are too bravehearted, Alcides,
in hastening to visit the gloomy dead.
The Parcae come at the set time.
None may delay when bidden,
none postpone the appointed date.
Once summoned, throngs are received by the urn.
    Another may be carried to many countries
by Renown; garrulous Rumour may praise him
through every city,
and raise him equal with the starry heavens;
another may ride high in a chariot.
For me, let my own land
hide me in a safe and secluded home.
White-haired old age comes to homebodies,
and the ignominious fortunes of a small house
have a lowly but firm foundation.

[15] The Fates, whose title Parcae is used in line 188.

alte virtus animosa cadit.

—Sed maesta venit crine soluto
Megara parvum comitata gregem,
tardusque senio graditur Alcidae parens.

AMPHITRYON

205 O magne Olympi rector et mundi arbiter,
iam statue tandem gravibus aerumnis modum
finemque cladi. nulla lux umquam mihi
secura fulsit; finis alterius mali
gradus est futuri. protinus reduci novus
210 paratur hostis; antequam laetam domum
contingat, aliud iussus ad bellum meat;
nec ulla requies, tempus aut ullum vacat,
nisi dum iubetur. sequitur a primo statim
infesta Iuno; numquid immunis fuit
215 infantis aetas? monstra superavit prius
quam nosse posset. gemina cristati caput
angues ferebant ora, quos contra obvius
reptabat infans igneos serpentium
oculos remisso lumine ac placido intuens;
220 artos serenis vultibus nodos tulit,
et tumida tenera guttura elidens manu
prolusit hydrae. Maenali pernix fera,
multo decorum praeferens auro caput,
deprensa cursu; maximus Nemeae timor
225 pressus lacertis gemuit Herculeis leo.
quid stabula memorem dira Bistonii gregis
suisque regem pabulum armentis datum,

Spirited valour falls from great height.

But look, sadly, her hair unfastened,
Megara approaches with her small flock of children,
and slowed by age comes Alcides' father.

ACT 2

AMPHITRYON

O great ruler of Olympus and lord of the universe, at long last set a limit to our heavy troubles, an end to disaster! No day has ever dawned for me free of anxiety; the end of one trouble is a stepping stone to the next. Straightway on his return a new enemy is produced; before he can reach his rejoicing home, he is journeying under orders to a new fight; there is no respite, no spare time, except while orders are being issued. Hostile Juno has pursued him right from the first; was even his infancy immune? He defeated monsters before he could recognise them.[16] Twin snakes with crested heads pushed their mouths forward; directly in their path crawled the infant, looking into the serpents' fiery eyes with a relaxed and benign gaze; he endured their tight coils with a calm expression, and in crushing their swollen throats with his tender hands he trained to face the hydra. The swift beast of Maenalus, that displayed a head graced with much gold, was caught by his pursuit; the mighty terror of Nemea, the lion, groaned under the pressure of Hercules' arms. Why mention the fearsome stables of the Bistonian herd, and the king given as fodder to his

---

[16] For details of the various exploits listed here, see Index under "Hercules."

solitumque densis hispidum Erymanthi iugis
Arcadia quatere nemora Maenalium suem,
230 taurumque centum non levem populis metum?
inter remotos gentis Hesperiae greges
pastor triformis litoris Tartesii
peremptus, acta est praeda ab occasu ultimo;
notum Cithaeron pavit Oceano pecus.
235 penetrare iussus solis aestivi plagas
et adusta medius regna quae torret dies
utrimque montes solvit ac rupto obice
latam ruenti fecit Oceano viam.
post haec adortus nemoris opulenti domos
240 aurifera vigilis spolia serpentis tulit.
quid? saeva Lernae monstra, numerosum malum,
non igne demum vicit et docuit mori,
solitasque pinnis condere obductis diem
petît ab ipsis nubibus Stymphalidas?
245 non vicit illum caelibis semper tori
regina gentis vidua Thermodontiae;
nec ad omne clarum facinus audaces manus
stabuli fugavit turpis Augei labor.
      Quid ista prosunt? orbe defenso caret.
250 sensere terrae pacis auctorem suae
abesse curis. prosperum ac felix scelus
virtus vocatur; sontibus parent boni,
ius est in armis, opprimit leges timor.
ante ora vidi nostra truculenta manu
255 natos paterni cadere regni vindices,

251 curis *Watt*: terris *EA*

own beasts, or the bristling Maenalian boar, that would jolt the Arcadian woods on the impenetrable slopes of Erymanthus, or the bull, no light threat to a hundred communities? Amidst the distant herds of the Hesperian land the triform herdsman of the Tartesian shore was killed, and the booty was driven from the farthest West; Cithaeron pastured cattle familiar to Ocean. When ordered to penetrate the regions of the summer sun—scorched kingdoms parched by noonday heat—he split the mountains apart, and by bursting that barrier he made a wide passage for Ocean to rush in.[17] After this he invaded the haunts of the opulent woodland, and took golden spoils from the unsleeping serpent. What of the fierce monster of Lerna, that manifold pest? Did he not defeat it at last by fire and teach it death? And the Stymphalian birds, which would hide the daylight with their shrouding wings—did he not fetch them down from the very clouds? He was not defeated by Thermodon's unwed, ever-virgin queen; and those hands, dauntless in every deed of renown, did not shirk the filthy labour of the Augean stable.

What good is all this? The world he guarded is closed to him. The earth has sensed that the source of its peace is away from his charge. Crime which prospers and flourishes is given the name of valour;[18] good people take orders from the wicked; might is right, and the laws are stifled by fear. Before my own eyes I saw sons fall by the aggressor's hand in defence of their father's kingdom, and the king

[17] The Straits of Gibraltar.

[18] John Marston has, "Mischief that prospers men do virtue call" (*The Malcontent* V.3); Ben Jonson, "Let 'hem call it mischief; / When it is past, and prosper'd, 'twill be virtue" (*Catiline* III.540f.).

ipsumque, Cadmi nobilis stirpem ultimam,
occidere; vidi regium capiti decus
cum capite raptum. quis satis Thebas fleat?
ferax deorum terra quem dominum tremit!
260 e cuius arvis eque fecundo sinu
stricto iuventus orta cum ferro stetit,
cuiusque muros natus Amphion Iove
struxit canoro saxa modulatu trahens,
in cuius urbem non semel divum parens
265 caelo relicto venit, haec quae caelites
recepit et quae fecit et (fas sit loqui)
fortasse faciet, sordido premitur iugo.
Cadmea proles atque Ophionium genus,
quo reccidistis! tremitis ignarum exulem,
270 suis carentem finibus, nostris gravem.
qui scelera terra quique persequitur mari
ac saeva iusta sceptra confregit manu
nunc servit absens fertque quae fieri vetat,
tenetque Thebas exul Herculeas Lycus.
275   Sed non tenebit. aderit et poenas petet
subitusque ad astra emerget; inveniet viam
aut faciet. adsis sospes et remees precor
tandemque venias victor ad victam domum.

MEGARA

Emerge, coniunx, atque dispulsas manu
280 abrumpe tenebras. nulla si retro via
iterque clausum est, orbe diducto redi,
et quidquid atra nocte possessum latet
emitte tecum. dirutis qualis iugis

269 ignarum *EA*: ignavum *Tpc*   277 precor *E*: tuis *A*

68

himself,[19] last of famous Cadmus' line, cut down; I saw the
royal adornment of his head torn from him, and the head
with it. Who could weep enough for Thebes? What a master that god-bearing land fears! She from whose fields and
fertile bosom warriors arose and stood ready with drawn
swords,[20] she whose walls Jove's son Amphion built, shifting the stones with his resonant music, she whose city the
father of the gods entered more than once, quitting the
heavens—this land which has received gods and created
gods, and (to speak no irreverence) perhaps *will* create
them, is weighed down beneath a degrading yoke. Children of Cadmus, race of Ophion, how far you have fallen!
You tremble before an unknown exile, shut out of his own
state and oppressive to ours. The one who hounds crimes
by land and sea, and smashed cruel sceptres with righteous
force, is now far away in servitude and endures what he
forbids elsewhere, while the exile Lycus holds the Thebes
of Hercules.

But not for long. *He* will be with us, seeking vengeance,
and suddenly emerge to the sight of the stars. He will find a
way, or else make one. Be with us, return in safety I pray,
and come at last in victory to your vanquished home.

MEGARA

Emerge, my husband! Dispel the darkness by force, break
it open! If there is no way back, if the path is closed, then
return by rending the earth, and release with you all that
lies in the grip of black night. Just as once you took your

[19] Creon, Megara's father, killed with his sons by the usurper
Lycus.

[20] They sprang from the dragon's teeth sown by Cadmus.

praeceps citato flumini quaerens iter
285 quondam stetisti, scissa cum vasto impetu
patuere Tempe—pectore impulsus tuo
huc mons et illuc cessit, et rupto aggere
nova cucurrit Thessalus torrens via—
talis, parentes liberos patriam petens,
290 erumpe rerum terminos tecum efferens,
et quidquid avida tot per annorum gradus
abscondit aetas redde, et oblitos sui
lucisque pavidos ante te populos age.
indigna te sunt spolia, si tantum refers
295 quantum imperatum est.
                              Magna sed nimium loquor
ignara nostrae sortis. unde illum mihi
quo te tuamque dexteram amplectar diem
reditusque lentos nec mei memores querar?
tibi, o deorum ductor, indomiti ferent
300 centena tauri colla; tibi, frugum potens,
secreta reddam sacra: tibi muta fide
longas Eleusin tacita iactabit faces.
tum restitutas fratribus rebor meis
animas, et ipsum regna moderantem sua
305 florere patrem. si qua te maior tenet
clausum potestas, sequimur; aut omnes tuo
defende reditu sospes aut omnes trahe.
—trahes, nec ullus eriget fractos deus.

AMPHITRYON

O socia nostri sanguinis, casta fide
310 servans torum natosque magnanimi Herculis,

287 cessit *Leo*: cecidit *EA*

stand, and by shattering the mountains you created a precipitous path for the rushing river, when Tempe was split open by your mighty onslaught—under your body's thrust the mountains were forced apart, and the Thessalian torrent raced through the broken barrier on its new course—so, in quest of your parents, children, country, burst forth, taking with you nature's boundaries; restore all that greedy time has hidden away through so many passing years, and drive out before you the self-forgetting throngs that fear the light. The spoils are unworthy of you, if you bring back only what was commanded!

But I speak too boldly, with no knowledge of my destiny. How can that day come, when I may clasp you and your right hand, and reproach you for so slow a return, so forgetful of me? For you, O leader of the gods, a hundred unbroken bulls will offer their necks; for you, lady of harvests,[21] I shall perform the mystic rites: for you, under its vow of secrecy, silent Eleusis will wave the long torches. Then I shall consider my brothers restored to life, and my father flourishing in command of his realm. But if some power greater than your own holds you imprisoned, we shall follow you. Either return safely and defend us all, or drag us all down. —You *will* drag us down, no god will rebuild our broken lives.

AMPHITRYON

Ally of our blood, chaste and faithful guardian of great-hearted Hercules' marriage bed and his sons: conceive

[21] Ceres.

meliora mente concipe atque animum excita.
aderit profecto, qualis ex omni solet
labore, maior.

MEGARA

Quod nimis miseri volunt,
hoc facile credunt.

AMPHITRYON

Immo quod metuunt nimis
315   numquam moveri posse nec tolli putant;
prona est timoris semper in peius fides.

MEGARA

Demersus ac defossus et toto insuper
oppressus orbe quam viam ad superos habet?

AMPHITRYON

Quam tunc habebat cum per arentem plagam
320   et fluctuantes more turbati maris
abît harenas bisque discedens fretum
et bis recurrens, cumque deserta rate
deprensus haesit Syrtium brevibus vadis
et puppe fixa maria superavit pedes.

MEGARA

325   Iniqua raro maximis virtutibus
Fortuna parcit. nemo se tuto diu
periculis offerre tam crebris potest;
quem saepe transit casus, aliquando invenit.
Sed ecce saevus ac minas vultu gerens
330   et qualis animo est talis incessu venit
aliena dextra sceptra concutiens Lycus.

---

321 abiit *A,Epc*: adiit Σ

better hopes, rouse your spirits! He will certainly be with us, and greater yet, as he is from every labour.

MEGARA
What the wretched deeply desire, they easily believe.

AMPHITRYON
No! What they deeply fear, they think can never be dislodged or removed. Fear's expectations always incline to the worse.

MEGARA
Submerged, buried, weighed down by the whole earth above him, what path does he have to the upper world?

AMPHITRYON
The same as he had when he escaped through the arid region, the sand in waves like a troubled sea, the waters which twice departed and twice returned—when his ship was abandoned and he stuck fast in the shallow Syrtes, and, with his vessel grounded, he surmounted the seas on foot.

MEGARA
Malicious Fortune rarely spares the greatest spirits. No one can confront such frequent dangers and survive for long. Disaster may miss a person repeatedly, but it finds him in the end.

But see, Lycus approaches, with threats in his expression, fierce in bearing as in spirit, brandishing the sceptre that belongs to another.

LYCUS

Urbis regens opulenta Thebanae loca
et omne quidquid uberis cingit soli
obliqua Phocis, quidquid Ismenos rigat,
335 quidquid Cithaeron vertice excelso videt,
[et bina findens Isthmos exilis freta]
non vetera patriae iura possideo domus
ignavus heres; nobiles non sunt mihi
avi nec altis inclitum titulis genus,
340 sed clara virtus. qui genus iactat suum,
aliena laudat. rapta sed trepida manu
sceptra obtinentur; omnis in ferro est salus;
quod civibus tenere te invitis scias,
strictus tuetur ensis. alieno in loco
345 haud stabile regnum est; una sed nostras potest
fundare vires iuncta regali face
thalamisque Megara; ducet e genere inclito
novitas colorem nostra. non equidem reor
fore ut recuset ac meos spernat toros;
350 quod si impotenti pertinax animo abnuet,
stat tollere omnem penitus Herculeam domum.
invidia factum ac sermo popularis premet?
ars prima regni est posse in invidia pati.
    —Temptemus igitur, fors dedit nobis locum:
355 namque ipsa, tristi vestis obtentu caput
velata, iuxta praesides astat deos,
laterique adhaeret verus Alcidae sator.

336 *deleted by B. Schmidt*

---

22 Line 336 (deleted): "and the narrow Isthmus separating two
straits."   23 Compare "A sceptre snatch'd with an unruly hand

LYCUS

[*Aside*] I rule the rich lands of the city of Thebes, and all the fertile soil that sloping Phocis surrounds, all that the Ismenos waters, all that Cithaeron beholds from its soaring peak.[22] These are no ancient rights of an ancestral house that I hold as an indolent heir; I do not have noble ancestors, nor a family distinguished by lofty titles, but glorious valour. A man who boasts of his family is praising others' achievements. But the hand trembles that holds a stolen sceptre; the only safety is in the sword; what you are aware of holding against the citizens' will is guarded by the naked blade.[23] Rule in another's place is not secure; yet there is one who can underpin my power if joined with me in a royal marriage: Megara.[24] From her famous family my newness will take on colour. I cannot think she will refuse and spurn my bed. But if she is self-willed and stubbornly denies me, I am resolved to eliminate Hercules' entire house. Will the deed be assailed by unpopularity and the people's gossip? The first art of kingship is to endure unpopularity.

Let us make the attempt, then, since chance has given us occasion: for she herself is standing by the protecting gods,[25] with head veiled in mourning, and close by her side clings the true begetter of Alcides.

/ Must be as boisterously maintain'd as gain'd" (Shakespeare, *King John* III.3(4).135f.).   [24] Voltaire adapts these lines in *Mérope* I.4.291–94: "J'ai besoin d'un hymen utile à ma grandeur, / Qui détourne de moi le nom d'usurpateur, / Qui fixe enfin les voeux de ce peuple infidèle, / Qui m'apporte pour dot l'amour qu'on a pour elle."   [25] I.e. by statues of those gods, which stand near the altar and shrine.

MEGARA

Quidnam iste, nostri generis exitium ac lues,
novi parat? quid temptat?

LYCUS

O clarum trahens
360 a stirpe nomen regia, facilis mea
parumper aure verba patienti excipe.
si aeterna semper odia mortales gerant,
nec coeptus umquam cedat ex animis furor,
sed arma felix teneat infelix paret,
365 nihil relinquent bella; tum vastis ager
squalebit arvis, subdita tectis face
altus sepultas obruet gentes cinis.
pacem reduci velle victori expedit,
victo necesse est.—particeps regno veni;
370 sociemur animis. pignus hoc fidei cape:
continge dextram. quid truci vultu siles?

MEGARA

Egone ut parentis sanguine aspersam manum
fratrumque gemina caede contingam? prius
extinguet ortus, referet occasus diem,
375 pax ante fida nivibus et flammis erit
et Scylla Siculum iunget Ausonio latus,
priusque multo vicibus alternis fugax
Euripus unda stabit Euboica piger.
patrem abstulisti, regna, germanos, larem,
380 patriam. quid ultra est? una res superest mihi
fratre ac parente carior, regno ac lare:
odium tui, quod esse cum populo mihi
commune doleo—pars quota ex isto mea est!

MEGARA

What new plan is he hatching, that scourge and ruin of our family? What is he attempting?

LYCUS

You who inherit a glorious name from your royal lineage, listen to my words for a moment with patience and indulgence. If mortals harbour eternal hatred forever, and rage once engendered never leaves their hearts, but the successful maintain arms and the unsuccessful prepare them—then war will leave nothing behind! The land will lie waste with its fields desolate, homes will be torched, and deep ash will overwhelm and bury the nations. To want peace restored is politic for the conqueror, and imperative for the conquered. Come, share my throne; let us have an alliance of hearts. Accept this assurance of good faith, take my hand. Why do you stand grim-faced and silent?

MEGARA

I take a hand spattered with my father's blood, and with the double slaughter of my brothers? Sooner shall the East quench the daylight and the West revive it, sooner will come staunch peace between snow and fire, and Scylla will link the shores of Sicily and Italy; sooner by far will the Euripus, which races in ebb and flow, stand with Euboea's waters motionless. You have stolen my father, kingdom, brothers, home, country. What else is there? One thing is left to me, dearer than brother and father, kingdom and home: hatred of you, which I share to my sorrow with the people—how small a portion of it is mine!

---

380 patriam *EA*: patrium *editio Patavina*

Dominare tumidus, spiritus altos gere:
385 sequitur superbos ultor a tergo deus.
Thebana novi regna: quid matres loquar
passas et ausas scelera? quid geminum nefas
mixtumque nomen coniugis nati patris?
quid bina fratrum castra? quid totidem rogos?
390 riget superba Tantalis luctu parens
maestusque Phrygio manat in Sipylo lapis.
quin ipse torvum subrigens crista caput
Illyrica Cadmus regna permensus fuga
longas reliquit corporis tracti notas.
395 haec te manent exempla. dominare ut libet,
dum solita regni fata te nostri vocent.

LYCUS

Agedum efferatas rabida voces amove,
et disce regum imperia ab Alcide pati.
ego rapta quamvis sceptra victrici geram
400 dextra, regamque cuncta sine legum metu
quas arma vincunt, pauca pro causa loquar
nostra. cruento cecidit in bello pater,
cecidere fratres? arma non servant modum;
nec temperari facile nec reprimi potest
405 stricti ensis ira; bella delectat cruor.
sed ille regno pro suo, nos improba
cupidine acti? quaeritur belli exitus,
non causa.—sed nunc pereat omnis memoria;
cum victor arma posuit, et victum decet
410 deponere odia. non ut inflexo genu

---

[26] Ino and Jocasta would fit both categories. Antiope, mother

Play the puffed-up despot, exercise your arrogance! An avenging god follows at the back of the proud. I know all about the Theban kingship. Need I speak of the mothers who have suffered and committed crimes?[26] Of the doubled infamy, and the intermingled names of husband, son, and father? Of the brothers' two armies, and their two pyres? The proud Tantalid mother is rigid with grief—a sombre stone wet with tears on Phrygian Sipylus.[27] Even Cadmus himself, as he traversed Illyria's realm in exile, raised a head made fearful by a crest, and left the long tracks of his trailing body. These precedents await you. Play the despot as you will, as long as the usual fate of our kingship beckons you.

LYCUS

Come now! Drop this wild and frenzied talk, and learn from Alcides to submit to kings' commands. Though I wield the stolen sceptre in my conquering hand, and have absolute power with no fear of laws (which are bested by weapons), I shall speak a few words in my defence. Did your father and brothers fall in the carnage of war? Weapons observe no bounds, and the anger of the drawn sword cannot easily be moderated or restrained; wars exult in blood. But was he fighting for his kingdom, while I was driven by shameless ambition? The question about war is its outcome, not its cause. But now let the past be completely forgotten; when the victor lays down arms, the vanquished should also lay aside hatred. I am not asking you to

of Amphion and Zethus, suffered persecution; Agave committed a crime against her son Pentheus.

[27] These references are respectively to Oedipus, to his sons Polynices and Eteocles, and to Tantalus' daughter Niobe.

regnantem adores petimus; hoc ipsum placet,
animo ruinas quod capis magno tuas.
es rege coniunx digna: sociemus toros.

MEGARA

Gelidus per artus vadit exsangues tremor.
415 quod facinus aures pepulit? haud equidem horrui,
cum pace rupta bellicus muros fragor
circumsonaret; pertuli intrepide omnia.
thalamos tremesco; capta nunc videor mihi.
gravent catenae corpus et longa fame
420 mors protrahatur lenta: non vincet fidem
vis ulla nostram. moriar, Alcide, tua.

LYCUS

Animosne mersus inferis coniunx facit?

MEGARA

Inferna tetigit, posset ut supera assequi.

LYCUS

Telluris illum pondus immensae premit.

MEGARA

425 Nullo premetur onere, qui caelum tulit.

LYCUS

Cogere.

MEGARA

Cogi qui potest nescit mori.

LYCUS

Effare thalamis quod novis potius parem
regale munus.

MEGARA

Aut tuam mortem aut meam.

do homage to your ruler on bended knee; I approve of the
fact that you bear your overthrow with great spirit. You are
a worthy wife for a king: let us make a marriage alliance.

MEGARA

A cold shudder runs through my stunned body. What outrage has struck my ears? *I* did not tremble when peace was
shattered and the din of war resounded around our walls; I
endured all that fearlessly. But marriage I shudder at; now
I recognise myself as a prisoner. Let chains burden my
body, let me face a lingering drawn-out death by slow starvation: no violence will overcome my loyalty. I shall die as
your wife, Alcides.

LYCUS

You take courage from a husband sunk in the underworld?

MEGARA

He visited the underworld to gain the upper world.

LYCUS

He is crushed by the weight of the vast earth.

MEGARA

No burden will crush the one who carried the heavens.

LYCUS

You will be forced.

MEGARA

One who can be forced does not know how to die.

LYCUS

Say what kingly gift I should prepare instead for our new
marriage.

MEGARA

Either your death or mine.

LYCUS

Moriere demens.

MEGARA

Coniugi occurram meo.

LYCUS

430   Sceptroque nostro potior est famulus tibi?

MEGARA

Quot iste "famulus" tradidit reges neci!

LYCUS

Cur ergo regi servit et patitur iugum?

MEGARA

Imperia dura tolle: quid virtus erit?

LYCUS

Obici feris monstrisque virtutem putas?

MEGARA

435   Virtutis est domare quae cuncti pavent.

LYCUS

Tenebrae loquentem magna Tartareae premunt.

MEGARA

Non est ad astra mollis e terris via.

LYCUS

Quo patre genitus caelitum sperat domos?

AMPHITRYON

Miseranda coniunx Herculis magni, sile:
440   partes meae sunt reddere Alcidae patrem
genusque verum. post tot ingentis viri
memoranda facta postque pacatum manu
quodcumque Titan ortus et labens videt,

LYCUS

You will die, madwoman.

MEGARA

Then I shall find my husband.

LYCUS

And is a slave more to you than my sceptered power?

MEGARA

How many kings that "slave" has delivered to death!

LYCUS

Then why does he serve a king and endure subjection?

MEGARA

Take away harsh commands: what will valour be?

LYCUS

You think being thrown to beasts and monsters is valour?

MEGARA

Valour consists of subduing what everyone fears.

LYCUS

The darkness of Tartarus covers that great boaster.

MEGARA

The path from earth to the stars is not a smooth one.

LYCUS

Who is his father, that he aspires to the gods' abodes?

AMPHITRYON

Piteous wife of great Hercules, speak no more. It is my part
to restore to Alcides his true father and lineage. After so
many impressive deeds by that great hero, after he brought
peace to all that the rising and setting Titan beholds, after

83

post monstra tot perdomita, post Phlegram impio
445 sparsam cruore postque defensos deos
nondum liquet de patre? mentimur Iovem?
Iunonis odio crede.

LYCUS

Quid violas Iovem?
mortale caelo non potest iungi genus.

AMPHITRYON

Communis ista pluribus causa est deis.

LYCUS

450 Famuline fuerant ante quam fierent dei?

AMPHITRYON

Pastor Pheraeos Delius pavit greges.

LYCUS

Sed non per omnes exul erravit plagas.

AMPHITRYON

Quem profuga terra mater errante edidit?

LYCUS

Num monstra saevas Phoebus aut timuit feras?

AMPHITRYON

455 Primus sagittas imbuit Phoebi draco.

LYCUS

Quam gravia parvus tulerit ignoras mala?

AMPHITRYON

E matris utero fulmine eiectus puer
mox fulminanti proximus patri stetit.

454 saevas* A: saeva E

he conquered so many monsters, after he defended the gods and spattered their enemies' blood over Phlegra, is there still any doubt about his father? Are we lying about Jove? Believe Juno's hatred!

LYCUS

Why profane Jove? Mortal kind cannot unite with heaven.

AMPHITRYON

That is the origin shared by many gods.

LYCUS

Had they been slaves before they could become gods?

AMPHITRYON

A cowhand from Delos pastured herds in Thessaly.[28]

LYCUS

But he did not drift in exile through every region.

AMPHITRYON

Though a fleeing mother bore him on a drifting land?

LYCUS

Did Phoebus face monsters or savage beasts?

AMPHITRYON

The first to stain Phoebus' arrows was a dragon.

LYCUS

Do you not know what serious trials he bore while small?

AMPHITRYON

A boy expelled by the lightning bolt from his mother's womb soon stood at the side of his lightning-wielding

[28] A reference to Apollo's servitude to Admetus.

quid? qui gubernat astra, qui nubes quatit,
460   non latuit infans rupis exesae specu?
sollicita tanti pretia natales habent,
semperque magno constitit nasci deum.

LYCUS

Quemcumque miserum videris, hominem scias.

AMPHITRYON

Quemcumque fortem videris, miserum neges.

LYCUS

465   Fortem vocemus cuius ex umeris leo,
donum puellae factus, et clava excidit
fulsitque pictum veste Sidonia latus?
fortem vocemus cuius horrentes comae
maduere nardo, laude qui notas manus
470   ad non virilem tympani movit sonum,
mitra ferocem barbara frontem premens?

AMPHITRYON

Non erubescit Bacchus effusos tener
sparsisse crines nec manu molli levem
vibrare thyrsum, cum parum forti gradu
475   auro decorum syrma barbarico trahit;
post multa virtus opera laxari solet.

LYCUS

Hoc Euryti fatetur eversi domus
pecorumque ritu virginum oppressi greges.
hoc nulla Iuno, nullus Eurystheus iubet:
480   ipsius haec sunt opera.

father.[29] What? Did he who governs the stars and shakes the clouds not lie concealed as an infant in a cave of a hollow cliff? Disquiet is the price of such high births, and there is always a great cost to being born a god.

LYCUS

If you see someone wretched, be sure that he is mortal.

AMPHITRYON

If you see someone resolute, you cannot call him wretched.

LYCUS

Can we call him resolute, when the lionskin and club fell from his shoulders and became a present for a girl,[30] and when his body gleamed bright in Sidonian dress? Can we call him resolute, when his shaggy hair was soaked in nard, and when he moved those renowned hands to the unmanly sound of the tambourine, encircling his fierce brow with an oriental turban?

AMPHITRYON

Delicate Bacchus does not blush to let his hair flow free, nor to shake a light thyrsus in his soft hand, when he steps daintily and trails his flowing garment, gorgeous with eastern gold. It is valour's habit to relax after much toil.

LYCUS

That is acknowledged by the overthrow of Eurytus' house, and the harrying of herds of maidens as if they were cattle. No Juno, no Eurystheus gave such commands: this is his own work.

[29] The boy was Bacchus, his mother Semele, his father Jupiter.
[30] Omphale.

87

AMPHITRYON

Non nosti omnia:
ipsius opus est caestibus fractus suis
Eryx et Eryci iunctus Antaeus Libys,
et qui hospitali caede manantes foci
bibere iustum sanguinem Busiridis;
485   ipsius opus est vulneri et ferro invius
mortem coactus integer Cycnus pati,
nec unus una Geryon victus manu.
eris inter istos—qui tamen nullo stupro
laesere thalamos.

LYCUS

Quod Iovi hoc regi licet:
490   Iovi dedisti coniugem, regi dabis;
et te magistro non novum hoc discet nurus,
etiam viro probante meliorem sequi.
sin copulari pertinax taedis negat,
vel ex coacta nobilem partum feram.

MEGARA

495   Umbrae Creontis et penates Labdaci
et nuptiales impii Oedipodae faces,
nunc solita nostro fata coniugio date!
nunc nunc, cruentae regis Aegypti nurus,
adeste multo sanguine infectae manus.
500   dest una numero Danais: explebo nefas.

485 invius *Heinsius*: obvius *EA*
490 dabis *EA*: dabit *(sc. Hercules) Leo*

HERCULES

AMPHITRYON

You do not know the whole story. It is his own work that Eryx was pulverized with the boxing gloves he chose, and that Eryx was joined by Libyan Antaeus; and that the altar dripping with strangers' gore drank the justly spilled blood of Busiris. It is his own work that Cycnus, impervious to wounds from weapons, was forced to suffer death unwounded,[31] and that Geryon, no single foe, was conquered single-handedly by him. You will join them—yet even they never defiled the marriage bed.

LYCUS

What Jove is allowed, a king is allowed. You provided a wife[32] to Jove, you shall provide one to a king; and from your teaching your daughter-in-law will learn this old lesson: that when even her husband approves, she should follow his superior. But if she stubbornly refuses to be joined in marriage, I shall have highborn children from her, even by force.

MEGARA

Ghost of Creon, house gods of Labdacus, and marriage torches of incestuous Oedipus, now grant the usual fate to our marriage! Now, you murderous daughters-in-law of King Aegyptus, be with us, your hands stained with copious blood. One Danaid is missing from your number: I shall complete the crime.

---

[31] Cycnus son of Mars, whom Hercules killed, is here conflated with Cycnus son of Neptune, who was impervious to weapons and was strangled to death by Achilles.

[32] I.e. your own wife Alcmene.

LYCUS

Coniugia quoniam pervicax nostra abnuis
regemque terres, sceptra quid possint scies.
complectere aras! nullus eripiet deus
te mihi, nec orbe si remolito queat
505 ad supera victor numina Alcides vehi.
—congerite silvas: templa supplicibus suis
iniecta flagrent, coniugem et totum gregem
consumat unus igne subiecto rogus.

AMPHITRYON

Hoc munus a te genitor Alcidae peto,
510 rogare quod me deceat, ut primus cadam.

LYCUS

Qui morte cunctos luere supplicium iubet
nescit tyrannus esse. diversa irroga:
miserum veta perire, felicem iube.
ego, dum cremandis trabibus accrescit rogus,
515 sacro regentem maria votivo colam.

AMPHITRYON

Pro numinum vis summa, pro caelestium
rector parensque, cuius excussis tremunt
humana telis, impiam regis feri
compesce dextram!—quid deos frustra precor?
520 ubicumque es, audi, nate.
                              Cur subito labant
agitata motu templa? cur mugit solum?
infernus imo sonuit e fundo fragor.
audimur! est est sonitus Herculei gradus.

CHORUS

O Fortuna viris invida fortibus,
525 quam non aequa bonis praemia dividis!

90

LYCUS

Since you obstinately refuse my marriage offer and threaten your king, you shall know what sceptered power can do. Yes, cling to your altar. No god will rescue you from me, not even if Alcides could heave the whole earth back and make his way triumphantly to the upper world and its gods. [*To attendants*] Pile up timber: let the shrine collapse in flames on its own suppliants; once fired, let a single pyre consume the wife and the whole flock.

AMPHITRYON

I request this favour, which is fitting for me to ask as Alcides' father, that I be first to fall.

LYCUS

A man who imposes the death penalty on all does not know how to be a tyrant. Inflict contrasting punishments: forbid the wretched to die, command the happy to do so. While the pyre grows with logs for burning, I shall worship the ruler of the seas with a vowed sacrifice.

AMPHITRYON

O high power of the gods, o ruler and father of the heavenly ones, whose hurled weapons set the human world trembling, check the impious hand of this cruel king! Why make vain prayers to the gods? Wherever you are, my son, hear me! Why is the shrine rocking and shaking with sudden movement? Why is the earth rumbling? A thunderous noise comes from the depths, from the underworld. We are heard! It *is* the sound of Hercules' step.

CHORUS

O Fortune, hostile to heroes,
how unfair to the good the rewards you assign!

Eurystheus facili regnet in otio;
Alcmena genitus bella per omnia
monstris exagitet caeliferam manum:
serpentis resecet colla feracia,
530   deceptis referat mala sororibus,
cum somno dederit pervigiles genas
pomis divitibus praepositus draco.
    Intravit Scythiae multivagas domos
et gentes patriis sedibus hospitas,
535   calcavitque freti terga rigentia
et mutis tacitum litoribus mare.
illic dura carent aequora fluctibus,
et, qua plena rates carbasa tenderant,
intonsis teritur semita Sarmatis.
540   stat pontus, vicibus mobilis annuis,
navem nunc facilis, nunc equitem pati.
illic quae viduis gentibus imperat,
aurato religans ilia balteo
detraxit spolium nobile corpori
545   et peltam et nivei vincula pectoris,
victorem posito suspiciens genu.
    Qua spe praecipites actus ad inferos,
audax ire vias irremeabiles,
vidisti Siculae regna Proserpinae?
550   illic nulla noto nulla favonio
consurgunt tumidis fluctibus aequora;

538 tenderant *A*: tenderent *E*

Eurystheus is to reign in effortless ease;
Alcmene's son in all manner of struggles
is to busy his heaven-bearing hands with monsters—
keep cutting the serpent's prolific necks,
bring back the apples from the cheated sisters,[33]
when the dragon guarding the precious fruits
has allowed his watchful eyes to sleep.
    He came among Scythia's nomad homes
and clans that are strangers to their fathers' dwellings;
he trod the frozen back of the sea,
hushed waters with silent shores.
There the hard surface is void of waves,
and where vessels had spread full sail,
a path is worn by the unshorn Sarmatae.
The sea stands still, but shifts with the year,
ready to bear now ships, now horsemen.
There she who commands an unwed race,[34]
her flanks bound with a gilded baldric,
stripped the glorious trophy from her body,
and her shield and the bonds of her snow-white breast,
looking up at her victor on bended knee.
    What purpose drove you to the precipitous
        underworld,
to travel boldly irretraceable paths,
and to see the realm of Sicilian Proserpine?
There no southerly, no westerly wind
causes seas to rise with swelling waves;

[33] The serpent is the Hydra; the sisters, the Hesperides.
[34] Hippolyte, queen of the Amazons.

non illic geminum Tyndaridae genus
succurrunt timidis sidera navibus;
stat nigro pelagus gurgite languidum,
555   et, cum Mors avidis pallida dentibus
gentes innumeras manibus intulit,
uno tot populi remige transeunt.
    Evincas utinam iura ferae Stygis
Parcarumque colos non revocabiles!
560   hic qui rex populis pluribus imperat,
bello cum peteres Nestoream Pylon,
tecum conseruit pestiferas manus
telum tergemina cuspide praeferens;
effugit tenui vulnere saucius
565   et mortis dominus pertimuit mori.
fatum rumpe manu: tristibus inferis
prospectus pateat lucis, et invius
limes det faciles ad superos vias.
    Immites potuit flectere cantibus
570   umbrarum dominos et prece supplici
Orpheus, Eurydicen dum repetit suam.
quae silvas et aves saxaque traxerat
ars, quae praebuerat fluminibus moras,
ad cuius sonitum constiterant ferae,
575   mulcet non solitis vocibus inferos
et surdis resonat clarius in locis.
deflent Eumenides Threiciam nurum,
deflent et lacrimis difficiles dei;
et qui fronte nimis crimina tetrica
580   quaerunt ac veteres excutiunt reos
flentes Eurydicen iuridici sedent.

553 sidera *EA*: sidere *Housman*

there no twin Tyndarids come to the aid
of fearful ships in starlike form.
The sea stands inert with its black flood,
and when Death, pale-faced with ravening teeth,
has brought innumerable throngs to the shades,
one oarsman transports so many peoples.
    May you vanquish the laws of cruel Styx,
and the irreversible distaffs of the Fates.
The king who here rules numerous peoples,
when you were attacking Nestor's Pylos,
raised his baneful hands against you,
wielding his triple-pointed weapon;
once injured with a slight wound, he fled—
the lord of death terrified to die.
Break through doom by force! For the gloomy
    underworld
let a view of the light be opened, and the impassable
boundary give easy passage to the upper world.
    Orpheus could sway the pitiless rulers
of the shades with songs and suppliant prayer,
when he sought back his Eurydice.
The art that had drawn trees, birds, and rocks,
that had caused rivers to tarry,
at whose sound beasts had stood still,
soothes the lower world with unwonted song,
and rings out clearer in those soundless places.
The Eumenides weep for the Thracian bride;
so too weep the gods who are proof against tears.
Even those who investigate crimes with sternest
brows and examine erstwhile culprits,
those seated judges weep for Eurydice.

tandem mortis ait "Vincimur" arbiter,
"evade ad superos, lege tamen data:
tu post terga tui perge viri comes,
585   tu non ante tuam respice coniugem,
quam cum clara deos obtulerit dies
Spartanique aderit ianua Taenari."
odit verus amor nec patitur moras:
munus dum properat cernere, perdidit.
590   Quae vinci potuit regia carmine,
haec vinci poterit regia viribus.

HERCULES

O lucis almae rector et caeli decus,
qui alterna curru spatia flammifero ambiens
illustre latis exeris terris caput,
595   da, Phoebe, veniam, si quid illicitum tui
videre vultus; iussus in lucem extuli
arcana mundi. tuque, caelestum arbiter
parensque, visus fulmine opposito tege;
et tu, secundo maria qui sceptro regis,
600   imas pete undas. quisquis ex alto aspicit
terrena, facie pollui metuens nova,
aciem reflectat oraque in caelum erigat
portenta fugiens. hoc nefas cernant duo,
qui advexit et quae iussit.
                    In poenas meas
605   atque in labores non satis terrae patent
Iunonis odio. vidi inaccessa omnibus,
ignota Phoebo quaeque deterior polus

---

594 latis *E*: laetis* *A*

At last death's ruler said, "We submit.
Go forth to the world, but with this proviso:
you may escort your husband, but behind him;
you may not look back on your wife
until bright daylight discloses the heavens,
and the door of Spartan Taenarus is near."
True love hates delays and cannot endure them:
in hurrying to behold his prize, he lost her.

The kingdom that could be conquered by song
can and will be conquered by force.

ACT 3

HERCULES

Lord of the life-giving light, glory of heaven, who circle through two expanses alternately[35] in your fiery chariot and reveal your glorious face to the broad lands: grant pardon, Phoebus, if your gaze has beheld what is forbidden. I brought earth's hidden things into the light under orders. And you, ruler and father of the heavenly gods, hold out the thunderbolt to shield your vision; and you who rule the seas with the second-drawn sceptre, make for your deepest waters. All who look from on high on earthly things, at risk of defilement from this strange sight, should turn their gaze away and lift their eyes to heaven, shunning such a monstrosity. Only two should behold this enormity: he who fetched it, she who ordered it.

For Juno's hatred the earth is not broad enough to afford me sufferings and toils. I have seen things inaccessible to all, unknown to Phoebus, those gloomy spaces which

---

[35] I.e. the hemispheres above and below the horizon.

obscura diro spatia concessit Iovi;
et, si placerent tertiae sortis loca,
610 regnare potui. noctis aeternae chaos
et nocte quiddam gravius et tristes deos
et fata vici; morte contempta redî.
quid restat aliud? vidi et ostendi inferos.
da si quid ultra est, iam diu pateris manus
615 cessare nostras, Iuno; quae vinci iubes?
—Sed templa quare miles infestus tenet
limenque sacrum terror armorum obsidet?

AMPHITRYON

Utrumne visus vota decipiunt meos,
an ille domitor orbis et Graium decus
620 tristi silentem nubilo liquit domum?
estne ille natus? membra laetitia stupent.
o nate, certa at sera Thebarum salus,
teneone in auras editum an vana fruor
deceptus umbra? tune es? agnosco toros
625 umerosque et alto nobilem trunco manum.

HERCULES

Unde iste, genitor, squalor et lugubribus
amicta coniunx? unde tam foedo obsiti
paedore nati? quae domum clades gravat?

AMPHITRYON

Socer est peremptus, regna possedit Lycus,
630 natos parentem coniugem leto petit.

HERCULES

Ingrata tellus, nemo ad Herculeae domus
auxilia venit? vidit hoc tantum nefas
defensus orbis?—cur diem questu tero?

the baser world has granted to infernal Jove; and if the regions of the third lot pleased me, I could have reigned there. The desolation of eternal night, an oppressiveness worse than night, the grim gods and the Fates—I overcame them; I flouted death and returned. What else remains? I have seen and revealed the underworld. Assign any further task, Juno, you have left my hands idle too long: what do you bid me conquer?

But why are there hostile soldiers in control of the shrine, and threatening weapons around the sacred entrance?

AMPHITRYON

Is hope deceiving my sight, or has that world conqueror, the pride of Greece, left the halls hushed by cheerless gloom? Is that my son? My body is stunned with joy. My son, sure though tardy saviour of Thebes, am I holding someone risen to the open air, or enjoying a false and empty apparition? Is it you? I recognise those sinews, those shoulders, that glorious hand with its mighty club.

HERCULES

Why are you in squalor, father, and my wife dressed in mourning? Why are my sons covered in loathsome filth? What disaster afflicts our house?

AMPHITRYON

Your father-in-law is slain; Lycus has seized the throne, and marks for death your sons, father, and wife.

HERCULES

Ungrateful land! Did no one come to the aid of Hercules' house? Did the world I protected watch this great iniquity? But why waste time in complaints? Though not my

mactetur impar, hanc ferat virtus notam
635 fiatque summus hostis Alcidae Lycus.
ad hauriendum sanguinem inimicum feror;
Theseu, resiste, ne qua vis subita ingruat.
me bella poscunt: differ amplexus, parens,
coniunxque differ. nuntiet Diti Lycus
640 me iam redisse.

THESEUS

Flebilem ex oculis fuga,
regina, vultum, tuque nato sospite
lacrimas cadentes reprime: si novi Herculem,
Lycus Creonti debitas poenas dabit.
lentum est "dabit": dat. hoc quoque est lentum: dedit.

AMPHITRYON

645 Votum secundet qui potest nostrum deus
rebusque lassis adsit. o magni comes
magnanime nati, pande virtutum ordinem,
quam longa maestos ducat ad manes via,
ut vincla tulerit dura Tartareus canis.

THESEUS

650 Memorare cogis acta securae quoque
horrenda menti. vix adhuc certa est fides
vitalis aurae; torpet acies luminum,
hebetesque visus vix diem insuetum ferunt.

AMPHITRYON

Pervince, Theseu, quidquid alto in pectore
655 remanet pavoris, neve te fructu optimo
frauda laborum: quae fuit durum pati,
meminisse dulce est. fare casus horridos.

634 impar *Fitch*: hostis *EA*

equal, he must be slaughtered; my valour must bear this stigma, and Alcides' final foe must be Lycus. I leave to drain his hateful blood; Theseus, remain here, in case of sudden attack. Battle calls me: postpone your embraces, father; wife, postpone them. Lycus must carry to Dis the news of my return.

THESEUS

Banish that tearful look from your eyes, O queen. You too, with your son safe, check your falling tears. If I know Hercules, Lycus will pay the penalty owed to Creon. "Will pay" is laggard, he *is* paying. That too is laggard, he *has* paid.[36]

AMPHITRYON

May God, who has the power, prosper our hopes and succour our distress. Great-souled companion of my great son, disclose the sequence of his heroic deeds: how long a path leads to the gloomy shades, and how the hound of Tartarus bore those galling chains.

THESEUS

You force me to recount deeds fearful to my mind even in safety. I scarcely have sure trust as yet in the life-giving air; my eyesight is dimmed, and my dull vision can hardly bear the unaccustomed light.

AMPHITRYON

Overcome such fear as remains lodged in your heart, Theseus. Do not cheat yourself of the best reward of toils: it is sweet to recollect what was hard to endure. Recount those fearful events.

[36] Compare Ben Jonson, *Catiline* III.3.174–76: "He shall die. / Shall, was too slowly said; he's dying. That / Is yet too slow; he's dead."

THESEUS

Fas omne mundi teque dominantem precor
regno capaci teque quam tota irrita
660   quaesivit Aetna mater, ut iure abdita
et operta terris liceat impune eloqui.
    Spartana tellus nobile attollit iugum,
densis ubi aequor Taenarus silvis premit.
hic ora solvit Ditis invisi domus
665   hiatque rupes alta et immenso specu
ingens vorago faucibus vastis patet
latumque pandit omnibus populis iter.
non caeca tenebris incipit primo via:
tenuis relictae lucis a tergo nitor
670   fulgorque dubius solis affecti cadit
et ludit aciem; nocte sic mixta solet
praebere lumen primus aut serus dies.
hinc ampla vacuis spatia laxantur locis,
in quae omne mersum pergat humanum genus.
675   nec ire labor est: ipsa deducit via.
ut saepe puppes aestus invitas rapit,
sic pronus aer urget atque avidum chaos,
gradumque retro flectere haud umquam sinunt
umbrae tenaces.
             Intus immenso sinu
680   placido quieta labitur Lethe vado
demitque curas; neve remeandi amplius
pateat facultas, flexibus multis gravem
involvit amnem, qualis incerta vagus
Maeander unda ludit et cedit sibi

659f. tota . . . Aetna* *EA*: amotam . . . Enna *Heimsoeth*: toto . . .
orbe *Schmidt*   660 iure *Par. Lat. 8030, 8035*: iura *EA*

THESEUS

I pray to the whole order of the universe, and to you[37] who rule the capacious kingdom, and you, sought in vain by your mother across the whole of Etna: may I speak with impunity of things rightfully hidden and buried in the earth.

There rises in the land of Sparta a far-famed ridge, where Cape Taenarus hems the sea with its dense forests. Here the house of hateful Dis opens its mouth; a tall cliff gapes wide, a cavernous abyss extends its vast jaws and spreads a broad path for all the nations. At the outset the way is not obscured by darkness: there falls a faint brightness from the light left behind, a twilight glow of the weakened sunshine, which baffles the eye. Such is the light, mingled with darkness, familiar at dawn or dusk. Then there open up empty regions, spaces extensive enough for all the human race to enter, once plunged into the earth. To travel is no toil: the path itself draws you down. As often a current sweeps ships unwillingly off course, so the downward breeze and the greedy void hurry you on, and the clutching shades never allow you to turn your steps backward.

In the immense abyss within, the River Lethe glides quietly with calm waters, and takes away cares; and lest an opening for return should ever appear, it entwines its sluggish stream in many winding turns, just as the wandering Meander plays with its puzzled waters, bends back on itself

---

[37] Theseus invokes Dis and then Proserpine.

---

670 affecti *Bentley*: afflicti *EA*

685 instatque dubius litus an fontem petat.
palus inertis foeda Cocyti iacet;
hic vultur, illic luctifer bubo gemit
omenque triste resonat infaustae strigis.
horrent opaca fronde nigrantes comae
690 taxo imminente quam tenet segnis Sopor,
Famesque maesta tabido rictu iacet
Pudorque serus conscios vultus tegit.
Metus Pavorque, Funus et frendens Dolor
aterque Luctus sequitur et Morbus tremens
695 et cincta ferro Bella; in extremo abdita
iners Senectus adiuvat baculo gradum.

AMPHITRYON
Estne aliqua tellus Cereris aut Bacchi ferax?

THESEUS
Non prata viridi laeta facie germinant,
nec adulta leni fluctuat Zephyro seges;
700 non ulla ramos silva pomiferos habet;
sterilis profundi vastitas squalet soli
et foeda tellus torpet aeterno situ—
rerumque maestus finis et mundi ultima.
immotus aer haeret et pigro sedet
705 nox atra mundo; cuncta marcore horrida,
ipsaque morte peior est mortis locus.

AMPHITRYON
Quid ille opaca qui regit sceptro loca:
qua sede positus temperat populos leves?

THESEUS
Est in recessu Tartari obscuro locus,

and presses forward, uncertain whether to head for the seacoast or its source. Here lies the foul swamp of the torpid Cocytus; here is the shriek of the vulture, there of the foreboding owl, and the grim echoing omen of the unlucky screech owl. Black bedraggled foliage hangs in shadowy fronds on an overhanging yew tree, the haunt of sluggish Sleep. There lies sad Hunger with wasted jaws, and Shame, too late, covers its guilty face. There are Fear and Panic, Death and gnashing Resentment; behind them black Grief, trembling Disease and steel-girt War; hidden at the back, feeble Old Age supports its steps with a stick.

AMPHITRYON

Is there any land productive of grain or wine?

THESEUS

There are no joyful grassy meadows of verdant aspect, no ripened grain rippling in the gentle west wind, no trees with fruit-laden branches; a barren desolation crusts over the Stygian soil, and the foul earth languishes in perpetual stagnation—sad end of things, the world's last estate. The air hangs motionless, and black night sits over the torpid world. Everything is rough and blighted, and the place of death is worse than death itself.

AMPHITRYON

What of him who holds sway in the shadowy region? From what seat does he govern the insubstantial throngs?

THESEUS

In a dark recess of Tartarus there is a place bound by thick

---

690 taxo imminente quam *EA*: taxum imminentem qua *Leo*
705 marcore *Richter*: maerore *EA*

710 quem gravibus umbris spissa caligo alligat.
a fonte discors manat hinc uno latex,
alter quieto similis (hunc iurant dei),
tacente sacram devehens fluvio Styga;
at hic tumultu rapitur ingenti ferox
715 et saxa fluctu volvit Acheron invius
renavigari. cingitur duplici vado
adversa Ditis regia, atque ingens domus
umbrante luco tegitur. hic vasto specu
pendent tyranni limina, hoc umbris iter,
720 haec porta regni. campus hanc circa iacet,
in quo superbo digerit vultu sedens
animas recentes. dira maiestas deo,
frons torva, fratrum quae tamen specimen gerat
gentisque tantae; vultus est illi Iovis,
725 sed fulminantis. magna pars regni trucis
est ipse dominus, cuius aspectus timet
quidquid timetur.

AMPHITRYON
Verane est fama inferis
iam sera reddi iura et oblitos sui
sceleris nocentes debitas poenas dare?
730 quis iste veri rector atque aequi arbiter?

THESEUS
Non unus alta sede quaesitor sedens
iudicia trepidis sera sortitur reis:
aditur illo Cnosius Minos foro,
Rhadamanthus illo, Thetidis hoc audit socer.
735 quod quisque fecit, patitur; auctorem scelus

728 iam *Ageno*: tam *EA*

fog and deep shadows. Here from a single source there flow disparate streams: the one, appearing at rest (by it the gods swear oaths), conveys the sacred Styx on its silent course; the other races fiercely with great turbulence and rolls rocks along in its current—Acheron, impassable to any recrossing. The palace of Dis is ringed in front by this pair of rivers, and the huge house is masked by a shadowing grove. Here is the cavernous arched doorway of the tyrant; this is the path for the shades, the gate of the kingdom. Around it lies a level space, where he sits with a haughty air to organize the newly arrived spirits. The god has a fearful majesty: his countenance is grim, but gives proof of his brothers' identity and his high birth; his face is that of Jove, but when hurling thunder. A large part of that realm's harshness is its lord, whose appearance is feared even by fearsome beings.

AMPHITRYON

Is the story true that belated justice is meted out to those below, and that guilty ones are duly punished though they have forgotten their crimes? Who is that lord of truth and arbiter of justice?

THESEUS

There is not just one investigator seated on a high bench and allotting overdue judgements to terrified defendants. Minos of Crete presides in one court, Rhadamanthus in another, and Thetis' father-in-law[38] hears cases in a third. What each man did, he suffers: the crime recoils on its per-

---

[38] Aeacus.

repetit, suoque premitur exemplo nocens.
vidi cruentos carcere includi duces
et impotentis terga plebeia manu
scindi tyranni. quisquis est placide potens
740 dominusque vitae servat innocuas manus
et incruentum mitis imperium regit
animaeque parcit, longa permensus diu
vivacis aevi spatia vel caelum petit
vel laeta felix nemoris Elysii loca,
745 iudex futurus. sanguine humano abstine
quicumque regnas: scelera taxantur modo
maiore vestra.

AMPHITRYON

　　　　　Certus inclusos tenet
locus nocentes? utque fert fama, impios
supplicia vinclis saeva perpetuis domant?

THESEUS

750 Rapitur volucri tortus Ixion rota;
cervice saxum grande Sisyphia sedet;
in amne medio faucibus siccis senex
sectatur undas; alluit mentum latex,
fidemque cum iam saepe decepto dedit,
755 perit unda in ore, poma destituunt famem.
praebet volucri Tityos aeternas dapes,
urnasque frustra Danaides plenas gerunt;
errant furentes impiae Cadmeides,
terretque mensas avida Phineas avis.

---

742 animaeque* E PCS: animoque T^{pc} recc.
743 vivacis Bentley: felicis EA

petrator, and the criminal is plagued by the precedent he set. I saw bloodstained leaders immured in prison, and a ruthless tyrant's back flayed by the hands of the plebs. But anyone who governs mildly, who keeps his hands guiltless as master of life and death, who conducts a gentle, bloodless reign and spares lives—he measures the long sweep of a life full of years, and then reaches either heaven or the happy setting of the blessed Elysian grove, to serve as judge. Avoid shedding human blood, all you who reign: your crimes are assessed with heavier penalties.

AMPHITRYON

Are the guilty imprisoned in a particular place? And are the godless curbed, as the story goes, by cruel punishments in eternal chains?

THESEUS

Ixion is whirled and racked on a speeding wheel; a huge rock rests on Sisyphus' neck. In mid-river an old man with parched jaws pursues the water;[39] it laps against his chin, and after inspiring his trust, though so often deceived, it vanishes from his mouth; the fruits leave his hunger cheated. Tityos furnishes the vulture with an eternal feast, and the Danaids carry full pitchers to no avail. The unnatural Cadmeids wander in madness, and gluttonous birds threaten Phineus' table.

[39] Tantalus.

AMPHITRYON

760 Nunc ede nati nobilem pugnam mei.
patrui volentis munus an spolium refert?

THESEUS

Ferale tardis imminet saxum vadis,
stupente ubi unda segne torpescit fretum.
hunc servat amnem cultu et aspectu horridus
765 pavidosque manes squalidus gestat senex.
impexa pendet barba, deformem sinum
nodus coercet, concavae lucent genae;
regit ipse longo portitor conto ratem.
hic onere vacuam litori puppem applicans
770 repetebat umbras; poscit Alcides viam;
cedente turba dirus exclamat Charon:
"Quo pergis audax? siste properantem gradum."
non passus ullas natus Alcmena moras
ipso coactum navitam conto domat
775 scanditque puppem. cumba populorum capax
succubuit uni; sedit et gravior ratis
utrimque Lethen latere titubanti bibit.
tum victa trepidant monstra, Centauri truces
[Lapithaeque multo in bella succensi mero]

   *   *   *   *   *

780 Stygiae paludis ultimos quaerens sinus
fecunda mergit capita Lernaeus labor.
  Post haec avari Ditis apparet domus.
hic saevus umbras territat Stygius canis,
qui trina vasto capita concutiens sono

---

769 vacuam *E*: vacuus *A*
779 *deleted and lacuna recognised by Fitch*

HERCULES

AMPHITRYON

Now recount my son's glorious struggle. Is it spoil he brings, or a willing gift from his uncle?

THESEUS

A deathly crag overhangs the slow-moving pool, where the sluggish river idles with languid waters. An old man with unkempt, filthy clothes and appearance tends this river and transports the shades. His beard hangs uncombed, his shapeless cloak is fastened with a knot, he has deep-sunk, blazing eyes. As ferryman, he controls his craft himself with a long pole. He was bringing the boat to shore empty of cargo to collect more shades. Alcides demanded room, but as the crowd gave way, dread Charon shouted, "Where are you heading so boldly? Check your hurried steps." Alcmene's son brooked no delay, but coerced the sailor into subjection with his own pole, and climbed aboard. The skiff, which could carry crowds, foundered beneath this one man; it settled overburdened in the water, and drank in the Lethe on each side as it rocked. Then the monsters he had conquered panicked, savage Centaurs . . . ;[40] seeking the farthest recesses of the Stygian swamp, the Lernaean labour submerged its prolific heads.

After this there came into sight the house of greedy Dis. Here the fierce Stygian hound keeps the shades in fear and guards the kingdom, tossing his triple heads with clamor-

---

[40] One or more lines, perhaps containing a reference to Geryon, have been lost. Line 779 is interpolated: "and Lapiths fired to fighting by much wine." The "Lernaean labour" is the Hydra (now a ghost).

785 regnum tuetur. sordidum tabo caput
lambunt colubrae, viperis horrent iubae
longusque torta sibilat cauda draco.
par ira formae: sensit ut motus pedum,
attollit hirtas angue vibrato comas
790 missumque captat aure subrecta sonum,
sentire et umbras solitus. ut propior stetit
Iove natus antro, sedit incertus canis
et uterque timuit.—ecce latratu gravi
loca muta terret; sibilat totos minax
795 serpens per armos. vocis horrendae fragor
per ora missus terna felices quoque
exterret umbras. solvit a laeva feros
tunc ipse rictus et Cleonaeum caput
opponit ac se tegmine ingenti tegit;
800 victrice magnum dextera robur gerens
huc nunc et illuc verbere assiduo rotat,
ingeminat ictus. domitus infregit minas
et cuncta lassus capita summisit canis
antroque toto cessit. extimuit sedens
805 uterque solio dominus et duci iubet;
me quoque petenti munus Alcidae dedit.
    Tum gravia monstri colla permulcens manu
adamante texto vincit. oblitus sui
custos opaci pervigil regni canis
810 componit aures timidus et patiens trahi,
erumque fassus, ore summisso obsequens,
utrumque cauda pulsat anguifera latus.
postquam est ad oras Taenari ventum, et nitor

793 et uterque *EA*: leviterque *Madvig*
799 tegit *E*: clepit *A*

ous noise. Snakes lick the heads foul with pus, his manes bristle with vipers, and a long serpent hisses in his twisted tail. His rage matches his appearance. As he heard the movement of feet, his shaggy coat bristled with quivering snakes, and he pricked up his ears to catch the sound, being practiced in hearing even ghosts. When Jove's son took his stand closer to the cave, the hound sat back uncertain, and each felt fear. Suddenly with deep barking he alarmed the silent region; the snakes hissed threateningly all over his shoulders. The din of his fearsome bark, emerging through his three mouths, frightened even the shades in bliss. Then the hero loosed the fierce, gaping jaws from his left shoulder, thrust out the Cleonaean head and screened himself with that huge shield.[41] Wielding the great tree trunk in his all-conquering right hand, he whirled it this way and that in constant blows, and redoubled his strikes. Mastered, the hound broke off its threats, wearily drooped all its heads and emerged from the cave that it filled. The two rulers quailed on their thrones and bade him be led away; they granted me too as a gift to Alcides' request.[42]

Then he stroked the monster's foul necks with his hand, and leashed them with adamantine chains. Forgetting himself, the unsleeping watchdog of the dark realm timidly laid back his ears and tolerated being led, acknowledging his master, submitting with lowered muzzles, and thumping each flank with his snaky tail. But after they reached the borders of Taenarus, and the brightness of the

[41] I.e. the pelt of the lion, called "Cleonaean" from Cleonae near Nemea.

[42] Theseus and Pirithous were held captive in Hades after attempting to abduct Proserpine.

percussit oculos lucis ignotae novos,
815 resumit animos victus et vastas furens
quassat catenas; paene victorem abstulit
pronumque retro vexit et movit gradu.
tunc et meas respexit Alcides manus;
geminis uterque viribus tractum canem
820 ira furentem et bella temptantem irrita
intulimus orbi. vidit ut clarum diem
et pura nitidi spatia conspexit poli,
[oborta nox est, lumina in terram dedit]
compressit oculos et diem invisum expulit
825 aciemque retro flexit atque omni petît
cervice terram; tum sub Herculeas caput
abscondit umbras.
              —Densa sed laeto venit
clamore turba frontibus laurum gerens,
magnique meritas Herculis laudes canit.

CHORUS
830 Natus Eurystheus properante partu
iusserat mundi penetrare fundum.
derat hoc solum numero laborum,
tertiae regem spoliare sortis.
ausus es caecos aditus inire,
835 ducit ad manes via qua remotos
tristis et nigra metuenda silva,
sed frequens magna comitante turba.
    Quantus incedit populus per urbes

814 novos *Ageno*: novus *Bücheler*: bono *EA*

unknown light struck his unaccustomed eyes, he regained
his spirit after defeat, and shook his great chains furiously;
he almost carried off his victor, unbalanced him and
dragged him back face-down. Then Alcides looked to my
hands too; with our twofold strength we dragged the
hound, mad with rage and struggling furiously, and
brought him into the world. Once he saw the bright daylight and glimpsed the clear expanses of the shining
heaven,[43] he shut his eyes tight to expel the hated light,
turned his gaze aside and lowered each of his necks to the
earth; then he hid his heads in Hercules' shadow.

But a throng crowd is approaching with joyful
shouts, wearing the laurel on their brows and singing the
well-deserved praises of great Hercules.

CHORUS

Eurystheus, first-born in haste,
had bidden you penetrate the world's foundations.[44]
This alone was missing from the count of the labours,
to plunder the king of the third-drawn realm.
You dared to enter those dark approaches,
where a path leads down to the distant shades
in gloom, made fearsome by black woods,
but filled with a great accompanying crowd.

As great as the throng which moves through city
streets,

[43] Line 823 (deleted): "darkness rose over him, he turned his
gaze to the ground."

[44] Juno hastened Eurystheus' birth, and so procured for him
the throne of Argos and power over Hercules.

ad novi ludos avidus theatri;
840 quantus Eleum ruit ad Tonantem,
quinta cum sacrum revocavit aestas;
quanta, cum longae redit hora nocti
crescere, et somnos cupiens quietos
Libra Phoebeos tenet aequa currus,
845 turba secretam Cererem frequentat
et citi tectis properant relictis
Attici noctem celebrare mystae:
tanta per campos agitur silentes
turba. pars tarda graditur senecta,
850 tristis et longa satiata vita;
pars adhuc currit melioris aevi:
virgines nondum thalamis iugatae
et comis nondum positis ephebi
matris et nomen modo doctus infans.
855 his datum solis, minus ut timerent,
igne praelato relevare noctem;
ceteri vadunt per opaca tristes.
qualis est vobis animus remota
luce cum maestus sibi quisque sensit
860 obrutum tota caput esse terra?
stat chaos densum tenebraeque turpes
et color noctis malus ac silentis
otium mundi vacuaeque nubes.

---

45 For the urban crowd likened to the throng of the dead, compare T. S. Eliot, *The Waste Land* I. The Burial of the Dead: "Unreal City, / Under the brown fog of a winter dawn, / A crowd flowed over London Bridge, so many, / I had not thought death had undone so many."

eager for the games at a new theatre;[45]
as great as that which rushes to Elean Jove,
when the fifth summer renews the festival;[46]
as great as the crowd when the season returns for
　　night
to lengthen, and, longing for restful sleep,
Libra holds Phoebus' chariot in balance—
the crowd that throngs Ceres' mysteries,[47]
as Athenian initiates leave their homes
and hasten to celebrate the holy night:
so great the crowd that is swept through the silent
fields. Some walk in slow old age,
gloomy and sated by long life;
others of better years are still running—
maidens not yet joined in marriage,
ephebes with hair not yet shorn,
and infants that have just learned the name of
　　mother.
For these alone, to reduce their fear,
torches may be carried to relieve the darkness;
the rest go sadly through the gloom.
What is your state of mind once the light
is lost, and each has a sorrowful sense
of being buried beneath the whole earth?
All around is turbid emptiness, unlovely darkness,
the sullen colour of night, the lethargy
of a silent world, and empty clouds.

[46] The Olympic Games, held near Elis every five years (by the inclusive reckoning of antiquity, but every four years by modern reckoning) in honour of Zeus/Jupiter.
[47] At Eleusis near Athens.

Sera nos illo referat senectus!
865   nemo ad id sero venit, unde numquam,
cum semel venit, potuit reverti;
quid iuvat durum properare fatum?
omnis haec magnis vaga turba terris
ibit ad manes facietque inerti
870   vela Cocyto. tibi crescit omne,
et quod occasus videt et quod ortus:
parce venturis; tibi, Mors, paramur.
sis licet segnis, properamus ipsi;
prima quae vitam dedit hora, carpit.

875   Thebis laeta dies adest.
aras tangite supplices,
pingues caedite victimas;
permixtae maribus nurus
sollemnes agitent choros;
880   cessent deposito iugo
arvi fertilis incolae.
pax est Herculea manu
Auroram inter et Hesperum,
et qua sol medium tenens
885   umbras corporibus negat;
quodcumque alluitur solum
longo Tethyos ambitu,
Alcidae domuit labor.
transvectus vada Tartari

---

48 Compare Thomas Hughes, *The Misfortunes of Arthur* I. 4:
"Thine (death) is all that East and West can see: / For thee we live,
our coming is not long: / Spare us but whiles we may prepare our

Late may old age carry us there!
No one comes too late to that from which,
once come, he never can return.
What is the good of hurrying harsh fate?
All this crowd that wanders the great earth
will join the shades and set sail
on lifeless Cocytus. For you grows all
that the rising and setting sun beholds;
be lenient, since we must come;
we are groomed for you, o Death.
You can be slow, we hasten of ourselves.
The hour that first gives life, erodes it.[48]

A joyful day for Thebes!
Touch the altars in thanksgiving,
sacrifice fattened animals.
Let young women in company with men
break into festival dances;
let the tillers of the fertile soil
set down the yoke and rest.
By the hand of Hercules there is peace
from the Dawn to the Evening Star,
and where the sun at its zenith
withholds shadows from bodies.
Every tract that is washed
by Tethys' long circuit
has been tamed by Alcides' toil.
He crossed the waters of Tartarus,

graves"; also Edward Young, *Night Thoughts* 5.719f.: "Our life is
nothing but our death begun; / As tapers waste, that instant they
take fire."

890   pacatis redit inferis.
        iam nullus superest timor:
        nil ultra iacet inferos.

        —Stantes sacrificus comas
        dilecta tege populo.

895 Ultrice dextra fusus adverso Lycus
     terram cecidit ore; tum quisquis comes
     fuerat tyranni iacuit et poenae comes.
     nunc sacra patri victor et superis feram,
     caesisque meritas victimis aras colam.
900 Te te laborum socia et adiutrix precor,
     belligera Pallas, cuius in laeva ciet
     aegis feroces ore saxifico minas;
     adsit Lycurgi domitor et Rubri Maris,
     tectam virenti cuspidem thyrso gerens,
905 geminumque numen Phoebus et Phoebi soror
     (soror sagittis aptior, Phoebus lyrae),
     fraterque quisquis incolit caelum meus
     non ex noverca frater.
                        Huc appellite
     greges opimos; quidquid Indi arvis secant
910 Arabesque odoris quidquid arboribus legunt
     conferte in aras, pinguis exundet vapor.
     populea nostras arbor exornet comas,
     te ramus oleae fronde gentili tegat,

909 Indi arvis secant *Schmidt*: Indorum seges *EA*: Leo raised
the possibility of a lacuna after 909

120

pacified the underworld, and returned.
Now no fear remains:
nothing lies beyond the underworld.

[*To Hercules as he enters*]
To sacrifice, crown your rough hair
with your beloved poplar.

ACT 4

HERCULES

Slain by my avenging right hand, Lycus fell sprawling face-
down on the ground. Then all who had been the tyrant's
associates died as associates of his punishment too. Now I
shall make offerings for my victory to my father and the
gods, and honour their altars as they deserve with sacrificed victims.

I pray to you, partner and helpmate in my toils, warlike
Pallas, on whose left arm the aegis issues fierce threats
with its petrifying face; I invoke the conqueror of Lycurgus
and of the Red Sea,[49] whose leafy thyrsus bears a concealed spearpoint, and the twin divinities, Phoebus and
Phoebus' sister (the sister more skilled with arrows, Phoebus with the lyre), and any brother of mine that dwells in
heaven—but not a brother by my stepmother. [*To attendants*] Drive here fattened flocks; bring to the altars the incense which Indians harvest in fields and Arabs gather
from perfumed trees; let fragrant clouds billow forth. A
wreath of poplar should adorn my hair; an olive branch
must crown you, Theseus, with the leaves of your own

[49] Bacchus.

Theseu; Tonantem nostra adorabit manus,
915 tu conditores urbis et silvestria
trucis antra Zethi, nobilis Dircen aquae
laremque regis advenae Tyrium coles.
—date tura flammis.

AMPHITRYON
Nate, manantes prius
manus cruenta caede et hostili expia.

HERCULES
920 Utinam cruorem capitis invisi deis
libare possem! gratior nullus liquor
tinxisset aras; victima haud ulla amplior
potest magisque opima mactari Iovi,
quam rex iniquus.

AMPHITRYON
Finiat genitor tuos
925 opta labores, detur aliquando otium
quiesque fessis.

HERCULES
Ipse concipiam preces
Iove meque dignas. stet suo caelum loco
tellusque et aequor; astra inoffensos agant
aeterna cursus, alta pax gentes alat;
930 ferrum omne teneat ruris innocui labor
ensesque lateant. nulla tempestas fretum
violenta turbet, nullus irato Iove
exiliat ignis, nullus hiberna nive

924 tuos *recc*.: tuus *EA*

people. My hand will worship the Thunderer; you are to venerate the city's founders, the woodland caves of fierce Zethus, Dirce's famous stream, and the Tyrian house gods of our foreign king.[50] [*Exit Theseus. To attendants:*] Throw the incense on the flames.

AMPHITRYON

Son, first purify your hands, which are dripping with your slaughtered enemy's blood.

HERCULES

I wish I could pour a libation to the gods with the blood of that hateful life! No more acceptable liquid would ever have stained the altars. No victim more choice or bounteous could be slaughtered to Jove than an unrighteous king.[51]

AMPHITRYON

Ask that your father end your toils, that peace and rest be granted at last to our weary spirits.

HERCULES

I shall pronounce prayers, ones worthy of Jove and of myself. May heaven stand in its place, and earth and sea. May the eternal stars pursue their courses unhindered. May deep peace nurture the nations, may iron be used only in the harmless toil of the countryside, and may swords be hidden away. May no violent storm disturb the seas, may no fire streak down from angry Jove, may no

---

[50] Cadmus, who came from Phoenicia.

[51] Milton renders, "There can be slain / No sacrifice to God more acceptable / Than an unjust and wicked king" (*The Tenure of Kings and Magistrates*, published after the execution of King Charles).

nutritus agros amnis eversos trahat.
935 venena cessent, nulla nocituro gravis
suco tumescat herba. non saevi ac truces
regnent tyranni. si quod etiamnum est scelus
latura tellus, properet, et si quod parat
monstrum, meum sit.
     —Sed quid hoc? medium diem
940 cinxere tenebrae. Phoebus obscuro meat
sine nube vultu. quis diem retro fugat
agitque in ortus? unde nox atrum caput
ignota profert? unde tot stellae polum
implent diurnae? primus en noster labor
945 caeli refulget parte non minima Leo
iraque totus fervet et morsus parat.
iam rapiet aliquod sidus: ingenti minax
stat ore et ignes efflat et rutilat, iubam
cervice iactans; quidquid autumnus gravis
950 hiemsque gelido frigida spatio refert
uno impetu transiliet, et verni petet
frangetque Tauri colla.

    AMPHITRYON
      Quod subitum hoc malum est?
quo, nate, vultus huc et huc acres refers
acieque falsum turbida caelum vides?

    HERCULES
955 Perdomita tellus, tumida cesserunt freta,
inferna nostros regna sensere impetus:
immune caelum est, dignus Alcide labor.
in alta mundi spatia sublimis ferar,
petatur aether: astra promittit pater.
960 —quid, si negaret? non capit terra Herculem

124

river fed with winter snows ravage the uptorn fields. May poisons disappear, and may no deadly herb swell with harmful juices. May no fierce and cruel tyrants reign. If the earth is even now to produce some wickedness, let it come quickly; if she is furnishing some monster, let it be mine.

But what is this? Midday is shrouded in darkness. Phoebus' face is obscured, though not by clouds. Who chases the daylight back and drives it to its dawning? Why is this strange night rearing its black head? Why are so many stars filling the heavens in daytime? Look, my first labour, the Lion, shines in a large segment of the sky, burns all over with anger and prepares to bite. Soon he will pounce on some constellation; he stands threatening with his huge jaws, breathes out fire and glows red, tossing the mane on his neck; in one bound he will overleap the signs brought round by unwholesome autumn and by chill winter in its frozen tract, and attack and break the neck of the Bull of spring.

AMPHITRYON

What is this sudden trouble? Why, son, are you turning your gaze keenly this way and that, and viewing an imaginary heaven with feverish eyes?

HERCULES

Earth is subdued, the swollen seas have yielded, the infernal realm has felt my onslaught: heaven is untouched, a labour worthy of Alcides. I must travel on high to the lofty expanses of the cosmos, and make for the sky: the stars are my father's promise. What if he should now refuse? The earth cannot contain Hercules, and at last yields him to the

---

948 rutilat *E*ac*A*: rutilam *E*pc

tandemque superis reddit. en ultro vocat
omnis deorum coetus et laxat fores,
una vetante. recipis et reseras polum?
an contumacis ianuam mundi traho?
965 dubitatur etiam? vincla Saturno exuam,
contraque patris impii regnum impotens
avum resolvam. bella Titanes parent
me duce furentes; saxa cum silvis feram
rapiamque dextra plena Centauris iuga.
970 iam monte gemino limitem ad superos agam:
videat sub Ossa Pelion Chiron suum,
in caelum Olympus tertio positus gradu
perveniet aut mittetur.

AMPHITRYON
                    Infandos procul
averte sensus; pectoris sani parum,
975 magni tamen, compesce dementem impetum.

HERCULES
Quid hoc? Gigantes arma pestiferi movent.
profugit umbras Tityos, ac lacerum gerens
et inane pectus quam prope a caelo stetit!
labat Cithaeron, alta Pallene tremit
980 marcentque Tempe. rapuit hic Pindi iuga,
hic rapuit Oeten, saevit horrendum Mimas.
flammifera Erinys verbere excusso sonat
rogisque adustas propius ac propius sudes
in ora tendit; saeva Tisiphone, caput

980 marcentque *A*: Macetumque *E*

world above.[52] See, the whole company of the gods spontaneously summons me and opens the doors, with one goddess forbidding it. Will you receive me and unbar the firmament? Or must I tear down the door of the stubborn heaven? Do you still hesitate? I shall strip off Saturn's chains, and against my unnatural father's unbridled rule I shall loose my grandfather. Let the Titans in rage prepare war under my leadership. I shall carry rocks and trees, and grasp ridges full of Centaurs in my right hand. With a pair of mountains I shall now construct a pathway to the world above: Chiron must see his Pelion set beneath Ossa. Then Olympus, placed as a third step, will reach to heaven—or else be hurled there.

AMPHITRYON

Banish these monstrous notions! Restrain the crazy impulses of your mind, which is great to be sure, but scarcely sane.

HERCULES

What is this? The pestilential Giants are in arms. Tityos has escaped the underworld, and stands so close to heaven, his chest all torn and empty! Cithaeron lurches, high Pallene shakes, and Tempe's beauty withers. One Giant has seized the peaks of Pindus, another has seized Oeta, and Mimas rages fearfully. The fire-bearing Fury is cracking her scourge, and pushing in my face stakes charred in pyres, closer and closer. Cruel Tisiphone, her head encircled with

---

[52] Compare the megalomania of Tamburlaine: "I might move the turning Spheres of heaven, / For earth and all this airy region / Cannot contain the state of Tamburlaine" (Christopher Marlowe, *2 Tamburlaine* IV.1.118–20).

985 serpentibus vallata, post raptum canem
portam vacantem clausit opposita face.
—sed ecce proles regis inimici latet,
Lyci nefandum semen. inviso patri
haec dextra iam vos reddet. excutiat leves
990 nervus sagittas. tela sic mitti decet
Herculea.

AMPHITRYON
Quo se caecus impegit furor?
vastum coactis flexit arcum cornibus
pharetramque solvit, strident emissa impetu
harundo; medio spiculum collo fugit
995 vulnere relicto.

HERCULES
Ceteram prolem eruam
omnesque latebras. quid moror? maius mihi
bellum Mycenis restat, ut Cyclopia
eversa manibus saxa nostris concidant.
huc eat et illuc valva deiecto obice
1000 rumpatque postes; columen impulsum labet.
perlucet omnis regia; hic video abditum
natum scelesti patris.

AMPHITRYON
En blandas manus
ad genua tendens voce miseranda rogat.
—scelus nefandum, triste et aspectu horridum!
1005 dextra precantem rapuit et circa furens
bis ter rotatum misit; ast illi caput
sonuit, cerebro tecta disperso madent.
at misera, parvum protegens natum sinu,

snakes, uses her outstretched torch to block the gateway,
left empty after the theft of the hound.

But look, here in hiding are my enemy's children, King
Lycus' vile seed. This hand will send you straightway to
join your hated father. My bowstring must shoot its swift
arrows. Yes, this is how Hercules' weapons should be fired!

AMPHITRYON

How far has his blind fury advanced? He has bent his huge
bow, drawing the tips together, and opened his quiver. The
reed whistles, shot with such force. The arrow hits the
middle of the neck, passes through and leaves the wound
behind.

HERCULES

I shall unearth the other offspring and all their hiding
places. Why delay? A greater struggle awaits me at Mycenae, to overthrow the Cyclopean walls with my bare
hands. Let the door fly this way and that, with its bar
knocked down, and smash the doorjambs. Let me push
against the roof ridge and dislodge it. Light pours through
the whole palace. Here I see hidden the son of a wicked
father. [*Exit into palace.*]

AMPHITRYON

[*Describing what he sees happening in the palace*] Look,
he stretches cajoling hands to touch his father's knees, and
begs in a pitiful voice. O monstrous crime, tragic and fearful to see! He caught the pleading child up in his hand,
whirled him around twice, three times, and flung him; his
head smashed, and spattered brains wetted the walls. But
poor Megara, shielding her little son in her bosom, rushes

---

999 valva *Baden*: aula *EA*: clava *Withof*   deiecto *E*: dis-
iecto *A*

Megara furenti similis e latebris fugit.

HERCULES

1010　Licet Tonantis profuga condaris sinu,
　　　petet undecumque temet haec dextra et feret.

AMPHITRYON

Quo misera pergis? quam fugam aut latebram petis?
nullus salutis Hercule infesto est locus.
amplectere ipsum potius et blanda prece
1015　lenire tempta.

MEGARA

　　　　　　Parce iam, coniunx, precor,
agnosce Megaram. natus hic vultus tuos
habitusque reddit; cernis, ut tendat manus?

HERCULES

Teneo novercam. sequere, da poenas mihi
iugoque pressum libera turpi Iovem—
1020　sed ante matrem parvulum hoc monstrum occidat.

AMPHITRYON

Quo tendis amens? sanguinem fundes tuum?
—pavefactus infans igneo vultu patris
perit ante vulnus, spiritum eripuit timor.
in coniugem nunc clava libratur gravis:
1025　perfregit ossa, corpori trunco caput
abest nec usquam est.—cernere hoc audes, nimis
vivax senectus? si piget luctus, habes
mortem paratam.—pectori tela indue,
vel stipitem istum caede monstrorum illitum

　　　1021 *attributed to Amphitryon by MN, to Megara by A, to Her-*
cules by E.　　　　1028 *pectori tela Axelson*: pectus in tela *EA*

130

like a madwoman from hiding. [*Megara rushes onstage from the palace, pursued by Hercules.*]

HERCULES

Though you flee and hide in the bosom of the Thunderer, this hand will find you and drag you from anywhere.

AMPHITRYON

Where are you running, poor woman? What escape or refuge are you looking for? There is no place of safety with Hercules as your enemy. Instead embrace him, and try to calm him with prayers and supplication.

MEGARA

Forbear now, my husband, I pray you, recognise your Megara. This is your son, who mirrors your face and bearing. Do you see how he stretches out his hands?

HERCULES

I have caught my stepmother. Follow me, receive your punishment, and free downtrodden Jove from a humiliating yoke. But before the mother let this little monster be killed. [*Exit with Megara and child.*]

AMPHITRYON

What is your mad purpose? Will you shed your own blood? [*Describing what he sees happening offstage*] Terrified by his father's blazing eyes, the child died before being wounded, terror snatched away his spirit. Against his wife now his heavy club is levelled; it smashed her bones, her head is gone from her truncated body, totally destroyed. Can you endure this sight, old age that has lived too long? If your grief is unbearable, you have a ready means of death. [*Calling to Hercules*] Come, plunge your arrows into my breast, or turn on me that club, smeared with the

131

1030 converte; falsum ac nomini turpem tuo
remove parentem, ne tuae laudi obstrepat.

CHORUS

Quo te ipse, senior, obvium morti ingeris?
quo pergis amens? profuge et obtectus late
unumque manibus aufer Herculeis scelus.

HERCULES

1035 Bene habet, pudendi regis excisa est domus.
tibi hunc dicatum, maximi coniunx Iovis,
gregem cecidi; vota persolvi libens
te digna, et Argos victimas alias dabit.

AMPHITRYON

Nondum litasti, nate; consumma sacrum.
1040 stat ecce ad aras hostia, expectat manum
cervice prona; praebeo, occurro, insequor:
macta.—quid hoc est? errat acies luminum
visusque maeror hebetat, an video Herculis
manus trementes? vultus in somnum cadit
1045 et fessa cervix capite summisso labat;
flexo genu iam totus ad terram ruit,
ut caesa silvis ornus aut portum mari
datura moles. vivis, an leto dedit
idem tuos qui misit ad mortem furor?
1050 sopor est: reciprocos spiritus motus agit.
detur quieti tempus, ut somno gravi
vis victa morbi pectus oppressum levet.
removete, famuli, tela, ne repetat furens.

1051 gravi *E*: gravis *A*

132

blood of monsters: make away with this sham father, this
blot on your name, lest he grate against your glory.

CHORUS LEADER

Why are you flinging yourself in death's path, old man?
What is your mad intention? Escape, stay hidden, and
spare the hands of Hercules this one crime.

HERCULES

[*Reentering*] It is well, the vile king's house is extermi-
nated. I consecrated and slaughtered this flock to you, wife
of almighty Jove; I have gladly fulfilled vows worthy of you,
and Argos will provide other victims for sacrifice.

AMPHITRYON

You have not yet made full offering, son; complete the
sacrifice. Look, the victim stands at the altar, his neck
bent, and awaits your hand. I present myself, willingly,
insistently: perform the killing! What is this? Are my eyes
failing, and grief dulling my sight, or do I see Hercules'
hands trembling? His eyes are closing in sleep, his head
sinking, his weary neck drooping. Now his knees bend and
his whole body collapses on the ground, as heavily as an ash
tree felled in the woods, or a mass of masonry dropped in
the sea to create a harbour. Are you alive, or killed by that
same frenzy which sent your loved ones to their death? It is
sleep: his breath comes and goes regularly. He must have
time for rest, so that deep sleep can overcome the violent
sickness and relieve his burdened mind. Remove his weapons, slaves, lest he revert to them in madness.

CHORUS

Lugeat aether
magnusque parens aetheris alti
1055 tellusque ferax
et vaga ponti mobilis unda,
tuque ante omnes
qui per terras tractusque maris
fundis radios
1060 noctemque fugas ore decoro,
fervide Titan:
obitus pariter
tecum Alcides vidit et ortus
novitque tuas utrasque domos.
Solvite tantis animum monstris,
solvite, superi;
1065 rectam in melius flectite mentem.
tuque, o domitor Somne malorum,
requies animi,
pars humanae melior vitae,
volucre o matris genus astriferae,
frater durae languide Mortis,
1070 veris miscens falsa, futuri
certus et idem pessimus auctor,
pax o rerum, portus vitae,
lucis requies noctisque comes,
qui par regi famuloque venis,
1075 pavidum leti genus humanum
cogis longam discere noctem:
placidus fessum lenisque fove,
preme devinctum torpore gravi;

1068 astriferae *Fitch*: astre(a)e *EA*

134

CHORUS

Let heaven mourn,
and the mighty father of high heaven;
fertile earth,
and the wandering waters of the restless deep;
and you above all,
who across the lands and the tracts of the sea
pour your radiance,
and rout the night with the beauty of your face,
blazing Titan:
like you, Alcides
has seen the place of your settings and risings,
and he knows both your homes.

Free his spirit from such monstrosities,
free him, you gods;
guide and turn his mind to a better state.
And you, o Sleep, subduer of troubles,
rest for the spirit,
sweeter part of human life;
winged child of a starry mother,[53]
languid brother of hardhearted Death,
who mingle falsehood with truth,
sure yet deceiving guide to the future,
peace of the world, haven of life,
rest from light and companion in darkness,
who come equally to king and slave,
and force all humans, fearful of death,
to gain knowledge of the long night:
calmly and gently soothe his exhaustion,
hold him bound in a deep coma;

[53] Night.

sopor indomitos alliget artus,
1080 nec torva prius pectora linquat,
quam mens repetat pristina cursum.
    En fusus humi
saeva feroci corde volutat
somnia—nondum est
tanti pestis superata mali—
1085 clavaeque gravi
lassum solitus mandare caput
quaerit vacua pondera dextra,
motu iactans bracchia vano.
nec adhuc omnes expulit aestus,
sed ut ingenti vexata noto
1090 servat longos unda tumultus
et iam vento cessante tumet.
pelle insanos fluctus animi;
redeat pietas virtusque viro.
vel sit potius
1095 mens vesano concita motu,
error caecus qua coepit eat:
solus te iam praestare potest
furor insontem;
proxima puris sors est manibus
nescire nefas.

1100 Nunc Herculeis
percussa sonent pectora palmis;
mundum solitos ferre lacertos

1091 Leo postulated a lacuna after 1091

54 For madness as preferable to knowledge of evils, cf. Shake-

136

let slumber fetter his unconquered limbs,
and let it not leave his wild breast,
till his mind regains its former tenor.

    Look, as he lies on the ground
violent dreams are whirling in his fierce
heart; not yet
is the powerful illness' poison overcome.
From his habit of resting
his head when weary on the heavy club,
he searches for its mass with his empty hand,
flinging his arms in fruitless movements.
He has not yet expelled all the surging madness,
as a sea buffeted by a strong south wind
keeps up a lengthy turbulence,
and its swell persists though the wind drops.
Drive the waves of madness from your spirit,
may the hero's goodness and heroism return.
Or rather
may your mind still race with insanity;
may blind error continue as it began:
the only thing now that can offer you
innocence is madness;
after pure hands, the next best fate
is ignorance of the evil.[54]

Now let Hercules'
palms beat his breast till it resounds;
let those arms, accustomed to bearing the sky,

speare, *King Lear* IV.6.281–84: "Better I were distract, / So should
my thoughts be sever'd from my griefs, / And woes by wrong imag-
inations lose / The knowledge of themselves."

verbera pulsent ultrice manu.
gemitus vastos audiat aether,
1105   audiat atri regina poli
vastisque ferox
qui colla gerit vincta catenis
imo latitans Cerberus antro.
resonet maesto clamore chaos
latique patens unda profundi
1110   et (qui melius
tua tela tamen senserat) aer.
pectora tantis obsessa malis
non sunt ictu ferienda levi:
uno planctu tria regna sonent.
1115   Et tu, collo decus ac telum
suspensa diu, fortis harundo,
pharetraeque graves,
date saeva fero verbera tergo;
caedant umeros robora fortes
stipesque potens
1120   duris oneret pectora nodis;
plangant tantos arma dolores.

Non vos patriae laudis comites
ulti saevos vulnere reges,
non Argiva membra palaestra
flectere docti
1125   fortes caestu fortesque manu—

1110 melius *A*: medius *E*

---

55 Hercules had shot the Stymphalian birds out of the air.

be struck by his avenging hands.
Let heaven hear his mighty groans,
let the queen of the dark world hear them,
and fierce Cerberus
where he skulks in his deep cave,
his necks still bound with mighty chains.
Let Chaos re-echo your sad cries,
and the open waters of the vast deep,
and the air—
though it felt your arrows to better purpose.[55]
The breast beset by such ills
cannot be struck lightly:
with one blow let three realms resound.

    And you, long hung from his neck
as glorious weapons, strong arrows
and heavy quiver,
rain savage lashes on his untamed back.
Let the powerful tree trunk
batter his stalwart shoulders
and tax his breast with its hard knots:
let his weapons mourn these immense sorrows.

You had not shared your father's glory
by violent punishment of cruel kings;[56]
you had not learnt
command of your limbs in a Greek palaestra,
hardy with boxing gloves and with bare hands;

[56] While the Chorus addresses the dead boys, their bodies and
Megara's are probably wheeled out on an *exostra/eccyclema*, so as
to be visible onstage, though understood by convention to remain
in the palace.

iam tamen ausi
telum Scythicis leve gorytis
missum certa librare manu,
tutosque fuga figere cervos
1130   nondumque ferae terga iubatae.
ite ad Stygios, umbrae, portus
ite, innocuae,
quas in primo limine vitae
scelus oppressit patriusque furor.
1135   ite, infaustum genus, o pueri,
noti per iter triste laboris.
—ite, iratos visite reges.

HERCULES

Quis hic locus, quae regio, quae mundi plaga?
ubi sum? sub ortu solis, an sub cardine
1140 glacialis Ursae? numquid Hesperii maris
extrema tellus hunc dat Oceano modum?
quas trahimus auras? quod solum fesso subest?
certe redîmus: unde prostrata domo
video cruenta corpora? an nondum exuit
1145 simulacra mens inferna? post reditus quoque
oberrat oculis turba feralis meis?
pudet fateri: paveo; nescioquod mihi,
nescioquod animus grande praesagit malum.
ubi es, parens? ubi illa natorum grege
1150 animosa coniunx? cur latus laevum vacat
spolio leonis? quonam abît tegimen meum

1149 es *E*: est *A*

but you were already
bold enough to aim and fire light arrows
from a Scythian quiver with an accurate hand,
and to transfix stags whose defence is flight,
or the back of a beast as yet unmaned.
Go to the harbour of the Styx;
go, innocent shades,
crushed on the very threshold of life
by the crime committed in your father's madness.
Go, you boys, you ill-fated children,
on the gloomy path of the famous labour.
Go to meet the angry rulers.[57]

ACT 5

HERCULES

What place is this, what region, what tract of the earth?
Where am I? Beneath the sun's rising, or beneath the turning point of the icy Bear? Can this be the limit set to
Ocean's waters by the farthest land on the western sea?
What air do I breath? What ground lies under my weary
body? Certainly I have returned: why do I see bloodstained bodies in a ruined house? Has my mind not yet cast
off images from the underworld? Even after my return
does a throng of the dead wander before my eyes? I confess with shame that I feel afraid. There is some ill, some
great ill, that my mind forebodes. Where are you, father?
Where is my wife, so proud of her flock of sons? Why is my
left side bare of the lionskin trophy? Where has it gone, my

[57] Dis and Proserpine, angered by Hercules' intrusion into
their realm.

idemque somno mollis Herculeo torus?
ubi tela? ubi arcus? arma quis vivo mihi
detrahere potuit? spolia quis tanta abstulit
1155 ipsumque quis non Herculis somnum horruit?
libet meum videre victorem, libet—
exsurge, virtus! quem novum caelo pater
genuit relicto? cuius in fetu stetit
nox longior quam nostra?
                —Quod cerno nefas?
1160 nati cruenta caede confecti iacent,
perempta coniunx. quis Lycus regnum obtinet,
quis tanta Thebis scelera moliri ausus est
Hercule reverso? quisquis Ismeni loca,
Actaea quisquis arva, qui gemino mari
1165 pulsata Pelopis regna Dardanii colis,
succurre, saevae cladis auctorem indica.
ruat ira in omnes: hostis est quisquis mihi
non monstrat hostem. victor Alcidae, lates?
procede, seu tu vindicas currus truces
1170 Thracis cruenti sive Geryonae pecus
Libyaeve dominos; nulla pugnandi mora est.
en nudus asto; vel meis armis licet
petas inermem.
            Cur meos Theseus fugit
paterque vultus? ora cur condunt sua?
1175 differte fletus. quis meos dederit neci
omnes simul, profare—quid, genitor, siles?
at tu ede, Theseu—sed tua, Theseu, fide.
uterque tacitus ora pudibunda obtegit
furtimque lacrimas fundit. in tantis malis
1180 quid est pudendum? numquid Argivae impotens

defence—a soft bed too for the sleep of Hercules? Where are my arrows, my bow? Who could strip my armour from me while I lived? Who stole such mighty spoils and had no dread of Hercules even in his sleep? I long to see my conqueror. Rouse yourself, my courage! What new son did my father leave heaven to sire? For whose begetting was night delayed longer than mine?

What evil do I see? My sons lie consumed by bloody slaughter, my wife lies slain. What Lycus holds the kingdom? Who dared encompass such crimes in Thebes once Hercules had returned? All you who dwell in the districts of Ismenos, the fields of Attica, and the realms of Dardan Pelops,[58] beaten by two seas: run to help, point out the source of this cruel carnage. My anger must pour out on all: my enemy is anyone who does not identify my enemy. Are you hiding, conqueror of Alcides? Come forth, whether you are avenging the fierce steeds of the blood-stained Thracian or the cattle of Geryon or the lords of Libya;[59] I make no delay in fighting. See, I stand here defenceless; you can use my own arms to attack me unarmed.

Why do Theseus and my father avoid my eyes? Why do they hide their faces? Postpone your tears. Speak out, father: who put to death all my loved ones at once? Why are you silent? Then *you* tell me, Theseus—no, as a true friend, Theseus! Each is silent, covering his face in shame and shedding hidden tears. What call is there for shame in such troubles? Can it be that the ruthless lord of Argos'

[58] In the Peloponnese. "Dardan" (i.e. Phrygian) alludes to Pelops' birth and childhood in Asia Minor.

[59] The Thracian is Diomedes; the Libyan lords are Antaeus and Busiris.

dominator urbis, numquid infestum Lyci
pereuntis agmen clade nos tanta obruit?
per te meorum facinorum laudem precor,
genitor, tuique nominis semper mihi
1185 numen secundum, fare: quis fudit domum?
cui praeda iacui?

AMPHITRYON
Tacita sic abeant mala.

HERCULES
Ut inultus ego sim?

AMPHITRYON
Saepe vindicta obfuit.

HERCULES
Quisquamne segnis tanta toleravit mala?

AMPHITRYON
Maiora quisquis timuit.

HERCULES
His etiam, pater
1190 quicquam timeri maius aut gravius potest?

AMPHITRYON
Cladis tuae pars ista quam nosti quota est!

HERCULES
Miserere, genitor, supplices tendo manus.
quid hoc? manus refugit: hic errat scelus.
unde hic cruor? quid illa puerili madens
1195 harundo leto? tincta Lernaea est nece.
iam tela video nostra. non quaero manum.

1195 Lernaea est *Leo*: Lernaea* *A*: Lernae *E*

144

city,[60] or a contingent of Lycus' men, angry over his death, has buried us in such catastrophe? By the fame of my deeds I beg you, father, and by your name, second only in holy power to me after Jove's: tell me, who has brought down our house? Whose victim have I been?

AMPHITRYON
These troubles must just pass in silence.

HERCULES
And I remain unavenged?

AMPHITRYON
Revenge often does harm.

HERCULES
Has anyone passively endured such troubles?

AMPHITRYON
Anyone who feared worse.

HERCULES
Can one fear anything, father, that is even worse or more painful than this?

AMPHITRYON
How little of your calamity you understand!

HERCULES
Have pity, father, I hold out my hands in supplication. What? He pulled back from my hands: the crime is lurking here. Why this blood? What of that shaft, soaked by a boy's death? It is steeped in the Hydra's fatal blood. *Now* I see my weapons. I need not ask about the hand. Who could

---

[60] Eurystheus.

quis potuit arcum flectere aut quae dextera
sinuare nervum vix recedentem mihi?
ad vos revertor, genitor: hoc nostrum est scelus?
1200   tacuere: nostrum est.

AMPHITRYON
        Luctus est istic tuus,
crimen novercae; casus hic culpa caret.

HERCULES
Nunc parte ab omni, genitor, iratus tona;
oblite nostri, vindica sera manu
saltem nepotes. stelliger mundus sonet
1205   flammasque et hic et ille iaculetur polus.
rupes ligatum Caspiae corpus trahant
atque ales avida; cur Promethei vacant
scopuli? vacat cur vertice immenso feras
volucresque pascens Caucasi abruptum latus
1210   nudumque silvis? illa quae Pontum Scythen
Symplegas artat hinc et hinc vinctas manus
distendat alto, cumque revocata vice
in se coibunt saxaque in caelum expriment
actis utrimque rupibus medium mare,
1215   ego inquieta montium iaceam mora.
quin structum acervans nemore congesto aggerem
cruore corpus impio sparsum cremo?
sic, sic agendum est; inferis reddam Herculem.

AMPHITRYON
Nondum tumultu pectus attonito carens
1220   mutavit iras, quodque habet proprium furor,
in se ipse saevit.

1208 vacat cur *Leo*: vagetur *E*: paretur *TpcCS*

have bent that bow, what hand flexed the string that barely yields to me? I turn to both of you again, father: is this crime mine? They are silent: it is mine.

AMPHITRYON

This grief is yours, but the crime is your stepmother's. Misfortune such as this carries no guilt.

HERCULES

Now thunder in anger, father, from every quarter. Though you have forgotten me, let your tardy hand at least avenge your grandsons. Let the starry heavens resound, and flames be darted from both poles. Let the Caspian crags and the ravenous bird pull apart my fettered body.[61] Why are Prometheus' cliffs empty? The sheer flank of Caucasus, bare of trees, which feeds wild beasts and birds on its vast heights—why is it empty? Let those Symplegades, which narrow the Scythian Pontus, hold my hands fastened on this side and that and stretch them apart over the deep; and when the rocks drive together on the recoil, and force up to heaven the sea caught between the closing crags, let me lie as an unresting buffer between the mountains. Why not collect timber, mound it up into a pyre and burn this body spattered with unnatural bloodshed? *This* is what must be done. I shall return Hercules to the underworld.

AMPHITRYON

His heart is not yet free of frenzied turmoil; his anger has shifted, and he turns his fury on himself—the hallmark of mad rage.

---

[61] Prometheus was fettered to a crag in the Caucasus, where a vulture preyed on his liver until Hercules rescued him.

147

HERCULES

Dira Furiarum loca
et inferorum carcer et sonti plaga
decreta turbae! si quod exilium latet
ulterius Erebo, Cerbero ignotum et mihi,
1225 hoc me abde, Tellus; Tartari ad finem ultimum
mansurus ibo.   Pectus o nimium ferum!
quis vos per omnem, liberi, sparsos domum
deflere digne poterit? hic durus malis
lacrimare vultus nescit. huc arcum date,
1230 date huc sagittas, stipitem huc vastum date.
tibi tela frangam nostra; tibi nostros, puer,
rumpemus arcus; at tuis stipes gravis
ardebit umbris; ipsa Lernaeis frequens
pharetra telis in tuos ibit rogos:
1235 dent arma poenas. vos quoque infaustas meis
cremabo telis, o novercales manus.

AMPHITRYON

Quis nomen usquam sceleris errori addidit?

HERCULES

Saepe error ingens sceleris obtinuit locum.

AMPHITRYON

Nunc Hercule opus est: perfer hanc molem mali.

HERCULES

1240 Non sic furore cessit extinctus pudor,
populos ut omnes impio aspectu fugem.
arma, arma, Theseu, flagito propere mihi
subtracta reddi. sana si mens est mihi,

HERCULES

Dread haunts of the Furies, prison of the underworld, regions reserved for the guilty throng! If any place of exile lies concealed beyond Erebus, unknown to Cerberus and to me, hide me there, Earth; I shall go to the farthest bound of Tartarus, never to return. O heart too fierce! Who can weep worthily for you children, scattered throughout the house? This face, hardened by sufferings, is incapable of weeping.

Give here my bow, give here my arrows, give here my great club. For you I shall break my arrows; for you, son, I shall smash my bow; for your shade the heavy club will be burned; the quiver too, packed with Lernaean arrows,[62] will be added to your pyre. My weapons must pay the penalty. And you that brought such ill-luck to my weapons, you stepmotherly hands, I shall burn you too.

AMPHITRYON

Whoever gave mistaken action the name of crime?

HERCULES

A great mistaken action often has the standing of a crime.

AMPHITRYON

Now there is call for a Hercules: bear this weight of disaster.

HERCULES

My sense of shame is not so far lost or erased by madness that I would scare off all peoples by my sacrilegious presence. My arms, my arms, Theseus, I demand that my stolen arms be quickly returned. If my mind is sane, give my

---

[62] Tipped with poison from the Hydra of Lerna.

referte manibus tela; si remanet furor,
1245 pater, recede: mortis inveniam viam.

AMPHITRYON

Per sancta generis sacra, per ius nominis
utrumque nostri, sive me altorem vocas
seu tu parentem, perque venerandos piis
canos, senectae parce desertae, precor,
1250 annisque fessis; unicum lapsae domus
firmamen, unum lumen afflicto malis
temet reserva. nullus ex te contigit
fructus laborum; semper aut dubium mare
aut monstra timui; quisquis in toto furit
1255 rex saevus orbe, manibus aut aris nocens,
a me timetur; semper absentis pater
fructum tui tactumque et aspectum peto.

HERCULES

Cur animam in ista luce detineam amplius
morerque nihil est; cuncta iam amisi bona,
1260 mentem arma famam coniugem natos manus,
etiam furorem. nemo polluto queat
animo mederi; morte sanandum est scelus.

AMPHITRYON

Perimes parentem.

HERCULES
Facere ne possim, occidam.

---

63 Compare George Chapman, *Byron's Tragedy* V.4.69–72:
"Why should I keep my soul in this dark light, / Whose black

hands back their weapons; if my madness remains, father, stand away; I shall find a path to death.

AMPHITRYON

By the sanctities of family bonds, by the rights of either of my names, whether you call me foster father or real parent, and by these grey hairs which should rightfully be venerated, show mercy to my lonely old age, I pray you, and to my weary years. Keep yourself alive as sole pillar of our fallen house, sole light in my affliction. I have received from you no benefit of your labours. Always I have feared either monsters or the uncertain sea; each cruel king that rages anywhere in the world, with guilt on his hands or altars, is a source of fear for me; always as your father I long for the enjoyment and touch and sight of you, my absent son.

HERCULES

There is no reason for me to keep my life lingering in this light any further. I have lost all of value: my mind, my weapons, glory, wife, sons, hands—even my madness.[63] No one could cure an infected spirit; the healing of the crime must be by death.

AMPHITRYON

You will kill your father.

HERCULES

To prevent my doing so, I shall die.

beams lighted me to lose myself? / When I have lost my arms, my fame, my mind, / Friends, brother, hopes, fortunes, and even my fury."

AMPHITRYON

Genitore coram?

HERCULES

Cernere hunc docui nefas.

AMPHITRYON

1265   Memoranda potius omnibus facta intuens
unius a te criminis veniam pete.

HERCULES

Veniam dabit sibi ipse, qui nulli dedit?
laudanda feci iussus; hoc unum meum est.
succurre, genitor, sive te pietas movet
1270   seu triste fatum sive violatum decus
virtutis. effer arma; vincatur mea
Fortuna dextra.

THESEUS

Sunt quidem patriae preces
satis efficaces, sed tamen nostro quoque
movere fletu. surge et adversa impetu
1275   perfringe solito. nunc tuum nulli imparem
animum malo resume, nunc magna tibi
virtute agendum est; Herculem irasci veta.

HERCULES

Si vivo, feci scelera; si morior, tuli.
purgare terras propero; iamdudum mihi
1280   monstrum impium saevumque et immite ac ferum
oberrat. agedum, dextra, conare aggredi
ingens opus, labore bis seno amplius.
ignave, cessas, fortis in pueros modo
pavidasque matres?—arma nisi dantur mihi,

AMPHITRYON

Before your father's eyes?

HERCULES

I taught him to watch evil.

AMPHITRYON

Look rather to your deeds, so impressive to all, and seek pardon from yourself for one misdeed.

HERCULES

Shall he pardon himself who pardoned no one? My praiseworthy deeds I did under orders; this alone is mine. Help me, father, whether moved by love or by this sad fate or by the dishonouring of my glorious valour. Bring out my weapons. I must win victory over Fortune by my right hand.

THESEUS

Your father's prayers are powerful enough, but let yourself be moved by my tears also. Rise up, break through adversity with your usual energy. Now regain that spirit of yours which is a match for any trouble, now you must act with great valour. Do not let Hercules give way to anger.

HERCULES

If I live, I committed those crimes; if I die, I suffered them. I am eager to cleanse the earth. An unnatural monster, savage, merciless, untamed, has long been ranging before me. Come, my right hand, attempt to undertake a gigantic task, greater than all twelve labours. Are you hesitating, coward—brave only against boys and fearful mothers? Unless my arms are given me, I shall fell the whole forest of

---

1270 fatum *A*: factum *E*

1285 aut omne Pindi Thracis excidam nemus
Bacchique lucos et Cithaeronis iuga
mecum cremabo, aut tota cum domibus suis
dominisque tecta, cum deis templa omnibus
Thebana supra corpus excipiam meum
1290 atque urbe versa condar, et, si fortibus
leve pondus umeris moenia immissa incident
septemque opertus non satis portis premar,
onus omne media parte quod mundi sedet
dirimitque superos, in meum vertam caput.

AMPHITRYON

1295 Reddo arma.

HERCULES

        Vox est digna genitore Herculis.
hoc en peremptus spiculo cecidit puer.

AMPHITRYON

Hoc Iuno telum manibus emisit tuis.

HERCULES

Hoc nunc ego utar.

AMPHITRYON

        Ecce quam miserum metu
cor palpitat pectusque sollicitum ferit.

HERCULES

1300 Aptata harundo est.

AMPHITRYON

        Ecce iam facies scelus
volens sciensque.

HERCULES

        Pande, quid fieri iubes?

Thracian Pindus, and burn Bacchus' groves and Cithaeron's mountain ridges along with myself; or else I shall
bring down on my body every building with its family and
master, the temples of Thebes with all their gods, and bury
myself beneath the ruins of the city; and if the falling walls
are too light a weight for these strong shoulders, and I am
not fully crushed and buried beneath the seven gates, then
I shall pull down on my head the whole mass that rests at
the centre of the firmament and keeps the gods separate.

AMPHITRYON

I return your weapons.

HERCULES

Those words are worthy of Hercules' father. See, by this
arrow my boy fell slain.

AMPHITRYON

This arrow was fired by Juno, using your hands.

HERCULES

Now *I* shall use it.

AMPHITRYON

See how my poor heart pounds with fear and beats against
my anxious breast.

HERCULES

The shaft is notched.

AMPHITRYON

See, now you will commit a crime intentionally and knowingly.

HERCULES

Tell me, what would you have me do?

AMPHITRYON

Nihil rogamus; noster in tuto est dolor:
natum potes servare tu solus mihi,
eripere nec tu. maximum evasi metum;
1305   miserum haud potes me facere, felicem potes.
sic statue, quidquid statuis, ut causam tuam
famamque in arto stare et ancipiti scias:
aut vivis aut occidis. hanc animam levem
fessamque senio nec minus fessam malis
1310   in ore primo teneo. tam tarde patri
vitam dat aliquis? non feram ulterius moram,
letale ferrum pectori impresso induam;
hic, hic iacebit Herculis sani scelus.

HERCULES

Iam parce, genitor, parce, iam revoca manum.
1315   succumbe, virtus, perfer imperium patris.
eat ad labores hic quoque Herculeos labor:
vivamus. artus alleva afflictos solo,
Theseu, parentis. dextra contactus pios
scelerata refugit.

AMPHITRYON

              Hanc manum amplector libens,
1320   hac nisus ibo, pectori hanc aegro admovens
pellam dolores.

HERCULES

              Quem locum profugus petam?
ubi me recondam, quave tellure obruar?
quis Tanais aut quis Nilus aut quis Persica

1312 ferrum pectori impresso *Fitch*: ferro pectus impresso
(-um *A*) *EA*   1317 afflictos *EA*: afflicti *recc.*

156

AMPHITRYON

I ask nothing. My grief has reached a safe place. You alone
can save my son for me, but even you cannot snatch him
from me.[64] I have got beyond my greatest fear. You cannot
make me wretched, but you can make me happy. Whatever
you decide, do so on the understanding that your glory and
the verdict about you is in a tight and critical position. Either you live, or you kill. I am holding on my very lips this
fragile life of mine, wearied with old age and no less wearied with troubles. Can anyone be so slow in granting his
father life? [*Taking a sword*] I shall not endure further delay, I shall set my breast against the deadly blade and thrust
it in. The crime lying here will belong to the sane Hercules.

HERCULES

Stop now, father, stop, draw back your hand. Give way,
my valour, endure my father's command. This labour must
be added to the Herculean labours: to live. Theseus, raise
up my father's body, collapsed on the ground. My crime-
stained hand shuns contact with one I love.

AMPHITRYON

But I grasp this hand gladly, I shall lean on it to walk, and
clasp it to my troubled breast to banish my griefs.

HERCULES

What place shall I seek out in exile? Where shall I hide myself, in what land be buried in oblivion? What Tanais or
what Nile or what Persian Tigris with its violent waters or

---

[64] Because if Hercules commits suicide, Amphitryon will die
with him (either through the shock to his weakened spirit, or by
suicide).

violentus unda Tigris aut Rhenus ferox
1325 Tagusve Hibera turbidus gaza fluens
abluere dextram poterit? Arctoum licet
Maeotis in me gelida transfundat mare
et tota Tethys per meas currat manus,
haerebit altum facinus. in quas impius
1330 terras recedes? ortum an occasum petes?
ubique notus perdidi exilio locum.
me refugit orbis, astra transversos agunt
obliqua cursus, ipse Titan Cerberum
meliore vultu vidit. o fidum caput,
1335 Theseu, latebram quaere longinquam, abditam;
quoniamque semper sceleris alieni arbiter
amas nocentes, gratiam meritis refer
vicemque nostris: redde me infernis, precor,
umbris reductum, meque subiectum tuis
1340 restitue vinclis; ille me abscondet locus—
sed et ille novit.

THESEUS
       Nostra te tellus manet.
illic solutam caede Gradivus manum
restituit armis; illa te, Alcide, vocat,
facere innocentes terra quae superos solet.

fierce Rhine or Tagus, turbid with Spanish treasure, can wash my right hand clean? Though chill Maeotis should pour its northern seas over me and all the Ocean stream across my hands, the deed will stay deeply ingrained.[65] To what lands will you withdraw when so unhallowed? Will you head to the sunrise or the sunset? By being known everywhere, I have forfeited a place for exile. The world shrinks from me, the stars turn aside and run their courses askew, even the Titan looked on Cerberus with a better countenance. O faithful friend, Theseus, search out a distant, obscure hiding place; and since as witness to others' crimes you always show love to the guilty,[66] pay me thanks and recompense for my service to you: return me, I pray you, to the shades of the underworld, and reinstate me in your chains as your replacement. That place will hide me—but it too knows me.

THESEUS

My land awaits you. There Gradivus had his hand purified of bloodshed and returned to warfare. That land summons you, Alcides, which customarily restores gods to innocence.

[65] Compare Shakespeare, *Macbeth* II.2.57f.: "Will all great Neptune's ocean wash this blood / Clean from my hand?"

[66] Specific instances are Pirithous and Oedipus, the latter given sanctuary by Theseus in Athens.

TROJAN WOMEN

INTRODUCTION

Background

After a ten-year siege, Troy has fallen to the Greeks. Its
warriors have died or fled into exile. During the sack, its
walls were toppled and its buildings burnt; its old king
Priam was butchered in his palace by young Pyrrhus. The
women of Troy have been taken into captivity and will soon
be distributed among the conquerors as slaves and concu-
bines. The Greeks are almost ready to set sail for home.

Summary

Act 1
Queen Hecuba reflects on the fall of Troy and the murder
of her husband Priam.

Ode 1. Hecuba leads the chorus of Trojan women in a
formal antiphonal lament for Troy, Hector, and Priam.

Act 2
Scene 1. A herald recounts the appearance of Achilles'
ghost over his grave mound, demanding that the princess
Polyxena be sacrificed to him. *Scene 2.* Pyrrhus and Agamemnon quarrel over this demand: Agamemnon resists it
as barbaric, while Pyrrhus insists on it as a mark of honour
to his all-conquering father. Agamemnon refers the ques-

163

tion to the prophet Calchas, who proclaims that not only Polyxena but also Hector's son Astyanax must be killed before the Greeks can sail.

Ode 2. Is there further existence to be faced after death, or does death end everything? The chorus contemplates this question, and concludes that death is a complete cessation.

Act 3

Warned by her dead husband Hector in a dream, Andromache hides their son Astyanax in Hector's tomb chamber. When Ulysses arrives to fetch the boy, Andromache almost convinces him that he is dead, but her nervousness betrays her. Ulysses' threat to destroy Hector's tomb is intended as a pressure tactic, but (unknown to him) it dooms the child anyway. Andromache brings him forth, pleads in vain for his life, and mourns his imminent loss.

Ode 3. The chorus catalogues the destinations in Greece to which its members may be sent as slaves.

Act 4

Helen has been sent to collect Polyxena, on the pretext of preparing her for marriage to Pyrrhus. Unable to maintain the pretence, she reveals the truth. She also announces the allocation of the other women to Greek masters, including that of Hecuba to Ulysses. Finally Pyrrhus enters and silently drags Polyxena away.

Ode 4. The chorus reflects that misery loves company, but that soon they will be separated from each other and from Troy.

Act 5

A messenger recounts the courageous deaths of Astyanax

and Polyxena. Hecuba laments that death has come to so many but avoided her.

Comment

Troades is unusual among Seneca's plays in having a large cast of characters, who are also varied in nationality (Trojan and Greek) and in type. Among them there is no single figure who could be called dominant or central, as Hercules and Medea are in their respective plays, though Hecuba is a symbol of community on the Trojan side. The play also has a double plot, one focussing on Polyxena and the other on Astyanax.

Yet despite this multiplicity, and despite local inconsistencies and disjunctions, the play feels strongly unified. Individual readers will define the unifying factors in different ways, but important among them is the play's structure. The two plots are closely parallel: each includes, first, a demand that a young Trojan be sacrificed; second, a fierce struggle over that demand; third, the narrative of each death. Furthermore these two plots are skilfully interwoven, with Act 2 focussing on Polyxena, Act 3 on Astyanax, Act 4 on Polyxena again, and Act 5 on the deaths of Astyanax and Polyxena in that order. And this double plot is framed at beginning and end by the single figure of Hecuba, a motherfigure for all Trojans.

Another unifying factor is the frame of reference of the Trojan War, shared by Greeks and Trojans. The play constantly recalls, allusively or explicitly, the war's events, from its beginnings in the Judgment of Paris, the abduction of Helen, and the delayed sailing from Aulis, to the tenth year of the war including Agamemnon's quarrel with Achilles, the deaths of Hector and Achilles, the sack of the city, and the butchery of Priam. In fact events in the play echo earlier episodes in the war: Pyrrhus' slaughter of Polyxena, for example, recalls his murder of the equally defenceless Priam. Agamemnon's quarrel with Pyrrhus in Act 2 reenacts two earlier events, his resistance to the demand for Iphigenia's sacrifice at Aulis, and his quarrel with Achilles over the captive Briseis. On both of those occasions he backed down, allowing Iphigenia's sacrifice and returning Briseis to Achilles; similarly here he backs down, for he knows that Calchas, once consulted, will endorse the sacrifice he has been resisting. Act 3, in which Ulysses outmatches Andromache in a deadly battle of wits, likewise recalls previous occasions when Ulysses defeated others by cunning and manipulation, for example Achilles on Scyros, Palamedes, and Ajax over the arms of Achilles. Though focussed towards the Trojans, then, the play also engages with the Greeks' experience of the war, past and present.[1]

Central to this tragedy is the experience of suffering, bereavement, loss of identity. Such a play could have become an oratorio of grief, concerned only with the passive aspect of suffering. But in fact Seneca's play has an active quality, showing how tragic experience arises from the dynamics of human interaction, from the issue of power in human life. Pyrrhus sees power as absolute, and military victory as granting the victor complete license over the

---

[1] The title "Trojan Women" is simply a label to identify the play, borrowed from Euripides' play which it slightly resembles. Seneca's play should not be read in light of the title as being "about" the experience of the Trojan women exclusively. It is not even certain that the title is Seneca's.

vanquished. Agamemnon takes the opposite view, that Troy's fall demonstrates the fragility of power (a lesson proclaimed also by Hecuba in the play's opening lines). But in the personal struggle for dominance between the two men, Agamemnon's humane views are not strong enough to withstand the ruthlessness of Pyrrhus, who is prepared to engulf fellow Greeks in his violent intentions. We also watch a desperate struggle of wills between Andromache and Ulysses, a struggle that Andromache comes close to winning at one point. Though Ulysses invokes destiny, he is himself convinced of the need to eliminate Astyanax in order to secure lasting peace: hence Andromache is right to insist on his personal responsibility. Yet the play also shows us that the ruthlessness of power has some justification in its own terms, since an adult Astyanax would indeed become a rallying point for Trojans; his mother sees him exclusively in this light, as a future avenger of Troy, a Hector redivivus. An element of brutality is built into the struggles of human life.

Out of the experience of life's brutality grows a perception of death as a haven. It is voiced first by Hecuba: despite its cruelty, Priam's death represents freedom from captivity with all its indignities (142–55). Vying with Hecuba, the chorus pictures Priam wandering happily in Elysium. The theme returns later, when Andromache encourages her son to see death as freedom, a means of rejoining free Trojans (790–91). Indeed both Astyanax and Polyxena face death with courage, and with active defiance of their murderers.

The theme of death as release is sounded in a different key in the sombre and beautiful second choral ode, which asserts that death terminates human consciousness and ex-

167

istence. How does this assertion relate to the picture of
Priam in Elysium in Ode 1? The salient point about each
view of death, as entrance into afterlife or as cessation, is
its consolatory value to the living. Similarly in his prose
works Seneca, without choosing between these two views
of death, emphasises the consolation which each can offer
(e.g. *To Polybius on Consolation* §9). That either view of
death can provide support is shown by the courageous
deaths of the two youngsters, Astyanax in expectation of
rejoining his father and other Trojans, Polyxena presumably in expectation of *not* surviving to become Achilles'
bride in the underworld. Ode 2, incidentally, does not respond to the events of Act 2, namely the reported appearance of Achilles' ghost: the chorus does not ask, "Do the
dead return to plague us?" but "Do we wretches have to
live on after death?" Like Odes 3 and 4, Ode 2 arises out of
the Trojan women's general situation, not out of specific
events.[2]

While the dead are in some sense fortunate, the survivors being taken into exile must face a different kind of
death, that of loss of their Trojan identity. This loss is particularly sharp because they identify so closely with Troy:

[2] A Senecan chorus cannot be assumed to be "present" during
the Acts, and its knowledge of events is only such as the dramatist
assigns it at any point: see section on "The Dramatic Tradition" in
the General Introduction. It is worth adding that although Ode 2
starts from the women's situation, it develops beyond it: the image
of line 373 does not relate to their situation, and the Epicurean
overtones of the ode belong more to the theme than the women.
Similarly in Greek tragedy choral odes sometimes develop from
particular situations into general reflections (e.g. the "Ode to
Man" in Sophocles' *Antigone*).

Hecuba is almost synonymous with the city, as mother of its princes; Andromache identifies herself entirely with Hector, who in turn was the wall and bulwark of the city. At the beginning the Trojan women, under Hecuba's leadership, can still constitute a Trojan community. But as they sail away to separate Greek destinations they will be able to locate Troy, the very foundation of their identity, only by the dark smoke of its destruction (1050–55). Hecuba stands finally desolate of everything, daughter, grandson, husband, even death itself, with a pathos that is all the more poignant because of her earlier resilience in the face of disaster.

Sources

The events surrounding Troy's fall are embedded in a rich literary, mythographic, and artistic tradition. Though the *Iliad* ends before Troy's fall and the *Odyssey* begins after it, the events between the two Homeric epics were covered in other early Greek epics now lost, the *Sack of Troy* and the *Little Iliad*. For Roman readers these events had gained new resonance through the national epic, Vergil's *Aeneid*, which not only retold Troy's fall vividly, but also celebrated the partial survival of Troy in exile, a degree of continuity between Troy and Rome. Seneca's audience would be alert to the many echoes of the *Aeneid* (particularly of Book 2) in his play, and would find its picture of Troy as utterly annihilated all the more stark by contrast. Seneca also echoes elements of Ovid's recounting of Polyxena's death in Book 13 of the *Metamorphoses*.

The sufferings of the Trojans after Troy's fall naturally provided subject matter for many dramas, but despite individual points of similarity, none seems likely to have been the exclusive *fons et origo* of Seneca's play. Sophocles' *Polyxena*, now lost, included an appearance of Achilles' ghost demanding Polyxena's death. Euripides' *Trojan Women*, despite an identical title and a basic similarity of situation to Seneca's play, is not at all close in plot or dramaturgy. Euripides' *Hecuba* is closer in some respects: it treats Polyxena's death and parallels it with the death of another young Trojan, Polydorus. All Roman dramas on these events have perished, including no doubt some unknown to us even by title. Accius' *Astyanax* included an attempt by Andromache to conceal her son, albeit in the hills, not in the tomb. It is conceivable (but no more) that Ennius' *Andromacha Aechmalotis* treated Polyxena's death as well as Astyanax'. The most likely hypothesis is that Seneca composed independently, while drawing on a great wealth of literary precedents. His practice elsewhere makes it improbable that he followed a single model closely or for any distance.

BIBLIOGRAPHY

Commentaries

A. J. Boyle, *Seneca's Troades: Introduction, Text, Translation and Commentary* (Leeds, 1994).

E. Fantham, *Seneca's Troades: a Literary Introduction with Text, Translation and Commentary* (Princeton, 1982).

A. J. Keulen, *L. Annaeus Seneca: Troades. Introduction, Text and Commentary* (Leiden etc., 2001).

Criticism

J. G. Fitch, "Seneca's *Troades* in a New Edition," *Classical Views* 29 (1985), 435–453.

G. Lawall, "Death and Perspective in Seneca's *Troades*," *CJ* 77 (1982), 244–252.

W. Schetter, "Sulla Struttura delle Troiane di Seneca," *Riv. Fil.* 93 (1965), 396–429; reprinted as "Zum Aufbau von Senecas Troerinnen," in Lefèvre (1972), 230–271.

M. Wilson, "The Tragic Mode of Seneca's *Troades*," in Boyle (1983), 27–60.

DRAMATIS PERSONAE

Trojans

HECUBA, *queen of Troy, widow of Priam, mother of many children including Hector*

ANDROMACHE, *widow of Hector and daughter-in-law of Hecuba*

OLD MAN, *attendant of Andromache*

ASTYANAX, *young son of Andromache*

POLYXENA (persona muta), *daughter of Hecuba*

CHORUS *of Trojan women*

Greeks

TALTHYBIUS, *herald of the army*

PYRRHUS, *son of Achilles, heir to the throne of Thessaly*

AGAMEMNON, *king of Mycenae, commander of the Greek forces against Troy*

CALCHAS, *priest and seer*

ULYSSES, *king of Ithaca, strategist of the defeat of Troy*

HELEN, *wife of Menelaus, Agamemnon's brother; her abduction by Paris, Hecuba's son, precipitated the Trojan War*

MESSENGER

SOLDIERS (personae mutae)

Scene

The action unfolds on the plains between the smouldering ruins of Troy and the shore. The setting is fluid and indefinite, except that Act III is set at Hector's burial mound.

TROADES

Quicumque regno fidit et magna potens
dominatur aula nec leves metuit deos
animumque rebus credulum laetis dedit,
me videat et te, Troia: non umquam tulit
5 documenta fors maiora, quam fragili loco
starent superbi. columen eversum occidit
pollentis Asiae, caelitum egregius labor;
ad cuius arma venit et qui frigidum
septena Tanain ora pandentem bibit
10 et qui renatum primus excipiens diem
tepidum rubenti Tigrin immiscet freto,
et quae vagos vicina prospiciens Scythas
ripam catervis Ponticam viduis ferit,
excisa ferro est; Pergamum incubuit sibi.
15 En alta muri decora congesti iacent
tectis adustis; regiam flammae ambiunt
omnisque late fumat Assaraci domus.

15–16 congesti . . . adustis *A*: congestis . . . adusti *E*

---

1 These lessons for rulers are echoed in Elizabethan drama:
"Those that are proud of fickle Empery, / And place their chiefest
good in earthly pomp: / Behold the Turk and his great Emperess"
(Christopher Marlowe, *1 Tamburlaine* V.2.290–92); "Never did

TROJAN WOMEN

ACT 1

HECUBA

Anyone who trusts in royal power, anyone who rules supreme in a great palace without fear of the fickle gods, anyone who surrenders his trusting heart to happiness, should look upon me, and upon you, Troy. Never did Fortune give greater proofs of how unstable the place is where the proud stand.[1] Overthrown and fallen is the pillar of mighty Asia, masterwork of the gods.[2] To its army came that warrior who drinks of the chill Tanais spreading wide its seven mouths,[3] and the one who first welcomes the reborn daylight and sends the warm Tigris on to join the crimson sea, and she who faces as neighbour the nomad Scyths and rides hard on the Pontic shore with her unwed hordes. Now it has been razed by the sword; Pergamum has collapsed on itself. See, the walls, those lofty glories, lie piled in ruins on the charred buildings; flames throng the palace, and smoke rises across the entire breadth of Assaracus'

Fortune greater instance give / In what frail state proud magistrates do live" (Thomas Storer, *Life and Death of Thomas Wolsey*).

[2] Troy's walls were built by Neptune and Apollo.

[3] Rhesus; the following references are to Memnon and the Amazon Penthesileia.

non prohibet avidas flamma victoris manus:
diripitur ardens Troia. nec caelum patet
20 undante fumo; nube ceu densa obsitus
ater favilla squalet Iliaca dies.
stat avidus irae victor et lentum Ilium
metitur oculis ac decem nondum ferus
ignoscit annis; horret afflictam quoque,
25 victamque quamvis videat, haud credit sibi
potuisse vinci. spolia populator rapit
Dardania; praedam mille non capiunt rates.

Testor deorum numen adversum mihi
patriaeque cineres teque rectorem Phrygum,
30 quem Troia toto conditum regno tegit,
tuosque manes quo stetit stante Ilium,
et vos meorum liberum magni greges,
umbrae minores: quidquid adversi accidit,
quaecumque Phoebas ore lymphato furens
35 credi deo vetante praedixit mala,
prior Hecuba vidi gravida nec tacui metus
et vana vates ante Cassandram fui.
non cautus ignes Ithacus aut Ithaci comes
nocturnus in vos sparsit aut fallax Sinon:
40 meus ignis iste est, facibus ardetis meis.

Sed quid ruinas urbis eversae gemis,
vivax senectus? respice infelix ad hos
luctus recentes; Troia iam vetus est malum.

23 nondum *Axelson*: tandem *EA*

---

4 Priam.
5 Hector, identified by the following words.

house. Yet the flames do not curb the conqueror's greedy hands: Troy is plundered while she burns. The sky is obscured by the billowing smoke; as though enveloped in thick cloud, the daylight is black and befouled with Ilium's ash. The conqueror stands insatiable in his anger and measures long-lingering Ilium with his gaze, and savagely refuses as yet to forgive the ten long years. He also shudders at her ruins, and though he sees her defeated, he cannot convince himself that her defeat was possible. Looters seize the Dardan spoils; those thousand ships cannot hold the plunder.

I call the gods to witness (hostile though they are to me), and the ashes of my country, and you, ruler of Phrygia,[4] now buried beneath your whole realm, covered by Troy, and *your* spirit[5]—as long as you stood, Ilium stood—and you great flocks of my children, less mighty shades: all disasters that have happened, all evils that Phoebus' priestess foretold in raving speech as the god denied her credence, I Hecuba saw first while great with child,[6] and I voiced my fears; I was a futile prophetess before Cassandra. It was not the wary Ithacan that scattered firebrands among you, nor the Ithacan's night-prowling companion, nor lying Sinon:[7] that fire is mine, you are burning with my brands.

But why, lingering old age, lament the downfall of a city that is overthrown? Ill-fated one, face these fresh griefs; Troy by now is an old distress. I saw the accursed sacrilege

---

[6] Hecuba while pregnant with Paris had dreamed of giving birth to a blazing firebrand, a portent of Troy's fall.   [7] The Ithacan is Ulysses; his companion in nighttime raids, Diomedes; Sinon's lies lulled the Trojans' suspicions of the Wooden Horse.

vidi execrandum regiae caedis nefas,
45 ipsasque ad aras maius admissum scelus
Aiacis ausis, cum ferox, saeva manu
coma reflectens regium torta caput,
alto nefandum vulneri ferrum abdidit;
quod penitus actum cum recepisset libens,
50 ensis senili siccus e iugulo redît.
placare quem non potuit a caede effera
mortalis aevi cardinem extremum premens
superique testes sceleris et quoddam sacrum
regni iacentis? ille tot regum parens
55 caret sepulcro Priamus et flamma indiget
ardente Troia.
            Non tamen superis sat est:
dominum ecce Priami nuribus et natis legens
sortitur urna, praedaque en vilis sequar.
hic Hectoris coniugia despondet sibi,
60 hic optat Heleni coniugem, hic Antenoris;
nec dest tuos, Cassandra, qui thalamos petat.
mea sors timetur, sola sum Danais metus.
    Lamenta cessant, turba captivae mea?
ferite palmis pectora et planctus date
65 et iusta Troiae facite. iamdudum sonet
fatalis Ide, iudicis diri domus.

CHORUS

Non rude vulgus lacrimisque novum
lugere iubes:
hoc continuis egimus annis,

---

46 Aiacis ausis *Bentley*: aeacis armis *E*: eacide armis *A*
saeva* *A*: scaeva* *E*: laeva *Gronovius*

of the king's murder, and a crime committed at the very altar greater than the outrage of Ajax, when the ferocious fellow,[8] bending back the king's head by the hair twisted in his cruel hand, buried his wicked blade in a deep wound. After he willingly received the deeply driven sword, it came out dry from the old man's throat. Who could not have been appeased from savage slaughter by a man closing on the last climacteric of mortal life, and by the gods witnessing the scene, and by a kind of sanctity belonging to fallen kingship? Priam, famous father of so many princes, has no tomb; he lacks a funeral fire, while Troy burns.

Yet this is not enough for the gods above: even now the urn is casting lots, selecting a master for the daughters and daughters-in-law of Priam, and I shall follow—see, a worthless prize! One man betroths Hector's wife to himself, another hopes for Helenus' wife, another for Antenor's; there is even someone who desires your bridal bed, Cassandra. My lot is feared, I alone frighten the Danaans.

Is your lamentation idle, my band of captive women? Strike your breasts with your hands, beat out the sounds of sorrow, and perform the funeral rites for Troy. For a long time now fateful Mt Ida should have been reechoing, home of the cursed judge.[9]

CHORUS

This is no untrained crowd, new to tears,
that you bid lament:
we have done this for years unbroken,

[8] Pyrrhus. The outrage of Ajax son of Oileus was to drag Cassandra from sanctuary at Athena's altar and rape her.

[9] An allusion to the Judgement of Paris.

ex quo tetigit
70   Phrygius Graias hospes Amyclas
secuitque fretum
pinus matri sacra Cybebae.
decies nivibus canuit Ide,
decies nostris nudata rogis,
75   et Sigeis trepidus campis
decimas secuit messor aristas,
ut nulla dies maerore caret,
sed nova fletus causa ministrat.
    Ite ad planctus,
80   miseramque leva, regina, manum:
vulgus dominam vile sequemur;
non indociles lugere sumus.

HECUBA

Fidae casus nostri comites,
solvite crinem;
85   per colla fluant maesta capilli
86   tepido Troiae pulvere turpes.
102   complete manus:
103   hoc ex Troia sumpsisse licet.
87   paret exertos turba lacertos;
veste remissa substringe sinus
uteroque tenus pateant artus.
90   cui coniugio pectora velas,
captive pudor?
cingat tunicas palla solutas,
vacet ad crebri verbera planctus

---

10 Paris was a guest of Menelaus at Sparta, near Amyclae,
when he seduced his wife Helen.

from the starting point
when the Phrygian guest touched at Greek
    Amyclae,[10]
and the pine sacred to Mother Cybele
cut through the deep.
Ten times Mt Ida has grown white with snows,
ten times bared for our pyres,
and on the plains of Sigeum the reaper
has cut ten harvests in fear,
while no day has been empty of grief,
but some new reason has furnished laments.

    Busy yourselves with blows of sorrow,
and you, our queen, raise your unhappy hand:
we the common crowd will follow our lady;
we are not unschooled in mourning.

HECUBA

Faithful companions of my fall,
unbind your hair;
let your locks flow over your necks in mourning,
filthy with the warm dust of Troy.
Fill your hands:
this much we *may* take from Troy.
The whole group must strip its shoulders in
    preparation:
drop your garments, fasten their folds around your
    hips,
let your bodies be bared down to the womb.
For what marriage do you cover your breasts,
you modest prisoners?
Tie your cloaks around your unfastened tunics,
free your hands

181

furibunda manus.
95   placet hic habitus,
placet: agnosco Troada turbam.
Iterum luctus redeant veteres,
solitum flendi vincite morem:
Hectora flemus.

CHORUS

Solvimus omnes
lacerum multo funere crinem;
100   coma dimissa est libera nodo
sparsitque cinis fervidus ora.
104   cadit ex umeris vestis apertis
105   imumque tegit suffulta latus;
iam nuda vocant pectora dextras.
Nunc, nunc vires exprome, dolor.
Rhoetea sonent litora planctu,
habitansque cavis montibus Echo
110   non, ut solita est,
extrema brevis verba remittat:
totos reddat Troiae gemitus.
audiat omnes pontus et aether.
Saevite, manus,
pulsu pectus tundite vasto;
115   non sum solito contenta sono:
Hectora flemus.

HECUBA

Tibi nostra ferit dextra lacertos
umerosque ferit tibi sanguineos,
tibi nostra caput dextera pulsat,
120   tibi maternis ubera palmis

to rain frenzied blows of mourning.
Yes, this appearance
is right: I recognise this group as Trojan.
Let your old griefs return once more,
but outdo the usual style of mourning:
it is Hector we mourn for.

CHORUS

We have all unbound
our hair, torn at many a funeral;
our locks are released and free,
and glowing ash has spattered our faces.
Our garments drop from our bared shoulders
and are fastened to cover our hips;
now our naked breasts demand blows.
Now our anguish must unleash its strength.
Let Rhoeteum's beaches resound to our mourning
    blows,
and let Echo, dwelling in the hollowed hills,
not return just the final words
with her usual brevity,
but give back fully Troy's groans of pain:
let sea and sky hear them all.
Hands, be violent,
strike my breasts with mighty blows!
I am not satisfied with the usual sound:
it is Hector we mourn for.

HECUBA

For you my right hand strikes my arms,
it strikes my shoulders for you till they bleed;
for you my right hand pounds my head;
for you my breasts lie torn

183

laniata iacent:
fluat et multo sanguine manet
quamcumque tuo funere feci
rupta cicatrix.
Columen patriae, mora fatorum,
125   tu praesidium Phrygibus fessis,
tu murus eras,
umerisque tuis
stetit illa decem fulta per annos;
tecum cecidit,
summusque dies Hectoris idem
patriaeque fuit.
130   Vertite planctus:
Priamo vestros fundite fletus;
satis Hector habet.

CHORUS

Accipe, rector Phrygiae, planctus,
accipe fletus, bis capte senex.
nil Troia semel te rege tulit,
135   bis pulsari
Dardana Graio moenia ferro
bisque pharetras passa Herculeas.
post elatos Hecubae partus
regumque gregem
postrema pater funera claudis,
140   magnoque Iovi victima caesus
Sigea premis litora truncus.

184

by a mother's fingers.
Every scar I made
at your funeral must burst open,
flow and stream with copious blood.
Pillar of our country, delayer of doom,
you were a protection for weary Phrygians,
you were a wall,
and by your shoulders
she stood buttressed for ten years;
with you she fell,
and Hector's last day was his country's also.
    Turn your mourning:
pour out your tears for Priam;
for Hector this suffices.

CHORUS

Receive our mourning, king of Phrygia;
receive our tears, twice-captured old man.
Nothing befell Troy just once in your reign:
twice she suffered
the battering of Dardan walls with Greek steel,
twice she suffered the arrows of Hercules.[11]
After Hecuba's young ones were carried to burial,
after that flock of princes,
you their father finally close the funeral train.
Butchered as a sacrifice to great Jove,[12]
you burden the Sigean shore, a headless corpse.

[11] Hercules captured Troy in Priam's childhood (see lines 718–28); his arrows were later instrumental in Troy's final fall, this time in Philoctetes' hands.

[12] Priam was killed at the altar of Jupiter in his own palace.

HECUBA

Alio lacrimas flectite vestras:
non est Priami miseranda mei
mors, Iliades.
145   "Felix Priamus" dicite cunctae:
liber manes vadit ad imos,
nec feret umquam
victa Graium cervice iugum;
non ille duos videt Atridas
nec fallacem cernit Ulixem;
150   non Argolici praeda triumphi
subiecta feret colla tropaeis;
non assuetas ad sceptra manus
post terga dabit,
currusque sequens Agamemnonios
aurea dextra vincula gestans
155   latis fiet pompa Mycenis.

CHORUS

"Felix Priamus" dicimus omnes:
secum excedens sua regna tulit.
nunc Elysii
nemoris tutis errat in umbris,
interque pias felix animas
160   Hectora quaerit.
Felix Priamus;
felix quisquis bello moriens
omnia secum consumpta tulit.

TROJAN WOMEN

HECUBA

Turn your tears elsewhere:
my Priam's death is not to be pitied,
women of Troy.
"Blest is Priam" you should all say:
he goes in freedom to the shades below,
and his neck will never
bear the yoke of the Greeks in defeat.
He does not see the two sons of Atreus,
he does not behold deceitful Ulysses;
he will not bear shoulders bowed beneath trophies,
as a prize in a triumphal Argive procession;
he will not proffer those hands, accustomed to the
    sceptre,
to be tied behind his back;
nor, following Agamemnon's chariot
in handcuffs of gold,
will he be paraded in spacious Mycenae.

CHORUS

"Blest is Priam" we all say:
in departing he has taken his kingdom with him.
Now he wanders among
the peaceful shadows of the Elysian grove,
and blest among the righteous spirits
he looks for Hector.
Blest is Priam;
blest is anyone who, dying in war,
has taken with him his whole destroyed world.

TALTHYBIUS

O longa Danais semper in portu mora,
165   seu petere bellum, petere seu patriam volunt!

CHORUS

Quae causa ratibus faciat et Danais moram
effare, reduces quis deus claudat vias.

TALTHYBIUS

Pavet animus, artus horridus quassat tremor.
maiora veris monstra (vix capiunt fidem)
170   vidi ipse, vidi. summa iam Titan iuga
170bis stringebat ortu, vicerat noctem dies,
cum subito caeco terra mugitu fremens
concussa totos traxit ex imo sinus;
movere silvae capita et excelsum nemus
fragore vasto tonuit et lucus sacer;
175   Idaea ruptis saxa ceciderunt iugis.
nec terra solum tremuit: et pontus suum
adesse Achillem sensit ac volvit vada.

    Tum scissa vallis aperit immensos specus,
et hiatus Erebi pervium ad superos iter
180   tellure fracta praebet ac tumulum levat.
emicuit ingens umbra Thessalici ducis,
Threicia qualis arma proludens tuis
iam, Troia, fatis stravit aut Neptunium

---

177 volvit *suggested as one possibility by Delz and Fitch*: stravit
EA

---

13 I.e. from Aulis; the parallel between the present delay and
that at Aulis is a frequent theme of this Act.

TROJAN WOMEN

ACT 2

TALTHYBIUS

How long the delay in port always for the Danaans, whether they want to head for war[13] or head for their homeland!

CHORUS

Tell us what cause creates delay for the ships and the Danaans, what god is blocking the homeward routes.

TALTHYBIUS

My mind feels fear, a shuddering tremor shakes my body. Things too unnatural to be true—they scarcely command belief—I saw with my own eyes, I saw them. The Titan was just grazing the mountain ridges as he rose, day had defeated night, when suddenly the earth shook with a muffled roar and heaved all of its inner recesses from the lowest depths. The treetops swayed; lofty woodland and sacred grove thundered with an awesome sound of breaking. On Ida rocks fell from the shattered ridges. Not only the earth trembled: the sea too sensed its own Achilles near,[14] and made its waters roll.

Then a newly opened chasm revealed measureless hollows, and the gaping maw of Erebus gave passage to the world above through the fractured earth, and eased the tomb's weight. Out darted the huge ghost of the Thessalian chief, looking as when he defeated Thracian arms, already in training for your doom, Troy, or when he struck down

---

[14] The sea responds to Achilles as son of the sea goddess Thetis.

189

cana nitentem perculit iuvenem coma,
185 aut cum inter acies Marte violento furens
corporibus amnes clausit et quaerens iter
tardus cruento Xanthus erravit vado,
aut cum superbo victor in curru stetit
egitque habenas Hectorem et Troiam trahens.
190 Implevit omne litus irati sonus:
"Ite, ite, inertes, debitos manibus meis
auferte honores, solvite ingratas rates
per nostra ituri maria! non parvo luit
iras Achillis Graecia et magno luet:
195 desponsa nostris cineribus Polyxene
Pyrrhi manu mactetur et tumulum riget."
haec fatus alta nocte divisit diem,
repetensque Ditem mersus ingentem specum
coeunte terra iunxit. immoti iacent
200 tranquilla pelagi, ventus abiecit minas,
placidumque fluctu murmurat leni mare,
Tritonum ab alto cecinit hymenaeum chorus.

PYRRHUS

Cum laeta pelago vela rediturus dares,
excidit Achilles, cuius unius manu
205 impulsa Troia, quidquid adiecit morae
illo remoto, dubia quo caderet stetit?
velis licet quod petitur ac properes dare,
sero es daturus: iam suum cuncti duces
tulere pretium. quae minor merces potest
210 tantae dari virtutis? an meruit parum
qui, fugere bellum iussus et longa sedens

Neptune's son[15] who gleamed with white hair; or when, in savage battle rage between the lines, he blocked rivers with corpses, and the Xanthus, seeking a way, wandered slowly with bloodstained waters; or when he stood victorious in his proud chariot and plied the reins, dragging Hector and Troy. The sound of his anger filled the whole shore: "Go on, you idlers, carry away the honours owed to my hands, launch your ungrateful ships—to travel through my seas! It cost Greece no small price to appease Achilles' wrath, and it will cost her dear. Let Polyxena, betrothed to my ashes, be sacrificed by Pyrrhus' hand and quench the tomb's thirst." After these words he separated the daylight from deep night: as he returned to Dis and plunged down, he sealed the vast abyss by the joining-up of the earth. Becalmed now lay the waters, the wind dropped its menace, the tranquil sea murmured with gentle waves, and a choir of Tritons sang a marriage hymn from the deep.

[*Enter Pyrrhus and Agamemnon, arguing*]

PYRRHUS

When you were setting sail joyfully for your return, did Achilles slip your mind? Troy had been dislodged by his hand alone, and, for the brief delay she gained by his removal, she stood only in doubt which way to fall! Even if you are willing and eager to grant his request, you will grant it too late: all the leaders have taken *their* prizes already. Can any smaller payment be granted for such valour? Or was he not sufficiently deserving? Though bidden to run away from war, to draw out a sedentary life in

---

[15] Cycnus. "Thracian arms" is obscure, but perhaps refers to Tenedos and Scyros (see lines 224–26).

aevum senecta ducere ac Pylii senis
transcendere annos, exuit matris dolos
falsasque vestes, fassus est armis virum?
215 Inhospitali Telephus regno impotens,
dum Mysiae ferocis introitus negat,
rudem cruore regio dextram imbuit,
fortemque eandem sensit et mitem manum.
cecidere Thebae, vidit Eetion capi
220 sua regna victus; clade subversa est pari
apposita celso parva Lyrnesos iugo,
captaque tellus nobilis Briseïde;
et causa litis regibus Chryse iacet,
et nota fama Tenedos, et quae pascuo
225 fecunda pingui Thracios nutrit greges
Scyros, fretumque Lesbos Aegaeum secans,
et cara Phoebo Cilla; quid quas alluit
vernis Caycus gurgitem attollens aquis?
Haec tanta clades gentium ac tantus pavor,
230 sparsae tot urbes turbinis vasti modo,
alterius esset gloria ac summum decus:
iter est Achillis; sic meus venit pater
et tanta gessit bella, dum bellum parat.
        Ut alia sileam merita, non unus satis
235 Hector fuisset? Ilium vicit pater,
vos diruistis. inclitas laudes iuvat
et clara magni facta genitoris sequi:
iacuit peremptus Hector ante oculos patris
patruique Memnon, cuius ob luctum parens

---

16 Thetis disguised him as a girl to prevent his fighting and dying at Troy, but through a ruse of Ulysses he picked up weapons
and so revealed his gender.

lengthy old age, and to outdo the years of the old man of Pylos, he stripped off his mother's tricks, the false clothes, and confessed himself a man by taking up arms.[16] Telephus, headstrong ruler of an inhospitable realm, who denied him entry to wild Mysia, was the first to stain that inexperienced hand with his royal blood, and found that hand both warlike and gentle. Thebes fell, and defeated Eetion saw his kingdom taken; toppled by a similar defeat was tiny Lyrnesos perched on its lofty ridge, and the land renowned for the capture of Briseis; Chryse too, cause of a quarrel for kings,[17] lies overthrown, and Tenedos renowned in story, and fertile Scyros which feeds Thracian herds with its rich pasture, and Lesbos cutting the Aegean Sea, and Cilla dear to Phoebus; what of the lands lapped by the Caycus, its flood swollen with springtime waters? Such a devastation of peoples as this, such dread, so many cities torn apart as if by a giant whirlwind, would have been another man's glory and highest renown, but in Achilles' case it was just a journey; so my father came, such wars he waged, while preparing for war.

To say nothing of his other services, would Hector alone not have been enough? Father conquered Troy, you people demolished it. I enjoy tracing the renowned accomplishments and glorious deeds of my great parent! Hector fell slain before his father's eyes and Memnon before his uncle's;[18] his mother, ashen-faced through grief for

[17] Agamemnon was forced to return his slave-woman Chryseis, captured in Chryse; in recompense he took Briseis, so precipitating the famous quarrel with Achilles.

[18] Priam was both father of Hector and uncle of Memnon, whose mother was Aurora the dawn goddess.

240 pallente maestum protulit vultu diem;
suique victor operis exemplum horruit,
didicitque Achilles et dea natos mori.
tum saeva Amazon ultimus cecidit metus.
Debes Achilli, merita si digne aestimas,
245 et si ex Mycenis virginem atque Argis petat.
dubitatur et iam placita nunc subito improbas,
Priamique natam Pelei nato ferum
mactare credis? at tuam natam parens
Helenae immolasti: solita iam et facta expeto.

AGAMEMNON

250 Iuvenile vitium est regere non posse impetum;
aetatis alios fervor hic primae rapit,
Pyrrhum paternus. spiritus quondam truces
minasque tumidi lentus Aeacidae tuli.
quo plura possis, plura patienter feras.
255   Quid caede dira nobiles clari ducis
aspergis umbras? noscere hoc primum decet,
quid facere victor debeat, victus pati.
violenta nemo imperia continuit diu,
moderata durant; quoque Fortuna altius
260 evexit ac levavit humanas opes,
hoc se magis supprimere felicem decet
variosque casus tremere metuentem deos
nimium faventes. magna momento obrui
vincendo didici. Troia nos tumidos facit
265 nimium ac feroces? stamus hoc Danai loco,
unde illa cecidit. fateor, aliquando impotens
regno ac superbus altius memet tuli;

---

19 Penthesilea, who came to Troy's aid after Hector's death.

him, ushered in a mournful day. His conqueror shuddered
at the lesson of his own deed, and Achilles learnt that even
a goddess' sons can die. Then the fierce Amazon fell, the
last threat.[19] If you set a worthy value on Achilles' services,
you even owe him a maiden from Mycenae and Argos, if
he should demand it. Are you still hesitating? Do you
suddenly now condemn approved policy, and consider it
brutal to sacrifice Priam's daughter to Peleus' son? Yet you,
a father, sacrificed your own daughter for Helen![20] What I
am demanding is now custom and practice.

AGAMEMNON

Young men have the failing of being unable to govern
impulse. In others such impetuous ardour is caused by
immaturity; in Pyrrhus, it is inherited. Once I tolerated
the harsh arrogance and threats of proud Aeacides.[21] The
greater your power, the greater should be your patience.

Why bespatter a renowned leader's glorious shade with
monstrous bloodshed? First one should understand what
actions the conqueror may rightly take, and the conquered
endure. Power used violently is held by no one for long;
used with restraint, it lasts. The higher Fortune raises and
exalts human might, the more the fortunate should humble themselves and tremble at shifting circumstance, fearing overly favourable gods. That greatness is crushed in a
moment I have learnt by conquering. Does Troy make us
too arrogant and self-assured? We Danaans stand in the
very place from which she fell. I admit, at one time I was
unrestrained and proud in government, bearing myself too

[20] The sacrifice of Iphigenia at Aulis allowed the Greeks to sail
to Troy to reclaim Helen.
[21] Achilles, grandson of Aeacus.

sed fregit illos spiritus haec quae dare
potuisset aliis causa, Fortunae favor.
270 tu me superbum, Priame, tu timidum facis.
ego esse quicquam sceptra nisi vano putem
fulgore tectum nomen et falso comam
vinclo decentem? casus haec rapiet brevis,
nec mille forsan ratibus aut annis decem;
275 non omnibus Fortuna tam lenta imminet.
    Equidem fatebor (pace dixisse hoc tua,
Argiva tellus, liceat): affligi Phrygas
vincique volui; ruere et aequari solo
etiam arcuissem; sed regi frenis nequit
280 et ira et ardens ensis et victoria
commissa nocti. quidquid indignum aut ferum
cuiquam videri potuit, hoc fecit dolor
tenebraeque, per quas ipse se irritat furor,
gladiusque felix, cuius infecti semel
285 vecors libido est. quidquid eversae potest
superesse Troiae, maneat; exactum satis
poenarum et ultra est. regia ut virgo occidat
tumuloque donum detur et cineres riget
et facinus atrox caedis ut thalamos vocent,
290 non patiar. in me culpa cunctorum redit;
qui non vetat peccare, cum possit, iubet.

PYRRHUS
Nullumne Achillis praemium manes ferent?

AGAMEMNON
Ferent, et illum laudibus cuncti canent,
magnumque terrae nomen ignotae audient.

---

280 ensis *Zwierlein*: hostis *EA*

high; but that arrogance was broken by the very cause that could have produced it in others, Fortune's favour. You make me proud, Priam, you make me fearful. Could *I* consider sceptered power to be anything but a name overlaid with false glitter, a deceiving bond to adorn the hair? Some quick calamity will snatch these things, perhaps without a thousand ships or ten years; Fortune's menace is not so long drawn out for all.

For my part I will admit it (may I say this without offence to you, Argive land): I wanted the Phrygians beaten down and defeated; but as for being ruined and levelled to the ground, I would actually have prevented it. Nevertheless tight reins cannot be kept on anger and the blazing sword and a victory turned over to night. Anything that might have been thought unworthy or barbarous was the work of bitterness and of darkness, through which frenzy intensifies itself, and of the successful sword, which once dyed in blood has an insane lust. Whatever can survive of Troy, let it remain. Enough reprisals and more have been exacted. That a princess should fall and be offered as a gift to the tomb and quench its ashes, and that they should call a cruel act of bloodshed "marriage," I will not permit. The guilt of all comes back to me: one who does not forbid wrongdoing, when he has the power, commands it.

PYRRHUS

Shall Achilles' ghost gain no reward?

AGAMEMNON

It shall, and all shall hymn him with praises, and lands unknown shall hear his great name. But if the dust is assuaged

295 quod si levatur sanguine infuso cinis,
opima Phrygii colla caedantur gregis,
fluatque nulli flebilis matri cruor.
quis iste mos est? quando in inferias homo est
impensus hominis? detrahe invidiam tuo
300 odiumque patri, quem coli poena iubes.

PYRRHUS

O tumide, rerum dum secundarum status
extollit animos, timide, cum increpuit metus,
regum tyranne! iamne flammatum geris
amoris aestu pectus ac veneris novae?
305 solusne totiens spolia de nobis feres?
hac dextra Achilli victimam reddam suam.
quam si negas retinesque, maiorem dabo
dignamque quam det Pyrrhus; et nimium diu
a caede nostra regia cessat manus
310 paremque poscit Priamus.

AGAMEMNON

Haud equidem nego
hoc esse Pyrrhi maximum in bello decus,
saevo peremptus ense quod Priamus iacet,
supplex paternus.

PYRRHUS

Supplices nostri patris
hostesque eosdem novimus. Priamus tamen
315 praesens rogavit; tu, gravi pavidus metu
nec ad rogandum fortis, Aiaci preces
Ithacoque mandas, clausus atque hostem tremens.

---

304 amoris aestu *Bentley*: amore subito *EA*

by the pouring-on of blood, have them cut the necks of prime cattle from a Phrygian herd, and let the blood that flows not bring grief to any mother. What kind of custom is *that*? When was human life expended on tomb offerings for a human? Lift the burden of odium and hatred from your father: you want him revered through reprisals!

PYRRHUS

You are proud-hearted while good fortune exalts your spirits, but faint-hearted at the clatter of danger, you tyrant of kings! *Now* is your heart inflamed with the fire of love, of a new passion? Are you alone to take spoils from us so often?[22] With this hand I shall pay Achilles the victim that is rightfully his. If you refuse and withhold her, I shall give a greater victim, a worthy one for Pyrrhus to give; indeed, my hand has rested too long from slaughtering kings, and Priam claims his peer.

AGAMEMNON

I certainly do not deny this to be Pyrrhus' greatest glory in war—that Priam, his father's suppliant, lies brutally killed by the sword.

PYRRHUS

I know my father's suppliants were his enemies too. But Priam pleaded in person: you, stricken with deep fear and lacking courage to plead, entrusted your prayers to Ajax and the Ithacan, shut away and trembling at your foe.

---

[22] The previous "spoil" was Briseis. The preceding line suggests lust as Agamemnon's motive in "stealing" both Briseis and Polyxena from Achilles.

AGAMEMNON

At non timebat tunc tuus, fateor, parens,
interque caedes Graeciae atque ustas rates
320   segnis iacebat, belli et armorum immemor,
levi canoram verberans plectro chelyn.

PYRRHUS

Tunc magnus Hector, arma contemnens tua,
cantus Achillis timuit, et tanto in metu
navalibus pax alta Thessalicis fuit.

AGAMEMNON

325   Nempe isdem in istis Thessalis navalibus
pax alta rursus Hectoris patri fuit.

PYRRHUS

Est regis alti spiritum regi dare.

AGAMEMNON

Cur dextra regi spiritum eripuit tua?

PYRRHUS

Mortem misericors saepe pro vita dabit.

AGAMEMNON

330   Et nunc misericors virginem busto petis?

PYRRHUS

Iamne immolari virgines credis nefas?

AGAMEMNON

Praeferre patriam liberis regem decet.

PYRRHUS

Lex nulla capto parcit aut poenam impedit.

AGAMEMNON

Certainly your father felt no fear at that time, I admit;
amidst the carnage of Greece and the burnt ships he lay
idle, forgetting war and weapons, striking his tuneful lyre
with a dainty pick.

PYRRHUS

At that time, though great Hector despised your weapons,
he feared Achilles' songs. Amidst such danger, there was
deep peace around the Thessalian shipways.

AGAMEMNON

Yes, and around those same Thessalian shipways of yours,
there was deep peace later for Hector's father.

PYRRHUS

It is the act of a great king to grant life to a king.

AGAMEMNON

Why then did *your* hand deprive the king of life?

PYRRHUS

Often a compassionate man will grant death rather than
life.

AGAMEMNON

And now as a compassionate man you seek a virgin for the
tomb?

PYRRHUS

So nowadays you consider sacrifice of virgins a crime?

AGAMEMNON

To put fatherland before children befits a king.

PYRRHUS

No law spares a prisoner, or forbids reprisal.

AGAMEMNON

Quod non vetat lex, hoc vetat fieri pudor.

PYRRHUS

335 Quodcumque libuit facere victori licet.

AGAMEMNON

Minimum decet libere cui multum licet.

PYRRHUS

His ista iactas, quos decem annorum gravi
regno subactos Pyrrhus exsolvit iugo?

AGAMEMNON

Hos Scyros animos?

PYRRHUS

Scelere quae fratrum caret.

AGAMEMNON

340 Inclusa fluctu—

PYRRHUS

Nempe cognati maris.
[Atrei et Thyestae nobilem novi domum]

AGAMEMNON

Ex virginis concepte furtivo stupro
et ex Achille nate, sed nondum viro—

PYRRHUS

Illo ex Achille, genere qui mundum suo,
345 sparsus per omne caelitum regnum, tenet:

341 *deleted by Friedrich*

---

23 An allusion to the crimes of Atreus and Thyestes (Agamem-

AGAMEMNON

What law does not forbid, a sense of restraint forbids.

PYRRHUS

The victor has a right to do whatever he pleases.

AGAMEMNON

He who has much right should please himself least.

PYRRHUS

Can you mouth such words to these men, who were crushed by your ten-year tyranny until Pyrrhus liberated them?

AGAMEMNON

Scyros produces such arrogance?

PYRRHUS

It is free of brothers' crimes.[23]

AGAMEMNON

Hemmed in by waves—

PYRRHUS

Yes, of our ancestral sea.[24]

AGAMEMNON

You were conceived through the furtive seduction of a virgin, fathered by Achilles, but before he came of age!

PYRRHUS

That same Achilles who holds the cosmos by a lineage branching into each of the gods' realms—the sea through

non's father and uncle) against each other. Scyros is Pyrrhus' island birthplace.

[24] Line 341 (deleted): "I know all about the distinguished house of Atreus and Thyestes."

Thetide aequor, umbras Aeaco, caelum Iove.

AGAMEMNON
Illo ex Achille, qui manu Paridis iacet.

PYRRHUS
Quem nec deorum comminus quisquam petît.

AGAMEMNON
Compescere equidem verba et audacem malo
350   poteram domare; sed meus captis quoque
scit parcere ensis. potius interpres deum
Calchas vocetur: fata si poscunt, dabo.
    Tu, qui Pelasgae vincla solvisti rati
morasque bellis, arte qui reseras polum,
355   cui viscerum secreta, cui mundi fragor
et stella longa semitam flamma trahens
dant signa fati, cuius ingenti mihi
mercede constant ora: quid iubeat deus
effare, Calchas, nosque consilio rege.

CALCHAS
360   Dant fata Danais quo solent pretio viam:
mactanda virgo est Thessali busto ducis;
sed quo iugari Thessalae cultu solent
Ionidesve vel Mycenaeae nurus,
Pyrrhus parenti coniugem tradat suo:
365   sic rite dabitur. Non tamen nostras tenet
haec una puppes causa: nobilior tuo,
Polyxene, cruore debetur cruor.

---

25 Thetis the sea goddess was Achilles' mother; Aeacus, judge
of the dead, was his paternal grandfather; Jupiter, father of
Aeacus, was his great-grandfather.

Thetis, the underworld through Aeacus, the heavens through Jove.[25]

AGAMEMNON
That same Achilles who lies dead by Paris' hand.

PYRRHUS
And whom not one god challenged in hand-to-hand fighting.

AGAMEMNON
In my position I could check your words and tame your recklessness with pain. But *my* sword is capable of sparing even prisoners. Instead, let the gods' spokesman Calchas be summoned; if Fate demands, I shall agree.

You who untied the fastenings of the Pelasgian fleet and the obstacles to war,[26] who unlock the heavens by your skill, to whom the hidden entrails, the sky's thunder-crash, and the star tracing a long fiery trail give signs of fate—and whose pronouncements cost me an enormous price: declare god's command, Calchas, and direct us with your counsel.

CALCHAS
Fate grants the Danaans passage at the customary price. The young woman is to be sacrificed on the Thessalian leader's tomb. Pyrrhus should deliver his father's wife to him in the costume in which brides of Thessaly are customarily married, or those of Ionia or Mycenae: so she will be given with proper rites. It is not, however, this cause alone that detains our ships. More illustrious blood is owed

---

[26] By revealing at Aulis that the fleet would be able to sail if Iphigenia was sacrificed.

quem fata quaerunt, turre de summa cadat
Priami nepos Hectoreus et letum oppetat.
370 tum mille velis impleat classis freta.

CHORUS

Verum est an timidos fabula decipit
umbras corporibus vivere conditis,
cum coniunx oculis imposuit manum
supremusque dies solibus obstitit
375 et tristis cineres urna coercuit?
non prodest animam tradere funeri,
sed restat miseris vivere longius?
an toti morimur nullaque pars manet
nostri, cum profugo spiritus halitu
380 immixtus nebulis cessit in aëra
et nudum tetigit subdita fax latus?
  Quidquid sol oriens, quidquid et occidens
novit, caeruleis Oceanus fretis
quidquid bis veniens et fugiens lavat,
385 aetas Pegaseo corripiet gradu.
quo bis sena volant sidera turbine,
quo cursu properat volvere saecula
astrorum dominus, quo properat modo
obliquis Hecate currere flexibus:
390 hoc omnes petimus fata, nec amplius,
iuratos superis qui tetigit lacus,
usquam est. ut calidis fumus ab ignibus
vanescit, spatium per breve sordidus;

---

[27] John Talbot renders (1686): "When any wretched Mortal
dies, / And his sad Kindred close his Eyes, / Does not Death finish
all his pain, / But must he die, to live again?"

than yours, Polyxena. The one whom fate requires, grandson of Priam through Hector, must fall from the tower's
height and meet his death. Then the fleet may fill the
straits with its thousand sails.

CHORUS

Is it true, or a tale to deceive the faint-hearted,
that spirits live on after bodies are buried,
when the spouse has placed a hand over the eyes,
and the final day has blocked out future suns,
and the grim urn has confined the ashes?
Is nothing gained in yielding the soul to death?
Are the wretched faced with further life?[27]
Or do we die wholly, and does no part of us
survive, once the spirit carried on the fugitive breath
has mingled with the mist and receded into the air,
and the kindling torch has touched the naked flesh?

All that is known to the rising or setting sun,
all that is laved by Ocean with its blue waters
twice approaching and twice fleeing,
time will seize at the pace of Pegasus.
As the twelve constellations fly at whirlwind speed,
as the lord of the stars[28] hastens apace
to roll on the centuries, in the way that Hecate
hurries to run on her slanting arcs:
so we all head for death. No longer does one
who has reached the pools[29] that bind the gods' oaths
exist at all. As smoke from burning fires
fades away, soiling the air for a brief space;

[28] I.e. the Sun, as at *Thyestes* 836.
[29] Those of the Styx.

ut nubes, gravidas quas modo vidimus,
395 arctoi Boreae dissipat impetus:
sic hic, quo regimur, spiritus effluet.
Post mortem nihil est, ipsaque mors nihil,
velocis spatii meta novissima.
spem ponant avidi, solliciti metum:
400 tempus nos avidum devorat et chaos.
mors individua est, noxia corpori
nec parcens animae. Taenara et aspero
regnum sub domino limen et obsidens
custos non facili Cerberus ostio
405 rumores vacui verbaque inania
et par sollicito fabula somnio.
quaeris quo iaceas post obitum loco?
quo non nata iacent.

ANDROMACHA

Quid, maesta Phrygiae turba, laceratis comas
410 miserumque tunsae pectus effuso genas
fletu rigatis? levia perpessae sumus,
si flenda patimur. Ilium vobis modo,
mihi cecidit olim, cum ferus curru incito
mea membra raperet, et gravi gemeret sono
415 Peliacus axis pondere Hectoreo tremens.
tunc obruta atque eversa quodcumque accidit
torpens malis rigensque sine sensu fero.
Iam erepta Danais coniugem sequerer meum,
nisi hic teneret: hic meos animos domat
420 morique prohibet; cogit hic aliquid deos

---

[30] After killing Hector, Achilles dragged his body before Troy's
walls. "Pelian" = cut on Mt Pelion in Thessaly, near Achilles'
kingdom.

as the leaden clouds that we saw just now
are scattered by the onset of northern Boreas:
so this spirit that rules us will flow away.
After death is nothing, and death itself is nothing,
the finishing line of a swiftly run circuit.
Let the greedy lay down their hopes, the anxious their
     fears:
greedy time and Chaos devour us.
Death is indivisible, destructive to the body
and not sparing the soul. Taenarus, and the kingdom
under its harsh lord, and Cerberus guarding
the entrance with its unyielding gate
—hollow rumours, empty words,
a tale akin to a troubled dream.
You ask where you lie after death?
Where unborn things lie.

ACT 3

ANDROMACHE

Sad crowd of Phrygian women, why tear your hair, beat
your breasts in sorrow and drench your cheeks with floods
of tears? Our past sufferings were trivial, if these sufferings deserve tears. For you Ilium fell just now, but for
me long ago, when the savage dragged *my* limbs behind
his speeding chariot, and the Pelian axle groaned deeply,
shuddering with Hector's weight.[30] *Then* I was overwhelmed and ruined: whatever happens now I endure
without feeling, dazed and numbed by adversity. I would
have escaped the Danaans and followed my husband by
now, if this one [*indicating Astyanax*] did not hold me: he
tames my spirit and prevents my death; he compels me still

209

adhuc rogare, tempus aerumnae addidit.
hic mihi malorum maximum fructum abstulit,
nihil timere. prosperis rebus locus
ereptus omnis, dura qua veniant habent.
425 miserrimum est timere, cum speres nihil.

SENEX
Quis te repens commovit afflictam metus?

ANDROMACHA
Exoritur aliquod maius ex magno malum.
nondum ruentis Ilii fatum stetit.

SENEX
Et quas reperiet, ut velit, clades deus?

ANDROMACHA
430 Stygis profundae claustra et obscuri specus
laxantur et, ne desit eversis metus,
hostes ab imo conditi Dite exeunt.
solisne retro pervium est Danais iter?
certe aequa mors est! turbat atque agitat Phrygas
435 communis iste terror; hic proprie meum
exterret animum noctis horrendae sopor.

SENEX
Quae visa portas? effer in medium metus.

ANDROMACHA
Partes fere nox alma transierat duas
clarumque septem verterant stellae iugum;
440 ignota tandem venit afflictae quies
brevisque fessis somnus obrepsit genis
(si somnus ille est mentis attonitae stupor):

---

424 dura *Bentley*: dira *EA*

to ask something of the gods, and prolongs my ordeal. He has robbed me of the best fruit of suffering: having no fear. All space for wellbeing is stolen, but affliction has a means of approach. It is utterly wretched to fear, when you have no hope.

OLD MAN

What sudden fear has touched you amidst your troubles?

ANDROMACHE

From great adversity some greater is arising. The doom of falling Ilium is not yet halted.

OLD MAN

And what disasters will god find, supposing he wishes?

ANDROMACHE

The barriers of the deep underworld and its dark caves are opening, and, lest the ruined should have nothing left to fear, their buried enemies are emerging from deepest Dis. Is the path back open only to Danaans? Surely death is impartial! That is a shared terror which disturbs and shakes the Phrygians, but my mind is filled with a private dread from this fearful night's dream.

OLD MAN

What vision do you bring word of? Disclose your fears before us all.

ANDROMACHE

The kindly night had completed perhaps two-thirds of her course, and the seven stars had turned their shining Wain: at last amidst my troubles an unfamiliar rest came to me, and a brief sleep stole over my weary eyes—if that stupor

211

cum subito nostros Hector ante oculos stetit,
non qualis ultro bella in Argivos ferens
445 Graias petebat facibus Idaeis rates,
nec caede multa qualis in Danaos furens
vera ex Achille spolia simulato tulit;
non ille vultus flammeum intendens iubar,
sed fessus ac deiectus et fletu gravis
450 similisque nostro, squalida obtectus coma.
iuvat tamen vidisse. tum, quassans caput,
"Dispelle somnos" inquit "et natum eripe,
o fida coniunx: lateat, haec una est salus.
omitte fletus. Troia quod cecidit gemis?
455 utinam iaceret tota! festina, amove
quocumque nostrae parvulam stirpem domus."
mihi gelidus horror ac tremor somnum excutit,
oculosque nunc huc pavida, nunc illuc ferens
oblita nati misera quaesivi Hectorem:
460 fallax per ipsos umbra complexus abît.
      O nate, magni certa progenies patris,
spes una Phrygibus, unica afflictae domus,
veterisque suboles sanguinis nimium inclita
nimiumque patri similis! hos vultus meus
465 habebat Hector, talis incessu fuit
habituque talis, sic tulit fortes manus,
sic celsus umeris, fronte sic torva minax
cervice fusam dissipans iacta comam.
o nate sero Phrygibus, o matri cito,
470 eritne tempus illud ac felix dies
quo Troici defensor et vindex soli
recidiva ponas Pergama et sparsos fuga

of a dazed mind is sleep. Suddenly Hector stood before my eyes, not as he looked when he carried the war forward against the Argives and attacked Greek ships with Idaean firebrands, or when he raged against the Danaans with much slaughter and took genuine spoils from a faked Achilles:[31] it was not that face directing its fiery radiant gaze, but one tired and downcast and heavy with weeping, and like my own, masked by filthy hair. Yet I was happy to see him. Then he shook his head and spoke: "Cast off sleep, my faithful wife, and rescue our son. He must be hidden, this is the only hope of safety. Leave off weeping. Are you lamenting Troy's fall? I wish she were completely fallen! Hurry, take the little offspring of our house away somewhere, anywhere!" Cold fear and trembling shook me out of sleep; turning my eyes fearfully this way and that, and forgetting my son, I searched piteously for Hector, but the delusive ghost slipped right through my embrace.

O son, true descendant of a great father, one hope for the Phrygians and only hope for our ruined house, all too famous as issue of ancient blood, and all too like your father! This countenance my Hector had, such he was in walk and bearing, so he carried his brave hands, so he squared his shoulders, so his stern brow conveyed a threat as he spread his flowing hair with a toss of his neck. O child born too late for the Phrygians, but too soon for your mother,[32] will that time come, that happy day, when you as defender and champion of Trojan soil will set up a resurgent Pergamum, bring home its citizens scattered in exile,

---

[31] Patroclus, who disguised himself in Achilles' armour, and was killed in battle by Hector.   [32] Before she could escape her sorrows by suicide (cf. 418–32).

cives reducas, nomen et patriae suum
Phrygibusque reddas? sed mei fati memor
475   tam magna timeo vota: quod captis sat est,
vivamus.
        Heu me, quis locus fidus meo
erit timori quave te sede occulam?
arx illa pollens opibus et muris deum,
gentes per omnes clara et invidiae gravis,
480   nunc pulvis altus; strata sunt flamma omnia,
superestque vasta ex urbe ne tantum quidem,
quo lateat infans. quem locum fraudi legam?
est tumulus ingens coniugis cari sacer,
verendus hosti, mole quem immensa parens
485   opibusque magnis struxit, in luctus suos
rex non avarus: optime credam patri—
sudor per artus frigidus totos cadit:
488   omen tremesco misera feralis loci.

SENEX
497   Miser occupet praesidia, securus legat.

ANDROMACHA
496   Quid quod latere sine metu magno nequit,
492   ne prodat aliquis?

SENEX
        Amove testes doli.

ANDROMACHA
493   Si quaeret hostis?

SENEX
        Urbe in eversa perît:
489   haec causa multos una ab interitu arcuit,
490   credi perisse.

and give the country and the Phrygians back their own name? But remembering my lot I fear such grand prayers. Let us live: this is enough for prisoners.

But alas, what place will be faithful to my fears? In what shelter shall I hide you? That citadel, strong in its resources and god-built walls, famed among all nations and irksome to envy, is now deep dust; every part is razed by fire, and of the whole desolate city not even enough survives to hide a child. What place shall I choose to cheat them? There is my dear husband's great burial mound, sacred, awe-inspiring to the enemy, built in immense bulk and at great cost by his father—a king who did not stint expense over his grief.[33] Best to entrust him to his father. A cold sweat runs down my body: I tremble wretchedly at the omen represented by the place of death.

OLD MAN

The wretched must seize protection, the untroubled can choose.

ANDROMACHE

But he cannot hide without great fear of betrayal.

OLD MAN

Have no witnesses to your ruse.

ANDROMACHE

And if the enemy search?

OLD MAN

He perished in the city's overthrow. This in itself has saved many from destruction—being thought to have perished.

---

[33] In ransoming Hector's body (*Iliad* 24.229–37) as well as in building his tomb.

ANDROMACHA
Vix spei quicquam est super:
491 grave pondus illum magna nobilitas premit.
494 quid proderit latuisse redituro in manus?

SENEX
495 Victor feroces impetus primos habet.

ANDROMACHA
498 Quis te locus, quae regio seducta invia
tuto reponet? quis feret trepidis opem?
500 quis proteget? qui semper, etiamnunc tuos,
Hector, tuere: coniugis furtum piae
serva et fideli cinere victurum excipe.
succede tumulo, nate—quid retro fugis?
turpesne latebras spernis? agnosco indolem:
505 pudet timere. spiritus magnos fuga
animosque veteres, sume quos casus dedit.
en intuere, turba quae simus super:
tumulus, puer, captiva: cedendum est malis.
sanctas parentis conditi sedes age
510 aude subire. fata si miseros iuvant,
habes salutem; fata si vitam negant,
habes sepulcrum.

SENEX
Claustra commissum tegunt;
quem ne tuus producat in medium timor,
procul hinc recede teque diversam amove.

ANDROMACHA
515 Levius solet timere, qui propius timet;
sed, si placet, referamus hinc alio pedem.

504 -ne *Richter*: -que *EA*

ANDROMACHE

Scarcely any hope is left: his noble birth is a great weight crushing him. What will he gain by hiding when he is bound to be recaptured?

OLD MAN

The conqueror's first onslaughts are the savage ones.

ANDROMACHE

What place, what remote inaccessible region will hold you safe? Who will bring help in our fear? Who protect us? Now as always, Hector, watch over your dear ones. Safeguard your loyal wife's secret love, and receive him faithfully beside your ashes, to live. Come to the burial mound, son. Why shrink back? Do you disdain concealment? I recognise your inborn character: you are ashamed to show fear. Put aside your proud, courageous attitudes of old, and adopt those which Fortune has assigned. Look, observe what a throng we survivors are: a grave mound, a boy, a captive woman. We must yield to misfortune. Come, steel yourself to enter your father's holy burial place. If fate helps the wretched, you have a refuge; if fate denies you life, you have a tomb.

OLD MAN

The vaults are protecting their charge. Lest your fear reveal him, depart far from here, withdraw elsewhere.

ANDROMACHE

Fear tends to be slighter if one is closer at hand. But if you so judge, let us retreat elsewhere.

SENEX

Cohibe parumper ora questusque opprime:
gressus nefandos dux Cephallanum admovet.

ANDROMACHA

Dehisce tellus, tuque, coniunx, ultimo
520 specu revulsam scinde tellurem et Stygis
sinu profundo conde depositum meum.
adest Ulixes, et quidem dubio gradu
vultuque: nectit pectore astus callidos.

ULIXES

Durae minister sortis hoc primum peto,
525 ut, ore quamvis verba dicantur meo,
non esse credas nostra: Graiorum omnium
procerumque vox est, petere quos seras domos
Hectorea suboles prohibet. hanc fata expetunt.
sollicita Danaos pacis incertae fides
530 semper tenebit, semper a tergo timor
respicere coget, arma nec poni sinet,
dum Phrygibus animos natus eversis dabit,
Andromacha, vester. augur haec Calchas canit;
et, si taceret augur haec Calchas, tamen
535 dicebat Hector, cuius et stirpem horreo.
generosa in ortus semina exsurgunt suos.
sic ille magni parvus armenti comes
primisque nondum cornibus findens cutem
cervice subito celsus et fronte arduus
540 gregem paternum ducit ac pecori imperat;
quae tenera caeso virga de trunco stetit,
par ipsa matri tempore exiguo subit
umbrasque terris reddit et caelo nemus;
sic male relictus igne de magno cinis

OLD MAN

Check your words for a moment and quell your protests:
the Cephallanian leader is directing his evil steps towards
us.

ANDROMACHE

Split open, Earth! You, my husband, cleave the earth, rend
it apart from its bottommost pit, and hide the treasure entrusted to you in the Stygian world's enfolding depths.
Ulysses is here, and with hesitant step and expression: he is
weaving cunning tricks in his heart.

ULYSSES

As the agent of a cruel fate I first ask this, that though
the words are spoken by my mouth, you not regard them
as mine. This is the speech of the Greek host and their
leaders, who are kept from their long-overdue homecom-
ing by Hector's child. The voice of the Fates demands
him. Nervous trust in uncertain peace will always possess
the Danaans, always fear at their back will force them
to glance around and not allow them to disarm, as long
as your son, Andromache, gives heart to the defeated
Phrygians. The prophet Calchas proclaims this; and if the
prophet Calchas were silent, yet Hector used to say so—
and I fear even an offspring of his. Seeds of good stock
grow up to match their ancestry. So the little calf accompanying great cattle, his budding horns not yet piercing the
skin, suddenly with neck high and lofty brow leads his
father's herd and commands the drove. The tender shoot
which survives from a felled trunk in a little time grows up
equal to its mother, and restores shade to the earth and a
leafy crown to heaven. In the same way embers carelessly
left after a great fire regain strength. Admittedly pain is no im-

545 vires resumit. Est quidem iniustus dolor
rerum aestimator; si tamen tecum exigas,
veniam dabis, quod bella post hiemes decem
totidemque messes iam senex miles timet
aliasque clades rursus ac numquam bene
550 Troiam iacentem. magna res Danaos movet,
futurus Hector. libera Graios metu.
haec una naves causa deductas tenet,
hic classis haeret. neve crudelem putes,
quod sorte iussus Hectoris natum petam:
555 petissem Oresten. patere quod victor tulit.

ANDROMACHA

Utinam quidem esses, nate, materna in manu,
nossemque quis te casus ereptum mihi
teneret, aut quae regio! non hostilibus
confossa telis pectus ac vinclis manus
560 secantibus praestricta, non acri latus
utrumque flamma cincta maternam fidem
umquam exuissem. nate, quis te nunc locus,
fortuna quae possedit? errore avio
vagus arva lustras? vastus an patriae vapor
565 corripuit artus? saevus an victor tuo
lusit cruore? numquid immanis ferae
morsu peremptus pascis Idaeas aves?

ULIXES

Simulata remove verba. non facile est tibi
decipere Ulixem: vicimus matrum dolos
570 etiam dearum. cassa consilia amove.
ubi natus est?

partial judge of things; but if you reflect, you will forgive the fact that after ten winters and as many harvests the soldiery, no longer young, fears wars and yet further slaughters and a Troy never truly lying at rest. It is a great matter that concerns the Danaans—a future Hector. Free the Greeks from fear. The ships are launched; this one cause delays them, for this the fleet is stayed. And do not think me cruel because the lot ordered me to demand Hector's son: I would have demanded Orestes. Endure what the victor bore.[34]

ANDROMACHE

Indeed I wish, my son, that you were under your mother's protection, or that I knew what chance, what region, had stolen and kept you from me. Never, not even if my breast were pierced with enemy weapons, or my hands were tight-bound with cutting bonds, or my body girt on each side with fierce flames, would I have cast off my loyalty as a mother. My son, what place, what destiny has you in its power? Are you roaming the countryside, lost in trackless wandering? Did the immense inferno of the city burn your body? Or did our cruel conqueror amuse himself with your bloody death? Perhaps you died in the jaws of some savage beast, and now feed the birds of Mt Ida?

ULYSSES

No more feigned words. It is not easy for you to fool Ulysses: I have defeated the tricks of mothers, even goddesses.[35] Set aside futile schemes. Where is your son?

[34] I.e. loss of a child (Iphigenia) by Agamemnon, to allow the fleet to sail.   [35] The plural probably generalises from a single event: Ulysses foiled the goddess Thetis' attempt to save her son Achilles by disguising him as a girl.

ANDROMACHA
Ubi Hector? ubi cuncti Phryges?
ubi Priamus? unum quaeris: ego quaero omnia.

ULIXES
Coacta dices sponte quod fari abnuis;
587 stulta est fides celare quod prodas statim.

ANDROMACHA
574 Tuta est, perire quae potest debet cupit.

ULIXES
575 Magnifica verba mors prope admota excutit.

ANDROMACHA
Si vis, Ulixe, cogere Andromacham metu,
vitam minare: nam mori votum est mihi.

ULIXES
Verberibus igni chalybe cruciatu eloqui
quodcumque celas adiget invitam dolor
580 et pectore imo condita arcana eruet:
necessitas plus posse quam pietas solet.

ANDROMACHA
Propone flammas, vulnera et diras mali
doloris artes et famem et saevam sitim
variasque pestes undique et ferrum inditum
585 visceribus ustis, carceris caeci luem,
et quidquid audet victor iratus timens:
588 animosa nullos mater admittit metus.

587 *placed after* 573 *by Zwierlein*
578 chalybe *Delz*: morte *EA*
585 ustis *A*: istis *E*
586 timens *EPT*: tumens *CS*

ANDROMACHE

Where is Hector? Where are all Phrygians? Where is
Priam? You look for the one, I look for my world.

ULYSSES

You will say under compulsion what you refuse to tell
freely. It is foolish loyalty to conceal what you must immediately betray.

ANDROMACHE

She who can die, who should and longs to, is safe.

ULYSSES

When death is brought close, it drives out grand words.

ANDROMACHE

Ulysses, if you want to coerce Andromache by fear,
threaten her with life: death is what I pray for.

ULYSSES

Lashes, fire, steel, torture—the pain of these will drive you
against your will to voice whatever you are hiding, and will
root out the inmost secrets of your heart. Necessity tends
to be stronger than devotion.

ANDROMACHE

Set forth flames, wounds, the dreadful arts of producing
fierce pain, hunger and cruel thirst, various scourges on
every side, iron fastened on my galled flesh, a dungeon's
pestilential darkness, and anything a victor dares to do
when he is angry and afraid. A courageous mother has no
room for fears.

ULIXES

Hic ipse, quo nunc contumax perstas, amor
590 consulere parvis liberis Danaos monet
post arma tam longinqua, post annos decem.
minus timerem quos facit Calchas metus,
si mihi timerem: bella Telemacho paras.

ANDROMACHA

Invita, Ulixe, gaudium Danais dabo:
595 dandum est; fatere quos premis luctus, dolor.
gaudete, Atridae, tuque laetifica, ut soles,
refer Pelasgis: Hectoris proles obît.

ULIXES

Et esse verum hoc qua probas Danais fide?

ANDROMACHA

Ita quod minari maximum victor potest
600 contingat, et me fata maturo exitu
facilique solvant ac meo condant solo,
et patria tellus Hectorem leviter premat,
ut luce caruit; inter extinctos iacet
datusque tumulo debita exanimis tulit.

ULIXES

605 Expleta fata stirpe sublata Hectoris
solidamque pacem laetus ad Danaos feram.—
quid agis, Ulixe? Danaidae credent tibi,
tu cui? parenti! fingit an quisquam hoc parens,
nec abominandae mortis auspicium pavet?
610 auspicia metuunt qui nihil maius timent.
fidem alligavit iure iurando suam.—

591 *A period is placed after* 591 *by Fitch, after* 590 *by earlier editors.*

224

ULYSSES

This very love, which now makes you stubborn and obsti-
nate, is what prompts the Danaans to take thought for their
own small children after such protracted fighting, after
ten years. I would be less frightened of the fears Calchas
raises, if I feared them for myself—but you are preparing
wars for Telemachus.

ANDROMACHE

I am loath, Ulysses, to give the Danaans cause for joy, but
give it I must. O my pain, confess the sorrow you are hiding. Rejoice, you sons of Atreus! And you—report joyful
news, as usual, to the Pelasgians: Hector's child is dead.

ULYSSES

And how do you prove to the Danaans that this is true?

ANDROMACHE

As I hope the worst the conqueror can threaten will come
true; as I hope the Fates will release me by a timely and
easy passing and hide me in my own soil, and that his native
earth will press lightly on Hector: so truly has he lost the
light; he lies among the dead, and entrusted to the tomb he
has received the due of those departed.

ULYSSES

I shall gladly bring the Danaans news of Fate fulfilled by
the removal of Hector's child, and of stable peace. [Aside]
What are you doing, Ulysses? The Danaans will believe
you, but whom will you believe? A parent! Yet would any
parent invent this story, and not shudder at the ominous
presage of death? They dread omens who have nothing
worse to fear. Yet she bound her word with an oath. But if

225

si peierat, timere quid gravius potest?
nunc advoca astus, anime, nunc fraudes, dolos,
nunc totum Ulixem; veritas numquam perit.
615 scrutare matrem. maeret, illacrimat, gemit;
sed huc et illuc anxios gressus refert
missasque voces aure sollicita excipit:
magis haec timet, quam maeret. ingenio est opus. —
Alios parentes alloqui in luctu decet;
620 tibi gratulandum est, misera, quod nato cares,
quem mors manebat saeva praecipitem datum
e turre, lapsis sola quae muris manet.

ANDROMACHA

Reliquit animus membra, quatiuntur, labant,
torpetque vinctus frigido sanguis gelu.

ULIXES

625 Intremuit: hac, hac parte quaerenda est mihi.
matrem timor detexit: iterabo metum.—
ite, ite celeres, fraude materna abditum
hostem, Pelasgi nominis pestem ultimam,
ubicumque latitat, erutam in medium date.—
630 bene est: tenetur. perge, festina, attrahe—
quid respicis trepidasque? iam certe perît.

ANDROMACHA

Utinam timerem! solitus ex longo est metus:
dediscit animus sero quod didicit diu.

ULIXES

Lustrale quoniam debitum muris puer

she is swearing falsely, what heavier blow could she be
fearing? Now, my mind, summon up your cunning, your
deceit, your trickery, everything that is Ulysses. The truth
is never lost. Observe this mother. She is grieving, weeping, groaning; yet she paces nervously up and down, and
strains her ears to catch each word spoken. She is more
fearful than mournful. My skills are needed.

[*Aloud*] Other parents should be consoled in their
grief, but you are to be congratulated, poor woman, for losing your son, since a cruel death awaited him, hurled headlong from the only tower that remains among the ruined
walls.

ANDROMACHE

[*Aside*] My limbs are fainting, shivering, collapsing, my
blood is congealed and frozen.

ULYSSES

[*Aside*] She trembled. *This* is the angle from which I must
test her. Fear unmasked the mother; I shall renew her terror. [*Aloud*] Go quickly, men: this enemy concealed by his
mother's trickery, this last bane of the Pelasgian cause, root
him out wherever he is hiding, bring him to light. [*To one
soldier, as if he has discovered the boy*] Well done! He is
caught. Come, hurry, drag him here. [*To Andromache*]
Why look around in alarm? Surely he is already dead.

ANDROMACHE

I wish I *were* afraid. It is just a long-established habit, this
anxiety: the mind is slow to unlearn a lesson learnt over
time.

ULYSSES

Since the boy has forestalled the lustral rite prescribed

227

635 sacrum antecessit nec potest vatem sequi
meliore fato raptus, hoc Calchas ait
modo piari posse redituras rates,
si placet undas Hectoris sparsi cinis
ac tumulus imo totus aequetur solo.
640 nunc ille quoniam debitam effugit necem,
erit admovenda sedibus sacris manus.

ANDROMACHA

Quid agimus? animum distrahit geminus timor:
hinc natus, illinc coniugis cari cinis.
pars utra vincet? testor immites deos,
645 deosque veros coniugis manes mei:
non aliud, Hector, in meo nato mihi
placere quam te. vivat, ut possit tuos
referre vultus.—prorutus tumulo cinis
mergetur? ossa fluctibus spargi sinam
650 disiecta vastis? potius hic mortem oppetat.—
poteris nefandae deditum mater neci
videre, poteris celsa per fastigia
missum rotari? potero, perpetiar, feram,
dum non meus post fata victoris manu
655 iactetur Hector.—hic suam poenam potest
sentire, at illum fata iam in tuto locant.
quid fluctuaris? statue, quem poenae extrahas.
ingrata, dubitas? Hector est illinc tuus—
erras, utrimque est Hector: hic sensus potens,
660 forsan futurus ultor extincti patris—
utrique parci non potest: quidnam facis?
serva e duobus, anime, quem Danai timent.

ULIXES

Responsa peragam; funditus busta eruam.

for the walls and cannot obey the prophet, carried off by a better fate, Calchas says that the ships can be ritually cleansed for their return, if the waves are appeased by the scattering of Hector's ashes and his entire tomb is levelled with the ground. Now, since that one has escaped the prescribed death, we shall have to lay hands on the sacred resting place.

ANDROMACHE

[*Aside*] What can I do? My mind is torn by twin fears: on the one side is my son, on the other my dear husband's ashes. Which will prevail? Witness the pitiless gods, and those true gods, the shades of my husband: I love nothing else, Hector, in my son but you. Let him live, to restore your features to life. But will the ashes be hurled from the tomb and sunk? Shall I allow the bones to be dispersed and scattered on the desolate waves? Better that this one should die. But can you, his mother, see him surrendered to monstrous murder, see him thrown whirling over the high battlements? I shall be able to, shall endure it, shall bear it, as long as my Hector is not tossed about after death by the victor's hand. Yet this one can still *feel* injury, while death now safeguards the other. Why are you wavering? Choose which one you will save from injury. Can you hesitate, ungrateful woman? On one side is your Hector—but no, Hector is on both sides. This one still has consciousness, and perhaps will be an avenger for his dead father. Both cannot be protected. What are you to do? From the two, my heart, save the one the Danaans fear.

ULYSSES

I shall fulfil the oracle and demolish the tomb utterly.

ANDROMACHA

Quae vendidistis?

ULIXES

Pergam et e summo aggere
665 traham sepulcra.

ANDROMACHA

Caelitum appello fidem
fidemque Achillis: Pyrrhe, genitoris tui
munus tuere.

ULIXES

Tumulus hic campo statim
toto iacebit.

ANDROMACHA

Fuerat hoc prorsus nefas
Danais inausum. templa violastis, deos
670 etiam faventes: busta transierat furor.
resistam, inermes offeram armatis manus,
dabit ira vires. qualis Argolicas ferox
turmas Amazon stravit, aut qualis deo
percussa Maenas entheo silvas gradu
675 armata thyrso terret atque expers sui
vulnus dedit nec sensit, in medios ruam
tumuloque cineris socia defenso cadam.

ULIXES

Cessatis et vos flebilis clamor movet

---

36 I.e. made its construction possible through the "sale" of

ANDROMACHE

The tomb you Greeks sold?[36]

ULYSSES

I shall proceed to tear apart the burial place, from the top of the mound down.

ANDROMACHE

I invoke the gods' honour, and Achilles' honour: Pyrrhus, protect the gift your father gave.

ULYSSES

Very soon this burial mound will lie scattered all over the plain.

ANDROMACHE

This was a sacrilege the Danaans had left undared. You violated temples, even gods favourable to you,[37] but your frenzy had bypassed tombs. I shall fight back, pit unarmed hands against armed might; anger will give me strength. As the fierce Amazon[38] felled Argive troops, or as a Maenad, god-smitten and with supernatural strides, strikes terror into the countryside armed with a thyrsus, and unaware of herself gives wounds but feels none, so I shall rush into the midst and die defending the tomb, fighting for its ashes.

ULYSSES

[*To soldiers*] Are you holding back? Are you swayed by a

Hector's body by Achilles, to which Andromache alludes again in 666–67.

[37] Pallas Athena supported the Greeks, but her temple in Troy was violated in the theft of the Palladium by Ulysses and Diomedes, and later in the rape of her priestess Cassandra.

[38] Penthesileia, Troy's ally.

furorque cassus feminae? iussa ocius
680 peragite.

ANDROMACHA

Me, me sternite hic ferro prius.
repellor, heu me. rumpe fatorum moras,
molire terras, Hector! ut Ulixem domes
vel umbra satis es.—arma concussit manu,
iaculatur ignes! cernitis, Danai, Hectorem?
685 an sola video?

ULIXES

Funditus cuncta eruam.

ANDROMACHA

Quid agis? ruina mater et natum et virum
prosternis una? forsitan Danaos prece
placare poteris. conditum elidet statim
immane busti pondus: intereat miser
690 ubicumque potius, ne pater natum obruat
prematque patrem natus.—Ad genua accido
supplex, Ulixe, quamque nullius pedes
novere dextram pedibus admoveo tuis.
miserere matris et preces placidus pias
695 patiensque recipe, quoque te celsum altius
superi levarunt, mitius lapsos preme:
misero datur quodcumque, Fortunae datur.
sic te revisat coniugis sanctae torus,
annosque, dum te recipit, extendat suos
700 Laerta; sic te iuvenis excipiat tuus,
et vota vincens vestra felici indole
aetate avum transcendat, ingenio patrem.

woman's tearful outcry and futile rage? Quickly, carry out your orders.

ANDROMACHE

Here, destroy *me* first with your swords. Oh, they drive me back. Break through death's barriers, force away the earth, Hector! Even as a ghost you are enough to master Ulysses. He brandished his weapons in his hands, he is hurling firebrands! Can you perceive Hector, you Danaans? Or do I alone see him?

ULYSSES

I shall overturn and level everything.

ANDROMACHE

[*Aside*] What are you doing? A mother destroying both son and husband in shared ruin? Perhaps you can soften the Danaans by an appeal. The one in hiding will be crushed this instant by the huge weight of the tomb: better that the poor child die anywhere else, than that father overwhelm son and son crush father.

I fall at your knees as a suppliant, Ulysses, and grasp your feet with this hand which has touched no man's feet before. Pity a mother; receive kindly and patiently my prayers of motherly love. The higher the gods have exalted your lofty station, the more gently you should tread on the fallen; gifts to the wretched are gifts to Fortune. So may your chaste wife's bed behold you once again, and Laertes lengthen his years until he receives you home; so may that young man of yours welcome you,[39] and exceeding your hopes in his natural gifts may he surpass his grandfather's

---

[39] Ulysses' wife is Penelope, his father Laertes, his son Telemachus.

miserere matris: unicum afflictae mihi
solamen hic est.

ULIXES
Exhibe natum et roga.

ANDROMACHA
705   Huc e latebris procede tuis,
flebile matris furtum miserae.
Hic est, hic est terror, Ulixe,
mille carinis.
Summitte manus,
dominique pedes
supplice dextra stratus adora,
710   nec turpe puta
quidquid miseros Fortuna iubet.
pone ex animo reges atavos
magnique senis
iura per omnes inclita terras,
excidat Hector, gere captivum,
715   positoque genu—
si tua nondum funera sentis—
matris fletus imitare tuae.
    Vidit pueri regis lacrimas
et Troia prior,
parvusque minas trucis Alcidae
720   flexit Priamus.
Ille, ille ferox,
cuius vastis viribus omnes
cessere ferae,
qui perfracto limine Ditis
caecum retro patefecit iter,
725   hostis parvi victus lacrimis

years and his father's intellect. Pity a mother: my sole comfort in distress is this boy.

ULYSSES

Produce your son, then pray.

ANDROMACHE

Come out here from your hiding place,
piteous secret of a wretched mother.
This is the source of terror, Ulysses,
for a thousand ships.
Hold out your arms;
at your master's feet
bow low and do homage with suppliant hand;
do not disdain
whatever Fortune demands of the wretched.
Put out of mind your royal ancestors
and the great old man
famed as lawgiver throughout the world;
forget Hector, play the captive,
and on bended knee,
if you do not yet sense your death,
copy your mother's weeping.
      An earlier Troy too
saw the tears of a boy-king:
Priam when small
turned aside the threats of ferocious Hercules.
Even that fierce hero,
to whose awesome strength all wild
beasts yielded,
who broke through the doorway of Dis
and opened up the dark path back,
was vanquished by the tears of his small foe.

"suscipe" dixit "rector habenas,
patrioque sede celsus solio;
sed sceptra fide meliore tene."
hoc fuit illo victore capi.
730   discite mites Herculis iras—
an sola placent Herculis arma?
iacet ante pedes
non minor illo supplice supplex
vitamque petit;
regnum Troiae quocumque volet
735   Fortuna ferat.

ULIXES

Matris quidem me maeror attonitae movet,
magis Pelasgae me tamen matres movent,
quarum iste magnos crescit in luctus puer.

ANDROMACHA

Has, has ruinas urbis in cinerem datae
740 hic excitabit? hae manus Troiam erigent?
nullas habet spes Troia, si tales habet.
non sic iacemus Troes, ut cuiquam metus
possimus esse. spiritus genitor facit?
sed nempe tractus. ipse post Troiam pater
745 posuisset animos, magna quos frangunt mala.
si poena petitur (quae peti gravior potest?)
famulare collo nobili subeat iugum,
servire liceat. aliquis hoc regi negat?

ULIXES

Non hoc Ulixes, sed negat Calchas tibi.

"Take up the reins of government," he said,
"and sit high on your father's throne,
but wield the sceptre with greater honesty."
Such was defeat by that conqueror.
Learn from Hercules' merciful anger.
Or do you admire only Hercules' fighting?
There lies at your feet
no less a suppliant than that suppliant,
asking for life;
for the kingship of Troy, Fortune may carry it
wherever she will.

ULYSSES

I am certainly moved by the grief of a devastated mother,
but more strongly moved by Pelasgian mothers, since your
boy is growing to bring them great sorrows.

ANDROMACHE

Shall *these* ruins of a city reduced to ashes be quickened by
this child? Shall these hands raise up Troy? Troy has no
hopes, if she has such as these. We Trojans are brought so
low, that we cannot be a fear to anyone. Does his father in-
spire him? Though of course he *was* dragged through the
dust. His father himself after Troy's fall would have given
up his pride, since pride is broken by great misfortunes. If
retribution is demanded, what heavier form can be demanded than this: let him wear the yoke of servitude on his
noble neck, permit him to be a slave. Does anyone refuse a
king this favour?

ULYSSES

Not Ulysses but Calchas refuses you this.

237

ANDROMACHA

750 O machinator fraudis et scelerum artifex,
virtute cuius bellica nemo occidit,
dolis et astu maleficae mentis iacent
etiam Pelasgi, vatem et insontes deos
praetendis? hoc est pectoris facinus tui.
755 nocturne miles, fortis in pueri necem,
iam solus audes aliquid et claro die.

ULIXES

Virtus Ulixis Danaidis nota est satis
nimisque Phrygibus. non vacat vanis diem
conterere verbis: ancoras classis legit.

ANDROMACHA

760 Brevem moram largire, dum officium parens
nato supremum reddo et amplexu ultimo
avidos dolores satio.

ULIXES

Misereri tui
utinam liceret. quod tamen solum licet,
tempus moramque dabimus. arbitrio tuo
765 implere lacrimis; fletus aerumnas levat.

ANDROMACHA

O dulce pignus, o decus lapsae domus
summumque Troiae funus, o Danaum timor,
genetricis o spes vana, cui demens ego
laudes parentis bellicas, annos avi
770 melius precabar: vota destituit deus.
Iliaca non tu sceptra regali potens
gestabis aula, iura nec populis dabis

770 melius *Garrod*: medius *EA*

238

ANDROMACHE

You inventor of deceit and craftsman of crimes! No one ever fell to your courage in battle, but even Pelasgians are brought low by the tricks and cunning of your destructive mind.[40] Do you blame the prophet and the guiltless gods? This is a deed of your own heart. Night-prowling soldier,[41] brave in killing a boy! Now you dare to act alone and in bright daylight.

ULYSSES

The courage of Ulysses is known well enough to the Danaans, and too well to the Phrygians. There is no leisure to waste the day in empty words: the fleet is weighing anchor.

ANDROMACHE

Grant me a brief delay, while I pay my son a mother's final service, and satisfy my yearning grief with a last embrace.

ULYSSES

I wish I were allowed to show you pity. But I shall give the only thing that is allowed, a respite of time. Take your fill of tears without constraint; weeping eases troubles.

ANDROMACHE

O sweet bond of love, o glory of our fallen house and final death of Troy, o menace to the Danaans, o fruitless hope of your mother, for whom I used to pray senselessly for glory in war like your father's, and more sensibly for long years like your grandfather's: god has cast aside my prayers. You will not carry Ilium's sceptre as ruler in a royal palace, you

---

40 Specifically Palamedes and Ajax, in addition to Iphigenia.
41 In raids with Diomedes under cover of darkness.

victasque gentes sub tuum mittes iugum,
non Graia caedes terga, non Pyrrhum trahes;
775   non arma tenera parva tractabis manu
sparsasque passim saltibus latis feras
audax sequeris, nec stato lustri die,
sollemne referens Troici lusus sacrum,
puer citatas nobilis turmas ages;
780   non inter aras mobili velox pede,
reboante flexo concitos cornu modos,
barbarica prisco templa saltatu coles.
o morte dira tristius leti genus!
flebilius aliquid Hectoris magni nece
785   muri videbunt.

ULIXES
Rumpe iam fletus, parens;
magnus sibi ipse non facit finem dolor.

ANDROMACHA
Lacrimas, Ulixe (parva quam petimus mora est)
concede paucas, ut mea condam manu
viventis oculos. occidis parvus quidem,
790   sed iam timendus. Troia te expectat tua:
i, vade liber, liberos Troas vide.

ASTYANAX
Miserere, mater.

ANDROMACHA
Quid meos retines sinus

781 reboante *Hemsterhuis*: revocante *EA*
787 lacrimas *E*: lacrimis *A*

---

[42] This game, in which boys engaged in equestrian battle maneuvers, allegedly originated in Troy, and Vergil describes it as

will not give laws to nations and bring conquered peoples under your yoke; you will not slaughter the Greeks in rout, you will not drag Pyrrhus; you will not handle small weapons in your tender hands, nor boldly pursue wild beasts scattered throughout broad forests; nor on the appointed lustral day, reenacting the traditional rite of the Trojan Game,[42] will you lead the galloping squadrons as their prince; nor moving swift-footed among the altars, as the curved horn resounds with frenzied rhythms, will you honour our Eastern temples in the age-old dance.[43] Oh, grimmer than dread death itself is the manner of your murder. The walls will see something more pitiful than the killing of great Hector.

ULYSSES

Break off your weeping now, mother; great grief sets itself no limit.

ANDROMACHE

Grant me a few tears, Ulysses—the respite I ask is small— to close his eyes while he still lives with my own hand. Yes, you are small to die, but already one to be feared. Your Troy awaits you: go in freedom, go to see free Trojans.

ASTYANAX

Have pity on me, mother.

ANDROMACHE

Why do you hug my breast and clutch your mother's hands,

conducted there under the leadership of several Trojan princes (*Aeneid* 5.545ff.). At Rome it was a traditional display, often used by emperors to parade their young heirs in public.

[43] Seneca here associates the ecstatic Eastern cult of Cybele with the Roman tradition of ritual dancing by the highborn Salii.

manusque matris, cassa praesidia, occupas?
fremitu leonis qualis audito tener
795 timidum iuvencus applicat matri latus,
at ille saevus matre summota leo
praedam minorem morsibus vastis premens
frangit vehitque: talis e nostro sinu
te rapiet hostis. oscula et fletus, puer,
800 lacerosque crines excipe et plenus mei
occurre patri. pauca maternae tamen
perfer querelae verba: "si manes habent
curas priores nec perit flammis amor,
servire Graio pateris Andromachen viro,
805 crudelis Hector? lentus et segnis iaces?
redît Achilles." sume nunc iterum comas
et sume lacrimas (quidquid e misero viri
funere relictum est), sume quae reddas tuo
oscula parenti. matris hanc solacio
810 relinque vestem: tumulus hanc tetigit meus
manesque cari. si quid hic cineris latet,
scrutabor ore.

ULIXES
Nullus est flendi modus:
abripite propere classis Argolicae moram.

CHORUS
Quae vocat sedes habitanda captas?
815 Thessali montes et opaca Tempe,
819 an maris vasti domitrix Iolcos?
821 parva Gyrtone sterilisque Tricce,
822 an frequens rivis levibus Mothone?
816 an viros tellus dare militares
aptior Pthie meliorque fetu

242

a useless protection? As a tender calf, hearing the lion's roar, fearfully presses against his mother's side, but the savage lion pushes the mother aside, and biting the smaller prey with its giant jaws breaks it and drags it off: so the enemy will snatch you from my breast. Collect these kisses and tears, child, and this torn hair, and filled with me hurry to your father. But deliver too a few words of your mother's reproach: "If spirits keep their former affections and love does not perish in the flames, why allow Andromache to serve a Greek man, callous Hector? Do you lie inert and unresponsive? Achilles returned!" Now once again take this hair and take these tears (the few that are left after my husband's sad funeral), take kisses to bring to your father. To comfort your mother leave this cloak, touched by my tomb and by the beloved dead. If any of his dust lurks here, my lips will discover it.

ULYSSES

There is no limit to weeping: [*to soldiers*] quickly, carry off this delay to the Argive fleet.

CHORUS

What place summons the captives to live there?
Thessaly's mountains and shaded Tempe,
or Iolcos tamer of the vast waste sea?[44]
Little Gyrtone and barren Tricce,
or Mothone abounding in swift streams?
Or the land fit for producing warriors,
Phthia, and stony Trachis,

[44] The *Argo*, according to myth the earliest ship, sailed from Iolcos.

816–18 *placed after 822 by Richter*

818	fortis armenti lapidosa Trachin,
823	quae sub Oetaeis latebrosa silvis
	misit infestos Troiae ruinis
825	non semel arcus?
	Olenos tectis habitata raris,
	virgini Pleuron inimica divae,
	an maris lati sinuosa Troezen?
	Pelion regnum Prothoi superbum,
830	tertius caelo gradus? (hic recumbens
	montis exesi spatiosus antro
	iam trucis Chiron pueri magister,
	tinnulas plectro feriente chordas,
	tunc quoque ingentes acuebat iras
835	bella canendo.)
820	Urbibus centum spatiosa Crete,
836	an ferax varii lapidis Carystos,
	an premens litus maris inquieti
	semper Euripo properante Chalcis?
	quolibet vento faciles Calydnae,
840	an carens numquam Gonoëssa vento
	quaeque formidat Borean Enispe?
	Attica pendens Peparethos ora,
	an sacris gaudens tacitis Eleusin?

*　　*　　*　　*　　*

	numquid Aiacis Salamina veri,
845	aut fera notam Calydona saeva,

⁸²⁰ *Placed after 835 by Fitch*
⁸⁴⁴ *Scaliger recognised a lacuna before 844; probably several lines are lost*

---

⁴⁵ Hercules used his bow in the first sack of Troy; later Phi-

better at breeding stalwart herds—
Trachis, which lurking under Oeta's woods
sent that dangerous bow more than once
    to Troy's destruction?[45]
Olenos, occupied by scattered homes,
Pleuron detested by the virgin goddess,
or Troezen curving the broad sea's edge?
Pelion, proud kingdom of Prothous,
third step to heaven? Reclining here
expansively in a cave of the fissured mountain,
Chiron, teaching a boy already savage,[46]
while his plectrum struck jangling strings,
was sharpening even then his mighty wrath
    by singing of wars.
Crete roomy enough for a hundred cities,
or Carystos rich in marbled stone,
or Chalcis thrust into the edge of the restless
sea on the ever hurrying Euripus?
The Calydnae, easy ports in any wind,
or Gonoessa never lacking wind,
and Enispe which fears the norther?
Peparethos clinging to Attica's shores,
or Eleusis exulting in its holy Mysteries?

    *   *   *   *   * [47]

not to Salamis home of the true Ajax,
or Calydon famed for its savage beast,

loctetes received it from Hercules on Mt Oeta, and employed it in
the second sack of Troy.   [46] Achilles.

  [47] The missing lines may have included a reference to the ter-
ritories of Ajax son of Oileus (cf. line 46); the "true Ajax" of the
next line is the son of Telamon.

quasque perfundit subiturus aequor
segnibus terras Titaressos undis?
Bessan et Scarphen, Pylon an senilem?
Pharin an Pisas Iovis et coronis
850   Elida claram?
Quolibet tristis miseras procella
mittat et donet cuicumque terrae,
dum luem tantam Troiae atque Achivis
quae tulit Sparte procul absit, absit
855 Argos et saevi Pelopis Mycenae,
Neritos parva brevior Zacyntho
et nocens saxis Ithace dolosis.
    Quod manet fatum dominusque quis te,
aut quibus terris, Hecabe, videndam
860 ducet? in cuius moriere regno?

HELENA

Quicumque hymen funestus, inlaetabilis
lamenta caedes sanguinem gemitus habet,
est auspice Helena dignus. eversis quoque
nocere cogor Phrygibus: ego Pyrrhi toros
865 narrare falsos iubeor, ego cultus dare
habitusque Graios. arte capietur mea
meaque fraude concidet Paridis soror.
fallatur: ipsi levius hoc equidem reor.
optanda mors est sine metu mortis mori.
870 quid iussa cessas agere? ad auctorem redit
sceleris coacti culpa.—Dardaniae domus
generosa virgo, melior afflictos deus

and those lands the Titaressos waters with its sluggish
stream before passing under the sea?
Bessa and Scarphe, or the old man's Pylos?
Pharis, or Pisa and Elis famed
    for Jove's victory wreaths?
Let the gloomy storm carry our misery
anywhere, make a gift of us to any land,
so long as Sparta, which bore such a scourge
for Troy and the Achaeans, is distant, and distant
Argos and cruel Pelops' Mycenae,
Neritos smaller than little Zacynthos,
and destructive Ithaca with its treacherous rocks.

    What fate and what master await you,
to what lands will they bring you, Hecuba,
for display? In whose kingdom will you die?

ACT 4

HELEN

[*Aside*] Any marriage that is funereal and joyless, that
brings lamentations, slaughters, blood, and groans, deserves Helen as its sponsor. Even when the Phrygians are
ruined, I am forced to harm them. I am ordered to tell a
false tale of union with Pyrrhus, to dress and adorn the
bride in Greek style. She, Paris' sister, will be snared by my
skill and destroyed by my deceit. Let her be deceived: for
her I think this is less painful. It is a death to be prayed for,
to die without fear of death. Why hesitate to carry out your
orders? The guilt for an enforced crime recoils on its
author.

[*To Polyxena*] Noble maiden of the house of Dardanus,
god has begun to look more kindly on the afflicted, and

247

respicere coepit, teque felici parat
dotare thalamo. tale coniugium tibi
875 non ipsa sospes Troia, non Priamus daret.
nam te Pelasgae maximum gentis decus,
878 cui regna campi lata Thessalici patent,
877 ad sancta lecti iura legitimi petit.
te magna Tethys teque tot pelagi deae
880 placidumque numen aequoris tumidi Thetis
suam vocabunt, te datam Pyrrho socer
Peleus nurum vocabit et Nereus nurum.
depone cultus squalidos, festos cape,
dedisce captam; deprime horrentes comas,
885 crinemque docta patere distingui manu.
hic forsitan te casus excelso magis
solio reponet. profuit multis capi.

ANDROMACHA

Hoc derat unum Phrygibus eversis malum,
gaudere. flagrant strata passim Pergama:
890 o coniugale tempus! an quisquam audeat
negare? quisquam dubius ad thalamos eat,
quos Helena suadet? pestis exitium lues
utriusque populi, cernis hos tumulos ducum
et nuda totis ossa quae passim iacent
895 inhumata campis? haec hymen sparsit tuus.
tibi fluxit Asiae, fluxit Europae cruor,
cum dimicantes lenta prospiceres viros,
incerta voti. perge, thalamos appara.
taedis quid opus est quidve sollemni face,
900 quid igne? thalamis Troia praelucet novis.
celebrate Pyrrhi, Troades, conubia,
celebrate digne: planctus et gemitus sonet.

plans to dower you with a blessed union. Not Troy itself while safe nor Priam could have offered you such a marriage. For the greatest glory of the Pelasgian race, whose broad kingdom extends over the plain of Thessaly, seeks you for the holy rites of lawful wedlock. Great Tethys and so many sea goddesses and Thetis, calm divinity of the swelling waves, will call you their own; when you are Pyrrhus' bride, Peleus as father-in-law will call you daughter, and so will Nereus. Remove these filthy clothes and accept festive ones, forget the role of captive; smooth your wild hair, and let your locks be parted by a skilled hand. This fall perhaps will place you on a loftier throne. Many have gained by captivity.

ANDROMACHE

For the ruined Phrygians this was the one woe missing—to rejoice. Pergamum's wreckage is blazing all around: an apt time for a wedding! Would anyone dare refuse? Would anyone hesitate to go to a marriage which Helen recommends? You pestilence, disaster, blight of both our peoples, do you see these burial mounds of the leaders, and the bare bones lying unburied everywhere across the plains? They were strewn by your marriage. It was for you the blood of Asia and Europe flowed, while you casually surveyed your menfolk battling, uncertain which to pray for. Go on, prepare the wedding! What need of pine brands and ceremonial torches, what need of fire? Troy lights the way for this strange wedding. Celebrate the nuptials of Pyrrhus, you Trojan women, celebrate them worthily—with sounds of blows and groaning.

HELENA

Ratione quamvis careat et flecti neget
magnus dolor, sociosque nonnumquam sui
905 maeroris ipsos oderit, causam tamen
possum tueri iudice infesto meam,
graviora passa. luget Andromacha Hectorem
et Hecuba Priamum? solus occulte Paris
lugendus Helenae est. durum et invisum et grave est
910 servitia ferre? patior hoc olim iugum,
annis decem captiva. prostratum Ilium est,
versi penates? perdere est patriam grave,
gravius timere. vos levat tantus mali
comitatus: in me victor et victus furit.
915 quam quisque famulam traheret incerto diu
casu pependit: me meus traxit statim
sine sorte dominus. causa bellorum fui
tantaeque Teucris cladis? hoc verum puta,
Spartana puppis vestra si secuit freta;
920 sin rapta Phrygiis praeda remigibus fui,
deditque donum iudici victrix dea,
ignosce Paridi. iudicem iratum mea
habitura causa est: ista Menelaum manent
arbitria. Nunc hanc luctibus paulum tuis,
925 Andromacha, omissis flecte—vix lacrimas queo
retinere.

ANDROMACHA

Quantum est Helena quod lacrimat malum!
cur lacrimat autem? fare quos Ithacus dolos,
quae scelera nectat: utrum ab Idaeis iugis
iactanda virgo est, arcis an celsae edito

HELEN

Though great bitterness is irrational and unbending, and sometimes hates even its fellow sufferers, nevertheless I can defend my cause before a hostile judge—for I have suffered worse. Is Andromache in mourning for Hector, and Hecuba for Priam? Only Helen's mourning for Paris has to be in secret. Is it harsh, hateful, oppressive to endure slavery? I have long endured that yoke, ten years a prisoner. Is Ilium overthrown, your guardian gods fallen? It is hard to lose one's country, but harder to be afraid of it. You are solaced by so large a companionship in suffering; I suffer the rage of both conqueror and conquered. Which woman each Greek would seize as slave has long hung in uncertainty; my master seized me immediately, without drawing lots. Was I the cause of the war, and of such disaster for Trojans? Believe this true, if a *Spartan* ship cut through *your* seas. But if I was plunder stolen by Phrygian sailors, a victorious goddess' gift to her judge,[48] Paris needs your forgiveness. My case certainly will have an angry judge: this decision awaits Menelaus. Now set your own grief aside a little, Andromache, and prevail on her [*indicating Polyxena*]—I can scarcely hold back my tears.

ANDROMACHE

How great the trouble that makes Helen weep! Yet why is she weeping? Tell us what tricks, what crimes the Ithacan is weaving. Is the maiden to be hurled from Mt Ida's ridge, or thrown from a jutting rock on the towering citadel? Not

---

[48] I.e. Venus' reward to Paris for his famous judgement.

---

913 tantus *Bentley*: tanti *EA*

251

930   mittenda saxo? num per has vastum in mare
volvenda rupes, latere quas scisso levat
altum vadosos Sigeon spectans sinus?
dic, fare quidquid subdolo vultu tegis.
leviora mala sunt cuncta, quam Priami gener
935   Hecubaeque Pyrrhus. fare, quam poenam pares
exprome, et unum hoc deme nostris cladibus,
falli: paratas perpeti mortem vides.

HELENA

Utinam iuberet me quoque interpres deum
abrumpere ense lucis invisae moras,
940   vel Achillis ante busta furibunda manu
occidere Pyrrhi, fata comitantem tua,
Polyxene miseranda, quam tradi sibi
cineremque Achilles ante mactari suum,
campo maritus ut sit Elysio, iubet.

ANDROMACHA

945   Vide ut animus ingens laetus audierit necem.
cultus decoros regiae vestis petit
et admoveri crinibus patitur manum.
mortem putabat illud, hoc thalamos putat.
At misera luctu mater audito stupet;
950   labefacta mens succubuit. assurge, alleva
animum et cadentem, misera, firma spiritum.
quam tenuis anima vinculo pendet levi!
minimum est quod Hecubam facere felicem potest.—
spirat, revixit. prima mors miseros fugit.

HECUBA

955   Adhuc Achilles vivit in poenas Phrygum?

flung into the desolate sea, tumbling down these cliffs which sheer-sided Sigeon raises, a lofty peak looking down on shallow bays? Speak, tell us what you are hiding beneath your deceitful looks. Any hurt is easier to bear than Pyrrhus as son-in-law to Priam and Hecuba. Tell us, reveal what torment you are preparing, and spare our sufferings one thing: being tricked. You see us prepared to endure death.

HELEN

I wish the gods' spokesman commanded me too to cut short with the sword this lingering in the hateful light, or to fall before Achilles' tomb by Pyrrhus' frenzied hand, sharing your fate, pitiable Polyxena: Achilles commands that you be delivered to him, sacrificed before his ashes, so that he can be a husband in the Elysian fields.

ANDROMACHE

See how her great spirit rejoiced to hear of her death. She welcomes being finely adorned in royal clothes, and allows a hand to touch her hair. That other prospect she saw as death, this she sees as marriage. But her unhappy mother is stunned to hear of this grief; her weakened mind has given way. [*To Hecuba*] Rise up, take heart and strengthen your failing courage, poor woman. Her frail life hangs on such a fragile bond! It would take very little to make Hecuba happy. But she breathes, she revives. Death is the first to shun the unhappy.

HECUBA

Is Achilles still living to scourge the Phrygians? Is he still

adhuc rebellat? o manum Paridis levem!
cinis ipse nostrum sanguinem ac tumulus sitit.
modo turba felix latera cingebat mea,
lassabar in tot oscula et totum gregem
960 dividere matrem. sola nunc haec est super,
votum, comes, levamen afflictae, quies;
haec totus Hecubae fetus, hac sola vocor
iam voce mater. dura et infelix age
elabere anima, denique hoc unum mihi
965 remitte funus.

ANDROMACHA
Inrigat fletus genas
imberque victo subitus e vultu cadit.
969 Nos, Hecuba, nos, nos, Hecuba, lugendae sumus,
970 quas mota classis huc et huc sparsas feret;
hanc cara tellus sedibus patriis teget.

HELENA
Magis invidebis, si tuam sortem scies.

ANDROMACHA
An aliqua poenae pars meae ignota est mihi?

HELENA
Versata dominos urna captivis dedit.

ANDROMACHA
975 Cui famula trador? ede: quem dominum voco?

HELENA
Te sorte prima Scyrius iuvenis tulit.

965b–66 *attributed to Andromache by Peiper, to Hecuba by EA*

fighting back? Oh, Paris' hand lacked power![49] His very ashes and tomb thirst for our blood. Just now a thriving family thronged around me; it was wearying just to share out my mother love among so many kisses, among my whole flock. Now she alone is left, my hope, companion, comfort in distress, and source of peace. She is Hecuba's whole brood, her voice alone now calls me mother. Come, you stubborn, ill-starred spirit, slip away, and finally spare me this one death.

ANDROMACHE

Her cheeks are flooded with weeping; a sudden flurry of tears falls from her defeated eyes. We, Hecuba, are the ones to be mourned—we, Hecuba, whom the fleet when it sails will scatter and carry in every direction. She will be covered by the dear earth in her ancestral homeland.

HELEN

You will envy her more when you know your own lot.

ANDROMACHE

Is any portion of my suffering unknown to me?

HELEN

The urn has been shaken and has given masters to the captives.

ANDROMACHE

To whom am I given as slave? Tell me, whom do I call master?

HELEN

On the first throw the young man from Scyros took you.

[49] Paris' bowshot to Achilles' heel was fatal—but too feeble (characteristically so, Hecuba implies) to lay his ghost too.

ANDROMACHA

Cassandra felix, quam furor sorti eximit
Phoebusque!

HELENA

Regum hanc maximus rector tenet.

HECUBA

967　Laetare, gaude, nata. quam vellet tuos
968　Cassandra thalamos, vellet Andromache tuos!
979　Estne aliquis Hecubam qui suam dici velit?

HELENA

980　Ithaco obtigisti praeda nolenti brevis.

HECUBA

Quis tam impotens ac durus et iniquae ferus
sortitor urnae regibus reges dedit?
quis tam sinister dividit captas deus?
quis arbiter crudelis et miseris gravis
985　eligere dominos nescit et [saeva manu
dat iniqua miseris fata? quis] matrem Hectoris
armis Achillis miscet? ad Ulixem vocor:
nunc victa, nunc captiva, nunc cunctis mihi
obsessa videor cladibus. domini pudet,
990　non servitutis. [Hectoris spolium feret
qui tulit Achillis?] sterilis et saevis fretis
inclusa tellus non capit tumulos meos.
Duc, duc, Ulixe, nil moror, dominum sequor;

967–68 *placed after* 978 *by Richter*
985b–86a *deleted by Peiper*
990b–91a *deleted by Leo*

ANDROMACHE
Lucky Cassandra, exempted from the lot by madness and by Phoebus!

HELEN
The mighty king of kings possesses her.

HECUBA
[*To Polyxena*] Rejoice, be glad, my daughter. How Cassandra or Andromache would wish for your marriage! Is there anyone who wants Hecuba to be called his?

HELEN
You fell to the Ithacan as his prize, unwanted and short-lived.

HECUBA
What caster of unjust lots has awarded royalty to royalty in this reckless, harsh, and brutal way? What god is so malign in distributing captives? What authority, cruel and oppressive to the wretched, is unfit to choose masters and couples the mother of Hector with the weapons of Achilles?[50] I am called to Ulysses. Now I recognise myself as defeated, a captive, beset by every disaster. I am ashamed of my master, not of slavery. That barren land, hemmed in by cruel seas, cannot hold my tomb.[51] Lead on, lead on, Ulysses; I do not hold back, I follow my master. But my destiny will

---

[50] Which had been awarded to Ulysses after Achilles' death. Between "and" and "couples" 985b–986a has been deleted: "callously hands out unjust destinies to the wretched? Who . . ."

[51] I.e. Ithaca is too meagre. Seneca also alludes to the mythical tradition that Hecuba died elsewhere than Ithaca. Before "That barren land," 990b–991a has been deleted: "Is the man who took the spoils of Achilles to take those of Hector?"

me mea sequentur fata: non pelago quies
995　tranquilla veniet, saeviet ventis mare

　　　　*　　*　　*　　*　　*

[et bella et ignes et mea et Priami mala]
dumque ista veniunt, interim hoc poenae loco est:
sortem occupavi, praemium eripui tibi. —
Sed incitato Pyrrhus accurrit gradu
1000　vultuque torvo. Pyrrhe, quid cessas? age
reclude ferro pectus et Achillis tui
coniunge soceros. perge, mactator senum,
et hic decet te sanguis.—abreptam trahit.
maculate superos caede funesta deos,
1005　maculate manes! quid precer vobis? precor
his digna sacris aequora: hoc classi accidat
toti Pelasgae, ratibus hoc mille accidat
meae precabor, cum vehar, quidquid rati.

CHORUS

Dulce maerenti populus dolentum,
1010　dulce lamentis resonare gentes;
lenius luctus lacrimaeque mordent,
turba quas fletu similis frequentat.
semper, a semper, dolor est malignus:
gaudet in multos sua fata mitti
1015　seque non solum placuisse poenae.
ferre quam sortem patiuntur omnes
　　　　nemo recusat.
　　Nemo se credet miserum, licet sit:
tolle felices. removeto multo

---

995 *Lacuna recognised after* 995 *by Leo;* 996 *deleted by Fitch*
1003 trahit *A:* trahe *E*　　　　1018–19 nemo se credet *and* tolle
felices *should perhaps be interchanged, as Madvig suggested*

258

follow *me*: no unruffled calm will come to the deep, the
winds will madden the seas . . . [52] And until these things
come, meanwhile this serves as punishment: I have appropriated your lot, and snatched your prize from you.

But Pyrrhus is rushing here, with hurried step and grim
face. Pyrrhus, why hesitate? Come, cut open my breast
with your sword and unite the parents-in-law of your dear
Achilles. Proceed, you butcher of the aged: this blood suits
you as well. He seizes her and drags her off. [*To Pyrrhus
and soldiers*] Stain the gods above with bloody slaughter,
stain the spirits of the dead! What should I pray to befall
you? I pray for seas to match rituals like these. Let the
whole Pelasgian fleet and its thousand ships suffer the
same fate as I shall pray, when I sail, to befall my own ship.

CHORUS

Sweet to one grieving is a host of mourners,
sweet that whole peoples are loud with laments;
gentler the sting of grief and tears
echoed by a crowd that is likewise weeping.
Always, always pain is malicious,
glad that its own fate falls on many,
that it was not suffering's only target.
No one objects to bearing a lot
    which all endure.
  No one will think himself wretched, though he is,
if you take away the fortunate. Remove those

---

[52] Line 996 (deleted): "—warfare and fires and all the troubles
that afflicted me and Priam." The lacuna after 995 may have con-
tained a reference to angry gods, exile, or lost companions.

1020   divites auro, removeto centum
       rura qui scindant opulenta bubus:
       pauperi surgent animi iacentes.
       est miser nemo nisi comparatus.

         Dulce in immensis posito ruinis,
1025   neminem laetos habuisse vultus.
       ille deplorat queriturque fatum,
       qui secans fluctum rate singulari
       nudus in portus cecidit petitos.
       aequior casum tulit et procellas,
1030   mille qui ponto pariter carinas
       obrui vidit tabulaque litus
       naufraga spargi, mare cum coactis
       fluctibus Corus prohibet reverti.

         Questus est Hellen cecidisse Phrixus,
1035   cum gregis ductor radiante villo
       aureo fratrem simul et sororem
       sustulit tergo medioque iactum
       fecit in ponto; tenuit querelas
       et vir et Pyrrha, mare cum viderent,
1040   et nihil praeter mare cum viderent
       unici terris homines relicti.

         Solvet hunc coetum lacrimasque nostras
       sparget huc illuc agitata classis,
       cum tuba iussi dare vela nautae
1045   et simul ventis properante remo
       prenderint altum fugietque litus.
       quis status mentis miseris, ubi omnis
       terra decrescet pelagusque crescet,

1044–45 cum tuba . . . et simul *Richter*: et tuba . . . cum simul *EA*

moneyed with much gold, remove those
who cleave rich acres with a hundred oxen:
the downcast spirits of the poor will rise.
No one is wretched except by comparison.
　　To one surrounded by massive ruins
it is sweet that no one has a joyful face.
That person deplores and laments his fate,
who cuts through waves in a lone vessel
and is stripped of everything but stumbles into port.
Calmer in bearing disaster and storms
is one who sees a thousand vessels together
overwhelmed at sea, and the shore strewn
with planks from shipwrecks, as a northwester piles
　　up
waves and prevents the sea from ebbing.
　　Phrixus lamented the fall of Helle,
when the flock's leader, shining-fleeced,
lifted brother and sister together
on his golden back, and then jettisoned one
in the midst of the sea; but Pyrrha and her man
both checked their laments, though they saw waters
and saw nothing besides waters,
the only humans left on earth.
　　This group will be sundered, our tears scattered
as the fleet is driven far and wide,
once the crews set sail at the trumpet's bidding
and, sped by oars as well as winds,
gain the open sea while the coast retreats.
What shall we wretches feel, as all
the landscape dwindles and the seascape grows,

celsa cum longe latitabit Ide?
1050 tum puer matri genetrixque nato,
Troia qua iaceat regione monstrans,
dicet et longe digito notabit:
"Ilium est illic, ubi fumus alte
serpit in caelum nebulaeque turpes."
1055 Troes hoc signo patriam videbunt.

NUNTIUS

O dura fata, saeva miseranda horrida!
quod tam ferum, tam triste bis quinis scelus
Mars vidit annis? quid prius referens gemam,
tuosne potius, an tuos luctus, anus?

HECUBA

1060 Quoscumque luctus fleveris, flebis meos.
sua quemque tantum, me omnium clades premit.
mihi cuncta pereunt; quisquis est Hecubae est miser.

NUNTIUS

Mactata virgo est, missus e muris puer;
sed uterque letum mente generosa tulit.

ANDROMACHA

1065 Expone seriem caedis, et duplex nefas
persequere; gaudet magnus aerumnas dolor
tractare totas. ede et enarra omnia.

NUNTIUS

Est una magna turris e Troia super,
assueta Priamo, cuius e fastigio
1070 summisque pinnis arbiter belli sedens
regebat acies. turre in hac blando sinu

and lofty Mt Ida is hidden in the distance?
Then boy to mother and mother to son,
showing the region where Troy lies,
will point it out from afar, and say:
"Ilium is there, where smoke twists high
into the heavens in squalid clouds."
By this sign Trojans will see their land.

ACT 5

MESSENGER

O cruel deaths, harsh and pitiable and horrible! What crime as grim and savage has Mars beheld in these twice five years? What shall I first tell with tears: your griefs [*to Andromache*] or yours, old woman?

HECUBA

Whatever griefs you weep, you will weep for mine. Individuals bear just their own disasters, but I bear everyone's. Every death touches me; anyone who is wretched touches Hecuba.

MESSENGER

The maiden is sacrificed, the boy thrown from the walls; but each bore death with a noble heart.

ANDROMACHE

Describe the sequence of killing, detail the double crime; great pain enjoys dwelling on its sorrow in full. Speak out, recount everything.

MESSENGER

There is one great tower of Troy surviving, a haunt of Priam's: from its lofty parapet, seated to weigh the fighting, he would govern the battlelines. On this tower he would

263

fovens nepotem, cum metu versos gravi
Danaos fugaret Hector et ferro et face,
paterna puero bella monstrabat senex.
1075 haec nota quondam turris et muri decus,
nunc saeva cautes, undique adfusa ducum
plebisque turba cingitur; totum coit
ratibus relictis vulgus. his collis procul
aciem patenti liberam praebet loco,
1080 his alta rupes, cuius in cacumine
erecta summos turba libravit pedes.
hunc pinus, illum laurus, hunc fagus gerit
et tota populo silva suspenso tremit.
extrema montis ille praerupti petit,
1085 semusta at ille tecta vel saxum imminens
muri cadentis pressit, atque aliquis (nefas)
tumulo ferus spectator Hectoreo sedet.
      Per spatia late plena sublimi gradu
incedit Ithacus parvulum dextra trahens
1090 Priami nepotem, nec gradu segni puer
ad alta pergit moenia. ut summa stetit
pro turre, vultus huc et huc acres tulit
intrepidus animo. qualis ingentis ferae
parvus tenerque fetus et nondum potens
1095 saevire dente iam tamen tollit minas
morsusque inanes temptat atque animis tumet:
sic ille dextra prensus hostili puer
ferox superbit. moverat vulgum ac duces
ipsumque Ulixem. non flet e turba omnium
1100 qui fletur; ac, dum verba fatidici et preces
concipit Ulixes vatis et saevos ciet
ad sacra superos, sponte desiluit sua
in media Priami regna.

gently fold his grandchild in his arms, and when Hector would turn the Danaans in panic and rout them with sword and firebrand, the old man would point out to the boy his father's fighting. This once famous tower and glory of the wall, now a grim crag, was surrounded by a crowd of leaders and rank and file pouring in from all sides; the whole throng left the ships and massed here. A hill provided a clear though distant view across open ground for some; for others a high cliff, on whose peak a crowd stood straining and poised on tip toe. A pine tree bore one man, a laurel another, a beech another; the whole woodland trembled with people hanging in it. Someone made for the edge of a sheer scarp, another put his weight on a half-burnt roof or a rock jutting from the collapsing wall, and—an outrage— one callous spectator took his seat on Hector's tomb.

Through the widely thronged area the Ithacan strode grandly, dragging by the hand Priam's little grandchild; but the boy's steps did not lag as he made his way to the high walls. When he stood forward on the top of the tower, he turned his alert gaze this way and that, fearless in spirit. As the tender little cub of a great beast, unable as yet to wreak havoc with its teeth, nevertheless rears up threateningly and tries feinting bites, swelling with courage, so the boy grasped by the enemy's hand was fiercely proud. He moved the people and their leaders and Ulysses himself. Of the whole crowd, he did not weep who was wept for. And while Ulysses pronounced the words and prayers of the fate-telling prophet and summoned the cruel gods to the ritual, he leapt down of his own accord, into the midst of Priam's kingdom.

1098 superbit *Leo*: superbe *EA*

ANDROMACHA

Quis Colchus hoc, quis sedis incertae Scytha
1105 commisit, aut quae Caspium tangens mare
gens iuris expers ausa? non Busiridis
puerilis aras sanguis aspersit feri,
nec parva gregibus membra Diomedes suis
epulanda posuit. quis tuos artus teget
1110 tumuloque tradet?

NUNTIUS

                    Quos enim praeceps locus
reliquit artus? ossa disiecta et gravi
elisa casu; signa clari corporis,
et ora et illas nobiles patris notas,
confudit imam pondus ad terram datum;
1115 soluta cervix silicis impulsu, caput
ruptum cerebro penitus expresso: iacet
deforme corpus.

ANDROMACHA

            Sic quoque est similis patri.

NUNTIUS

Praeceps ut altis cecidit e muris puer,
flevitque Achivum turba quod fecit nefas,
1120 idem ille populus aliud ad facinus redît
tumulumque Achillis. cuius extremum latus
Rhoetea leni verberant fluctu vada;
adversa cingit campus, et clivo levi
erecta medium vallis includens locum
1125 crescit theatri more. concursus frequens
implevit omne litus. hi classis moras
hac morte solvi rentur, hi stirpem hostium
gaudent recidi; magna pars vulgi levis

ANDROMACHE

What Colchian, what nomad Scythian perpetrated this?
What lawless tribe from the edge of the Caspian Sea dared
this? Not even savage Busiris' altar was sprinkled with the
blood of a boy; Diomedes did not set out young limbs for
his animals to feed on.[53] Who will cover your body and con-
sign it to the tomb?

MESSENGER

What body did that steep place leave? His bones were
wrenched apart and smashed by the heavy fall. The features of that illustrious form, his face and those noble
traces of his father, were disfigured as his weight hit the
ground below. His neck was broken by the impact against
stone, the skull split with the entire brain forced out. He
lies a shapeless corpse.

ANDROMACHE

Even in this he is like his father.

MESSENGER

After the boy fell headlong from the high walls and the
Achaean crowd wept for the outrage it had done, that same
host turned back to another crime and to Achilles' burial
mound. Its far edge is beaten by the soft waves of the
Rhoetean strait; around the facing side is level ground; a
gently rising valley-side, which encloses the intervening
space, slopes up in the form of a theatre. The gathering
crowd filled the entire shore. Some regarded this death
as resolving the fleet's delay, others were glad to have enemy stock cut away; most of the shallow mob detested

[53] Busiris was notorious for performing human sacrifice, Diomedes for feeding human flesh to his horses.

odit scelus spectatque. nec Troes minus
1130 suum frequentant funus et pavidi metu
partem ruentis ultimam Troiae vident:
cum subito thalami more praecedunt faces
et pronuba illi Tyndaris, maestum caput
demissa. "Tali nubat Hermione modo"
1135 Phryges precantur, "sic viro turpis suo
reddatur Helena." terror attonitos tenet
utrosque populos. Ipsa deiectos gerit
vultus pudore, sed tamen fulgent genae
magisque solito splendet extremus decor,
1140 ut esse Phoebi dulcius lumen solet
iamiam cadentis, astra cum repetunt vices
premiturque dubius nocte vicina dies.
stupet omne vulgus: [et fere cuncti magis
peritura laudant] hos movet formae decus,
1145 hos mollis aetas, hos vagae rerum vices;
movet animus omnes fortis et leto obvius,
[Pyrrhum antecedit; omnium mentes tremunt]
mirantur ac miserantur.
                              Ut primum ardui
sublime montis tetigit, atque alte edito
1150 iuvenis paterni vertice in busti stetit,
audax virago non tulit retro gradum;
conversa ad ictum stat truci vultu ferox.
tam fortis animus omnium mentes ferit,
novumque monstrum est Pyrrhus ad caedem piger.
1155 ut dextra ferrum penitus exactum abdidit,
subitus recepta morte prorupit cruor
per vulnus ingens. nec tamen moriens adhuc

1143b–44a *deleted by Zwierlein*   1147 *deleted by Zwierlein*

the crime—and gazed. No less than them the Trojans thronged their own funeral, and watched frightened the final act of Troy's fall. Suddenly, as at a wedding, torches led the procession, and the Tyndarid[54] as matron escorting the bride, hanging her head in sorrow. "May Hermione wed like this," prayed the Phrygians, "may degraded Helen be restored so to her husband!" Both peoples were held paralysed by dread. She herself lowered her gaze in modesty, but her eyes were radiant nonetheless, and her beauty shone forth more than usual at its ending, as Phoebus' light is always lovelier at the moment of setting, when the stars take up the cycle and failing daylight is threatened by night's closeness. The whole crowd was awestruck.[55] Some were moved by her beauty, some by her tender years, some by life's shifting changes; all were moved by the braveness of her spirit, facing death head-on;[56] they marvelled and felt pity.

Once she reached the height of the steep mound, and the young man took his position on the high-raised summit of his father's burial place, the dauntless heroine did not step back: she stood facing the blow, frowning defiance. So brave a spirit struck everyone's mind, and there was a strange prodigy—Pyrrhus reluctant to kill. When his hand did plunge the blade-thrust deep into her, and then withdrew the death weapon, blood suddenly erupted through the massive wound. Nevertheless in dying she still main-

[54] Helen, nominally daughter of Tyndareus, though actually of Jupiter. Hermione is her daughter by Menelaus.
[55] Line 1143b–44a (deleted): "and all tend to praise more highly what is about to be lost."   [56] Line 1147 (deleted): "she went ahead of Pyrrhus. The minds of all feared, . . ."

deponit animos: cecidit, ut Achilli gravem
factura terram, prona et irato impetu.
1160 uterque flevit coetus — et timidum Phryges
misere gemitum, clarius victor gemit.
hic ordo sacri. non stetit fusus cruor
humove summa fluxit: obduxit statim
saevusque totum sanguinem tumulus bibit.

HECUBA

1165 Ite, ite, Danai, petite iam tuti domos;
optata velis maria diffusis secet
secura classis. concidit virgo ac puer:
bellum peractum est. quo meas lacrimas feram?
ubi hanc anilis expuam leti moram?
1170 natam an nepotem, coniugem an patriam fleam?
an omnia an me? sola mors votum meum,
infantibus violenta virginibus venis,
ubique properas saeva; me solam times
vitasque, gladios inter ac tela et faces
1175 quaesita tota nocte, cupientem fugis.
non hostis aut ruina, non ignis meos
absumpsit artus: quam prope a Priamo steti!

NUNTIUS

Repetite celeri maria, captivae, gradu:
iam vela puppis laxat et classis movet.

tained her pride: she fell, so as to make the earth heavy for Achilles, face downward and with angry force. Each group wept, but the Phrygians uttered timid laments, while the victor lamented more loudly. Such was the order of the ritual. The spilt gore did not stand or flow on the ground's surface: immediately the tomb swallowed and savagely drank down all the blood.

HECUBA

Go, go, you Danaans, now you can head for your homes in safety. Let the fleet spread its sails and cut through the longed-for seas without a care. A maiden and boy have fallen: the war is finished. Where shall I take my tears? Where shall I spew out this obstacle to an old woman's death?[57] Shall I weep for daughter or grandchild, husband or country? For my whole world, or for myself? O death, my only prayer, you come with violence to infants and to girls, everywhere you appear with savage haste; you fear me alone and shun me. Though I sought you all night amid swords and spears and firebrands, you flee from my desire. No enemy or collapsing building, no fire consumed my body; yet how close I stood to Priam!

MESSENGER

Head quickly towards the sea, you prisoners; already the ships are unfurling their sails and the fleet is moving.

---

[57] *Mora* (obstacle or delay) refers primarily to her life-breath (*spiritus*).

PHOENICIAN WOMEN

INTRODUCTION

Background

After recognising the terrible deeds he had committed
in ignorance, Oedipus abdicated and left Thebes; he is
now wandering as an outcast, accompanied only by his devoted daughter Antigone. His two sons agreed to share the
throne by ruling alternately, but Eteocles, who ruled first,
refused to yield the throne. The ousted Polynices therefore secured external help by marrying the daughter of
Adrastus, king of Argos, who then raised an army to support the claims of his new son-in-law. This army with its
seven champions, the famous "Seven Against Thebes," is
now about to attack the city. Jocasta has lived on at Thebes
after Oedipus' downfall, not committed suicide as in Sophocles' *Oedipus the King* and Seneca's *Oedipus*.

Comment

This dramatic text is intriguing in form because of its
apparent incompleteness: it lacks a chorus, it has insufficient dramatic material for the usual five Acts of a
Senecan play, and it breaks off abruptly at line 664. What
exists falls into two sections, the first concerned with
Oedipus and his daughter in exile, the second with his
mother-wife Jocasta and their warring sons at Thebes.

275

The two segments of the play present a strong contrast between the characters of the two parents. Jocasta, the loving mother, is equally devoted to both sons (though more sympathetic to the wronged Polynices), and prepared to risk her own life by intervening physically between them on the battlefield. Oedipus, in contrast, is as wild as the countryside through which he roams, like King Lear on the heath; he is filled with guilt and self-loathing which extends to others also, as he bitterly hopes that his sons will destroy each other and Thebes. In fact the first section of the play, in which Oedipus vehemently longs for death while Antigone attempts to dissuade him, can be seen typologically as one of the Passion-Restraint scenes characteristic of Senecan drama; Oedipus' sudden yielding at the end (306–19), in response not to Antigone's arguments but to her supplication, has a particularly close analogue in Phaedra's yielding to supplication by her Nurse (*Pha* 250).

For a Roman audience, a key to this contrast between the two parents lies in the term *pietas* and the related adjective *pius* with its opposite *impius*. *Pietas* denotes right and natural relationships between family members, particularly parents and children, and a corresponding right relationship of humans to gods. Jocasta's love for her sons, then, embodies *pietas* in contrast to Oedipus' involuntary *impietas* against his parents and deliberate rejection of a father's duty towards his sons; Oedipus' attitude in turn is set against Antigone's *pietas*, as her brothers' *impietas* towards each other is set against Jocasta's love for them. But this is no equal match, since in a family so filled with inversion, *pietas* is tragically compromised in every manifestation. For Jocasta to show *pietas* towards one son risks showing *impietas* towards the other. For Oedipus the very idea of right relationships in the past or future is inconceivable. Such expressions of *pietas* as occur in the play frequently carry incestuous overtones of excessive physical or emotional closeness between father and daughter, mother and son. These themes are underlined by the repeated use in the play of familial terms, "mother," "brother" etc., almost to the exclusion of proper names.

In his portrayal of Oedipus, Seneca gives an intense exploration of the experience of guilt—an irrational burden of guilt for deeds which were, after all, done in ignorance. This guilt colours Oedipus' whole perception of the world, so that he regards himself as still contaminating earth, air, and water, and hears every human voice as a reminder of his deeds. In retrojecting the guilt of incest and parricide back into the very womb, in hallucinating the threatening father-figure of Laius, in his self-loathing, he embodies (as he does in Seneca's *Oedipus*) the dynamics of an Oedipus complex, even though that condition was not psychoanalytically defined in antiquity. What is added to this guilt is a perverse insistence on defining an identity for himself (and even for his sons) in this terrible personal history, and on achieving a radical self-determination by taking punishment into his own hands. This impulse is akin to the old intransigent heroic ethos (see the section on "Self and the World" in the General Introduction). What becomes more evident in Seneca is that such self-determination desperately excludes other means of self-fashioning that would be less harmful, less paradoxically self-destructive.

Jocasta's intercession with Polynices had a Roman analogue in the tradition of Coriolanus confronted by his mother as he marched on Rome (a tradition dramatised in

277

Shakespeare's *Coriolanus*), while the conflict of the brothers had a parallel in the fratricide of Romulus, Rome's leg-
endary founder. The succession of Roman civil wars in the
first century B.C. had left a deep sense of inherited guilt in
following generations, a feeling expressed in the two leading epics of the later first century A.D.: the *Pharsalia* or
Civil War of Seneca's nephew Lucan deals directly with
the war between Pompey and Caesar ("war between kin,"
cognatas acies, since the two men were related by marriage), while Statius' *Thebaid* returns to the mythical analogue of the "war between brothers" (*fraternas acies*) at
Thebes. Both epics are strongly influenced by the themes
and atmosphere of Seneca's tragedies.

Assuming that the play is incomplete, its composition
could have been abandoned for any number of reasons; or,
if it is indeed Seneca's last play, it could have been left
unfinished at his death in A.D. 65. We cannot tell whether
the two existing segments should be seen as two Acts,[1] nor
how Seneca would have developed the plot into a regular
five-Act structure. It is a reasonable guess that, if the play
had been expanded, events would have led to the mutual
slaughter of the two brothers on the battlefield and the
subsequent suicide of Jocasta out of grief, and that these
deaths would have been reported by a Messenger to
Oedipus in his remote hiding place. An alternative hypothesis has been proposed that the text is actually complete,

---

[1] In addition to the obvious break at 362, some critics find Act
divisions at 319 and 442, giving four Acts in total. On this analysis
Acts II and III are either unfinished or unusually short and light-
weight by Senecan standards.

and represents an essay in innovative dramatic form, which dispenses with the chorus and with conventional constraints such as the unity of place (Tarrant 1978, 229f., 251–53).

The A manuscripts call Seneca's play *The Thebaid*, but this is properly a title for an epic, not a drama. E calls it *Phoenician Women*: this title could go back to Seneca, in which case it could indicate an intention to use a chorus of Phoenician women, as Euripides did; but the title could equally well have been added later because of the resemblance between portions of the Senecan and Euripidean plays.

Sources

An antecedent for the first part of Seneca's play is Sophocles' *Oedipus at Colonus*. But there are also great differences, amounting to complete reversals, in the locale and its significance, and in the meaning of Oedipus' desire to end his life. We cannot tell whether Seneca is responding directly to Sophocles' play, or to intermediate versions, or both. A seemingly closer antecedent for the second part of Seneca's text is Euripides' *Phoenician Women*. That play, for example, contains an episode in which Jocasta pleads with her sons in Thebes, and a later episode in which she hastens to intercede with them on the battlefield, only to find them already mortally wounded. One might infer that Seneca has adapted these two episodes into his single scene of Jocasta intervening between her still living sons on the battlefield. But in fact such a scene is attested long before Seneca wrote.[2] Seneca's imagination was no doubt fuelled by many versions including Euripides', rather than by Euripides exclusively. Above all, it is tempting to think that the bringing together in one play of Oedipus in exile and Jocasta in Thebes, in order to compare and contrast the attitudes of the two parents, is Seneca's innovation; but this too must remain no more than a guess.

BIBLIOGRAPHY

A. Barchiesi, "L'Incesto e il Regno," in *Seneca: Le Fenicie* (Venice, 1988), 9–39, 101–09.

E. Fantham, *"Nihil iam iura naturae valent*: Incest and Fratricide in Seneca's *Phoenissae,"* in Boyle (1983), 61–76.

M. Frank, *Seneca's Phoenissae: Introduction and Commentary* (Leiden etc., 1995).

[2] Etruscan vase paintings of the second century B.C. show Jocasta and Antigone restraining the brothers as they prepare to fight (*LIMC* 4.1 p. 29 # 13, 14). In the first century B.C. Propertius speaks in passing of Jocasta interceding between the battling brothers (2.9.49f.), as if that scene were familiar to his audience.

DRAMATIS PERSONAE

OEDIPUS, *former king of Thebes, blind*
ANTIGONE, *his daughter*
MESSENGER *from Thebes*
JOCASTA, *wife and mother of Oedipus*
ATTENDANT *of Jocasta*
POLYNICES *and* ETEOCLES, *sons of Oedipus and
    Jocasta, now on the brink of war with each other*

Scene

*The first section of the play (to line 362) is set in wild coun-
tryside in the territory of Thebes. The second section takes
place at Thebes, initially on the battlements or palace roof,
and then on the battlefield outside the city walls. The time
is three years after Eteocles came to the throne following
his father's downfall and abdication.*

281

PHOENISSAE

OEDIPUS

Caeci parentis regimen et fessi unicum
patris levamen, nata, quam tanti est mihi
genuisse vel sic, desere infaustum patrem.
in recta quid deflectis errantem gradum?
5   permitte labi; melius inveniam viam,
quam quaero, solus, quae me ab hac vita extrahat
et hoc nefandi capitis aspectu levet
caelum atque terras. quantulum hac egi manu!
non video noxae conscium nostrae diem,
10   sed videor. hinc iam solve inhaerentem manum
et patere caecum qua volet ferri pedem.
ibo, ibo qua praerupta protendit iuga
meus Cithaeron, qua peragrato celer
per saxa monte iacuit Actaeon suis
15   nova praeda canibus, qua per obscurum nemus
silvamque opacae vallis instinctas deo
egit sorores mater et gaudens malo
vibrante fixum praetulit thyrso caput;
vel qua cucurrit, corpus invisum trahens,
20   Zethi iuvencus, qua per horrentes rubos
tauri ferocis sanguis ostentat fugas;
vel qua alta maria vertice immenso premit
Inoa rupes, qua scelus fugiens suum

PHOENICIAN WOMEN

OEDIPUS

Guidance for your blind parent, only solace for your weary
father, my daughter: to me it is worth the cost to have produced you, even as it happened; but abandon your ill-fated
father. Why do you turn my wandering steps aside onto the
straight path? Allow me to stray; when alone I shall better
find the path I am searching for, the path that can draw
me from this life, and free heaven and earth from seeing
this unspeakable body. How little I accomplished with this
hand! I cannot see the daylight that witnessed my wrongdoing, but I can be seen. Now release your hand from its
grip on mine, and let my blind feet travel where they will. I
shall go, I shall go where my own Cithaeron extends its
sheer ridges, where Actaeon swiftly traversed the rocky
mountain and fell as strange prey for his own hounds,
where through the dark grove, the glen shaded with trees,
a mother led her god-ridden sisters, and gleeful in her ruin
displayed on her quivering thyrsus a head fixed there;[1]
or where the bull of Zethus ran, dragging a hated body,
where the fierce bull's flight through the tangled brambles
is traced in blood; or where Ino's crag looms over the deep

[1] The reference is to Agave's tearing apart of her son Pentheus.

novumque faciens mater insiluit freto
25　mersura natum seque—felices quibus
fortuna melior tam bonas matres dedit!
　　　Est alius istis noster in silvis locus,
qui me reposcit: hunc petam cursu incito;
non haesitabit gressus, huc omni duce
30　spoliatus ibo. quid moror sedes meas?
mortem, Cithaeron, redde et hospitium mihi
illud meum restitue, ut expirem senex
ubi debui infans; recipe supplicium vetus.
semper cruente saeve crudelis ferox,
35　cum occidis et cum parcis, olim iam tuum
est hoc cadaver: perage mandatum patris,
iam et matris. animus gestit antiqua exequi
supplicia.
　　　　　Quid me, nata, pestifero tenes
amore vinctum? quid tenes? genitor vocat.
40　sequor, sequor, iam parce! sanguineum gerens
insigne regni Laius rapti furit;
en ecce, inanes manibus infestis petit
foditque vultus. nata, genitorem vides?
ego video. tandem spiritum inimicum expue,
45　desertor anime, fortis in partem tui.
omitte poenae languidas longae moras
mortemque totam recipe. quid segnis traho
quod vivo? nullum facere iam possum scelus?
possum miser, praedico: discede a patre,
50　discede virgo. timeo post matrem omnia.

---

[46] poenae languidas longae moras *Grotius*: poenas* languidas
longae* morae* *EA*

seas from its immense height, where a mother, fleeing
from her own crime and committing a new one, leapt into
the strait to drown her child and herself: lucky those to
whom a better fortune gave such good mothers!

There is another place, my place, in those forests, that
calls me back.[2] I shall make for it in urgent haste, my steps
will not falter, I shall go there bereft of any guide. Why
keep my own abode waiting? Give me back my death,
Cithaeron; restore to me that lodging place of mine, so I
may die in old age where I should have died in infancy;
receive the long overdue punishment. Always bloody, savage, cruel, ferocious, when you kill and when you spare!
This carcass was yours long ago. Carry out my father's command—my mother's too, now. My spirit is eager to execute
the punishment of old.

Why, daughter, do you hold me bound by this pestilential love? Why hold me? My father calls. I follow, I follow,
stop now! Laius rages, bearing the bloodied symbol of his
stolen kingship; see, he attacks my empty eyes and claws at
them with his malevolent hands. Daughter, can you see my
father? I can see him! Finally spew out this hated life, my
spirit—you quitter, brave only against a portion of yourself! Drop these idle delays in your long postponed punishment, and accept death in full. Why do I sluggishly drag
out such life as I have? Am I incapable now of committing a
crime? I *am* capable, wretched man, I give warning: leave
your father, leave while a virgin. After my mother I fear
everything.

[2] The place on Mt Cithaeron where his father Laius intended
that he should die of exposure as an infant.

ANTIGONA

Vis nulla, genitor, a tuo nostram manum
corpore resolvet, nemo me comitem tibi
eripiet umquam. Labdaci claram domum,
opulenta ferro regna germani petant;
55   pars summa magno patris e regno mea est,
pater ipse. non hunc auferet frater mihi
Thebana rapto sceptra qui regno tenet,
non hunc catervas alter Argolicas agens;
non si revulso Iuppiter mundo tonet
60   mediumque nostros fulmen in nexus cadat
manum hanc remittam. prohibeas, genitor, licet,
regam abnuentem, derigam inviti gradum.
in plana tendis? vado. praerupta appetis?
non obsto, sed praecedo. quo vis utere
65   duce me, duobus omnis eligitur via.
perire sine me non potes, mecum potes.
hic alta rupes arduo surgit iugo
spectatque longe spatia subiecti maris:
vis hanc petamus? nudus hic pendet silex,
70   hic scissa tellus faucibus ruptis hiat:
vis hanc petamus? hic rapax torrens cadit
partesque lapsi montis exesas rotat:
in hunc ruamus? dum prior, quo vis eo.
non deprecor, non hortor. extingui cupis
75   votumque, genitor, maximum mors est tibi?
si moreris, antecedo; si vivis, sequor.
sed flecte mentem, pectus antiquum advoca
victasque magno robore aerumnas doma;
resiste: tantis in malis vinci mori est.

ANTIGONE

Father, no force shall loosen my hold on your body, no one shall ever tear me from your side. Let my brothers strive with the sword for Laius' glorious house and his rich kingdom; the chief part of our father's great kingdom—our father himself—is mine. He shall not be taken from me by the brother who holds Thebes' sceptre by theft of the throne, nor by the other who leads squadrons from Argos. Not even if Jove should thunder, rending the heavens, and the bolt should fall right between our close bodies, would I release this hand. Though you forbid me, father, I shall guide you despite refusals, direct your unwilling steps. Do you head for level ground? I come too. Do you make for the cliffs? I do not hinder you, but go before you. Use me as your guide to any goal, any path is chosen for both of us. You cannot perish without me, but with me you can. Here a high crag rises to a lofty peak, looking far out over the reaches of the sea beneath it: do you want us to make for that? Here a bare rock is poised, here the rent earth yawns open in a broken chasm: do you want us to make for that? Here a sweeping torrent falls, and whirls around eroded fragments of a fallen hillside: should we plunge into that? I go wherever you wish—only before you. I do not plead against anything, I do not urge anything. Do you long for annihilation, father, is death your chief prayer? If you die, I go before; if you live, I follow. But change your thinking, summon up your courage of old, and vanquish your troubles with sturdy resolve. Fight back; amid such evils, to die is a defeat.

OEDIPUS

80 Unde in nefanda specimen egregium domo?
unde ista generi virgo dissimilis suo?
Fortuna, cedis? aliquis est ex me pius?
non esset umquam, fata bene novi mea,
nisi ut noceret. ipsa se in leges novas
85 Natura vertit: regeret in fontem citas
revolutus undas amnis et noctem afferet
Phoebea lampas, Hesperus faciet diem;
ut ad miserias aliquid accedat meas,
pii quoque erimus.
                              Unica Oedipodae est salus,
90 non esse salvum. liceat ulcisci patrem
adhuc inultum. dextra quid cessas iners
exigere poenas? quidquid exactum est adhuc,
matri dedisti. mitte genitoris manum,
animosa virgo: funus extendis meum
95 longasque vivi ducis exequias patris.
aliquando terra corpus invisum tege;
peccas honesta mente, pietatem vocas
patrem insepultum trahere. qui cogit mori
nolentem in aequo est quique properantem impedit;
100 occidere est vetare cupientem mori.
nec tamen in aequo est; alterum gravius reor:
malo imperari quam eripi mortem mihi.
desiste coepto, virgo: ius vitae ac necis
meae penes me est. regna deserui libens,
105 regnum mei retineo. si fida es comes,
ensem parenti trade, sed notum nece
ensem paterna. tradis? an nati tenent

<hr>

85 vertit *E*: vertet *A*

OEDIPUS

How did this paragon arise in our unspeakable house?
Where did she come from, this maid so unlike her own
family? Fortune, are you failing? Is some child of mine
natural? It would not be—I know my fate well enough—
except to do harm. Nature is changing, following new laws:
rivers will double back and return their swift waters to
their source; Phoebus' lamp will bring night, Hesperus will
set up the day; so that something can be added to my
misery, we will actually be a natural family.

The only safety for Oedipus is not to be saved. Let me
avenge my father, who is still unavenged. My right hand,
why so remiss in exacting punishment? What has been exacted so far, you paid to my mother. Let go your father's
hand, noble maid. You are protracting my funeral, pro-
longing the exequies for your still-living father. At long last
hide this hateful body in the earth! You do wrong, though
with honourable intentions; you call it loyalty to drag about
your unburied father. One who hinders a man in haste to
die is the equal of one who forces an unwilling man to die.
Forbidding a man to die who desires to is the same as killing him. No, the two are not equal, I think the first more
harsh: I would rather have death imposed on me than with-
held from me. Cease your efforts, girl. The rights over my
own life and death belong to me. I abandoned the kingship
gladly, but I keep the kingship over myself. If you are a
faithful companion, hand your father a sword—but the
sword notorious for his father's murder. Are you handing it

cum regno et illum? faciet, ubicumque est, opus.
ibi sit; relinquo. natus hunc habeat meus,
110   sed uterque.
             Flammas potius et vastum aggerem
compone; in altos ipse me immittam rogos,
haerebo ad ignes, funebrem accendam struem,
pectusque solvam durum et in cinerem dabo
hoc quidquid in me vivit. ubi saevum est mare?
115   duc ubi sit altis prorutum saxis iugum,
ubi torva rapidus ducat Ismenos vada,
duc ubi ferae sint, ubi fretum, ubi praeceps locus,
si dux es. illuc ire morituro placet,
ubi sedit alta rupe semifero dolos
120   Sphinx ore nectens. derige huc gressus pedum,
hic siste patrem. dira ne sedes vacet,
monstrum repone maius. hoc saxum insidens
obscura nostrae verba fortunae loquar,
quae nemo solvat. quisquis Assyrio loca
125   possessa regi scindis et Cadmi nemus
serpente notum, sacra quo Dirce latet,
supplex adoras, quisquis Eurotan bibis
Spartenque fratre nobilem gemino colis,
quique Elin et Parnason et Boeotios
130   colonus agros uberis tondes soli:
adverte mentem. saeva Thebarum lues
luctifica caecis verba committens modis
quid simile posuit, quid tam inextricabile?
"Avi gener patrisque rivalis sui,
135   frater suorum liberum et fratrum parens;

---

112 accendam *Fitch*: ascendam *A*: escendam *E*

me? Or do my sons hold it too, along with the throne? Wherever it is, it will do its work: let it stay there, I relinquish it. Let my son have it—*each* son.

Instead, gather a great mound for the flames. I shall throw myself on the lofty pyre, embrace the fires, make the funeral pile blaze up; I shall melt this hard breast, and reduce to ashes whatever still lives in me. Where is the cruel sea? Guide me where there are high boulders from a tumbled mountain ridge, or where the rushing Ismenos guides its savage waters; guide me where there are wild beasts, where there are straits, where there is some precipitous place, if you are my guide. My wish is to go to die in that place where the Sphinx sat on her high crag, weaving her craft from half-bestial lips. Direct my steps there, there seat your father. Lest that terrible abode be empty, place a greater monster there. Seated on that rock I shall utter the dark words of my fate, which none can solve. All you who plough the land settled by the Assyrian king[3] and make reverent supplication in Cadmus' grove, famed for its serpent, where Dirce's sacred spring lies hidden; all you who drink of the Eurotas and dwell in Sparta famed for twin brothers;[4] all you countrymen whose herds graze Elis and Parnassus and Boeotia's fertile fields: give me your attention. That cruel scourge of Thebes, that linked together calamitous words in dark measures—what riddle did she pose like this, or as impenetrable? "He was son-in-law to his grandfather, rival to his father, brother to his own children and parent to his brothers; the grandmother in one

3 Cadmus, Thebes' founder, who came from Phoenicia; "Assyrian" virtually = "Asiatic" here.

4 Castor and Pollux.

uno avia partu liberos peperit viro,
sibi et nepotes." monstra quis tanta explicet?
ego ipse, victae spolia qui Sphingis tuli,
haerebo fati tardus interpres mei.

140   Quid perdis ultra verba? quid pectus ferum
mollire temptas precibus? hoc animo sedet,
effundere hanc cum morte luctantem diu
animam et tenebras petere; nam sceleri haec meo
parum alta nox est: Tartaro condi iuvat,
145 et si quid ultra Tartarum est. tandem libet
quod olim oportet. morte prohiberi haud queo.
ferrum negabis? noxias lapsu vias
claudes et artis colla laqueis inseri
prohibebis? herbas quae ferunt letum auferes?
150 quid ista tandem cura proficiet tua?
ubique mors est; optime hoc cavit deus.
eripere vitam nemo non homini potest,
at nemo mortem; mille ad hanc aditus patent.
nil quaero: dextra noster et nuda solet
155 bene animus uti. dextra, nunc toto impetu,
toto dolore, viribus totis veni.
non destino unum vulneri nostro locum:
totus nocens sum: qua voles mortem exige.
effringe corpus corque tot scelerum capax
160 evelle, totos viscerum nuda sinus;
fractum incitatis ictibus guttur sonet
laceraeve fixis unguibus venae fluant.
aut derige iras quo soles: haec vulnera

162 -ve μ: -ne A: -que E

_____

5 This image is popular in later drama, e.g. John Marston, *An-*

labour bore children for her man, but for herself grand-children as well." Who could unravel such a monstrosity? Even I, who triumphed over the Sphinx, would be slow and stumbling in interpreting my fate.

Why waste your words any further? Why try to soften my fierce heart with your prayers? It is settled in my spirit to pour out this life that has long wrestled with death, and to seek darkness—for this night is not deep enough for my crime; I long to hide in Tartarus, or whatever lies beyond Tartarus. What was long my duty is at last my desire. I cannot be restrained from death. Will you deny me a sword? Will you close off paths that threaten a fall, and restrain me from setting my neck in a tight noose? Will you remove herbs that bring death? Tell me, what will this care of yours achieve? Everywhere there is death. God made excellent provision for this. Anyone can deprive a person of life, but no one of death; a thousand doorways open onto it.[5] I require nothing: my right hand, even unarmed, has been well used before by my spirit. Come now, my hand, with all your force, all your pain, all your strength. I do not fix on any one place for wounding; all of me is guilty, exact death where you will. Break open my body and tear out this heart, capable of so many crimes, lay bare all my coiling guts; smash my throat with forceful blows so it chokes, or implant your nails to tear my veins so they flood. Or else direct your anger as before; pull open these wounds, drench

---

tonio and Mellida 3.2: "[Death]'s a goodfellow, and keeps open house: / A thousand thousand ways lead to his gate, / To his wide-mouthed porch, when niggard life / Hath but one little, little wicket in"; John Webster, *Duchess of Malfi* 4.2: "I know death hath ten thousand several doors / For men to take their exits."

rescissa multo sanguine ac tabe inriga;
165 hac extrahe animam duram, inexpugnabilem.
       Et tu, parens, ubicumque poenarum arbiter
     astas mearum: non ego hoc tantum scelus
     ulla expiari credidi poena satis
     umquam, nec ista morte contentus fui,
170 nec me redemi parte: membratim tibi
     perire volui. debitum tandem exige.
     nunc solvo poenas, tunc tibi inferias dedi.
     ades atque inertem dexteram introrsus preme
     magisque merge! timida tunc parvo caput
175 libavit haustu, vixque cupientes sequi
     eduxit oculos. haeret etiamnunc mihi
     ille animus; haesit, cum recusantem manum
     pressere vultus. audies verum, Oedipu:
     minus eruisti lumina audacter tua,
180 quam praestitisti. nunc manum cerebro indue:
     hac parte mortem perage qua coepi mori.

ANTIGONA

     Pauca, o parens magnanime, miserandae precor
     ut verba natae mente placata audias.
     non te ut reducam veteris ad speciem domus
185 habitumque regni flore pollentem inclito
     peto aut ut iras, temporum haud ipsa mora
     fractas, remisso pectore ac placido feras.
     at hoc decebat roboris tanti virum,
     non esse sub dolore nec victum malis
190 dare terga. non est, ut putas, virtus, pater,

---

[177] haesit *Fitch*: haeret* *EA*

them with blood and gore, and by this route drag out this tough and impregnable life.

And you, my father, wherever you stand to witness my punishment: I did not believe that such a crime as mine could be properly expiated by any punishment, ever; I was not satisfied with this much death,[6] I did not redeem myself by partial payment: I wanted to die for you limb by limb. But now at last exact your debt. *Now* I am paying the penalty, *then* I gave you a funeral offering. Stand close and press my feeble hand further in, plunge it deeper! Slight and timid the libation it poured from my head then: it scarely drew out the eyes that were eager to follow. My spirit is still hesitating, as it hesitated when my eyes thrust themselves upon my reluctant hand. You will hear the truth, Oedipus: you plucked out your eyes less boldly than you offered them. Now plunge your hand into the brain. Bring death to completion through that part where I began to die.

ANTIGONE

My great-souled father, I pray you calm your mind and listen to a few words from your pitiable daughter. I do not seek to lead you back to the past splendour of our house, or to your royal state, flourishing in power and renown; nor do I ask you to brook with a calm and tranquil heart this anger that has not been broken even by the interval of time. Yet it would become a man of such stalwart strength not to be ruled by pain, nor to turn tail in defeat before troubles. Valour does not consist in fearing life,[7] as you suppose,

---

[6] I.e. his blindness, a partial death: cf. lines 170–71 and 180.

[7] I.e. Oedipus' willingness to face death is not courageous if based on a desire to escape life.

timere vitam, sed malis ingentibus
obstare nec se vertere ac retro dare.
qui fata proculcavit ac vitae bona
proiecit atque abscidit et casus suos
195   oneravit ipse, cui deo nullo est opus,
quare ille mortem fugiat aut quare petat?
utrumque timidi est: nemo contempsit mori
qui concupivit. cuius haud ultra mala
exire possunt, in loco tuto est situs.
200   quis iam deorum, velle fac, quicquam potest
malis tuis adicere? iam nec tu potes
nisi hoc, ut esse te putes dignum nece—
non es, nec ulla pectus hoc culpa attigit.
et hoc magis te, genitor, insontem voca,
205   quod innocens es dis quoque invitis.
                                Quid est
quod te efferarit, quod novos suffixerit
stimulos dolori? quid te in infernas agit
sedes, quid ex his pellit? ut careas die?
cares. ut altis nobilem muris domum
210   patriamque fugias? patria tibi vivo perît.
natos fugis matremque? ab aspectu omnium
Fortuna te summovit, et quidquid potest
auferre cuiquam mors, tibi hoc vita abstulit.
regni tumultus? turba fortunae prior
215   abscessit a te iussa. quem, genitor, fugis?

OEDIPUS

Me fugio, fugio conscium scelerum omnium
pectus, manumque hanc fugio et hoc caelum et deos

---

196 fugiat *Lipsius*: cupiat *EA*

father, but in confronting vast troubles without turning aside or retreating. A man who has trampled on fate, who has torn off and thrown away life's blessings, who has added burdens to his own misfortunes, who has no need of any god—why should he shun death or seek it? Each action betokens a fearful man: no one who desires death is indifferent to it. One whose troubles can go no further has reached a place of safety. What god now could add anything to your troubles, even if he wished? You yourself cannot add anything—except to think yourself deserving of death. But you are not, no blame attaches to this heart of yours. And you have all the more reason to call yourself guiltless, father, in that you are innocent even despite the gods' intentions.

What is it that has maddened you and goaded your pain anew? What purpose drives you to the world below, and forces you out of this world? To be without the daylight? You *are* without it. To shun our home and fatherland, famed for its high walls? Our fatherland is dead to you while you live. Do you shun sons and mother? Fortune has removed you from the sight of all, and everything that death could take from anyone, life has taken from you. The turmoil of kingship? Those who thronged around your former fortunes have left at your command. Whom, father, do you flee?

OEDIPUS

I flee myself, I flee a conscience burdened with all those crimes, I flee this hand and these heavens and gods, and I

et dira fugio scelera quae feci innocens.
ego hoc solum, frugifera quo surgit Ceres,
220 premo? has ego auras ore pestifero traho?
ego laticis haustu satior aut ullo fruor
almae parentis munere? ego castam manum
nefandus incestificus execrabilis
attrecto? ego ullos aure concipio sonos,
225 per quos parentis nomen aut nati audiam?
utinam quidem rescindere has quirem vias,
manibusque adactis omne qua voces meant
aditusque verbis tramite angusto patet
eruere possem! nata, iam sensum tui,
230 quae pars meorum es criminum, infelix pater
fugissem. inhaeret ac recrudescit nefas
subinde, et aures ingerunt quidquid mihi
donastis, oculi. cur caput tenebris grave
non mitto ad umbras Ditis aeternas? quid hic
235 manes meos detineo? quid terram gravo
mixtusque superis erro? quid restat mali?
regnum parentes liberi, virtus quoque
et ingeni sollertis eximium decus
periere, cuncta sors mihi infesta abstulit.
240 lacrimae supererant: has quoque eripui mihi.
    Absiste: nullas animus admittit preces
novamque poenam sceleribus quaerit parem.
—et esse par quae poterit? infanti quoque
decreta mors est. fata quis tam tristia
245 sortitus umquam? videram nondum diem
uterique nondum solveram clausi moras,
et iam timebar. protinus quosdam editos
nox occupavit et novae luci abstulit:
mors me antecessit. aliquis intra viscera

flee the terrible crimes I did in innocence. Am I still burdening this earth, where fruitful crops arise? Am I breathing this air with my pestilential mouth? Do I slake my thirst with draughts of water, or enjoy the gifts of our kindly mother? Do I lay my hand on this chaste hand, though evil, incestuous, accursed? Do my ears take in any sounds through which I can hear the name of parent or son? If only I could cut off these pathways, drive in my hands and root out every avenue for voices, every narrow passageway open to words! Then, daughter, your ill-fated father would have escaped awareness of you, who are part of my crimes. The evil is embedded in me and breaks open repeatedly, and my ears force on me all that my eyes have spared me. Why do I not plunge this head, burdened with gloom, into the eternal shades of Dis? Why do I keep this ghost of myself back here? Why encumber the earth and wander mingling with the living? What evil is left? My kingdom, parents, children are lost, even my valour and the high renown of my skilled intellect; a hostile fortune has taken all from me. Tears were left: I robbed myself even of them.

Keep away—my spirit listens to no prayers: it is seeking a new punishment to match my crimes. And yet what could match them? Death was decreed for me even as an infant. Who has ever drawn so grim a fate? I had not yet seen the daylight, not yet escaped the restraint of the closed womb, and already I was feared. Some have been captured by night immediately after birth, and snatched from the newly seen light; for me death came before birth. Others

250   materna letum praecoquis fati tulit:
sed numquid et peccavit? abstrusum, abditum
dubiumque an essem sceleris infandi reum
deus egit; illo teste damnavit parens
calidoque teneros transuit ferro pedes,
255   et in alta nemora pabulum misit feris
avibusque saevis quas Cithaeron noxius
cruore saepe regio tinctas alit.
sed quem deus damnavit, abiecit pater,
mors quoque refugit. praestiti Delphis fidem:
260   genitorem adortus impia stravi nece.
hoc alia pietas redimet: occidi patrem,
sed matrem amavi. proloqui hymenaeum pudet
taedasque nostras? has quoque invitum pati
te coge poenas! facinus ignotum efferum
265   inusitatum fare quod populi horreant,
quod esse factum nulla non aetas neget,
quod parricidam pudeat. in patrios toros
tuli paterno sanguine aspersas manus
scelerisque pretium maius accepi scelus.
270   leve est paternum facinus: in thalamos meos
deducta mater, ne parum sceleris foret,
fecunda. nullum crimen hoc maius potest
Natura ferre.
                Si quod etiamnum est tamen,
qui facere possent dedimus. abieci necis
275   pretium paternae sceptrum et hoc iterum manus
armavit alias. optime regni mei
fatum ipse novi: nemo sine sacro feret
illud cruore. magna praesagit mala
paternus animus. iacta iam sunt semina
280   cladis futurae: spernitur pacti fides;

have suffered premature death in the mother's womb; but did they do wrong as well? Hidden and unknown, my very existence uncertain, I was tried by a god for an unspeakable crime; on his evidence my father condemned me, pierced my tender feet through with hot iron, and dispatched me to the deep woods as food for the wild beasts and birds that baneful Cithaeron feeds and taints repeatedly with the blood of kings. But the one condemned by the god and cast away by his father was shunned by death too. I stayed faithful to Delphi: I attacked my father and brought him down—an unnatural killing. Another, natural relationship will atone for this: I killed my father, but I loved my mother! Am I ashamed to speak out about our marriage and wedlock? Force yourself, though unwilling, to endure this punishment too! Tell of that deed, unheard-of, brutish, unprecedented—one that nations would shudder at, one that each age would refuse to believe occurred, one that would bring shame to a parricide. Into my father's bed I took these hands spattered with my father's blood; and as a reward for my crime I accepted a greater crime. My deed against my father is trivial: into my bedroom was led my mother—lest there should be an insufficiency of crime, a *prolific* mother. Nature can bear no crime greater than this.

Yet, if there still is one, we have produced those capable of committing it. I cast away the sceptre that rewarded my father-killing, and it has armed other hands again. I know very well the fate of my kingdom: no one will bear that sceptre without accursed blood. My spirit, a father's, presages great evils. Already sown are the seeds of future disaster: the pledges of the pact are disregarded; one of

hic occupato cedere imperio negat,
ius ille et icti foederis testes deos
invocat et Argos exul atque urbes movet
Graias in arma. non levis fessis venit
285 ruina Thebis: tela flammae vulnera
instant et istis si quod est maius malum,
ut esse genitos nemo non ex me sciat.

ANTIGONA

Si nulla, genitor, causa vivendi tibi est,
haec una abunde est, ut pater natos regas
290 graviter furentes. tu impii belli minas
avertere unus tuque vecordes potes
inhibere iuvenes, civibus pacem dare,
patriae quietem, foederi laeso fidem.
vitam tibi ipse si negas, multis negas.

OEDIPUS

295 Illis parentis ullus aut aequi est amor,
avidis cruoris imperi armorum doli,
diris, scelestis, breviter ut dicam, meis?
certant in omne facinus et pensi nihil
ducunt, ubi illos ira praecipites agit,
300 nefasque nullum per nefas nati putant.
non patris illos tangit afflicti pudor,
non patria: regno pectus attonitum furit.
scio quo ferantur, quanta moliri parent,
ideoque leti quaero maturi viam
305 morique propero, dum in domo nemo est mea
nocentior me.   Nata, quid genibus meis
fles advoluta? quid prece indomitum domas?
unum hoc habet Fortuna quo possim capi,

302

them refuses to cede the power he has appropriated; the other invokes the rights of the treaty they struck and the gods that witnessed it, and in exile he rouses Argos and the cities of Greece to arms. No light destruction is coming upon weary Thebes: weapons, flames, wounds are imminent, and any evil worse than these, so that no one can fail to know that they are my sons.

ANTIGONE
If you have no reason for living, father, this one reason is amply sufficient, that as a father you may rule your sons in their grievous rage. Only you can avert the threat of an unnatural war, only you can restrain these mad young men, and give peace to the citizens, calm to the country, good faith to the broken treaty. If you deny life to yourself, you deny it to many.

OEDIPUS
Do they have any love for parent or for justice, being greedy for blood, power, arms, treachery, being hideous, criminal—in short, sons of mine? They compete in every kind of ill deed, they have no scruples when anger drives them headlong; born through evil, they think nothing evil. No respect for their ruined father touches them, no thought for their country: in their hearts is a raging frenzy for the throne. I know where they are headed, what they are ready to perpetrate, and for that very reason I am seeking a path to an early death, hastening to die, while there is no one in my house guiltier than I.

Daughter, why do you throw yourself weeping at my knees? Why do you tame my untamed spirit with your prayers? Fortune has this one means to take me, unde-

invictus aliis; sola tu affectus potes
310　mollire duros, sola pietatem in domo
　　docere nostra. nil grave aut miserum est mihi
　　quod te sciam voluisse; tu tantum impera:
　　hic Oedipus Aegaea transnabit freta
　　iubente te, flammasque quas Siculo vomit
315　de monte tellus igneos volvens globos
　　excipiet ore, seque serpenti offeret
　　quae saeva furto nemoris Herculeo furit;
　　iubente te praebebit alitibus iecur,
　　iubente te vel vivet.

NUNTIUS

320　Exemplum in ingens regia stirpe editum
　　Thebae paventes arma fraterna invocant,
　　rogantque tectis arceas patriis faces.
　　non sunt minae, iam propius accessit malum.
　　nam regna repetens frater et pactas vices
325　in bella cunctos Graeciae populos agit;
　　septena muros castra Thebanos premunt.
　　succurre, prohibe pariter et bellum et scelus.

OEDIPUS

　　Ego ille sum qui scelera committi vetem
　　et abstineri sanguine a caro manus
330　doceam? magister iuris et amoris pii
　　ego sum? meorum facinorum exempla appetunt,
　　me nunc sequuntur; laudo et agnosco libens,

feated as I am by other means. You alone can soften my hard heart, you alone in our family can teach me natural feelings. Nothing that I know you want is grievous or painful for me; you have only to command it. Oedipus, this Oedipus, will swim the Aegean sea at your bidding;[8] he will swallow the flames which the earth spews from the mountain in Sicily, jetting out fiery masses; he will confront the fierce serpent enraged by Hercules' theft from the grove; at your bidding he will offer his liver to vultures; at your bidding he will even live.

MESSENGER

Thebes, in fear of fighting between brothers, calls for help on the man born of royal stock as a great exemplar, and asks you to protect our fathers' homes from the flames. These are not just threats, the evil has come closer. For one brother, demanding his turn on the throne as agreed, is stirring all the nations of Greece to war; seven separate encampments menace the walls of Thebes. Help quickly, proscribe the war and the accompanying crime.

OEDIPUS

Am I the man to forbid crimes to be committed, and teach hands to abstain from the blood of loved ones? Am I a guide to lawfulness and natural love? They are emulating the example of my deeds, they are following me now; I praise them and acknowledge them gladly, I urge them to

---

[8] This evokes the feat of Leander, who swam the Hellespont for love. The following lines adapt the traditional and hyperbolic eagerness of lovers to go through fire or fetch the apples of the Hesperides. Vultures tearing at the liver recall the punishment of Tityos and Prometheus.

exhortor, aliquid ut patre hoc dignum gerant.
agite, o propago clara, generosam indolem
335   probate factis, gloriam ac laudes meas
superate et aliquid facite propter quod patrem
adhuc iuvet vixisse! facietis, scio:
sic estis orti. scelere defungi haud levi,
haud usitato tanta nobilitas potest.
340   ferte arma, facibus petite penetrales deos
frugemque flamma metite natalis soli,
miscete cuncta, rapite in exitium omnia,
disicite passim moenia, in planum date,
templis deos obruite, maculatos lares
345   conflate, ab imo tota considat domus,
urbs concremetur—primus a thalamis meis
incipiat ignis.

NUNTIUS

      Mitte violentum impetum
doloris ac te publica exorent mala,
auctorque placidae liberis pacis veni.

OEDIPUS

350   Vides modestae deditum menti senem
placidaeque amantem pacis ad partes vocas?
tumet animus ira, fervet immensum dolor,
maiusque quam quod casus et iuvenum furor
conatur aliquid cupio. non satis est adhuc
355   civile bellum: frater in fratrem ruat.
nec hoc sat est: quod debet, ut fiat nefas
de more nostro, quod meos deceat toros,
date arma matri!

do something worthy of this father of theirs. Come on, my glorious issue, prove your noble ancestry by your deeds, surpass my fame and renown, and achieve something to make your father glad that he lived till now! You will do it, I know: you were born to it. Such high birth cannot make do with ordinary or trivial crime. Bring weapons, attack the Penates with firebrands, reap the grain of your native land with fire, confound everything, hurl all into destruction, fling the city walls down on every side and level them, crush gods beneath their temples, melt the statues of our sullied housegods, let our whole house collapse to its foundations, let the city be cremated—and let the fire begin first at my marriage chamber.

MESSENGER

Check this violent outburst of your pain! Let the sufferings of the people prevail on you; come to sanction peace and calm among your children.

OEDIPUS

Do you see an old man given to temperate thoughts? Is it a lover of peace and calm you call to take your side? My spirit is swelling with anger, my pain is burning beyond measure, and I want some outcome greater than the random efforts of young men's madness. A war that is just a civil war is insufficient:[9] let brother rush upon brother! Nor is that enough. As must happen so there can be an outrage after my style, one appropriate to my marriage bed, let your mother have your weapons!

---

[9] Compare the opening of Lucan's *Pharsalia*: "I sing of a war beyond civil war" (*bella . . . plus quam civilia*).

307

Nemo me ex his eruet
silvis: latebo rupis exesae cavo
360 aut saepe densa corpus abstrusum tegam.
hinc aucupabor verba rumoris vagi
et saeva fratrum bella, quod possum, audiam.

IOCASTA

Felix Agave! facinus horrendum manu
qua fecerat gestavit, et spolium tulit
365 cruenta nati maenas in partes dati;
fecit scelus, sed misera non ultra suo
sceleri occucurrit. hoc leve est quod sum nocens:
feci nocentes. hoc quoque etiamnunc leve est:
peperi nocentes. derat aerumnis meis,
370 ut et hostem amarem! bruma ter posuit nives
et tertia iam falce decubuit Ceres,
ut exul errat natus et patria caret
profugusque regum auxilia Graiorum rogat.
gener est Adrasti, cuius imperio mare
375 qui findit Isthmos regitur; hic gentes suas
septemque secum regna ad auxilium trahit
generi. quid optem quidve decernam haud scio.
regnum reposcit: causa repetentis bona est,
mala sic petentis. vota quae faciam parens?
380 utrimque natum video. nil possum pie
pietate salva facere; quodcumque alteri
optabo nato fiet alterius malo.
sed utrumque quamvis diligam affectu pari,
quo causa melior sorsque deterior trahit

358 eruet *Fitch*: eruat *EA*
375 qui *Fitch*: quod *EA*   findit *Gronovius*: cingit *EA*

No one shall root me out of these woods. I shall lurk in the cave of a hollowed cliff, or shelter in hiding behind dense brush. From here I shall catch at the words of straying rumours, and hear as best I can of the brothers' savage warfare.

[*The scene now shifts to the battlements or palace roof of the city of Thebes.*]

JOCASTA

Lucky Agave! She carried that horrific deed in the hand that had committed it, a bloodstained maenad bearing spoils of her dismembered son; she committed the crime, but beyond that the poor woman did not come face to face with her crime. That I am guilty is a trivial thing: I have made others guilty. Even this too is trivial: I have born sons who are guilty. My troubles were incomplete without my loving my enemy as well! Thrice has winter laid down its snows, and the third harvest has now dropped before the sickle, while my son has been wandering as a fugitive, deprived of his fatherland, and asking as an exile for the help of Greece's kings. He has married the daughter of Adrastus, whose sway governs the Isthmus that sunders the sea; *he* draws his own people and seven kingdoms with him to assist his son-in-law. I do not know what I should hope for or decide. He demands his kingdom back: his cause is good when he seeks it back, but bad when he seeks it thus. As a parent, what prayers should I make? On each side I see a son. I can do nothing loyally without destroying my loyalty; any hopes I have for one son will harm the other if realized. Yet, though I love each with equal affection, my spirit inclines where it is pulled by the better

385 inclinat animus semper infirmo favens;
miseros magis Fortuna conciliat suis.

SATELLES

Regina, dum tu flebiles questus cies
terisque tempus, saeva nudatis adest
acies in armis; aera iam bellum cient
390 aquilaque pugnam signifer mota vocat.
septena reges bella dispositi parant,
animo pari Cadmea progenies subit,
cursu citato miles hinc atque hinc ruit.
vide ut atra nubes pulvere abscondat diem
395 fumoque similes campus in caelum erigat
nebulas, equestri fracta quas tellus pede
summittit. et, si vera metuentes vident,
infesta fulgent signa, subrectis adest
frons prima telis, aurea clarum nota
400 nomen ducum vexilla praescriptum ferunt.
i, redde amorem fratribus, pacem omnibus,
et impia arma matris opposita impedi.

ANTIGONA

Perge, o parens, et concita celerem gradum,
compesce tela, fratribus ferrum excute,
405 nudum inter enses pectus infestos tene.
aut solve bellum, mater, aut prima excipe.

IOCASTA

Ibo, ibo et armis obvium opponam caput,
stabo inter arma. petere qui fratrem volet,
petat ante matrem. tela, qui fuerit pius,
410 rogante ponat matre; qui non est pius

---

388 adest *E*: stetit *A*

cause and the worse situation, for it always favours the weak; misfortune brings the wretched closer to their loved ones.

ATTENDANT

My queen, while you waste time in raising tearful laments, the fierce battlelines are before us with weapons bared; even now trumpets arouse war, and the standard bearer calls for fighting by advancing the eagle. The seven kings at their different stations each prepare for battle; with matching spirit the seed of Cadmus advance towards them, and soldiers on both sides hurry at the double. See how a black pall of dust blots out the daylight, and how the plain lifts skyward clouds that resemble smoke, rising from the earth broken by the hooves of the cavalry! And, if those in fear can see true, threatening standards are gleaming, the front ranks are in position with weapons raised, and banners bear the leaders' names clearly inscribed in letters of gold. Go, restore love to the brothers and peace to all: check this unnatural warfare by interposing as a mother.

ANTIGONE

Go on, mother, speed with all haste, restrain their weapons, dash the steel from the brothers' hands, stand firm with your breast bared between the opposing swords! Either break up the fighting, mother, or be first to suffer it.

JOCASTA

I *shall* go and interpose my body against their weapons, take my stand between their weapons. The one who wants to attack his brother must attack his mother first. He who will be loyal must lay down arms at his mother's request; he

incipiat a me. fervidos iuvenes anus
tenebo, nullum teste me fiet nefas;
aut si aliquod et me teste committi potest,
non fiet unum.

ANTIGONA

         Signa collatis micant
415   vicina signis, clamor hostilis fremit;
scelus in propinquo est: occupa, mater, preces.
et ecce motos fletibus credas meis,
sic agmen armis segne compositis venit.

SATELLES

Procedit acies tarda, sed properant duces.

IOCASTA

420   Quis me procellae turbine insanae vehens
volucer per auras ventus aetherias aget?
quae Sphinx vel atra nube subtexens diem
Stymphalis avidis praepetem pinnis feret?
aut quae per altas aëris rapiet vias
425   Harpyia saevi regis observans famem,
et inter acies proiciet raptam duas?

SATELLES

Vadit furenti similis aut etiam furit.
sagitta qualis Parthica velox manu
excussa fertur, qualis insano ratis
430   premente vento rapitur aut qualis cadit
delapsa caelo stella, cum stringens polum
rectam citatis ignibus rumpit viam,
attonita cursu fugit et binas statim

who is disloyal must begin with me. I, an old woman, shall restrain these blazing young men, no outrage shall occur while I look on; or if any can be committed even while I look on, it will not be the only one to occur.[10]

ANTIGONE
Standards are glittering near opposing standards, battle-cries are resounding, crime is close at hand: forestall it with your prayers, mother! And see, you could believe them moved by my tears, so listlessly do the armies come on, with their weapons at rest.

ATTENDANT
The ranks advance slowly, but the leaders are hastening.

JOCASTA
What swift wind will lift me in the maelstrom of a maddened storm and carry me through the open air? What Sphinx, what Stymphalian bird with its black cloud veiling the daylight will bear me in flight on its greedy wings? Or what Harpy, that oversees the starvation of the savage king, will snatch me away through the air's lofty pathways and fling its plunder down between the two battlelines? [*She hastens down to the battlefield*]

ATTENDANT
She presses on like a madwoman, or truly is mad. As an arrow flies swiftly when shot from a Parthian's hand, as a ship is whirled along by the thrust of an insane gale, or as a shooting star falls from the sky, scoring the heavens and smashing a direct path with its speeding fires: so she has flown apace in her frenzy, and straightway separated the

10 Probably the meaning is that if either man attacks his brother, he will have to attack his mother also.

diduxit acies. victa materna prece
435 haesere bella, iamque in alternam necem
illinc et hinc miscere cupientes manus
librata dextra tela suspensa tenent.
paci favetur, omnium ferrum latet
cessatque tectum—vibrat in fratrum manu.
440 laniata canas mater ostendit comas,
rogat abnuentes, irrigat fletu genas.
negare matri, qui diu dubitat, potest.

IOCASTA

In me arma et ignes vertite, in me omnis ruat
una iuventus quaeque ab Inachio venit
445 animosa muro quaeque Thebana ferox
descendit arce: civis atque hostis simul
[hunc petite ventrem, qui dedit fratres viro]
haec membra passim spargite ac divellite!
ego utrumque peperi: ponitis ferrum ocius?
450 an dico et ex quo? dexteras matri date,
date dum piae sunt. error invitos adhuc
fecit nocentes, omne Fortunae fuit
peccantis in nos crimen; hoc primum nefas
inter scientes geritur. in vestra manu est,
455 utrum velitis: sancta si pietas placet,
donate matri bella; si placuit scelus,
maius paratum est: media se opponit parens.
proinde bellum tollite aut belli moram.
    Sollicita cui nunc mater alterna prece
460 verba admovebo? misera quem amplectar prius?

---

447 *deleted by Axelson*

314

two battlelines. Conquered by a mother's prayer, the warfare has halted. Now, though keen to join battle from each side in mutual slaughter, they hold their weapons suspended, their right hands poised. Peace wins the day; everyone's weapons are sheathed and idle—but in the brothers' hands they still quiver. The mother displays and tears her white hair, begs as they shake their heads, drenches her cheeks with tears. One who hesitates so long can deny his mother's request.

JOCASTA

[*Between her two sons and their armies*] Turn against me your weapons and fires, against me let all warriors charge as one, both the spirited men who come from Inachus' walls and the fierce fighters who descend from the Theban citadel. Fellow townsman and enemy, together[11] tear these limbs asunder, scatter them in all directions! I bore you both: will you lay aside your swords at once? Or must I also say from what father? Give your mother your right hands, give them while they are loyal. Previously it was an error that made us guilty without our intent, the blame was entirely that of Fortune transgressing against us; this is the first outrage committed knowingly amongst us. Your choice is in your hands: if you decide on sacrosanct loyalty, give up the war for your mother; but if you decide on crime, a greater one is to hand: your parent sets herself between you. So do away with war, or with this hindrance to war.

[*Aside*] As an anxious mother praying to each in turn, on which of them shall I now deploy my words? Poor woman,

11 Line 447 (deleted): "aim at this belly, that produced brothers for my husband."

in utramque partem ducor affectu pari.
hic afuit; sed pacta si fratrum valent,
nunc alter aberit. ergo iam numquam duos
nisi sic videbo?
                    Iunge complexus prior,
465 qui tot labores totque perpessus mala
longo parentem fessus exilio vides.
accede propius, claude vagina impium
ensem et trementem iamque cupientem excuti
hastam solo defige. maternum tuo
470 coire pectus pectori clipeus vetat:
hunc quoque repone. vinculo frontem exue
tegimenque capitis triste belligeri leva
et ora matri redde. quo vultus refers
acieque pavida fratris observas manum?
475 affusa totum corpus amplexu tegam,
tuo cruori per meum fiet via.
quid dubius haeres? an times matris fidem?

POLYNICES

Timeo; nihil iam iura naturae valent.
post ista fratrum exempla ne matri quidem
480 fides habenda est.

IOCASTA

                    Redde iam capulo manum,
astringe galeam, laeva se clipeo inserat:
dum frater exarmatur, armatus mane.
    Tu pone ferrum, causa qui ferri es prior.
si pacis odium est, furere si bello placet,
485 indutias te mater exiguas rogat,
ferat ut reverso post fugam nato oscula
vel prima vel suprema. dum pacem peto,

whom shall I embrace first? I am drawn to each side with
equal affection. I have missed this one; but if the brothers'
agreement holds, now I shall miss the other. So shall I
never see the two of them from now, except like this?

[*To Polynices*] You must be first to join me in an embrace, who set your eyes on your parent after so many toils
and troubles, wearied with long exile. Come nearer, enclose this unnatural sword in its sheath, and fix in the
ground this spear which trembles and longs to be dis-
charged. Your shield prevents your mother's breast from
uniting with your breast: set it aside too. Take off this bond
from your brows, raise the grim sheathing of your warlike
head, and restore your features to your mother. [*He obeys*]
Why do you look away and watch your brother's hand with
fearful eyes? I shall encompass you and protect your whole
body with my embrace, the path to your blood will be
through mine. Why do you linger in doubt? Are you afraid
to trust your mother?

POLYNICES

I *am* afraid: the laws of nature have no power any longer.
After this example of brothers, I must not trust even my
mother.

JOCASTA

Then return your hand to the swordhilt, fasten on your
helmet, thrust your left arm into the shield. While your
brother disarms, remain under arms.

[*To Eteocles*] You, who first occasioned the sword, must
lay the sword aside. If you hate peace, if you choose the
rage of war, your mother asks you for a brief truce, so that
now my son has returned from exile I can enjoy his kisses,
the first of many or the last. While I plead for peace, disarm

317

audite inermes. ille te, tu illum times?
ego utrumque, sed pro utroque. quid strictum abnuis
490   recondere ensem? qualibet gaude mora:
id gerere bellum cupitis, in quo est optimum
vinci. vereris fratris infesti dolos?
quotiens necesse est fallere aut falli a suis,
patiare potius ipse quam facias scelus.
495   sed ne verere: mater insidias et hinc
et rursus illinc abiget. exoro? an patri
invideo vestro? veni ut arcerem nefas
an ut viderem propius? hic ferrum abdidit,
reclinis hastae parma defixae incubat.
500   Ad te preces nunc, nate, maternas feram,
sed ante lacrimas. teneo longo tempore
petita votis ora. te profugum solo
patrio penates regis externi tegunt,
te maria tot diversa, tot casus vagum
505   egere! non te duxit in thalamos parens
comitata primos nec sua festas manu
ornavit aedes nec sacra laetas faces
vitta revinxit. dona non auro graves
gazas socer, non arva, non urbes dedit:
510   dotale bellum est. hostium es factus gener,
patria remotus, hospes alieni laris,
externa consecutus, expulsus tuis,
sine crimine exul. ne quid e fatis tibi
desset paternis, hoc quoque ex illis habes,

---

[12] So Sophia speaks to her sons in Beaumont and Fletcher, *The Bloody Brother*: "Know yet, my sons, when of necessity / You must deceive or be deceived, 'tis better / To suffer treason than to act

yourselves to hear me. Does he fear you, you him? I fear each of you, but for the sake of each. Why hesitate to sheathe the drawn sword? Be glad of any delay: you both want to wage a war in which the best outcome is defeat. Do you fear treachery from your hated brother? When the need is to deceive one's kin or be deceived by them, one should suffer crime oneself rather than commit it.[12] But do not fear: your mother will ward off treachery, both from this side and again from that. Do I win my plea? Or must I envy your father?[13] Did I come to avert an outrage, or to watch it closer at hand? This one has sheathed his sword, his spear is grounded with the shield leaning tilted against it.

[*Turning to Polynices*] Now I shall offer my prayers as a mother to you, my son—but first my tears. After so long a time I hold the face I prayed for. You are exiled from your fatherland and sheltered by the hearthgods of a foreign king; you have been driven wandering by so many misfortunes, so many distant seas. Your mother did not lead and accompany you to your first marriage bed, nor decorate the festive house with her own hand, nor wreath holy ribbons around the joyful torches. Your father-in-law did not give you gifts of treasure heavy with gold, nor lands, nor cities: the dowry is war. You have become the son-in-law of our enemy, separated from your fatherland, guest in another's home, pursuing foreign possessions, expelled from your own, an exile without a charge against you. Lest you should lack any part of your father's fate, you have this

the traitor—/ And in a war like this, in which the glory / Is his that's overcome."

13 For his blindness, which protects him from terrible sights.

319

515 errasse thalamis. Nate post multos mihi
remisse soles, nate suspensae metus
et spes parentis, cuius aspectum deos
semper rogavi, cum tuus reditus mihi
tantum esset erepturus, adventu tuo
520 quantum daturus: "Quando pro te desinam"
dixi "timere?"; dixit inridens deus:
"Ipsum timebis." nempe nisi bellum foret,
ego te carerem; nempe si tu non fores,
bello carerem. triste conspectus datur
525 pretium tui durumque, sed matri placet.
　　　Hinc modo recedant arma, dum nullum nefas
Mars saevus audet. hoc quoque est magnum nefas,
tam prope fuisse. stupeo et exsanguis tremo,
cum stare fratres hinc et hinc video duos
530 sceleris sub ictu. membra quassantur metu:
quam paene mater maius aspexi nefas,
quam quod miser videre non potuit pater!
licet timore facinoris tanti vacem
videamque iam nil tale, sum infelix tamen
535 quod paene vidi. per decem mensum graves
uteri labores perque pietatem inclitae
precor sororis et per irati sibi
genas parentis, scelere quas nullo nocens,
erroris a se dura supplicia exigens,
540 hausit: nefandas moenibus patriis faces
averte, signa bellici retro agminis
flecte. ut recedas, magna pars sceleris tamen
vestri peracta est: vidit hostili grege
campos repleri patria, fulgentes procul
545 armis catervas vidit, equitatu levi
Cadmea frangi prata et excelsos rotis

portion of it too—a mistaken marriage. Son, returned to
me after many dawns; son, hope and fear of your anxious
parent, for sight of whom I constantly asked the gods,
even though your return was bound to deprive me of just
as much as it would bestow on me through your arrival:
"When shall I cease," I said, "to fear for you?"—and the
god said mockingly, "It is his very self you will fear." Yes, if
war were not here, I would be without you; yes, if you were
not here, I would be without war. Grim is the price of seeing you and harsh, but your mother accepts it.

Only let your troops fall back from here, while savage
Mars ventures no outrage. Even this is a great outrage, to
have been so close. I am stunned, I turn pale and tremble,
when I see two brothers standing here and here, in easy
range of crime. My body shakes with fear: how nearly I,
your mother, saw a greater outrage than that which your
poor father balked at seeing! Though now I have no fear of
such a deed and see nothing of the sort, yet I am ill-fated in
having almost seen it. By my womb's heavy pangs through
those ten months[14] I pray you, by the loyalty of your renowned sister, by the eyes of your self-castigating father—
eyes which, guilty of no crime, but exacting harsh self-pun-
ishment for his mistake, he gouged out: turn away these accursed torches from the walls of your fatherland, turn back
the standards of your warlike host! Even if you retreat, yet
the great part of your crime is already carried out: your
fatherland has seen its plains filled with a hostile horde,
has seen squadrons glittering far off in armour, Cadmean
meadows trampled by swift cavalry, leaders flying about in

[14] I.e. the ten months (by the inclusive counting of antiquity)
during which she was pregnant with Polynices.

volitare proceres, igne flagrantes trabes
fumare, cineri quae petunt nostras domos,
fratresque (facinus quod novum et Thebis fuit)
550 in se ruentes. totus hoc exercitus,
hoc populus omnis, utraque hoc vidit soror
genetrixque vidit: nam pater debet sibi
quod ista non spectavit. occurrat tibi
nunc Oedipus, quo iudice erroris quoque
555 poenae petuntur.
                Ne, precor, ferro erue
patriam ac penates neve, quas regere expetis,
everte Thebas. quis tenet mentem furor?
petendo patriam perdis? ut fiat tua,
vis esse nullam? quin tuae causae nocet
560 ipsum hoc quod armis uris infestis solum
segetesque adultas sternis et totos fugam
edis per agros. nemo sic vastat sua;
quae corripi igne, quae meti gladio iubes
aliena credis. rex sit ex vobis uter,
565 manente regno quaerite.
                Haec telis petes
flammisque tecta? poteris has Amphionis
quassare moles? nulla quas struxit manus
stridente tardum machina ducens onus,
sed convocatus vocis et citharae sono
570 per se ipse summas venit in turres lapis:
haec saxa franges? victor hinc spolia auferes,
victosque duces patris aequales tui
matresque ab ipso coniugum raptas sinu

572 victosque *PCS*: vinctosque *ET*

322

their high chariots, the blaze and smoke of firebrands seeking to reduce our homes to ashes, and brothers (a deed unknown even in Thebes) rushing upon each other. This sight has been witnessed by the whole army, by the entire people, by each of your sisters, and by your mother—for your father is indebted to himself alone that he did not watch it. Think now about Oedipus, who judges that punishment is required even for a mistake.

Do not uproot your fatherland and housegods with the sword, I pray you; do not overthrow the very Thebes you seek to rule. What madness holds your mind? You wreck your country in gaining it? You want it erased so that it may be yours?[15] Already you hurt your cause by the very act of ravaging the land with hostile arms, flattening grown crops and creating an exodus throughout the countryside. No one devastates his own possessions so; what you bid put to the torch and reaped with the sword, you regard as another's. In determining which of you will be king, let the kingdom survive!

Will you attack these buildings with weapons and flames? Will you be able to shake these bastions of Amphion? No hands built them by moving ponderous masses on creaking machinery; the stones were mustered by the sound of his voice and lyre, and rose by themselves to the tops of the towers. Will you smash these rocks? Will you carry off spoils from here as vanquisher? Shall vanquished leaders, contemporaries of your own father, and mothers torn from their husbands' very arms, be dragged off in

[15] These paradoxes appealed to Thomas Hughes, *The Misfortunes of Arthur* 2.2: "You lose your country, whiles you win it thus: / To make it yours, you strive to make it none."

saevus catena miles imposita trahet?
575 adulta virgo, mixta captivo gregi,
Thebana nuribus munus Argolicis eat?
an et ipsa, palmas vincta post tergum datas,
mater triumphi praeda fraterni vehar?
potesne cives leto et exitio datos
580 videre passim? moenibus caris potes
hostem admovere, sanguine et flamma potes
implere Thebas? tam ferus durum geris
saevumque in iras pectus? et nondum imperas.
quid sceptra facient? pone vesanos, precor,
585 animi tumores teque pietati refer.

POLYNICES

Ut profugus errem semper? ut patria arcear
opemque gentis hospes externae sequar?
quid paterer aliud, si fefellissem fidem?
si peierassem? fraudis alienae dabo
590 poenas, at ille praemium scelerum feret?
Iubes abire. matris imperio obsequor—
da quo revertar. regia frater meus
habitet superba, parva me abscondat casa—
hanc da repulso; liceat exiguo lare
595 pensare regnum. coniugi donum datus
arbitria thalami dura felicis feram,
humilisque socerum lixa dominantem sequar?
in servitutem cadere de regno grave est.

IOCASTA

Si regna quaeris nec potest sceptro manus
600 vacare saevo, multa quae possint peti
in orbe toto quaelibet tellus dabit.
hinc nota Baccho Tmolus attollit iuga,

324

to Bacchus, where lie broad tracts of productive land, and where the Pactolus with its heavy, opulent stream floods the fields with gold; the Meander winds its vagrant waters through equally fruitful acres, and the swift Hermus cuts through fertile plains. In another region is Gargara, dear to Ceres, and the rich soil encircled by the Xanthus, swollen with Mt Ida's snows. Here, where the Ionian Sea relinquishes its name, as Sestos opposite Abydos narrows the strait,[16] or where it veers closer to the East and looks on Lycia with its many protective harbours—here seek out a kingdom with the sword; let your doughty father-in-law bear arms against these peoples, let him win these nations and deliver them to your sceptre: but consider *this* kingdom as still held by your father. Better is exile for you than a return such as this: your exile is due to another's crime, but your return will be due to your own. Better use these forces of yours to seek a new realm unblemished by crime. Indeed your very brother will accompany your troops and fight for you. Go, and wage a war in which your father and mother can support you as you fight. A kingdom won with crime is more burdensome than any exile.

Picture now the mishaps of war, the unsure vicissitudes of inconstant Mars. Though you draw with you the entire might of Greece, though your soldiers deploy their weapons far and wide, the fortunes of war always stand in doubt. Mars decides everything; two men, however unevenly matched, are made equal by the sword. Both hopes and

16 The Hellespont. The gist of lines 610–13 is "anywhere on the Ionian coast, from its northern to its southern limit."

Fors caeca versat. praemium incertum petis,
certum scelus. favisse fac votis deos
omnes tuis—cessere et aversi fugam
635   petiere cives, clade funesta iacens
obtexit agros miles: exultes licet
victorque fratris spolia deiecti geras,
frangenda palma est. quale tu hoc bellum putas,
in quo execrandum victor admittit nefas,
640   si gaudet? hunc quem vincere infelix cupis,
cum viceris, lugebis. infaustas age
dimitte pugnas, libera patriam metu,
luctu parentes.

POLYNICES
Sceleris et fraudis suae
poenas nefandus frater ut nullas ferat?

IOCASTA
645   Ne metue. poenas et quidem solvet graves:
regnabit. est haec poena. si dubitas, avo
patrique crede; Cadmus hoc dicet tibi
Cadmique proles. sceptra Thebano fuit
impune nulli gerere—nec quisquam fide
650   rupta tenebat illa: iam numeres licet
fratrem inter istos.

ETEOCLES
Numeret, est tanti mihi
cum regibus iacere. te turbae exulum
ascribo.

651–64 *Grotius assigned these speeches to Eteocles and Polynices: according to EA, the speakers continue to be Polynices and
Jocasta.*

fears are tossed about by blind Chance. The reward you seek is unassured, but assured the crime. Suppose your prayers are favoured by all the gods—citizens have given ground and fled, soldiers lie covering the fields in mortal carnage: though you exult and bear spoils from your overthrown brother as victor, yet the palm of victory must be broken. What sort of war do you think it is, where the victor commits a detestable outrage if he celebrates? You have a hapless desire to defeat this man, yet you will mourn him after defeating him! Come, drop this accursed fight; free your country from fear and your parents from grief.

POLYNICES

So my evil brother is to receive no punishment for his treacherous crime?

JOCASTA

Do not fear. He will suffer a punishment, a heavy one indeed: he will reign. This is a punishment. If you doubt it, believe your grandfather and father; Cadmus will tell you this, and Cadmus' descendants. No Theban has been able to wield the sceptre with impunity—and yet none held it by breaking faith: already you may count your brother among them.

ETEOCLES

[*Intervening*] Let him count me so! For me it is worth the price to lie with kings. [*To Polynices*] You I number among the motley crowd of exiles.

POLYNICES
Regna, dummodo invisus tuis.

ETEOCLES
Regnare non vult, esse qui invisus timet.
655   simul ista mundi conditor posuit deus,
odium atque regnum. regis hoc magni reor,
odia ipsa premere. multa dominantem vetat
amor suorum; plus in iratos licet.
qui vult amari, languida regnat manu.

POLYNICES
660   Invisa numquam imperia retinentur diu.

ETEOCLES
Praecepta melius imperi reges dabunt;
exilia tu compone. pro regno velim—

POLYNICES
Patriam penates coniugem flammis dare?

ETEOCLES
Imperia pretio quolibet constant bene.

POLYNICES

Rule, then, but only as one hated by your people.

ETEOCLES

He who fears to be hated has no appetite for ruling. The god who created the world set these things together: hatred and kingship. I think it the mark of a great king, actually to crush hatred. A monarch is much constrained by his people's love; their anger gives him more freedom. One who wants to be loved rules with a feeble hand.

POLYNICES

Hated power is never held for long.

ETEOCLES

Kings will give better advice about power; you should organise your exile. For kingship I would be willing—

POLYNICES

To give fatherland, housegods, wife to the flames?

ETEOCLES

Power is well purchased at any price.[17]

---

[17] Here the play breaks off. The theme of the ruthless lust for power echoes into Renaissance drama, e.g. Shakespeare 3 *Henry VI* 1.2, "But for a kingdom any oath may be broken; / I would break a thousand oaths, to reign one year." For the thought of line 654 and *Oedipus* 703f. cf. Ben Jonson, *Sejanus* 2.2, "Whom hatred frights, / Let him not dream of sovereignty," and John Marston, *Malcontent* 5.3, "Who cannot bear with spite, he cannot rule."

MEDEA

INTRODUCTION

Background

Medea, daughter of King Aeetes, grew up in the remote kingdom of Colchis, well versed in her country's magic lore. When Jason arrived with the Argonauts in quest of the kingdom's treasure, the Golden Fleece, Medea fell in love with him. She employed her magic skills to help him accomplish the trials set by Aeetes, including the yoking of a fire-breathing bull to the plough, and to overcome the ever wakeful serpent that guarded the Fleece. To slow down her father's pursuit as she escaped with Jason and the Fleece on the *Argo*, she killed and dismembered her brother Absyrtus, and scattered his limbs on the sea.

After the *Argo* returned safely to Jason's hometown of Iolcos, Medea brought about the murder of his evil uncle Pelias by trickery. Forced as a result to flee once more, Medea and Jason settled in Corinth and had two sons. But now they are under threat from the army of Acastus, Pelias' son, who seeks to avenge his father. Jason has undertaken, in the interests of securing royal protection, to marry Creusa, daughter of the king of Corinth, Creon. But Medea regards this as an act of betrayal, and is enraged by it.

MEDEA

Summary

Act 1
Alone, Medea invokes many gods, including those of marriage and of the underworld. She expresses fantasies of revenge against Creusa, Creon, and Jason.

Ode 1. In a hymn celebrating Jason's marriage to Creusa, the chorus invokes the gods of marriage and praises the beauty of bride and groom.

Act 2
Stunned by the reality of the marriage, Medea exculpates Jason in her mind and puts all the blame on Creon. Creon enters to enforce her immediate banishment from Corinth. Medea pleads her case as one who saved the Argonauts' lives. Creon finally grants her a stay of exile for the remainder of the day.

Ode 2. The theme is the disruption of the primal age of innocence and stability by the first sailors, particularly the Argonauts. The Argonauts unleashed against themselves the dangers of the sea, and the dangerous Medea. A coda speaks of the seas as now fully open to travel, and destined to reveal lands as yet unknown.

Act 3
Approached by Jason, Medea bitterly recounts all she has done for him. Jason argues that the new marriage provides protection, particularly for their sons, against Acastus. Finally accepting that he is lost to her, Medea pretends acquiescence, but as soon as he leaves she begins preparations for revenge against Creusa.

Ode 3. The violence of a wronged wife exceeds that of

nature's destructive forces. The deaths of individual Argonauts represent the sea's revenge for their violation of its
domain. The chorus prays for the safety of Jason, who is
endangered on both counts.

Act 4
Medea gathers poisons from far and wide by her magic,
and invokes Hecate to ensure their efficacy. Precious
clothes are imbued with the seeds of fire, and sent to
Creusa as a pretended wedding present.

Ode 4. The chorus expresses fear over the threat posed
by Medea's continued presence.

Act 5
A messenger tersely reports the destruction of Creusa,
Creon, and the royal palace by fire emanating from
Medea's gifts. Medea, after an intense self-debate, kills
one of her sons. As Jason approaches with followers, she
climbs to the roof of the house. There she achieves her
fullest revenge by killing the other son in Jason's sight. She
departs through the air in a chariot drawn by dragons.

Comment

Seneca's play embodies a gradual development in Medea's plans for vengeance. Her visions of revenge in Act 1
have more to do with fantasy than reality. But then three
blows fall: the marriage hymn brings home the reality of
Jason's new marriage; she is faced with imminent exile; and
she realises finally, towards the end of Act 3, that Jason is
lost to her. Hence by the end of Act 3 she is initiating practical preparations to destroy Creusa. The intention of killing her own children develops at a less conscious level. She

notes in Act 3 the general possibility of wounding Jason through the children,[1] but she sets it aside while preparing the attack on Creusa. Only in Act 5, when assured of the destruction of Creusa and Creon, does she think again about Jason and the children; the possibility of infanticide, which has formed at some level below consciousness, now emerges into her conscious mind, and she reacts to it first with horror.

Within this portrayal of gradually developing revenge there are more gradations and variations than might appear on first reading. That Medea feels some residual love for Jason, as well as anger, is clear from her desperate attempt to find excuses for him at the beginning of Act 2. In Acts 2 and 3 there is some truth, and so pathos, in her pleas that she gave up everything for Jason, that she saved the lives of the Argonauts, and that Jason at least, if no one else, should exculpate her for the crimes she did earlier for his sake. Irony, scorn, honesty, dissembling are present at various moments in these confrontations with Creon and Jason. Act 4 show her confidence and pride in her "barbarian" skills as a witch. At the end what drives her to infanticide is not only desire for revenge, but the combination of that desire with guilt over the earlier murder of her brother (lines 958–71). An actress playing this role, then, would need to portray much more than the vehement anger which is its leading characteristic.

---

[1] Lines 549–50; this possibility could be realised in various ways, e.g. by abducting the children. Medea's earlier words, "My revenge is born, already born" (line 25), clearly mean in context that the *character* of the children, if they take after their parents, will be a kind of revenge—though the audience will hear a foreshadowing of the infanticide.

Relationships to nature are important in this play. The Argonauts are portrayed in Ode 2 as initiating a process of technological control over nature. But Medea by birth has a more participatory relationship to nature, as granddaughter of the Sun and child of a people skilled in witchcraft, i.e. in arcane knowledge of potent plants and in an ability to share in nature's powers. Admittedly such activity itself represents a kind of control of nature, but one used for temporary and immediate needs, not for mercantile or geopolitical domination. Medea has laid aside these "barbarian" skills while part of the civilised order of a Greek city, but once excluded from that polity, she reverts to her old capabilities. Her alignment with nature deepens as the play advances. Ode 3 associates her vengefulness with the revenge of the sea on the trespassing Argonauts, many of whom died by the natural forces of fire and water. It is traditional to use imagery of fire and flood to convey the power of anger and love, as is done at the beginning of Ode 3. But as the ode develops and is followed by Act 4, the association grows stronger than that of imagery alone.

Though Medea defines her self-debate in Act 5 as between "mother" and "wife," the infanticide wipes out both aspects of her relationship to Jason; indeed, it wipes out the entire relationship, so that she feels momentarily as if she were the young Colchian princess once again (982–83). But she is actually the mature Medea. What she achieves, what she has been working towards throughout the play, is an autonomous selfhood, untramelled, able to impose itself on others. She realises herself fully, achieves a personal power far beyond that of any other figure in the play, and magnified by her association with the power of moon and earth, fire and sea. "Now I am Medea; my genius has grown through evils" (910). At one level, this line plays on her name: "I am the woman who thinks, who has cunning intelligence," in allusion to the roots mēd- and mēt-.[2] At another level it has a metadramatic quality: "I am that Medea famed for doing these deeds, that Medea whose story will be read millennia later." But its primary suggestion is, "I have reached the fulness of my selfhood, the potential that was always within me."

Responses to this triumph will be as varied as its audiences. A didactic reading seems unpersuasive: one does not discourage an audience from anger by showing its success, nor by suggesting that the forces of nature contribute to it. Of course we know that ordinary human beings must not behave as Medea does (a knowledge that constitutes one of the discontents of civilisation)—that raging anger and violence are abhorrent in any functional society, that infanticide destroys the mother almost as surely as her children. Perhaps we also perceive, at least in retrospect, that this Medea is torn between conflicting passions (rage, love, hate, motherly affection, guilt) and between conflicting identities (wife, mother, Colchian, criminal) which preclude any possibility of real selfhood. But to focus on such moral reservations *during* the play would be to resist the imaginative, vicarious, symbolic experience it offers: the experience of the amoral fulfilment gained by demonstrating one's personal power over enemies who would deny it. Medea is like other intransigent heroes of myth such as Ajax, who, when denied the arms of Achilles which he considered his right, planned to slaughter the

---

[2] Such etymological play on the name Medea is found also at Pindar, *Pythian Ode* 4.27, and at Euripides, *Medea* 402.

whole Greek leadership. This intransigence can have such strength that it becomes a kind of greatness. These solitary heroes have power that reaches far beyond their own existence, whether from the grave as with Ajax, or from the stage and the printed page as with Medea.

Sources

Seneca will have been thoroughly familiar with the Medea myth, and with at least some of the many dramatic and literary treatments of it in both Greek and Latin, of which only a few survive. No doubt he composed independently, making use of this treasury of material as appropriate, rather than following the armature of any particular version. It is unlikely that he worked directly from Euripides, whose drama characteristically scales down Medea's heroic stature to something more like ordinary human identity. Apollonius of Rhodes had described the young Medea's infatuation with Jason in his *Argonautica*; that love story coloured Vergil's account of Dido's obsessive passion in *Aeneid* 4, which in turn coloured Seneca's portrait of the mature Medea, though Seneca also knew Apollonius' epic directly. Seneca's beloved Ovid had recounted Medea's story, particularly the episodes in Colchis and Iolcos, in Book 7 of the *Metamorphoses*, and had voiced Medea's reproaches to the unfaithful Jason in *Heroides* 12. Each of these versions influences many turns of phrase and thought in Seneca's drama, and we would surely find the same to be true of Ovid's drama *Medea*, if it had survived. Odes 2 and 3 of Seneca's play allude frequently to Horace's *Odes*, and particularly to ode 3 of Book 1, whose theme is similarly the transgressive nature of human seafaring.

MEDEA

Setting

Beyond the fact that the play unfolds in Corinth, the dramatic setting is fluid and indefinite, as often in Seneca. After Act 1, whose setting is indeterminate, the events of lines 56–669 clearly occur in public space, which however is given only fleeting definition and redefinition.[3] In Act 4 the setting is gradually redefined, by Medea's conducting of her ritual, as a more private space within or behind her house; the altar mentioned there would be represented by the stage altar in a theatrical production. Only at the end of the play does location become more specific and integral to the action, when Medea leaves the stage and climbs to the roof of her house.

BIBLIOGRAPHY

Commentaries

C. D. N. Costa, *Seneca. Medea, Edited with Introduction and Commentary* (Oxford, 1973).

H. M. Hine, *Seneca, Medea, with an Introduction, Text, Translation and Commentary* (Warminster, 2000).

---

3 Lines 177 and 380 mention Creon's palace and Medea's house respectively. These two lines are primarily entrance announcements, which also characterize the persons entering (Creon as peremptory, Medea as impetuous). They should probably not be amplified into anything as definite as a two-door set with Creon's palace adjacent to Medea's house. Indeed at the beginning of Act 5 it appears that Creon's palace is some distance away.

SENECA

Criticism

H. Fyfe, "An Analysis of Seneca's Medea," in Boyle (1983), 77–93.

C. Gill, "Two Monologues of Self-Division: Euripides, *Medea* 1021–80 and Seneca, *Medea* 893–977," in P. Hardie, M. Whitby, edd., *Homo Viator: Classical Essays for J. Bramble* (Bristol, 1987), 25–37.

J. Henderson, "Poetic Technique and Rhetorical Amplification: Seneca *Medea* 579–669," in Boyle (1983), 94–113.

D. and E. Henry, "Loss of Identity: "Medea superest"? A Study of Seneca's *Medea*," *C Phil.* 62 (1967), 169–181.

J. L. Sanderson, E. Zimmerman, edd., *Medea: Myth and Dramatic Form. Five plays by Euripides, Seneca, Jean Anouilh, Robinson Jeffers, Maxwell Anderson* (Boston, 1967).

J.-A. Shelton, "Seneca's *Medea* as Mannerist Literature," *Poetica* 11 (1979), 38–82.

DRAMATIS PERSONAE

MEDEA, *daughter of Aeetes king of Colchis, and wife of Jason*

NURSE *of Medea*

CREON, *king of Corinth*

JASON, *from Iolcos in Thessaly, onetime leader of the Argonautic expedition to Colchis in quest of the Golden Fleece*

TWO SONS *of Medea and Jason (personae mutae)*

MESSENGER

CHORUS OF CORINTHIANS, *sympathetic to Jason and hostile to Medea*

Scene

The play takes place in Corinth (see Introduction).

MEDEA

Di coniugales, tuque genialis tori,
Lucina, custos, quaeque domituram freta
Tiphyn novam frenare docuisti ratem,
et tu, profundi saeve dominator maris,
5   clarumque Titan dividens orbi diem,
tacitisque praebens conscium sacris iubar
Hecate triformis—quosque iuravit mihi
deos Iason, quosque Medeae magis
fas est precari: noctis aeternae chaos,
10   aversa superis regna manesque impios
dominumque regni tristis et dominam fide
meliore raptam, voce non fausta precor.
nunc, nunc adeste, sceleris ultrices deae,
crinem solutis squalidae serpentibus,
15   atram cruentis manibus amplexae facem;
adeste, thalamis horridae quondam meis
quales stetistis: coniugi letum novae
letumque socero et regiae stirpi date.
    Mihi peius aliquid, quod precer sponso, manet:

19 manet *Leo*: malum *EA*

---

1 The teacher was Pallas Athena, the ship the *Argo*.

344

MEDEA

ACT 1

MEDEA

Gods of marriage! And you, Lucina, keeper of the marriage bed; and you who taught Tiphys to bridle the novel ship that would tame the seas;[1] and you, ferocious tamer of the deep sea;[2] and Titan, apportioning bright daylight to the world; and three-formed Hecate, granting your witnessing beams to silent rituals! Gods by whom Jason swore oaths to me, and those to whom Medea more rightly directs her prayers: chaos of eternal night, realms faced away from life above, unholy spirits of the dead, lord of the gloomy realm, and lady[3] stolen like me but shown better loyalty: I pray to you with words not of good omen. Be present now, you goddesses who avenge crime,[4] your hair bristling with loosened snakes, your bloody hands grasping a black torch; be present, as once you stood unkempt and fearful around my marriage chamber. Bring death on this new wife, death on the father-in-law and the whole royal stock.

For the bridegroom I have a worse prayer in store: may

2 Neptune.
3 Dis and Proserpine.
4 The Furies.

20   vivat. per urbes erret ignotas egens
       exul pavens invisus incerti laris;

23a,22b iam notus hospes limen alienum expetat;

22a,23b me coniugem optet, quoque non aliud queam
       peius precari, liberos similes patri

25   similesque matri. parta iam, parta ultio est:
       peperi.

              Querelas verbaque in cassum sero?
       non ibo in hostes? manibus excutiam faces
       caeloque lucem! spectat hoc nostri sator
       Sol generis, et spectatur, et curru insidens

30   per solita puri spatia decurrit poli?
       non redit in ortus et remetitur diem?
       da, da per auras curribus patriis vehi,
       committe habenas, genitor, et flagrantibus
       ignifera loris tribue moderari iuga:

35   gemino Corinthos litori opponens moras
       cremata flammis maria committat duo.

       Hoc restat unum, pronubam thalamo feram
       ut ipsa pinum, postque sacrificas preces
       caedam dicatis victimas altaribus.

40   per viscera ipsa quaere supplicio viam,
       si vivis, anime, si quid antiqui tibi
       remanet vigoris. pelle femineos metus,
       et inhospitalem Caucasum mente indue.
       quodcumque vidit Phasis aut Pontus nefas,

45   videbit Isthmos. effera ignota horrida,
       tremenda caelo pariter ac terris mala
       mens intus agitat: vulnera et caedem et vagum

---

     5 Hilaire-Bernard de Longepierre adapts these lines into a
chant-like prayer (*Médée* 2.1): "Ou plutôt donne-moi tes chevaux

he live. May he wander through unknown cities in want, in exile, in fear, hated and homeless; may he seek out men's doors, by this time a notorious guest; may he long for me as his wife, and—I can make no worse prayer—for children resembling their father and resembling their mother. My revenge is born, already born: I have given birth.

Am I stringing together futile words and complaints? Shall I not attack my enemies? I shall dash the bridal torches from their hands, and the light from heaven. Does the Sun, the sower of my family's seed, behold this? And is he beheld? Does he sit in his chariot and race along his usual course through an unclouded sky? Not return to the East and re-traverse the day? Grant me to ride through the air in my ancestral chariot, entrust me with the reins, father, and allow me to guide the fiery steeds with blazing traces: Corinth, which blocks a pair of gulfs, must be consumed by flames and let the two seas converge.[5]

This alone remains, that I carry the bridesmaid's torch myself into the chamber, and after sacrificial prayers slaughter the victims on a consecrated altar. Through the very guts find a path to punishment, my spirit, if you are alive, if there is any of your old energy left. Drive out womanish fears, and plant the forbidding Caucasus in your mind. Every outrage that Phasis or Pontus saw, the Isthmus will see. Savage, unheard-of, horrible things, evils fearful to heaven and earth alike, my mind stirs up within me: wounds and slaughter and death creeping from limb

à conduire, / En poudre dans ces lieux je saurais tout réduire; / Je tomberai sur l'Isthme avec ton char brûlant, / J'abymerai Corinthe et son peuple insolent, / J'écraserai ses rois, et ma fureur barbare / Unira les deux mers que Corinthe sépare."

funus per artus. levia memoravi nimis;
haec virgo feci. gravior exsurgat dolor:
50   maiora iam me scelera post partus decent.
accingere ira, teque in exitium para
furore toto. paria narrentur tua
repudia thalamis. quo virum linquis modo?
hoc quo secuta es. rumpe iam segnes moras:
55   quae scelere parta est, scelere linquenda est domus.

CHORUS

Ad regum thalamos numine prospero
qui caelum superi quique regunt fretum
adsint cum populis rite faventibus.
Primum sceptriferis colla Tonantibus
60   taurus celsa ferat tergore candido;
Lucinam nivei femina corporis
intemptata iugo placet; et asperi
Martis sanguineas quae cohibet manus,
quae dat belligeris foedera gentibus
65   et cornu retinet divite copiam,
donetur tenera mitior hostia.
Et tu, qui facibus legitimis ades,
noctem discutiens auspice dextera,
huc incede gradu marcidus ebrio,
70   praecingens roseo tempora vinculo.
Et tu, quae, gemini praevia temporis,
tarde, stella, redis semper amantibus:
te matres, avide te cupiunt nurus
quamprimum radios spargere lucidos.

---

[6] Pax or Peace.   [7] Hymen, god of marriage.

[8] Lucifer, heralding dawn, and Hesperus, heralding night too
slowly for lovers, were sometimes regarded as the same star in antiquity, cf. *Pha* 749–52, *Ag* 819–21.

to limb. But these things I talk of are too slight; I did all this as a girl. My bitterness must grow more weighty: greater crimes become me now, after giving birth. Arm yourself in anger, prepare to wreak destruction with full rage. Let the story they tell of your divorce match that of your marriage. How should you leave your husband? Just as you followed him. Now break off sluggish delays; in crime you gained your home, in crime you must leave it.

CHORUS

At this royal wedding in divine support
may the gods who rule heaven on high and rule the sea
be present, along with the people in due favouring
   silence.
First to the sceptred Thunderers
a white-backed bull must offer his high-raised neck.
Lucina must be appeased by a female of snowwhite
   body,
untried by the yoke; and she who restrains
the bloodstained hands of savage Mars,
grants treaties to warring nations
and stores abundance in her rich horn,[6]
must be given a tender sacrifice, as one more gentle.
And you who attend the torches of lawful unions,
dispelling darkness with a propitious hand,[7]
approach with your languid, drunken steps,
wreathing your brows in a rose garland.
And you, star that herald both halves of the day,
and ever return too slowly for lovers:[8]
matrons desire you, young women ardently desire you
to scatter your bright beams with all speed.

75   Vincit virgineus decor
    longe Cecropias nurus,
    et quas Taygeti iugis
    exercet iuvenum modo
    muris quod caret oppidum,
80   et quas Aonius latex
    Alpheosque sacer lavat.
    Si forma velit aspici,
    cedent Aesonio duci
    proles fulminis improbi
85   aptat qui iuga tigribus,
    nec non, qui tripodas movet,
    frater virginis asperae,
    cedet Castore cum suo
    Pollux caestibus aptior.
90   Sic, sic, caelicolae, precor,
    vincat femina coniuges,
    vir longe superet viros.
  Haec cum femineo constitit in choro,
  unius facies praenitet omnibus.
95 sic cum sole perit sidereus decor,
  et densi latitant Pleiadum greges,
  cum Phoebe solidum lumine non suo
  orbem circuitis cornibus alligat.
  ‹sponso si cupido conspicitur, pudor
  perfundit teneros purpureus genas.›

98 *lacuna after* 98 *identified by Leo; supplement by Fitch,
adapted from that of Leo*

The maiden's beauty far
outdoes Cecropian brides,
and those from the unwalled town[9]
who are exercised like young men
on Taygetus' mountainsides,
and those the Aonian stream
and holy Alpheus bathes.
  Should he wish to be judged for looks,
the Aesonian hero will surpass
the child of the ruthless lightning
who harnesses tigers to his chariot,
and the one that shakes the tripods,
brother of the fierce virgin;[10]
surpass Castor and his twin
Pollux, the abler boxer.
  Just so, I pray the heavens,
as a woman may she outdo wives,
as a man may he far surpass husbands.

When she takes her place in a women's dance,
her face alone outshines them all.
So the stars' beauty fails before the sun,
and the clustered Pleiads are hidden
when Phoebe in borrowed light
clasps her full orb with encircling horns.
‹If she is beheld by her eager bridegroom, a blush
of modesty suffuses her soft cheeks.›

---

[9] Sparta.
[10] The lightning's child is Bacchus; the tripod-shaker is Phoebus Apollo, brother of Phoebe/Diana.

351

ostro sic niveus puniceo color
100 perfusus rubuit, sic nitidum iubar
pastor luce nova roscidus aspicit.
    Ereptus thalamis Phasidis horridi,
effrenae solitus pectora coniugis
invita trepidus prendere dextera,
105 felix Aeoliam corripe virginem,
nunc primum soceris sponse volentibus.
    Concesso, iuvenes, ludite iurgio,
hinc illinc, iuvenes, mittite carmina:
rara est in dominos iusta licentia.

110 Candida thyrsigeri proles generosa Lyaei,
multifidam iam tempus erat succendere pinum;
excute sollemnem digitis marcentibus ignem.
festa dicax fundat convicia fescenninus,
solvat turba iocos. tacitis eat illa tenebris,
115 si qua peregrino nubit fugitiva marito.

MEDEA
Occidimus: aures pepulit hymenaeus meas.
vix ipsa tantum, vix adhuc credo malum.
hoc facere Iason potuit, erepto patre
patria atque regno sedibus solam exteris

---

11 Lyaeus = Bacchus, whose "fair and noble" son is Hymen.

Such is the blush of snowwhite colour suffused
by scarlet dye; so the bright dawn rays
are viewed at first light by a shepherd amidst the dew.

 Rescued from a marriage bed of daunting Phasis,
inured to fondling the breast of an untamed wife
in fear, with reluctant hands,
seize the Aeolian maid with good fortune, for the first
  time now
a bridegroom with consent from your parents-in-law.

 Indulge, young men, in tolerated insults,
to and fro, young men, toss answering verses:
rarely is license sanctioned against our masters.

Fair and noble child of Lyaeus the thyrsus-bearer,[11]
now is the time to kindle the torch of fine-split
  pinewood;
swing out the ceremonial fire in your languid fingers.
Let the sharp-tongued Fescennine verses pour their
  festive abuse,
let the crowd give rein to jokes; and let any runaway girl
who weds with a foreign husband pass in silent darkness.

ACT 2

MEDEA

I am finished: the wedding hymn has struck my ears. I can
scarcely believe it myself, still scarcely believe such disaster. Could Jason have done this? After robbing me of my
father, my fatherland, my kingdom, could he callously

120 deserere durus? merita contempsit mea
qui scelere flammas viderat vinci et mare?
adeone credit omne consumptum nefas?
incerta vecors mente non sana feror
partes in omnes. unde me ulcisci queam?
125 utinam esset illi frater! est coniunx: in hanc
ferrum exigatur. hoc meis satis est malis?
si quod Pelasgae, si quod urbes barbarae
novere facinus quod tuae ignorent manus,
nunc est parandum. scelera te hortentur tua
130 et cuncta redeant: inclitum regni decus
raptum et nefandae virginis parvus comes
divisus ense, funus ingestum patri
sparsumque ponto corpus et Peliae senis
decocta aëno membra. funestum impie
135 quam saepe fudi sanguinem—et nullum scelus
irata feci: saevit infelix amor.

    Quid tamen Iason potuit, alieni arbitrî
iurisque factus? debuit ferro obvium
offerre pectus—melius, a melius, dolor
140 furiose, loquere. si potest, vivat meus,
ut fuit, Iason; si minus, vivat tamen,
memorque nostri muneri parcat meo.
Culpa est Creontis tota, qui sceptro impotens
coniugia solvit, quique genetricem abstrahit
145 natis, et arto pignore astrictam fidem
dirimit: petatur, solus hic poenas luat,
quas debet. alto cinere cumulabo domum;
videbit atrum verticem flammis agi
Malea longas navibus flectens moras.

---

12 Whom she could kill as she killed her own brother.

abandon me by myself in a foreign country? Did he hold my services cheap, though he had seen fire and sea over-powered by my crime? Is he so confident that my evil is completely used up? Perplexed and frenzied and mad-dened I turn one way and another. Where could I find re-venge? If only *he* had a brother![12] He has a wife: let the sword be thrust into her. Is this sufficient for my wrongs? If Pelasgian or barbarian cities have discovered some deed that your hands do *not* know, you must prepare to do it now. Your own crimes must urge you on, every one of them must return: the famous ornament of my kingdom stolen, the criminal girl's little companion cut apart with the sword,[13] his death thrust in his father's face, his body scat-tered on the sea, and the limbs of old Pelias boiled in a cauldron. How often have I spilled blood fatally—kindred blood! And yet I did no crime from anger; the cruelty came from my unhappy love.

Yet what could Jason do, as subject to another's power and authority? He should have offered his breast to the sword! No, don't say that, raging voice of my pain. If he can, may he live as he was, as my Jason; if not, may he still live, may he remember me and be gentle with the gift I gave him.[14] The blame is entirely Creon's: in the tyranny of power he breaks up marriages, drags a mother away from her children, and severs a loyalty bound by firm pledges. He must be my target, he alone must be punished, as he deserves. I shall bury his home deep in ashes; the black plume raised by the flames will be seen at Malea, the turn-ing point in ships' long detours.

---

[13] The references are to the Golden Fleece and her brother Absyrtus: see "Background" in Introduction.   [14] His life.

NUTRIX

150 Sile, obsecro, questusque secreto abditos
   manda dolori. gravia quisquis vulnera
   patiente et aequo mutus animo pertulit,
   referre potuit; ira quae tegitur nocet;
   professa perdunt odia vindictae locum.

MEDEA

155 Levis est dolor qui capere consilium potest
   et clepere sese; magna non latitant mala.
   libet ire contra.

NUTRIX

   Siste furialem impetum,
   alumna; vix te tacita defendit quies.

MEDEA

Fortuna fortes metuit, ignavos premit.

NUTRIX

160 Tunc est probanda, si locum virtus habet.

MEDEA

Numquam potest non esse virtuti locus.

NUTRIX

Spes nulla rebus monstrat afflictis viam.

MEDEA

Qui nil potest sperare, desperet nihil.

NUTRIX

Abiere Colchi, coniugis nulla est fides,
165 nihilque superest opibus e tantis tibi.

MEDEA

Medea superest: hic mare et terras vides
ferrumque et ignes et deos et fulmina.

NURSE

Be silent, I beg you, hide your grievances, lock them away in secret resentment. One who endures deep wounds mutely, with cool patience, can repay them; anger concealed wreaks havoc; hatred declared loses its chance for revenge.

MEDEA

The pain is slight that can deliberate and dissemble; great sufferings do not skulk in hiding. I want to attack head-on!

NURSE

Control your impulsive rage, my child; even silence and stillness can hardly protect you.

MEDEA

Fortune fears the brave, but crushes cowards.

NURSE

Courage is praiseworthy when it is in place.

MEDEA

It can never happen that courage is out of place.

NURSE

No hope points a way for your battered fortunes.

MEDEA

One who can feel no hope need feel no despair.

NURSE

Colchis is lost, there is no loyalty in your husband, and nothing remains of your great wealth.

MEDEA

Medea remains: *here* you see sea and land, steel and fire, gods and thunderbolts.

NUTRIX

Rex est timendus.

MEDEA

Rex meus fuerat pater.

NUTRIX

Non metuis arma?

MEDEA

Sint licet terra edita.

NUTRIX

170 Moriere.

MEDEA

Cupio.

NUTRIX

Profuge.

MEDEA

Paenituit fugae.

NUTRIX

Medea—

MEDEA

Fiam.

NUTRIX

Mater es.

MEDEA

Cui sim vides.

NURSE

A king must be feared.

MEDEA

My father was a king.

NURSE

You do not fear arms?

MEDEA

Not even if sprung from the earth.[15]

NURSE

You will die.

MEDEA

I desire it.

NURSE

Escape!

MEDEA

I regret escaping.

NURSE

Medea—

MEDEA

I shall become her.

NURSE

You are a mother.

MEDEA

You see by whom.

[15] Like the armed soldiers that sprang from the dragon's teeth sown by Jason in Colchis.

NUTRIX

Profugere dubitas?

MEDEA

Fugiam, et ulciscar prius.

NUTRIX

Vindex sequetur.

MEDEA

Forsan inveniam moras.

NUTRIX

Compesce verba, parce iam, demens, minis
175 animosque minue; tempori aptari decet.

MEDEA

Fortuna opes auferre, non animum potest.
Sed cuius ictu regius cardo strepit?
ipse est Pelasgo tumidus imperio Creo.

CREO

Medea, Colchi noxium Aeetae genus,
180 nondum meis exportat e regnis pedem?
molitur aliquid: nota fraus, nota est manus.
cui parcet illa quemve securum sinet?
abolere propere pessimam ferro luem
equidem parabam: precibus evicit gener.
185 concessa vita est, liberet fines metu
abeatque tuta. Fert gradum contra ferox
minaxque nostros propius affatus petit.
arcete, famuli, tactu et accessu procul,
iubete sileat. regium imperium pati

---

172 et *A*: sed *E*: at *Ascensius*

MEDEA

NURSE

You hesitate to escape?

MEDEA

I shall escape, *and* take vengeance first.

NURSE

Retaliation will come after you.

MEDEA

Perhaps I shall find delays.[16]

NURSE

Control your words, give up your threats now, crazy woman, subdue your proud spirit; it is right to adapt to circumstances.

MEDEA

Fortune can take away my wealth, but not my spirit. But who pounds the palace doors, creaking on their hinges? It is himself, swollen with Pelasgian power: Creon.

CREON

Medea, that noxious child of Colchian Aeetes—is she not yet withdrawing from my realm? She is contriving something: her cunning is well known, so is her handiwork. Whom will she spare, whom will she leave untroubled? For my part I was planning to eliminate this evil infection quickly with the sword, but my son-in-law's prayers prevailed. She has been granted life: let her free the land of fear and depart in safety.

She advances fiercely against me, and with a threatening air seeks closer speech. Keep her away, servants, well away from contact or access; bid her be silent. She must

16 As she delayed her father's pursuit.

190 aliquando discat. Vade veloci via
monstrumque saevum horribile iamdudum avehe!

MEDEA

Quod crimen aut quae culpa multatur fuga?

CREO

Quae causa pellat, innocens mulier rogat.

MEDEA

Si iudicas, cognosce; si regnas, iube.

CREO

195 Aequum atque iniquum regis imperium feras.

MEDEA

Iniqua numquam regna perpetuo manent.

CREO

I, querere Colchis.

MEDEA

Redeo: qui avexit, ferat.

CREO

Vox constituto sera decreto venit.

MEDEA

Qui statuit aliquid parte inaudita altera,
200 aequum licet statuerit, haud aequus fuit.

CREO

Auditus a te Pelia supplicium tulit?
sed fare, causae detur egregiae locus.

finally learn to endure a king's authority. [*To Medea*] Depart with haste, and remove at long last a savage and fearful horror!

MEDEA
What crime, what guilt is being punished by exile?

CREON
An innocent woman asks the cause of her expulsion.

MEDEA
If you are acting as judge, investigate the case; if as king, give orders.

CREON
You must endure a king's command, just or unjust.

MEDEA
Unjust kingship never remains unbroken.

CREON
Go and complain to the Colchians.

MEDEA
I am going, but he who brought me away should take me back.

CREON
Your words come too late, my decree is decided.

MEDEA
He who decides an issue without hearing one side has not been just, however just the decision.

CREON
Was Pelias given a hearing by you before being punished? But speak on, let us give your excellent case a chance.

MEDEA

Difficile quam sit animum ab ira flectere
iam concitatum, quamque regale hoc putet,
205 sceptris superbas quisquis admovit manus,
qua coepit ire, regia didici mea.
quamvis enim sim clade miseranda obruta,
expulsa supplex sola deserta, undique
afflicta, quondam nobili fulsi patre,
210 avoque clarum Sole deduxi genus.
quodcumque placidis flexibus Phasis rigat,
Pontusque quidquid Scythicus a tergo videt,
palustribus qua maria dulcescunt aquis,
armata peltis quidquid exterret cohors
215 inclusa ripis vidua Thermodontiis,
hoc omne noster genitor imperio regit.
generosa, felix, decore regali potens
fulsi: petebant tunc meos thalamos proci,
qui nunc petuntur. rapida Fortuna ac levis
220 praecepsque regno eripuit, exilio dedit.
      Confide regnis, cum levis magnas opes
huc ferat et illuc casus! hoc reges habent
magnificum et ingens, nulla quod rapiat dies:
prodesse miseris, supplices fido lare
225 protegere. solum hoc Colchico regno extuli,
decus illud ingens Graeciae et florem inclitum,
praesidia Achivae gentis et prolem deum,
servasse memet. munus est Orpheus meum,
qui saxa cantu mulcet et silvas trahit,
230 geminumque munus Castor et Pollux meum est,
satique Borea, quique trans Pontum quoque
summota Lynceus lumine immisso videt,
omnesque Minyae: nam ducum taceo ducem,

364

MEDEA

How difficult it is to turn a mind from anger once it is aroused, and how kingly it appears, to one who has laid his proud hands on the sceptre, to continue a course once begun, I learned in my own royal home. For though I am overwhelmed by pitiable disaster, exiled, a suppliant, alone, abandoned, afflicted on every side, yet once I shone in my noble father's light, and traced my bright ancestry from the Sun my grandfather. All that the Phasis waters with its gentle meanders, all that Scythian Pontus sees on its far side, where the sea is freshened by the waters of the marshes, all that is threatened by the unwed fighters with crescent shields, whose bound is the Thermodon River— all this my father rules as his domain. Highborn, happy, I shone in royal power and splendour. Then suitors pursued me for marriage, men I now pursue. Fortune, so swift and fickle and precipitate, snatched me from my kingdom, and delivered me to exile.

So feel confident in your kingship, while fickle chance carries great wealth this way and that! This is the immense and magnificent asset of kings, which no day can steal from them: to help the wretched, to give suppliants protection under a safe roof. The only thing I brought away from my kingdom in Colchis was this, that the great and the glorious flower of Greece, bulwark of the Achaeans, offspring of gods, was saved by me. My gift is Orpheus, who charms rocks and draws forests with his song; my twin gift is Castor and Pollux; so too the seed of Boreas, and Lynceus who by focussing his gaze sees things even far across the Pontus, and all the Minyans. You see I say nothing of the leaders'

pro quo nihil debetur; hunc nulli imputo;
235 vobis revexi ceteros, unum mihi.
    Incesse nunc et cuncta flagitia ingere:
fatebor. obici crimen hoc solum potest,
Argo reversa. virgini placeat pudor
paterque placeat: tota cum ducibus ruet
240 Pelasga tellus, hic tuus primum gener
tauri ferocis ore flagranti occidet.
[fortuna causam quae volet nostram premat,
non paenitet servasse tot regum decus.]
quodcumque culpa praemium ex omni tuli,
245 hoc est penes te. si placet, damna ream;
sed redde crimen. sum nocens, fateor, Creo;
talem sciebas esse, cum genua attigi
fidemque supplex praesidis dextrae petî.
terra hac miseriis angulum et sedem rogo
250 latebrasque viles: urbe si pelli placet,
detur remotus aliquis in regnis locus.

CREO

Non esse me qui sceptra violentus geram,
nec qui superbo miserias calcem pede,
testatus equidem videor haud clare parum
255 generum exulem legendo et afflictum et gravi
terrore pavidum, quippe quem poenae expetit
letoque Acastus regna Thessalica obtinens.
senio trementem debili atque aevo gravem
patrem peremptum queritur et caesi senis
260 discissa membra, cum dolo captae tuo

242–43 *deleted by Zwierlein*
248 dextrae* *A*: dextra *E*

leader, for whom nothing is owed; for him I count no one my debtor; the rest I brought back for all of you, but him alone for myself.

Now censure me, hurl all kinds of shameful behaviour at me: I shall admit to them. But the only crime I can be charged with is the safe return of the *Argo.* Suppose the maiden should opt for modesty, opt for her father: the entire Pelasgian land will perish, following its leaders, and this son-in-law of yours will fall at the outset before the fierce bull's fiery breath.[17] But such profit as I gained by all my guilt is in your hands. If you so determine, condemn the accused—but give back her crime! I am guilty, I admit it, Creon; you knew me to be so, when I touched your knees in supplication and sought the promise of protection given by your hand. I ask for a corner where my misery can dwell in this land, a paltry hiding place. If your decision is expulsion from the city, let me be granted some remote spot in your kingdom.

CREON

That I am not a man to wield the sceptre with violence, nor to trample misery under proud feet, I think I have demonstrated with sufficient clarity, by choosing as son-in-law one exiled and afflicted and terrified by grave fears, through being sought for punishment and death by Acastus, who holds the kingship of Thessaly. His grievance is that his father, trembling in frail old age and heavy with years, was murdered, his old body cut and dismembered,

---

[17] Lines 242–43 (deleted): "Let Fortune in any form trample on my cause, yet I do not regret having saved so many famous princes."

piae sorores impium auderent nefas.
potest Iason, si tuam causam amoves,
suam tueri: nullus innocuum cruor
contaminavit, afuit ferro manus
265 proculque vestro purus a coetu stetit.
Tu, tu malorum machinatrix facinorum,
feminea cui nequitia ad audendum omnia,
robur virile est, nulla famae memoria,
egredere, purga regna, letales simul
270 tecum aufer herbas, libera cives metu,
alia sedens tellure sollicita deos.

MEDEA

Profugere cogis? redde fugienti ratem
vel redde comitem. fugere cur solam iubes?
non sola veni. bella si metuis pati,
275 utrumque regno pelle. cur sontes duos
distinguis? illi Pelia, non nobis iacet.
fugam, rapinas adice, desertum patrem
lacerumque fratrem, quidquid etiamnunc novas
docet maritus coniuges, non est meum:
280 totiens nocens sum facta, sed numquam mihi.

CREO

Iam exisse decuit. quid seris fando moras?

MEDEA

Supplex recedens illud extremum precor,
ne culpa natos matris insontes trahat.

CREO

Vade: hos paterno ut genitor excipiam sinu.

---

18 I.e. with Acastus. 19 Of the Golden Fleece.

MEDEA

when his loyal sisters dared commit a disloyal outrage,
taken in by your trickery. Jason can defend his case, if you
separate your case from it: no blood stained his innocence,
his hand did not touch the sword, and he kept himself
clean and clear of intercourse with them and you. You, you
architectress of wicked crimes, who have a woman's evil
willingness to dare anything, along with a man's strength,
and no thought of reputation: leave, cleanse my kingdom,
take your deadly herbs with you, free my citizens of fear,
and dwell in some other land while you harass the gods.

MEDEA

You force me to flee? For my flight give me back my ship,
or give back my companion. Why do you bid me flee alone?
I did not arrive alone. If you fear the prospect of war,[18] expel us both from your kingdom. Why distinguish between
two guilty parties? It is for his benefit, not mine, that Pelias
lies dead. Add running away, robbery,[19] desertion of a father, butchery of a brother, all that this husband teaches
his new wives even now: it is not mine. I incurred guilt so
often, but never for myself.

CREON

You should have gone by now. Why spin out delays by
talking?

MEDEA

As I depart, I make this last imploring prayer, that the guilt
of the mother should not drag down her innocent sons.

CREON

Go: I will shelter them in my fatherly embrace like their
own parent.

369

MEDEA

285 Per ego auspicatos regii thalami toros,
per spes futuras perque regnorum status,
Fortuna varia dubia quos agitat vice,
precor: brevem largire fugienti moram,
dum extrema natis mater infigo oscula,
290 fortasse moriens.

CREO

Fraudibus tempus petis.

MEDEA

Quae fraus timeri tempore exiguo potest?

CREO

Nullum ad nocendum tempus angustum est malis.

MEDEA

Parumne miserae temporis lacrimis negas?

CREO

Etsi repugnat precibus infixus timor,
295 unus parando dabitur exilio dies.

MEDEA

Nimis est, recidas aliquid ex isto licet;
et ipsa propero.

CREO

Capite supplicium lues,
clarum priusquam Phoebus attollat diem
nisi cedis Isthmo. Sacra me thalami vocant,
300 vocat precari festus Hymenaeo dies.

CHORUS

Audax nimium qui freta primus
rate tam fragili perfida rupit,

370

MEDEA

By the auspicious bed of this royal marriage, by your hopes for the future and by the condition of kingship, always buffeted by the vicissitudes of uncertain Fortune, I pray you: generously grant a brief stay of exile, while I plant my last kisses on my children as their mother—perhaps a dying mother.

CREON

You are seeking time for treachery.

MEDEA

What fear of treachery can there be in so brief a time?

CREON

No time is too short for the wicked to do harm.

MEDEA

You refuse a wretched woman time that is insufficient even for tears?

CREON

Even though my rooted fear opposes your prayers, a single day will be granted you to prepare for exile.

MEDEA

It is too much, you can cut it down: I too am in haste.

CREON

You will be punished by death if you do not leave the Isthmus before Phoebus raises the bright day. Now the marriage rites call me, and the day sacred to Hymenaeus calls me to prayer.

CHORUS

Daring, too daring, the man who first broke into
the treacherous seas with a boat so fragile;

371

terrasque suas post terga videns
animam levibus credidit auris,
305   dubioque secans aequora cursu
potuit tenui fidere ligno,
inter vitae mortisque vias
nimium gracili limite ducto.
    Nondum quisquam sidera norat,
310   stellisque, quibus pingitur aether,
non erat usus;
nondum pluvias Hyadas poterat
vitare ratis,
non Oleniae lumina caprae,
nec quae sequitur flectitque senex
315   Arctica tardus plaustra Bootes;
nondum Boreas, nondum Zephyrus
nomen habebant.
    Ausus Tiphys
pandere vasto carbasa ponto
320   legesque novas scribere ventis:
nunc lina sinu tendere toto,
nunc prolato pede transversos
captare notos,
nunc antemnas
medio tutas ponere malo,
325   nunc in summo religare loco,
cum iam totos
avidus nimium navita flatus
optat et alto
rubicunda tremunt sipara velo.

315 arctica* *A*: attica *E*

who, seeing his own land left behind him,
committed his life to the fickle breezes,
and cutting the seas on an unsure course
could put his trust in thin wooden planks;
slender, too slender the margin drawn
between the paths of life and death.

    Not yet were the constellations known;
there was no use
of the stars that embellish the heavens;
not yet could a boat
avoid the rainy Hyades,
nor the bright Olenian Goat,
nor the Northern Wain which the slow old man
Bootes follows and guides.
Not yet did Boreas, not yet did Zephyrus
possess a name.

    Tiphys dared
to spread his canvas on the vast waste sea
and write new laws for the winds:
now to strain the ropes with sails full-bellied,
now to advance
one sheet to catch the cross-winds;
now to set
the yards safely at mid-mast,
now to fasten them at the highest point,
when the sailor, all too greedy,
is hoping to catch the full gusts,
and above the lofty sail
the scarlet topsails tremble.

Candida nostri saecula patres
330 videre, procul fraude remota.
sua quisque piger litora tangens
patrioque senex factus in arvo,
parvo dives,
nisi quas tulerat natale solum
335 non norat opes.
bene dissaepti foedera mundi
traxit in unum Thessala pinus
iussitque pati verbera pontum
partemque metus fieri nostri
340 mare sepositum.
Dedit illa graves improba poenas
per tam longos ducta timores,
cum duo montes, claustra profundi,
hinc atque illinc subito impulsu
⟨rupe coacta⟩
velut aetherio gemerent sonitu,
345 spargeret astra
nubesque ipsas mare deprensum.
Palluit audax Tiphys et omnes
labente manu misit habenas;
Orpheus tacuit torpente lyra,
ipsaque vocem perdidit Argo.
350 Quid cum Siculi virgo Pelori,
rabidos utero succincta canes,
omnes pariter solvit hiatus?
quis non totos horruit artus

343 *lacuna after* 343 *recognised and supplement proposed by*
Fitch

Our forefathers saw bright eras
with crime and deceit far distant.
Homely, touching no shores but their own,
they grew to old age on their fathers' land,
and, rich with little,
beyond what their native soil had yielded
they knew no wealth.
The covenants of this well-separated world
were dragged together by Thessaly's pinewood boat
which bade the deep suffer lashes,[20]
and bade the sea, once alien,
become part of our fears.

That wanton boat suffered heavy punishment,
passing through such lengthy terrors,
when the two sea-stacks, barriers of the deep,
their facing ⟨cliffs driven together⟩[21]
by a sudden force,
groaned with a sound like that from heaven,
and the sea trapped between them
sprinkled the stars and the very clouds.
Daring Tiphys grew pale, and dropped
all the guide ropes from his unnerved hand;
Orpheus fell silent, his lyre dumbfounded,
and the *Argo* herself lost her voice.
What of the time when the maid of Sicilian Pelorus,
her womb girt round with rabid dogs,
opened all her gaping throats at once?
Who did not shudder in every limb

[20] The boat is the *Argo*, the lashes those of oars.
[21] Translating the supplement. The sea-stacks are the Symplegades.

375

totie[m] no latrante malo?
Quid [...] Ausonium dirae pestes
voce [...]ra mare mulcerent,
cum [...]ia resonans cithara
Thrac[io] Orpheus
solita[m ca]ntu retinere rates
Paene [co]egit Sirena sequi?
Quid fuit huius pretium cursus?
aurea pellis
maiusque mari Medea malum,
merces prima digna carina.

Nunc iam cessit pontus et omnes
patitur leges.
non Pallalia compacta manu
regum referens inclita remos
quaeritur Argo:
quaelibet altum cumba pererrat.
Terminus omnis motus, et urbes
muros terra posuere nova.
nil qua fuerat sede reliquit
pervius orbis;
Indus gelidum potat Araxen,
Albin Persae Rhenumque bibunt.
Venient annis saecula seris,
quibus Oceanus vincula rerum
laxet, et ingens pateat tellus,
Tethysque novos detegat orbes
nec sit terris ultima Thule.

355
360
365
370
375

376

at the multiple barking of a single monster?
What of the time the Ausonian sea was calmed
by the melodious voices of those dread dangers,
when with answering music from his Pierian lyre
Thracian Orpheus
almost compelled the Sirens to follow,
though they used to hold ships fast by their song?
    What was the prize gained by this voyage?
The Golden Fleece
and Medea, an evil worse than the sea,
fit merchandise for the first vessel.

These days the sea has yielded,
and endures all laws.
No need of a boat framed by Pallas,
bringing home princely rowers,
a famous *Argo*:
any little rowboat wanders over the deep.
All boundaries are removed, and cities
have established their walls in new lands.
Nothing is left where it once belonged
by a world open to access.
The Indian drinks the cold Araxes,
Persians the Albis and the Rhine.
    There will come an epoch late in time
when Ocean will loosen the bonds of the world
and the earth lie open in its vastness,
when Tethys will disclose new worlds
and Thule not be the farthest of lands.[22]

---

[22] From the sixteenth century on, these lines were sometimes
read as prophesying the discovery of the Americas by Europeans.

NUTRIX

380 Alumna, celerem quo rapis tectis pedem?
resiste et iras comprime ac retine impetum.
Incerta qualis entheos gressus tulit
cum iam recepto maenas insanit deo
Pindi nivalis vertice aut Nysae iugis,
385 talis recursat huc et huc motu effero,
furoris ore signa lymphati gerens.
flammata facies, spiritum ex alto citat,
proclamat, oculos uberi fletu rigat,
renidet; omnis specimen affectus capit.
390 haeret minatur aestuat queritur gemit.
quo pondus animi verget? ubi ponet minas?
ubi se iste fluctus franget? exundat furor.
non facile secum versat aut medium scelus:
se vincet. irae novimus veteris notas.
395 magnum aliquid instat, efferum immane impium.
vultum Furoris cerno. di fallant metum!

MEDEA

Si quaeris odio, misera, quem statuas modum,
imitare amorem. regias egone ut faces
inulta patiar? segnis hic ibit dies,
400 tanto petitus ambitu, tanto datus?
dum terra caelum media libratum feret,
nitidusque certas mundus evolvet vices,
numerusque harenis derit, et solem dies,
noctem sequentur astra, dum siccas polus
405 versabit Arctos, flumina in pontum cadent,
numquam meus cessabit in poenas furor,

MEDEA

ACT 3

NURSE

My child, where are you rushing in such haste from the house? Stop, curb your anger, control your aggression!

Like an ecstatic maenad taking erratic steps, crazed and possessed by the god, on snowy Pindus' peak or Nysa's ridges, so she keeps running here and there with wild movements, with signs of frenzied rage in her expression. Her face is blazing, she draws deep breaths, she shouts out, weeps floods of tears, beams with joy; she shows evidence of each and every emotion. She hesitates, threatens, fumes, laments, groans. Which way will the weight of her mind come down? Where will she implement her threats? Where will that wave break? Her rage is cresting. It is no simple or moderate crime she is contemplating: she will outdo herself. I know the hallmarks of her old anger. Something great is looming, savage, monstrous, unnatural. I see the face of Rage. May the gods prove my fears wrong!

MEDEA

[*To herself*] If you wonder, poor wretch, what limit to put on your hatred, copy your love. Am I to endure this royal marriage unavenged? Shall this day go by idly, after being sought and granted through such insistence? While the earth at the centre shall bear the balanced heavens, and the shining skies unroll their unerring changes, while sands are numberless, while day attends the sun and the stars attend night, while the Pole keeps the Bears circling and unsinking, and rivers fall to the sea, my rage will never

crescetque semper. quae ferarum immanitas,
quae Scylla, quae Charybdis Ausonium mare
Siculumque sorbens, quaeve anhelantem premens
410   Titana tantis Aetna fervebit minis?
non rapidus amnis, non procellosum mare
pontusve coro saevus aut vis ignium
adiuta flatu possit inhibere impetum
irasque nostras. sternam et evertam omnia.
415   Timuit Creontem ac bella Thessalici ducis?
amor timere neminem verus potest.
sed cesserit coactus et dederit manus:
adire certe et coniugem extremo alloqui
sermone potuit: hoc quoque extimuit ferox.
420   laxare certe tempus immitis fugae
genero licebat: liberis unus dies
datus est duobus. non queror tempus breve:
multum patebit. faciet hic faciet dies
quod nullus umquam taceat. invadam deos
425   et cuncta quatiam.

NUTRIX

                 Recipe turbatum malis,
era, pectus, animum mitiga.

MEDEA

                Sola est quies,
mecum ruina cuncta si video obruta;
mecum omnia abeant. trahere, cum pereas, libet.

NUTRIX

Quam multa sint timenda, si perstas, vide.
430   nemo potentes aggredi tutus potest.

slacken in seeking revenge, but grow ever greater. What savagery of wild beasts, what Scylla, what Charybdis sucking in the Ausonian and Sicilian seas, what Etna crushing the panting Titan, will blaze with such menace as mine? No whirling river, no stormy ocean, no sea enraged by northwesters, no force of fire aided by gales, could check the momentum of my anger. I shall overturn and flatten everything.

Did he fear Creon, and war with the Thessalian leader? True love is incapable of fearing anyone. But grant that he was forced to give way and surrender: certainly he could have approached his wife and comforted her in a last conversation—yet even this the fierce hero feared to do. Certainly he had scope as son-in-law to postpone the bitter moment of exile; yet for two children a single day is granted. I do not complain about the short time: it will go far. Today—today will achieve what no tomorrow will fail to speak of. I shall attack the gods, and shake the world.

NURSE

Regain control of your heart, so disturbed by troubles, my lady, calm your anger.

MEDEA

The only peace is if I see the world overwhelmed along with me in ruin. Let everything fall along with me. It is sweet to wreak havoc as you perish.

NURSE

Think how many dangers there are, if you persist. No one can attack the powerful in safety.

IASON

O dura fata semper et sortem asperam,
cum saevit et cum parcit ex aequo malam!
remedia quotiens invenit nobis deus
periculis peiora! si vellem fidem
435   praestare meritis coniugis, leto fuit
caput offerendum; si mori nollem, fide
misero carendum. non timor vicit fidem,
sed trepida pietas; quippe sequeretur necem
proles parentum. sancta si caelum incolis
440   Iustitia, numen invoco ac testor tuum:
nati patrem vicere. quin ipsam quoque,
etsi ferox est corde nec patiens iugi,
consulere natis malle quam thalamis reor.
constituit animus precibus iratam aggredi.
445   atque ecce, viso memet exiluit, furit,
fert odia prae se; totus in vultu est dolor.

MEDEA

Fugimus, Iason, fugimus. hoc non est novum,
mutare sedes; causa fugiendi nova est:
pro te solebam fugere. discedo, exeo,
450   penatibus profugere quam cogis tuis.
ad quos remittis? Phasin et Colchos petam
patriumque regnum quaeque fraternus cruor
perfudit arva? quas peti terras iubes?
quae maria monstras? Pontici fauces freti,
455   per quas revexi nobilem regum manum
adulterum secuta per Symplegadas?
parvamne Iolcon, Thessala an Tempe petam?
quascumque aperui tibi vias, clausi mihi.

MEDEA

JASON

[*To himself*] How harsh fate always is, how hard my luck, just as bad when it is lenient as when hostile! How often god finds us remedies worse than the dangers! If I wanted to keep faith with my wife as she deserves, I had to yield up my life; if I wanted not to die—poor man, I had to break faith. It was not fear that prevailed over faith, but a father's anxiety, seeing that the death of the parents would have been followed by the children. Holy Justice, if you dwell in heaven, I call your divinity to witness: the sons won out over the father. Indeed, I think even she, fierce-hearted though she is and unyielding, would place her sons' interests before her marriage. My mind is resolved to tackle the angry woman with an appeal.

And look, as she sees me she leaps up, becomes furious, shows her hatred; all her resentment is in her face.

MEDEA

I have fled before, Jason, I am fleeing now. There is nothing new in changing my dwelling place, but the reason for my flight is new: I used to flee for your sake. I depart, I leave, since you force me to forsake your hearth and home. But to whom are you returning me? Shall I make for Phasis and the Colchians, my father's kingdom, and the fields soaked in my brother's blood? What lands do you bid me head for? What seas do you point me to? The mouth of the Pontic strait, through which I brought back the famed band of princes, following an adulterer through the Symplegades? Should I head for little Iolcos, or Thessalian Tempe? Each path I opened for you, I closed for myself.

383

quo me remittis? exuli exilium imperas
460 nec das.
          Eatur. regius iussit gener:
nihil recuso. dira supplicia ingere:
merui. cruentis paelicem poenis premat
regalis ira, vinculis oneret manus,
clausamque saxo noctis aeternae obruat:
465 minora meritis patiar. ingratum caput,
revolvat animus igneos tauri halitus,
interque saevos gentis indomitae metus
armifero in arvo flammeum Aeetae pecus,
hostisque subiti tela, cum iussu meo
470 terrigena miles mutua caede occidit;
adice expetita spolia Phrixei arietis,
somnoque iussum lumina ignoto dare
insomne monstrum, traditum fratrem neci
et scelere in uno non semel factum scelus,
475 ausasque natas fraude deceptas mea
secare membra non revicturi senis.
[aliena quaerens regna, deserui mea]
per spes tuorum liberum et certum larem,
per victa monstra, per manus, pro te quibus
480 numquam peperci, perque praeteritos metus,
per caelum et undas, coniugî testes mei,
miserere, redde supplici felix vicem.
ex opibus illis, quas procul raptas Scythae
usque a perustis Indiae populis agunt,
485 quas quia referta vix domus gazas capit,
ornamus auro nemora, nil exul tuli

---

475 ausasque *Heinsius*: iussasque *EA*
477 *deleted by Zwierlein*

Where are you sending me back? You order the exile into exile, but do not provide it.

But go I must; the royal son-in-law has ordered it; I make no protest. Heap dreadful punishments on me: I have deserved them. Let the king's anger crush your mistress with bloody tortures, burden my hands with chains and bury me in a stony prison of unending night: my sufferings will be less than I deserve. Ungrateful creature! Wind your thoughts back to the fiery breath of the bull, the flame-darting beast of Aeetes encountered, amidst the savage threats of that untamed nation, on the field that bore arms, and the spears of the sudden foe, when at my bidding the earthborn soldiers fell in mutual slaughter.[23] Think too of the long-sought spoil from Phrixus' ram, of the unsleeping monster bidden to close his eyes in unfamiliar sleep, of the brother put to death (a single crime involving many acts of crime), of the daughters that dared through my trickery to dismember a father who would never revive.[24] By your hopes in your children, by your well-established house, by the monsters I overcame, by these hands which I never spared in your cause, by our bygone fears, by sky and sea, witnesses of my marriage: pity me; in your good fortune make recompense to your suppliant. Of all the wealth the Scythians bring from afar as plunder, even from India's scorched peoples—treasures which our brimful house can scarcely hold, so that we deck the trees with gold—I

[23] The dragon's teeth sown by Jason in the furrows cut by the fire-breathing bull grew into armed warriors, who (thanks to Medea) attacked each other rather than Jason.

[24] The father was Pelias. Line 477 (deleted): "Seeking another's kingdom, I abandoned my own."

nisi fratris artus: hos quoque impendi tibi.
tibi patria cessit, tibi pater frater pudor.
hac dote nupsi; redde fugienti sua.

IASON

490 Perimere cum te vellet infestus Creo,
lacrimis meis evictus exilium dedit.

MEDEA

Poenam putabam: munus, ut video, est fuga.

IASON

Dum licet abire, profuge teque hinc eripe:
gravis ira regum est semper.

MEDEA

                   Hoc suades mihi,
495 praestas Creusae: paelicem invisam amoves.

IASON

Medea amores obicit?

MEDEA

             Et caedem et dolos.

IASON

Obicere crimen quod potes tandem mihi?

MEDEA

Quodcumque feci.

IASON

          Restat hoc unum insuper,
tuis ut etiam sceleribus fiam nocens.

brought nothing into exile save my brother's limbs: these too I expended on you. My fatherland fell to you,[25] my father, my brother, my modesty. This was the dowry I married with: give the fugitive back what is hers.

JASON

When Creon in rancour wanted to destroy you, my tears prevailed on him to grant you exile.

MEDEA

I thought it was punishment, but I see exile is a gift.

JASON

While you are allowed to leave, get away, escape from here: the anger of kings is always harsh.

MEDEA

Your good advice to me is a favour to Creusa: you are removing her hated rival.

JASON

Medea accuses me of having a love interest?

MEDEA

And of murder and treachery.

JASON

In the end, what crime can you charge me with?

MEDEA

All I have done.

JASON

This is the one remaining step, that I should actually become guilty of your crimes.

---

[25] A play on two senses of *cedo*, (1) "yield place to," (2) "pass into the possession of."

MEDEA

500 Tua illa, tua sunt illa: cui prodest scelus,
is fecit. omnes coniugem infamem arguant,
solus tuere, solus insontem voca:
tibi innocens sit quisquis est pro te nocens.

IASON

Ingrata vita est cuius acceptae pudet.

MEDEA

505 Retinenda non est cuius acceptae pudet.

IASON

Quin potius ira concitum pectus doma,
placare natis.

MEDEA

Abdico eiuro abnuo.
meis Creusa liberis fratres dabit?

IASON

Regina natis exulum, afflictis potens.

MEDEA

510 Ne veniat umquam tam malus miseris dies,
qui prole foeda misceat prolem inclitam,
Phoebi nepotes Sisyphi nepotibus.

IASON

Quid, misera, meque teque in exitium trahis?
abscede, quaeso.

MEDEA

Supplicem audivit Creo.

MEDEA

They are yours, they are yours: he who gains by a crime, committed it. Though everyone condemns your wife as infamous, you alone should defend her, you alone call her guiltless; one who is guilty for your sake should be innocent in your eyes.

JASON

There is no gratitude for a life one is ashamed of receiving.

MEDEA

One need not hold onto a life one is ashamed of receiving.

JASON

Instead of this, get control of your angry heart, be friends again with our sons.

MEDEA

I disown them, forswear them, repudiate them! Shall Creusa provide brothers for my children?

JASON

A queen for the sons of exiles, a powerful person for the distressed.

MEDEA

May we wretches never see the evil day that would mix renowned offspring with base offspring, Phoebus' descendants with the descendants of Sisyphus.

JASON

Why, wretched woman, are you dragging both me and yourself into destruction? Leave, I beseech you.

MEDEA

Creon listened to my entreaty.

389

IASON

515 Quid facere possim, loquere.

MEDEA

Pro me vel scelus.

IASON

Hinc rex et illinc.

MEDEA

Est et his maior metus:
Medea. nos conflige, certemus sine,
sit pretium Iason.

IASON

Cedo defessus malis.
et ipsa casus saepe iam expertos time.

MEDEA

520 Fortuna semper omnis infra me stetit.

IASON

Acastus instat.

MEDEA

Propior est hostis Creo:
utrumque profuge. non ut in socerum manus
armes, nec ut te caede cognata inquines,
Medea cogit: innocens mecum fuge.

IASON

525 Et quis resistet, gemina si bella ingruant,
Creo atque Acastus arma si iungant sua?

MEDEA

His adice Colchos, adice et Aeeten ducem,

---

516 his *E*: hic *A*   517 conflige *Avantius*: confligere *EA*

JASON

Tell me what I can do.

MEDEA

For me? Even a crime.

JASON

A king is here, a king there.[26]

MEDEA

There is an even greater threat than these: Medea. Set us face to face, let us fight it out, and let Jason be the prize.

JASON

I give up, worn out by troubles. Even you should fear the odds of chance, which you have tested many times.

MEDEA

I have always risen above Fortune in every form.

JASON

Acastus is close by.

MEDEA

A nearer enemy is Creon: escape from both of them. Medea does not compel you to arm yourself against your father-in-law, nor to stain yourself with kindred blood. Keep your innocence, and flee with me.

JASON

And who will resist if war besets us with double strength, if Creon and Acastus join their forces?

MEDEA

Add the Colchians, add Aeetes to lead them, combine the

26 Creon and Acastus.

Scythas Pelasgis iunge: demersos dabo.

IASON

Alta extimesco sceptra.

MEDEA

Ne cupias vide.

IASON

530 Suspecta ne sint, longa colloquia amputa.

MEDEA

Nunc summe toto Iuppiter caelo tona,
intende dextram, vindices flammas para,
omnemque ruptis nubibus mundum quate!
nec deligenti tela librentur manu
535 vel me vel istum: quisquis e nobis cadet
nocens peribit; non potest in nos tuum
errare fulmen.

IASON

Sana meditari incipe
et placida fare. si quod ex soceri domo
potest fugam levare solamen, pete.

MEDEA

540 Contemnere animus regias, ut scis, opes
potest soletque. liberos tantum fugae
habere comites liceat, in quorum sinu
lacrimas profundam. te novi nati manent.

IASON

Parere precibus cupere me fateor tuis;
545 pietas vetat: namque istud ut possim pati,
non ipse memet cogat et rex et socer.

Scythians with the Pelasgians: I shall bury them.

JASON

I fear exalted sceptres.

MEDEA

Or perhaps you desire them.

JASON

Cut short this long exchange, lest it arouse suspicion.

MEDEA

Now, highest Jupiter, thunder across the whole sky! Stretch forth your right hand, make ready your avenging flames, rend the clouds and shake the whole world! And in levelling its weapons your hand need not choose between me and him: whichever of us falls, the guilty will die; against us your thunderbolt can make no error.

JASON

Start thinking sensibly, speak calmly! If anything from my father-in-law's house can comfort and lighten your exile, ask for it.

MEDEA

My mind has the power and habit, as you know, of disdaining the wealth of kings. Only allow me to have the children as companions in my exile, in whose embrace I can pour out my tears. You have the prospect of new sons.

JASON

I admit I would like to obey your appeal, but fatherly love for them forbids. Not even my king and father-in-law himself could force me to endure that. This is my reason for

haec causa vitae est, hoc perusti pectoris
curis levamen. spiritu citius queam
carere, membris, luce.

MEDEA
Sic natos amat?
550 bene est, tenetur, vulneri patuit locus.
Suprema certe liceat abeuntem loqui
mandata, liceat ultimum amplexum dare.
gratum est. et illud voce iam extrema peto,
ne, si qua noster dubius effudit dolor,
555 maneant in animo verba. melioris tibi
memoria nostri sedeat; haec irae data
oblitterentur.

IASON
Omnia ex animo expuli,
precorque et ipse, fervidam ut mentem regas
placideque tractes: miserias lenit quies.

MEDEA
560 Discessit. itane est? vadis oblitus mei
et tot meorum facinorum? excidimus tibi?
numquam excidemus. hoc age, omnes advoca
vires et artes. fructus est scelerum tibi
nullum scelus putare. vix fraudi est locus:
565 timemur. hac aggredere, qua nemo potest
quicquam timere. perge, nunc aude, incipe
quidquid potest Medea, quidquid non potest.
Tu, fida nutrix, socia maeroris mei
variique casus, misera consilia adiuva.
570 est palla nobis, munus aetheriae domus
decusque regni, pignus Aeetae datum
a Sole generis; est et auro textili

394

MEDEA

living, this is the solace for my heart, so scorched by cares. I would sooner be deprived of my breath, of my body, of the light.

MEDEA

[*Aside*] Does he love his sons so much? Good, he is caught! The place to wound him is laid bare. [*To Jason*] At least you must allow me in departing to tell them my last instructions and give my final embrace. I thank you. And now lastly I make this request, that any words poured out by my distracted pain should not stay in your mind. Let the memory of my better self remain with you, and let these words that yielded to anger be effaced.

JASON

I have banished them all from my mind. And I make my own request, that you will govern your passionate mind and behave calmly. Misery is eased by composure.

MEDEA

He has left. Is it true? You go oblivious of me, and all my deeds? Am I forgotten for you? I shall never be forgotten. To work, summon all your strengths and skills. The benefit of your crimes is that you think nothing a crime. There is scant room to deceive them: I am feared. Attack at the point where no one can fear anything. Press on! Now is the time for daring, and for undertaking all that Medea can do, and all that she *cannot* do.

You, loyal nurse, companion of my grief and my varied fortunes, must assist my unhappy plans. I have a robe, a present to my heaven-born family, the glory of our throne, given Aeetes by the Sun as an assurance of his parentage. I

---

570 aetheriae* *A*: aetherium *E*

monile fulgens, quodque gemmarum nitor
distinguit aurum, quo solent cingi comae.
575 haec nostra nati dona nubenti ferant,
sed ante diris inlita ac tincta artibus.
vocetur Hecate. sacra letifica appara:
statuantur arae, flamma iam tectis sonet.

CHORUS

Nulla vis flammae tumidive venti
580 tanta, nec teli metuenda torti,
quanta cum coniunx viduata taedis
    ardet et odit:

non ubi hibernos nebulosus imbres
Auster advexit, properatque torrens
585 Hister et iunctos vetat esse pontes
    ac vagus errat;

non ubi impellit Rhodanus profundum,
aut ubi in rivos nivibus solutis
sole iam forti medioque vere
590   tabuit Haemus.

caecus est ignis stimulatus ira
nec regi curat patiturve frenos
aut timet mortem; cupit ire in ipsos
    obvius enses.

595 Parcite, o divi, veniam precamur,
vivat ut tutus mare qui subegit.
sed furit vinci dominus profundi
    regna secunda.

have also a necklace that gleams with woven gold, and the golden thing set off with bright gems that usually encircles my hair. My sons are to bear these as my gifts to the bride—but first my dread arts must anoint and tincture them. Hecate must be invoked. Prepare the deadly rites. An altar must be set up, and flames must sound in the house.

CHORUS

No violence of flame or swelling wind,
no fearful violence of a whirling spear,
matches a wife bereft of her marriage,
    burning and hating:

not when the south wind carries the mists
and rains of winter, and the Hister rushes
in spate and forbids the joining of bridges
    and strays from its course;

not when the Rhone drives into the deep,
or when, with its snows melting into streams
under the strength of the mid-spring sun,
    Mt Haemus thaws.

Blind is the fire whipped up by anger,
careless of control, impatient of curbs,
fearless of death, longing to attack
    straight against swords.

Mercy, you gods! We pray for pardon;
he who tamed the sea, let him live in safety.
But the lord of the deep is enraged at the conquest
    of the second realm.

ausus aeternos agitare currus
600 immemor metae iuvenis paternae
quos polo sparsit furiosus ignes
    ipse recepit.

constitit nulli via nota magno:
vade qua tutum populo priori,
605 rumpe nec sacro violente sancta
    foedera mundi.

Quisquis audacis tetigit carinae
nobiles remos, nemorisque sacri
Pelion densa spoliavit umbra,
610 quisquis intravit scopulos vagantes
et tot emensus pelagi labores
barbara funem religavit ora
raptor externi rediturus auri,
exitu diro temerata ponti
615   iura piavit.

Exigit poenas mare provocatum.
Tiphys imprimis, domitor profundi,
liquit indocto regimen magistro.
litore externo, procul a paternis
620 occidens regnis tumuloque vili
tectus ignotas iacet inter umbras.
Aulis amissi memor inde regis
portibus lentis retinet carinas
    stare querentes.

---

27 Phaethon, who drove the chariot of his father the Sun.

He who dared to drive the eternal chariot,[27]
the youth who forgot his father's bounds,
after wildly showering fire through the heavens
    suffered fire himself.

The familiar path costs no one dear;
walk where people before found safety,
and do not violently break the inviolate
    pacts of the world.

All who handled the famous oars
of that daring ship and stripped Mt Pelion
of the dense shade of its sacred wood,
all who entered between the drifting crags
and after traversing such toils at sea
berthed against a barbaric coast
to return as plunderers of foreign gold,
have atoned with a dreadful death for trespass
    on the rights of the deep.

The sea exacts punishment for their challenge.
First and foremost Tiphys, tamer of the deep,
left the tiller to an untrained master.
On a foreign shore, far from his father's
realm in death, with a paltry tomb
for covering, he lies among unknown shades.
Hence Aulis, remembering its lost king,
holds vessels back in its still harbour,
    as they chafe at idleness.

625　Ille vocali genitus Camena,
　　　cuius ad chordas modulante plectro
　　　restitit torrens, siluere venti,
　　　cui suo cantu volucris relicto
　　　adfuit tota comitante silva,
630　Thracios sparsus iacuit per agros,
　　　at caput tristi fluitavit Hebro;
　　　contigit notam Styga Tartarumque,
　　　　　non rediturus.

　　　Stravit Alcides Aquilone natos,
635　patre Neptuno genitum necavit
　　　sumere innumeras solitum figuras;
　　　ipse post terrae pelagique pacem,
　　　post feri Ditis patefacta regna,
　　　vivus ardenti recubans in Oeta
640　praebuit saevis sua membra flammis,
　　　tabe consumptus gemini cruoris
　　　　　munere nuptae.

　　　Stravit Ancaeum violentus ictu
　　　saetiger; fratrem, Meleagre, matris
645　impius mactas, morerisque dextra
　　　matris iratae. meruere cuncti:
　　　morte quod crimen tener expiavit
　　　Herculi magno puer inrepertus,
　　　raptus, heu, tutas puer inter undas?

---

28 Calliope ("the beautiful-voiced one"): her son was Orpheus.
29 Orpheus had entered the underworld previously, and returned from it on that occasion.

That famous son of the sweet-voiced Muse,[28]
at the sound of whose strings, played by the pick,
torrents stood still, winds fell silent,
birds forgot their own singing, and came
with the whole forest dancing attendance—
he lay dead and scattered over Thracian fields,
while his head floated down the gloomy Hebrus;
he reached the familiar Styx and Tartarus,
    with no hope of return.[29]

Alcides felled the sons of Aquilo,
he killed the young man fathered by Neptune,[30]
given to adopting countless shapes;
but after bringing peace to land and sea
and uncovering the realm of savage Dis,
he surrendered his limbs to the cruel flames,
lying back, still living, on burning Oeta,
consumed by the poison of the dual blood,[31]
    gift of his wife.

Ancaeus was felled by the violent thrust
of the boar; Meleager wrongfully slays
his mother's brother, and dies at the hand
of his angered mother. All these deserved death;
but what crime was atoned by the death of the tender
boy that great Hercules never recovered,[32]
poor boy, dragged down amidst safe waters?

[30] Periclymenus.
[31] The commingled blood of the hydra and of the centaur Nessus.
[32] Hylas.

650   ite nunc, fortes, perarate pontum
             fonte timendo.

    Idmonem, quamvis bene fata nosset,
    condidit serpens Libycis harenis;
    omnibus verax, sibi falsus uni,
655   concidit Mopsus caruitque Thebis.
    ille si vere cecinit futura,
657   exul errabit Thetidis maritus;
661   fulmine et ponto moriens Oilei
660a   ⟨pro suo natus⟩ patrioque pendet
660b   crimine poenas.

658   Igne fallaci nociturus Argis
659   Nauplius praeceps cadet in profundum;
662   coniugis fatum redimens Pheraei
    uxor impendes animam marito.
    ipse qui praedam spoliumque iussit
665   aureum prima revehi carina
    [ustus accenso Pelias aëno]
    arsit angustas vagus inter undas.
    Iam satis, divi, mare vindicastis:
          parcite iusso.

NUTRIX

670 Pavet animus, horret: magna pernicies adest.
immane quantum augescit et semet dolor
accendit ipse vimque praeteritam integrat.

658–59 *transposed after* 660, *and* 661 *transposed before* 660, *by
Peiper, who also recognised the lacuna in* 660; *the supplement is
Zwierlein's*   661 Oilei *D. Heinsius:* oyleus *E:* cyleus *A*
    666 *deleted by Peiper*

Go ahead, brave men, plough through the seas,
　　with danger in a spring!

Idmon, though well aware of fate,
was buried in Libya's sands by a serpent;
true seer for all, false only for himself,
Mopsus fell dead, parted from Thebes.
If he sang truly of the future,
Thetis' husband will wander in exile;
dying by lightning and sea, Oileus'
〈son〉 will pay penalty 〈for his own〉
　　and his father's crime.

Planning harm for Argos with deceiving fire,
Nauplius will fall sheer into the deep;
replacing her Pheraean spouse in death,
the wife[33] will expend her life for her husband.
Even he who ordered the plunder, the golden
spoil brought back on that first ship,
seethed while wandering in narrow waters.[34]
Enough reparations, you gods, for the sea:
　　spare one under orders.

ACT 4

NURSE

My heart shudders with fear: great devastation is near. It is
monstrous how her resentment grows, feeds its own fires,
renews its past violence. I have often seen her raging,

---

[33] Alcestis.　　[34] Line 666 is an explanatory interpolation:
"Pelias, boiled in the heated cauldron."

vidi furentem saepe et aggressam deos,
caelum trahentem: maius his, maius parat
675   Medea monstrum. namque ut attonito gradu
evasit et penetrale funestum attigit,
totas opes effudit, et quidquid diu
etiam ipsa timuit promit, atque omnem explicat
turbam malorum, arcana secreta abdita;
680   et triste laeva comprecans sacrum manu
pestes vocat quascumque ferventis creat
harena Libyae quasque perpetua nive
Taurus coercet frigore Arctoo rigens,
et omne monstrum. tracta magicis cantibus
685   squamifera latebris turba desertis adest.
hic saeva serpens corpus immensum trahit
trifidamque linguam exertat et quaerit quibus
mortifera veniat; carmine audito stupet,
tumidumque nodis corpus aggestis plicat
690   cogitque in orbes. "Parva sunt" inquit "mala
et vile telum est, ima quod tellus creat.
caelo petam venena. iam iam tempus est
aliquid movere fraude vulgari altius.
huc ille vasti more torrentis iacens
695   descendat anguis, cuius immensos duae,
maior minorque, sentiunt nodos ferae
(maior Pelasgis apta, Sidoniis minor),
pressasque tandem solvat Ophiuchus manus
virusque fundat; adsit ad cantus meos
700   lacessere ausus gemina Python numina,
et Hydra et omnis redeat Herculea manu

680 comprecans *E*: complicans *A*

404

assailing the gods, drawing down the heavens; greater than that, greater still is the monstrosity Medea is preparing. For after going out with frenzied steps and reaching her inner sanctum of death, she pours out her entire resources, brings forth everything that even she has long feared, and deploys all her host of evils, occult, mysterious, hidden things. Making prayers at the sinister shrine with her left hand,[35] she summons all plagues produced by the sand of burning Libya, and all those locked in the everlasting snow of the Taurus, frozen by Arctic cold, and every monster. Hauled out by her magic spells, the scaly throng desert their lairs and approach. Here a fierce serpent hauls its vast body, flicks out its three-forked tongue and casts about for those to whom it can bring death; at the sound of her spell it is mesmerised, twines its swollen body into folds upon folds, forces it into coils.

"Too small," she says, "are the evils, too ordinary the weapons that earth below produces: I must seek my poisons from heaven. Now is the time to embark on something loftier than ordinary criminality. That snake must descend here who lies like a vast torrent, whose gigantic coils are felt by the two beasts,[36] the greater and the less (the greater useful to Pelasgians, the less to Sidonians); Ophiuchus must finally release his gripping hands and let the venom pour out. My chants must summon Python, who dared provoke the twin deities;[37] the Hydra must return, with each snake that was cut away by Hercules' hand, re-

[35] It was customary to touch or hold the altar while praying; use of the left hand here is ill-omened.   [36] I.e. the two Bears, between which coils the constellation Draco.

[37] Phoebus Apollo and his sister Phoebe/Diana.

succisa serpens, caede se reparans sua.
tu quoque relictis pervigil Colchis ades,
sopite primum cantibus, serpens, meis."
705   Postquam evocavit omne serpentum genus,
congerit in unum frugis infaustae mala:
quaecumque generat invius saxis Eryx,
quae fert opertis hieme perpetua iugis
sparsus cruore Caucasus Promethei,
711   et quîs sagittas divites Arabes linunt
710   pharetraque pugnax Medus aut Parthi leves,
aut quos sub axe frigido sucos legunt
lucis Suebae nobiles Hercyniis;
quodcumque tellus vere nidifico creat
715   aut rigida cum iam bruma discussit decus
nemorum et nivali cuncta constrinxit gelu,
quodcumque gramen flore mortifero viret,
dirusve tortis sucus in radicibus
causas nocendi gignit, attrectat manu.
720   Haemonius illas contulit pestes Athos,
has Pindus ingens, illa Pangaei iugis
teneram cruenta falce deposuit comam;
has aluit altum gurgitem Tigris premens,
Danuvius illas, has per arentes plagas
725   tepidis Hydaspes gemmifer currens aquis,
nomenque terris qui dedit Baetis suis
Hesperia pulsans maria languenti vado.
haec passa ferrum est, dum parat Phoebus diem,
illius alta nocte succisus frutex;
730   at huius ungue secta cantato seges.
    Mortifera carpit gramina ac serpentium
saniem exprimit, miscetque et obscenas aves

newing itself through its own laceration. You too must leave Colchis and come, unsleeping serpent, lulled for the first time by my chants."

After summoning the whole league of serpents, she collects together the poisons of ominous plants: all those engendered on the impassable crags of Mt Eryx, those borne by the Caucasus, sprinkled with Prometheus' blood, on its perpetually snow-covered ridges; and those with which the rich Arabs smear their arrows, and the Medes, warlike archers, and fleet Parthians; or those juices collected under the cold pole by Suebian women, famed for their Hercynian forests; all that earth bears in nest-building springtime, or when frozen winter has scattered the glory of the woods and gripped the world in snowy cold; every plant that burgeons with deadly flowers, every kind of injurious sap that breeds in twisted roots the sources of harm: all these she handles. Some toxic plants were contributed by Haemonian Athos, others by the vast Pindus; another yielded up its tender foliage to her bloody sickle on the ridges of Pangaeum. Some were nurtured by the Tigris, which submerges its deep flood; some by the Danube, others by the gem-bearing Hydaspes that flows through parched regions with its tepid waters, and the Baetis that gives its land a name and pushes into the Hesperian sea with a sluggish current. One felt the knife while Phoebus was preparing day, another's stalk was cut at midnight, another was snipped by her fingernail under a spell.

She plucks the deadly herbs and bleeds the snakes of their venom; she mixes in also unwholesome birds, the

---

710 *transposed after* 711 *by Gronovius*
713 Hercyniis *Avantius*: Hyrcaniis* EA

maestique cor bubonis et raucae strigis
exsecta vivae viscera. haec scelerum artifex
735   discreta ponit: his rapax vis ignium,
his gelida pigri frigoris glacies inest.
addit venenis verba non illis minus
metuenda. Sonuit ecce vesano gradu
canitque. mundus vocibus primis tremit.

MEDEA

740   Comprecor vulgus silentum vosque ferales deos
et Chaos caecum atque opacam Ditis umbrosi domum,
Tartari ripis ligatos squalidae Mortis specus.
supplicîs, animae, remissis currite ad thalamos novos:
rota resistat membra torquens, tangat Ixion humum,
745   Tantalus securus undas hauriat Pirenidas.
gravior uni poena sedeat coniugis socero mei:
lubricus per saxa retro Sisyphum volvat lapis.
vos quoque, urnis quas foratis inritus ludit labor,
Danaides, coite: vestras hic dies quaerit manus.
750   Nunc meis vocata sacris, noctium sidus, veni
pessimos induta vultus, fronte non una minax.

---

38 Hecate, often represented as triple-headed, is frequently
identified with the moon (as here) and Diana; below she is invoked by various names, Phoebe, Trivia, Dictynna, daughter of
Perses.

heart of a boding horned owl and entrails cut from a living screech owl. There are things the artificer of crimes keeps separate: some contain the tearing violence of fire, others the icy chill of numbing cold. To her poisons she adds words that are no less fearful. There! the sound of her maddened steps and her chanting. The world trembles at her first words.

MEDEA

I invoke the thronging silent dead, and you the gods of
the grave,
and sightless Chaos, and the shadowy home of dark-
enshrouded Dis,
the cavernous halls of squalid Death, enclosed by
Tartarus' streams.
Eased of your torments, run, you ghosts, to this strange
marriage rite;
the wheel that tortures limbs may stop, Ixion touch the
ground,
and Tantalus may swallow down Pirene's stream in
peace.
But may heavier punishment rest on one, my husband's
marriage relation:
over the rocks may the slippery stone roll Sisyphus back
downhill.
And you who are mocked by fruitless toil with pitchers
pierced by holes,
assemble here, you Danaids: this day demands your
hands.
Now summoned by my rites appear, you heavenly
globe of night,
displaying your most hostile looks, with menace in every
face.[38]

Tibi more gentis vinculo solvens comam
secreta nudo nemora lustravi pede,
et evocavi nubibus siccis aquas
755 egique ad imum maria, et Oceanus graves
interius undas aestibus victis dedit;
pariterque mundus lege confusa aetheris
et solem et astra vidit, et vetitum mare
tetigistis, Ursae. temporum flexi vices:
760 aestiva tellus horruit cantu meo,
coacta messem vidit hibernam Ceres.
violenta Phasis vertit in fontem vada,
et Hister, in tot ora divisus, truces
compressit undas, omnibus ripis piger.
765 sonuere fluctus, tumuit insanum mare
tacente vento; nemoris antiqui domus
amisit umbras vocis imperio meae.
[die relicto Phoebus in medio stetit,
Hyadesque nostris cantibus motae labant]
770 Adesse sacris tempus est, Phoebe, tuis.

Tibi haec cruenta serta texuntur manu,
        novena quae serpens ligat,
tibi haec Typhoeus membra quae discors tulit,
        qui regna concussit Iovis.
775 vectoris istic perfidi sanguis inest,
        quem Nessus expirans dedit.

760 horruit *Markland*: floruit *EA*
768–69 *deleted by Fitch*

For you I have loosed my hair in the style of my people
and paced your sequestered groves with naked feet;
I have summoned water out of rainless clouds,
and forced the sea to its depths: Ocean withdrew
his heavy waves, as his tides were overpowered.
With the laws of heaven confounded, the world has seen
both sun and stars together, and the Bears have touched
the forbidden sea. I have changed the pattern of the
    seasons:
the summer earth has frozen under my spells,
and Ceres was compelled to see a winter harvest.
The Phasis turned his violent stream to its source,
and the Hister, with so many separate mouths,
    constrained
its savage waters in every branch to stillness.
Waves have crashed, the maddened seas have swelled
with the wind silent; the shelter of the ancient woods
has lost its shade at the bidding of my voice.[39]

    The moment is right to attend your ritual, Phoebe.

For you this wreath is woven with bloodstained hand
      and tied with serpents nine;
for you these limbs, borne by discordant Typhon,
      who shook the throne of Jove.
This holds the blood of the treacherous ferryman,
      given by Nessus as he died.

[39] Lines 768–69 (deleted): "Phoebus has stopped at the zenith, forgoing the day, / and the Hyades move unsteadily through my spells."

Oetaeus isto cinere defecit rogus,
  qui virus Herculeum bibit.
piae sororis, impiae matris, facem
780   ultricis Althaeae vides.
reliquit istas invio plumas specu
  Harpyia, dum Zeten fugit.
his adice pinnas sauciae Stymphalidos
  Lernaea passae spicula.
785 Sonuistis, arae, tripodas agnosco meos
  favente commotos dea.

   Video Triviae currus agiles,
   non quos pleno lucida vultu
   pernox agitat,
790   sed quos facie lurida maesta,
   cum Thessalicis vexata minis
   caelum freno propiore legit.
   sic face tristem pallida lucem
   funde per auras;
   horrore novo terre populos,
795   inque auxilium, Dictynna, tuum
   pretiosa sonent aera Corinthi.
    Tibi sanguineo
   caespite sacrum sollemne damus,
   tibi de medio rapta sepulcro
800   fax nocturnos sustulit ignes,
   tibi mota caput
   flexa voces cervice dedi,

---

[40] Witches, whose stronghold was Thessaly, were believed capable of causing eclipses of the moon.

MEDEA

Into this ash the Oetaean pyre burnt down,
    that drank the poison of Hercules.
See here the brand of vengeful Althaea, the loyal
    sister, disloyal mother.
This plumage was left in an inaccessible cave
    by the Harpy in flight from Zetes;
add to it the feathers of the wounded Stymphalian bird,
    struck by Lernaean arrows.
A sound from the altar: I recognise that my tripods
    have been moved by the favouring goddess.

        I see the coursing chariot of Trivia—
        not as it looks when she drives full-faced
        in nightlong brightness,
        but when she is sallow and gloomy-faced,
        tormented by Thessalian threats,[40]
        and skirts the sky with closer reins.
        Pour dismal light with this pallid glare
        through the atmosphere;
        terrify the nations with newfound dread,
        and in your aid, Dictynna, let precious
        vessels of bronze resound in Corinth.[41]
            For you on bloodstained turf I perform
        the proper sacrifice;
        for you a brand stolen from the midst
        of a burial has raised its fire in darkness.
        For you I have given tongue,
        with arching neck and tossing head;

[41] Witches' spells could be counteracted by the loud clashing of metal; Corinth was noted for its precious bronze vessels.

tibi funereo de more iacens
passos cingit vitta capillos,
tibi iactatur
805   tristis Stygia ramus ab unda,
tibi nudato pectore maenas
sacro feriam bracchia cultro.
manet noster sanguis ad aras:
assuesce, manus, stringere ferrum
810   carosque pati posse cruores—
sacrum laticem percussa dedi.

Quodsi nimium saepe vocari
quereris votis, ignosce, precor:
causa vocandi,
815   Persei, tuos saepius arcus
una atque eadem est semper, Iason.

Tu nunc vestes tinge Creusae,
quas cum primum sumpserit, imas
urat serpens flamma medullas.
820   Ignis fulvo clausus in auro
latet obscurus,
quem mihi caeli qui furta luit
viscere feto
dedit et docuit
condere vires arte, Prometheus.
dedit et tenui
825   sulphure tectos Mulciber ignes,
et vivacis fulgura flammae
de cognato Phaethonte tuli.

for you, hanging down in funeral style,
this wool band circles my spreading hair.
For you I wave
a sombre branch from the Stygian stream.
For you like a maenad with breast bared
I shall strike my arms with the holy knife.
My blood must flow onto the altar.
Rehearse, my hands, how to draw the steel
and endure the shedding of your own dear blood.
With a blow I have offered the flowing sacrament.

But if you protest at too frequent a summons
from my entreaties, forgive me, I pray:
my reason for summoning your crescent too often,
daughter of Perses,
is always one and the same: Jason.

[*To Nurse*] You must now tincture the clothes for
    Creusa,
so the moment she wears them, crawling flame
may burn its way deep into her bones.
Enclosed and lurking in the tawny gold
is shrouded fire:
the one who pays for his theft from heaven
with the tissue that grows in him
gave it me and taught me
to store its power by craft: Prometheus.
Mulciber too
gave me fire concealed in fine-grained sulphur,
and I gathered the flashes of living flame
from the kindred body of Phaethon.

habeo mediae dona Chimaerae,
habeo flammas
830   usto tauri gutture raptas,
quas permixto felle Medusae
tacitum iussi servare malum.
    Adde venenis stimulos, Hecate,
donisque meis
semina flammae condita serva:
835   fallant visus tactusque ferant,
meet in pectus venasque calor,
stillent artus ossaque fument
vincatque suas flagrante coma
nova nupta faces.
    Vota tenentur:
840   ter latratus audax Hecate
dedit, et sacros edidit ignes
face lucifera.

Parata vis est omnis. huc natos voca,
pretiosa per quos dona nubenti feras.
845   Ite, ite, nati, matris infaustae genus,
placate vobis munere et multa prece
dominam ac novercam. vadite et celeres domum
referte gressus, ultimo amplexu ut fruar.

CHORUS

Quonam cruenta maenas
850   praeceps amore saevo

---

843 parata *Watt*: peracta *EA*

I possess gifts from the belly of Chimaera,[42]
I possess flames
caught from the scorched throat of the bull,
which I compounded with Medusa's venom
and bade to preserve their harm in secret.

Give the spur to my poisons, Hecate,
and in my gifts
keep the seeds of fire concealed.
Let them cheat the gaze, be inert to the touch,
but let heat pass into her heart and veins,
let her limbs melt, her bones smoulder,
and let this new bride with her blazing hair
outshine her own torches.

My prayers are received:
thrice has bold Hecate vouchsafed the barking
of dogs, and set off uncanny fires
with her light-bearing torch.

My violent powers are fully prepared. [*To Nurse*] Call the
children here, so you can convey the precious gifts through
them to the bride.

Go now, my sons, born to a cursed mother: win over for
yourselves the heart of your lady and stepmother with this
gift and many prayers. Go, and return home quickly, so I
may enjoy a final embrace.

CHORUS
Where is the bloodstained maenad
being driven impetuously

[42] Literally, from her "middle": of her three parts (lion's front,
goat's middle, serpent's tail) the midmost was thought to produce
fire.

rapitur? quod impotenti
facinus parat furore?
vultus citatus ira
riget, et caput feroci
855 quatiens superba motu
regi minatur ultro.
    quis credat exulem?

Flagrant genae rubentes,
pallor fugat ruborem.
860 nullum vagante forma
servat diu colorem.
huc fert pedes et illuc,
ut tigris orba natis
cursu furente lustrat
865 Gangeticum nemus.

Frenare nescit iras
Medea, non amores;
nunc ira amorque causam
iunxere: quid sequetur?
870 quando efferet Pelasgis
nefanda Colchis arvis
gressum, metuque solvet
regnum simulque reges?
Nunc, Phoebe, mitte currus
875 nullo morante loro,
nox condat alma lucem,
mergat diem timendum
    dux noctis Hesperus.

by savage love? What crime
is she planning in uncurbed fury?
Her face is sharpened with anger
and set; her head is tossing
with fierce and arrogant movements
and she actually threatens the king.
  Who would think her an exile?

Her cheeks are red and inflamed,
then the red is displaced by pallor;
she keeps no colour for long,
her appearance ever shifting.
She paces to and fro,
as a tigress robbed of her children
roams in a raging onrush
  the Ganges' wooded banks.

Medea cannot rein in
her feelings of love or anger.
Now anger and love have joined
their forces: what will follow?
When will the evil Colchian
make her way from Pelasgian
fields, and free from fear
the kingdom along with its kings?
Now, Phoebus, run your chariot
with no restraint from the reins:
friendly night must hide the sunlight,
and this fearful day be buried
  by Hesperus, leader of night.

NUNTIUS

Periere cuncta! concidit regni status;
880 nata atque genitor cinere permixto iacent.

CHORUS

Qua fraude capti?

NUNTIUS

Qua solent reges capi:
donis.

CHORUS

In illis esse quis potuit dolus?

NUNTIUS

Et ipse miror, vixque iam facto malo
potuisse fieri credo.

CHORUS

Quis cladis modus?

NUNTIUS

885 Avidus per omnem regiae partem furit
ut iussus ignis: iam domus tota occidit,
urbi timetur.

CHORUS

Unda flammas opprimat.

NUNTIUS

Et hoc in ista clade mirandum accidit:
alit unda flammas, quoque prohibetur magis,
890 magis ardet ignis; ipsa praesidia occupat.

NUTRIX

Effer citatum sede Pelopea gradum,
Medea, praeceps quaslibet terras pete.

420

MEDEA

ACT 5

MESSENGER

All is lost! The fortunes of the kingdom are fallen; daughter
and father lie with their ashes intermingled.

CHORUS

How were they trapped?

MESSENGER

As kings are always trapped: by gifts.

CHORUS

What trickery could have been in them?

MESSENGER

I too am amazed, and though the evil is done, I can hardly
believe it possible.

CHORUS

What is the extent of the disaster?

MESSENGER

The greedy fire rages through every part of the palace as
if under orders; already the building has collapsed completely, and they fear for the city.

CHORUS

Water must smother the flames.

MESSENGER

A further marvel has happened in this disaster: water feeds
the flames, and the more they try to check the fire, the
more it blazes; it commandeers the very defences.

NURSE

Make your escape swiftly from the land of Pelops, Medea,
race to reach some other country, no matter where.

MEDEA

Egone ut recedam? si profugissem prius,
ad hoc redirem. nuptias specto novas.
895 quid, anime, cessas? sequere felicem impetum.
pars ultionis ista, qua gaudes, quota est!
amas adhuc, furiose, si satis est tibi
caelebs Iason. quaere poenarum genus
haud usitatum, iamque sic temet para:
900 fas omne cedat, abeat expulsus pudor;
vindicta levis est quam ferunt purae manus.
incumbe in iras teque languentem excita,
penitusque veteres pectore ex imo impetus
violentus hauri. quidquid admissum est adhuc,
905 pietas vocetur. hoc agam et faxo sciant
quam levia fuerint quamque vulgaris notae
quae commodavi scelera. prolusit dolor
per ista noster; quid manus poterant rudes
audere magnum, quid puellaris furor?
910 Medea nunc sum: crevit ingenium malis.
iuvat, iuvat rapuisse fraternum caput,
artus iuvat secuisse et arcano patrem
spoliasse sacro, iuvat in exitium senis
armasse natas. quaere materiam, dolor:
915 ad omne facinus non rudem dextram afferes.
    Quo te igitur, ira, mittis, aut quae perfido
intendis hosti tela? nescioquid ferox
decrevit animus intus et nondum sibi
audet fateri. stulta properavi nimis:
920 ex paelice utinam liberos hostis meus
aliquos haberet! quidquid ex illo tuum est,

905 agam *Richter*: age *EA*

MEDEA

I retreat? If I had fled before, I would return for this; I am watching a new kind of wedding! Why are you slackening, my spirit? Follow up your successful attack. How small a part of your revenge is this that thrills you! You are still in love, mad spirit, if it is enough for you that Jason be wifeless. Search out some exceptional kind of punishment, and prepare yourself in this fashion now: let all right be gone, let any sense of shame be expelled; the vengeance is trivial that is gained by pure hands. Bear down on your anger, awaken your sluggish spirits, and fiercely draw out the old aggression from deep in your heart's core. Let any deed committed so far be called love of family. I shall set to work, and make them understand how trivial, of what common stamp were the crimes I did to oblige others. Through them my pain was just practicing. What great deed could be dared by untrained hands, by the fury of a girl? Now I am Medea: my genius has grown through evils.[43] I am glad, yes glad, to have torn away my brother's head, glad to have cut up his limbs and plundered my father of his hidden holy object, glad to have armed the daughters to destroy the old man.[44] Just find the means, my pain: to any crime you will bring a well-trained hand.

So where are you driving, my anger, what weapons are you aiming at your faithless enemy? The spirit within me has determined on some brutality, but dare not yet acknowledge it to itself. Fool, I have been too hasty! If only my enemy had some children by his mistress! No: all that is

---

[43] I.e. the *ingenium* (inborn nature and talent) denoted by her name, which means "the thinking/inventive woman," has come to maturity. [44] Pelias.

Creusa perit. placuit hoc poenae genus,
merito placuit. ultimum, agnosco, scelus
animo parandum est. liberi quondam mei,
925 vos pro paternis sceleribus poenas date.

Cor pepulit horror, membra torpescunt gelu
pectusque tremuit. ira discessit loco
materque tota coniuge expulsa redit.
egone ut meorum liberum ac prolis meae
930 fundam cruorem? melius, a, demens furor!
incognitum istud facinus ac dirum nefas
a me quoque absit. quod scelus miseri luent?
scelus est Iason genitor et maius scelus
Medea mater. occidant, non sunt mei;
935 pereant, mei sunt. crimine et culpa carent,
sunt innocentes, fateor: et frater fuit.
quid, anime, titubas? ora quid lacrimae rigant
variamque nunc huc ira, nunc illuc amor
diducit? anceps aestus incertam rapit;
940 ut saeva rapidi bella cum venti gerunt,
utrimque fluctus maria discordes agunt
dubiumque fervet pelagus, haud aliter meum
cor fluctuatur: ira pietatem fugat
iramque pietas. cede pietati, dolor.

945 Huc, cara proles, unicum afflictae domus
solamen, huc vos ferte, et infusos mihi
coniungite artus. habeat incolumes pater,
dum et mater habeat. urget exilium ac fuga:
iam iam meo rapientur avulsi e sinu,
950 flentes, gementes. osculis pereant patris,
periere matris. rursus increscit dolor
et fervet odium, repetit invitam manum

424

yours by him has Creusa for a mother. This path of punishment is decided on, rightly decided on. My spirit must prepare, I recognise, for its ultimate crime. Children once mine, you must pay the penalty for your father's crimes.

My heart is struck with horror, my limbs freeze, my breast trembles. Anger retreats, and the mother returns, with the wife utterly banished. Could I shed the blood of my children, my own youngsters? Do not say so, mad rage! Let that unheard-of deed, that abomination, be left untouched by me as well. What crime will the poor boys pay for? The crime is having Jason as their father, and the worse crime is having Medea as their mother. Let them fall, since they are not mine; let them perish, since they are mine. They are free of guilt and blame, they are innocent, I admit: my brother was, too. Why do you vacillate, my spirit? Why are tears wetting my face, and anger leading me to shift in one direction, love in another? Conflicting currents whirl me from side to side. Just as, when the whirling winds wage savage warfare, the contending waves drive the seas both ways, and the waters seethe in confusion: so my heart wavers; anger puts mother love to flight, then mother love, anger. Give way to love, my pain.

Here, my dear young ones, sole comfort of a troubled house, bring yourselves here, hug me and press your bodies against mine. Let your father have you safe and sound, as long as your mother can have you too. But exile and flight are close. At any moment they will be snatched and torn from my embrace, in tears, in distress. Let them be lost to their father's kisses, they are lost to their mother's. Once more my pain grows and my hatred burns, the Erinys

---

923 agnosco *E*: magno *A*

antiqua Erinys. ira, qua ducis, sequor.
utinam superbae turba Tantalidos meo
955 exisset utero, bisque septenos parens
natos tulissem! sterilis in poenas fui.
fratri patrique quod sat est, peperi duos.

    Quonam ista tendit turba Furiarum impotens?
quem quaerit aut quo flammeos ictus parat,
960 aut cui cruentas agmen infernum faces
intentat? ingens anguis excusso sonat
tortus flagello. quem trabe infesta petit
Megaera? cuius umbra dispersis venit
incerta membris? frater est, poenas petit.
965 dabimus, sed omnes. fige luminibus faces,
lania, perure, pectus en Furiis patet.
Discedere a me, frater, ultrices deas
manesque ad imos ire securas iube;
mihi me relinque et utere hac, frater, manu
970 quae strinxit ensem. victima manes tuos
placamus ista.

               Quid repens affert sonus?
parantur arma, meque in exitium petunt.
excelsa nostrae tecta conscendam domus
caede incohata. perge tu mecum comes.
975 tuum quoque ipsa corpus hinc mecum aveham.
nunc hoc age, anime. non in occulto tibi est
perdenda virtus; approba populo manum.

IASON

Quicumque regum cladibus fidus doles,
concurre, ut ipsam sceleris auctorem horridi

of old demands my reluctant hand again. Anger, where you lead, I follow. If only the throng of the proud Tantalid had issued from my womb, and I had born and mothered twice seven children! I was barren for revenge. Yet I gave birth to two, enough for my brother and my father.

What is the target of this wild throng of Furies? Whom are they hunting, whom are they threatening with fiery blows? At whom is the hellish band pointing its bloody torches? A huge snake hisses, entwined in a lashing whip. Whom is Megaera seeking with her bludgeon? Whose shade approaches ill-defined with limbs dispersed? It is my brother, he seeks amends. We shall pay them, yes, every one. Drive torches into my eyes, mutilate me, burn me: see, my breast is open to the Furies.

Bid the avenging goddesses draw back from me, brother, and return to the deep shades assured of their purpose. Leave me to myself, and act, brother, through this hand that has drawn the sword. With this sacrifice I placate your shade. [*She kills one son. At that moment, sounds of pursuit are heard from offstage.*]

What is the meaning of this sudden noise? They are obtaining arms and searching for me to kill me. I shall climb to the lofty roof of our house, now the killing has begun. [*To the living son*] Come, you, in company with me. [*To the dead son*] Your body too I shall carry away with me in my own arms. To work now, my spirit! You must not waste your valour in obscurity; have the people applaud your handiwork!

JASON

All loyal citizens grieved by the downfall of the royal family, rally to me, so we may catch the perpetrator of this

980 capiamus. huc, huc, fortis armiferi cohors,
conferte tela, vertite ex imo domum.

MEDEA

Iam iam recepi sceptra germanum patrem,
spoliumque Colchi pecudis auratae tenent;
rediere regna, rapta virginitas redît.

985 o placida tandem numina, o festum diem,
o nuptialem! vade: perfectum est scelus—
vindicta nondum: perage, dum faciunt manus.
quid nunc moraris, anime? quid dubitas? potens
iam cecidit ira? paenitet facti, pudet.

990 quid, misera, feci? misera? paeniteat licet,
feci. voluptas magna me invitam subit,
et ecce crescit. derat hoc unum mihi,
spectator iste. nil adhuc facti reor:
quidquid sine isto fecimus sceleris perît.

IASON

995 En ipsa tecti parte praecipiti imminet.
huc rapiat ignes aliquis, ut flammis cadat
suis perusta.

MEDEA

Congere extremum tuis
natis, Iason, funus ac tumulum strue.
coniunx socerque iusta iam functis habent

1000 a me sepulti; natus hic fatum tulit,
hic te vidente dabitur exitio pari.

IASON

Per numen omne perque communes fugas
torosque, quos non nostra violavit fides,
iam parce nato. si quod est crimen, meum est:

fearful crime. Here, bring your weapons here, brave band of warriors, overturn the house from its foundations.

MEDEA

[*Aside*] Now in this moment I have recovered my sceptre, brother, father, and the Colchians hold the spoil of the golden ram. My realm is restored, my stolen maidenhood restored. O gods benign at last, o festive day, o wedding day! Depart, you have brought crime to fulfilment—but not yet so revenge: finish it, while your hands are accomplishing things. Why delay now, my spirit? Why hesitate? Has your powerful anger already flagged? I regret what I have done, I feel ashamed. What have I done, poor woman? Poor woman? Whatever my regrets, I have done it. A great sense of pleasure steals over me unbidden, and it is still growing. This was the one thing I lacked, this spectator. I think nothing has been done as yet: such crime as I did without him was lost.

JASON

Look, there she is, leaning over us from the edge of the roof. Rush fire here, one of you, so she can fall consumed by her own flames.

MEDEA

Heap up a final pyre for your sons, Jason, and build them a tomb. Your wife and father-in-law have what is owed the dead, buried by me; this son has met his doom, and before your eyes this one will be given a matching death.

JASON

By every divinity, by our shared exile and shared bed, not betrayed by any infidelity of mine, spare our son now. If there is any guilt, it is mine. I surrender myself to death,

1005   me dedo morti; noxium macta caput.

MEDEA

Hac qua recusas, qua doles, ferrum exigam.
i nunc, superbe, virginum thalamos pete,
relinque matres.

IASON
Unus est poenae satis.

MEDEA

Si posset una caede satiari manus,
1010   nullam petisset. ut duos perimam, tamen
nimium est dolori numerus angustus meo.
in matre si quod pignus etiamnunc latet,
scrutabor ense viscera et ferro extraham.

IASON

Iam perage coeptum facinus (haud ultra precor),
1015   moramque saltem supplicîs dona meis.

MEDEA

Perfruere lento scelere, ne propera, dolor:
meus dies est; tempore accepto utimur.

IASON

Infesta, memet perime.

MEDEA
Misereri iubes.

bene est, peractum est. plura non habui, dolor,
1020   quae tibi litarem. lumina huc tumida alleva,
ingrate Iason. coniugem agnoscis tuam?

sacrifice my guilty life.

MEDEA

I shall drive the sword just here where you forbid me to, where it hurts you. Go on now, arrogant man, seek out virgins' bedrooms, and abandon mothers.

JASON

One boy is enough to punish me.

MEDEA

If this hand could have been content with one slaughter, it would not have aspired to any. Even if I kill two, the number is still too limited for my pain. If some love pledge is hiding even now in my mothering body, I shall probe my vitals with the sword, drag it out with steel.

JASON

Now finish the deed you have begun—I make no further prayers—and at least spare me this drawing-out of my punishment.

MEDEA

Relish your crime in leisure, my pain, do not hurry. This day is mine, I am using the time I was granted.

JASON

Kill *me*, violent woman.

MEDEA

You bid me have pity. [*She kills the second son.*] Good, it is finished. I had no more to offer you, my pain, in atonement. Raise your tear-swollen eyes here, ungrateful Jason. Do you recognise your wife? This is how I always escape.[45]

---

[45] I.e. "amidst murders" (those of Absyrtus and Pelias) and/or "in this chariot" (as she escaped from Iolcos).

sic fugere soleo. patuit in caelum via:
squamosa gemini colla serpentes iugo
summissa praebent. recipe iam natos parens;
1025 ego inter auras aliti curru vehar.

IASON

Per alta vade spatia sublime aetheris;
testare nullos esse, qua veheris, deos.

1026 sublime aetheris *Bothe*: sublimi aethere *Farnaby*: sublimi
aetheri *E* (1009–27 *missing in A*)

MEDEA

A path has opened to heaven: twin serpents offer their scaly necks bowed to the chariot yoke. Now recover your sons as their parent. I shall ride through the air in my winged chariot.

JASON

Travel on high through the lofty spaces of heaven, and bear witness where you ride that there are no gods.

PHAEDRA

INTRODUCTION

Background

In his early years Theseus was among the youths sent by Athens as tribute to King Minos of Crete, to be sacrificed to the Minotaur. Theseus managed, however, to slay the Minotaur and to escape from the labyrinth with the help of Minos' daughter Ariadne, who had fallen in love with him. They fled together from Crete, but Theseus left Ariadne behind on the island of Naxos.

Succeeding to the throne of Athens on his return from Crete, Theseus married the Amazon queen Antiope, by whom he had a son Hippolytus. Hippolytus, now a young man himself, has inherited the striking good looks of both his parents. In nature, however, he is a true Amazon, despising love, marriage, and settled life, and devoting himself to a vigorous outdoor life of hunting.

Later Theseus killed Antiope in mysterious circumstances, and married Phaedra, the sister of Ariadne. She bore him two sons. But then Theseus was persuaded by his close friend Pirithous to accompany him on a reckless expedition to abduct Proserpine, queen of the underworld. He has been absent now for four years. Phaedra, left alone with Hippolytus, has fallen passionately in love with her handsome stepson.

Summary

Prelude. Hippolytus makes preparations for a hunt with his attendants.

Act 1
Phaedra speaks of her obsessive passion for Hippolytus, while the Nurse attempts to bring her to her senses. Phaedra veers towards suicide as the only escape; to forestall that, the Nurse undertakes to approach Hippolytus.

Ode 1. The chorus sings of Cupid's power over humans, gods, and animals.

Act 2
Phaedra's frenzy increases. The Nurse engages Hippolytus in debate and criticizes him for rejecting sex and pleasure, which are natural and proper to human life. Hippolytus defends his way of life as innocent, free of the guilt which he associates with cities and with womankind. Phaedra interrupts and confesses her love to Hippolytus, who flees in horror. The Nurse raises a hue and cry, accusing Hippolytus of rape.

Ode 2. The theme is Hippolytus' beauty, and the dangers associated with such beauty.

Act 3
Theseus returns to Athens from the underworld. Believing Phaedra's accusation of rape, he curses Hippolytus with the third of three wishes granted him by his father Neptune.

Ode 3. The theme is the moral chaos of human life, contrasted with the order of the heavens.

Act 4

A messenger recounts Hippolytus' death: a monstrous bull
from the sea terrified his horses; thrown from his chariot,
he was dragged in the reins and torn apart.

Ode 4. Fortune's blows single out the mighty: Theseus
is an instance.

Act 5

Phaedra expresses anguish over Hippolytus' broken body,
reveals the truth, and commits suicide. Theseus envisages
punishments for his own guilt and lays out his son's body
for funeral.

Comment

The title *Phaedra*, even if authentic (the A MSS call the
play *Hippolytus*), is simply a label and should not be read
as indicating that the play focusses on one figure. This is a
tragedy of three people, each of whom bears a large share
of responsibility.

The prelude sets the initial focus on Hippolytus, and
presents him as energetic and enthusiastic. (Modern an-
tipathy to hunting per se should not be retrojected onto
the ancient world.) His easy assumption of dominance
over the natural world will be cast in an ironic light by his
eventual fate, but the prelude stands outside the tragedy. A
more complex picture emerges, however, from his justification of his way of life in Act 2. No one responsive to
wild nature can fail to appreciate his exaltation of the freedom and beauty found there. But his obsessive harping on
the corruption found in cities and women makes it clear

439

that the countryside represents for him an escape made necessary by a paranoia about human guilt and corruption. His escapism is confirmed later in the Act, where his only means of dealing with Phaedra's advances is to flee to the "woods and wild beasts" (718).

The unreality of Hippolytus' understanding of nature is confirmed by the choral odes. Ode 1 recognises the power of *amor* among wild animals as well as among humans and gods; ode 2 warns that Hippolytus' beauty will not be safe-guarded by the forests, since Dryads and Pans are hardly unsusceptible to beauty. Even the goddess Diana herself, traditionally characterized as fiercely chaste (witness Actaeon), is here portrayed as amorously interested in handsome young men (309–16, 422, 785–94), so that there is no divine warrant for Hippolytus' devotion to chastity.

The Phaedra portrayed in this play changes and fluctuates in response to her emotional impulses and the developing situation. From the outset the imagery of love's fire, and of a ship swept away by the current, suggests that her passion will quickly overwhelm such self-control as she possesses. Her passion is equated with "madness" (*furor*). Already at the end of Act 1 she is drifting into pure fantasy about the potential reactions of Hippolytus and others to her passion (225–45). By the beginning of Act 2, perhaps after a time lapse covered by ode 1, she is more fully in the grip of frenzy, as indicated both by the Nurse's description and by the dressing scene. Her approach to Hippolytus is impulsive, with no plan of attack in mind, as is clear from the fact that she takes her cues from Hippolytus' words. The motivation of her behaviour in Act 4 is only lightly sketched, and can be read variously: perhaps, as at the end of Act 3, she is overwhelmed by the situation and simply acquiesces in the Nurse's initiative, until the sight of Hippolytus' broken body in Act 5 confronts her with the reality of what she has done.

The forces contributing to Phaedra's passion are indicated skilfully and succinctly. They include a desperate loneliness in this alien land and in the absence of the once-loved Theseus (89–98). Hippolytus would be a replacement for Theseus—not just a replacement, however, but a reincarnation of a more youthful Theseus, as Phaedra makes explicit in comparing the son's attractive looks to the father's (646–66). When Hippolytus dutifully promises to fill his absent father's place for Phaedra (633), he voices unconsciously her strongest desire. What Seneca is dramatising, then, is that dynamic within the family through which sexuality can become incestuous, being misdirected from the spouse towards a child (here stepchild) with tragic results.

Whereas Hippolytus associates the wild country with innocence, Phaedra associates it with monstrous sexuality as a result of her mother Pasiphae's bestial passion, the product of which was the Minotaur. Though Phaedra's claim to be a helpless victim of Venus is exploded by the Nurse's vigorous commonsense, it is clear that she has an inherited predisposition to sensuality. Like the countryside, hunting too is eroticized for her: in her enclosed female world, she longs for the forceful energy of the hunter, longs to hurl stiff javelins with her soft hand (111). And in her fantasy the quarry of the hunt will be Hippolytus himself (233–41).

But she is also characterised by another emotional impulse, which is designated *pudor*, a sense of modesty, shame, and honour. When the Nurse makes a desperate emotional plea to her, it is *pudor* that causes Phaedra to yield (250), in one of those abrupt but understandable changes of heart characteristic of Senecan drama. Similarly, after Hippolytus rejects her advances, she welcomes the possibility of dying at his hands *salvo pudore*, "with honour safe" (712). In fact *pudor* is a leading motive in her successive flirtations with death, finally consummated in Act 5. Supposedly a last safeguard for chastity, death itself becomes eroticised as it represents penetration by Hippolytus' sword.

This portrayal of Phaedra is essentially new, though it includes elements of previous portrayals. Seneca presents dramatically a woman of intense emotions, but weak-willed, a woman who veers wildly between one impulse and another, even in the space of a few lines. Her mental and emotional confusion continues right into her suicide speech, which contains varied and even contradictory elements: anguish and guilt over Hippolytus' death, desire to share his death and even pursue him in the underworld, desire to salvage some honour, hatred of Theseus and horror at the prospect of living on as his wife. Though it is an understandable impulse of critics to look for some moral redemption in her moment of suicide, such redemption is hard to find here or elsewhere in Senecan drama.

It would be easy to be impatient with Theseus as a blundering male heroic type: as he rashly accompanied Pirithous on a madcap adventure to the underworld, so now he hastily believes Phaedra and condemns his son. Yet sorrow seems a more appropriate response as the tragedy proceeds inexorably. Exhausted on his return to the upper world, this Theseus lacks both the address and the wisdom to deal with an unexpected crisis. In fact from the moment of his appearance Theseus is a figure thematically associated with death.

The play's closing scene bears some resemblance to the final episode of Euripides' *Bacchae*, in which Pentheus' dismembered body was similarly brought on stage, though the loss of part of that episode after line 1329 means that we cannot tell how close the resemblance was. It is a reasonable guess that Seneca heightens the horror, particularly by dwelling on the unrecognisability of one fragment of the body (1265–66). The horror of that moment, however, is not unrelated to theme and context. This scene enacts the ritual of laying out a body (which here involves reassembling a body)—a ritual which asserts human identity in the face of death's annihilation. The ritual is particularly poignant here because a parent performs it for a child: having contributed to making the body originally, he now tries hopelessly to remake it. Theseus attempts the task of a creator as he "counts out limbs" to his son and "fashions his body" (*corpus fingit*, 1264–65). But the word *fingit* can mean also "feigns, fabricates," and that sense is reinforced in what follows; the arbitrariness of setting a formless piece of the body "not in its proper place, but in an empty place," underlines the impossibility of restoring the body in any real sense.

From one viewpoint human beings are the source of their own destruction in this play, Hippolytus through escapism, Phaedra through self-indulgent emotionalism, Theseus through thoughtlessness. Yet they can also be seen as victims of forces greater than themselves, in particular Nature (read sexuality) and ancestry, and of external circumstances, and of an uncaring god. Their punishment is out of all proportion to their responsibility. The response shaped by the play is not one of moral condemnation, but rather of compassion. Such a tragic effect is comparable to that of many Greek tragedies. Yet the tone is darker and more Senecan: there is no resolution of the hatred between Phaedra and Theseus, for each closes by cursing the other; and there is no evidence of either human or divine order in the world of this play, where a god intervenes only to destroy the innocent.

Sources

The strongest and most immediate influence on Seneca's portrait of Phaedra lay in Ovid's *Heroides*. Almost every line of *Heroides* 4, the imaginary letter from Phaedra to Hippolytus, is echoed in some way in Seneca's play. But there is more change and development in Seneca's Phaedra. The Ovidian letter is in a minor key, an overtly artificial construct; to reread Phaedra's opening words in Seneca after reading the letter is to return to a major mode, to the sweeping power of drama.

There had been three well known Greek dramas on these mythical events, the *Phaedra* of Sophocles, now lost, and two *Hippolytus* plays of Euripides, of which the earlier is lost while the later survives. In the surviving play Phaedra is desperately determined to resist her desire, to say nothing to Hippolytus, and to preserve her reputation. A famous scene from this play, showing Phaedra in delirium (176–238), is integrated into Seneca's depiction of Phaedra's developing frenzy (358–403). Seneca's messenger speech is also modelled loosely on Euripides', with colouring from Ovid's *Metamorphoses* (15.497–529); otherwise the surviving *Hippolytus* play contributes little directly to

Seneca's play.[1] Reconstruction of the two lost plays is precarious, and we cannot be sure that Seneca knew either of them. In the earlier *Hippolytus* it seems likely that Phaedra approached Hippolytus directly, and may have been quite forthright in pursuing her desire. In Seneca too she approaches her stepson directly, but her hesitancy probably comes from Ovid rather than from Euripides. About Sophocles' play one of the few reliable details is that Theseus was absent in Hades, rather than elsewhere. In Seneca this detail (not necessarily drawn directly from Sophocles) serves to associate Theseus thematically with the world of death.

BIBLIOGRAPHY

Commentaries

A. J. Boyle, *Seneca's Phaedra: Introduction, Text, Translation and Notes* (Liverpool, 1987).

M. Coffey and R. Mayer, *Seneca: Phaedra* (Cambridge etc., 1990).

Criticism

A. J. Boyle, "In Nature's Bonds; a Study of Seneca's *Phaedra*," *ANRW* II 32.2 (1985), 1284–1347.

[1] Seneca's Ode 1, on the power of love, may have been suggested by an ode at the corresponding point in Euripides' play 525ff., cf. 447ff.), but the development of the topic is quite different. Seneca's lines on desire in the animal kingdom are overtly indebted to Book 3 of Vergil's *Georgics*.

P. J. Davis, "Vindicat Omnes Natura Sibi: a Reading of Seneca's Phaedra," in Boyle (1983), 114–27.

J. J. Gahan, "*Imitatio* and *aemulatio* in Seneca's *Phaedra*," *Latomus* 46 (1987), 380–87 (specifically on Act 5).

P. Grimal, "L'originalité de Sénèque dans la tragédie de Phèdre," *Rev. Ét. Lat.* 41 (1963), 297–314; also in *Rome: la littérature et l'histoire* 1 (Rome, 1986), 557–73.

D. Henry and B. Walker, "Phantasmagoria and Idyll: an Element of Seneca's Phaedra," *G&R* 13 (1966) 223–39.

C. Segal, "Senecan Baroque: the Death of Hippolytus in Seneca, Ovid, Euripides," *TAPA* 114 (1984), 311–25.

——— *Language and Desire in Seneca's Phaedra* (Princeton, 1986).

Heaven-sent is that fire (believe its victims)
and all too powerful.
Where the earth is girdled by the deep salt sea
and where the bright stars run their courses
through the very heavens,
the implacable boy holds sovereignty.
In the watery depths his arrows are felt
by the sea-blue throng of Nereids,
who cannot allay those flames with the sea.
His fires are felt by winged creatures.
Roused by Venus, a bullock boldly
undertakes war for the whole herd.
If they fear the loss of their mates,
timid stags issue challenges to battle,
and with their roaring
they signal the madness engendered in them.
At that time swarthy India dreads
the banded tigers;
the boar sharpens his wounding tusks
at that time, with foam covering his muzzle;
Carthaginian lions shake their manes
when love has moved them;
then the woods echo with savage growls.
The leviathan of the maddened seas feels love,
the elephant too.
    Nature asserts her power over all.
Nothing is immune,
and hatred vanishes when love commands;
inveterate anger yields to that fire.
To end my song:
love-cares conquer stepmothers' cruelty.

PHAEDRA

HIPPOLYTUS

Ite, umbrosas cingite silvas
summaque montis iuga Cecropii!
celeri planta lustrate vagi
quae saxoso loca Parnetho
subiecta iacent,
quae Thriasiis vallibus amnis
rapida currens verberat unda;
scandite colles
semper canos nive Riphaea.
   Hac, hac alii
qua nemus alta texitur alno,
qua prata iacent
quae rorifera mulcens aura
Zephyrus vernas evocat herbas,
ubi per graciles
levis Ilisos labitur agros
piger et steriles
amne maligno radit harenas.
   Vos qua Marathon tramite laevo
saltus aperit,
qua comitatae gregibus parvis
nocturna petunt pabula fetae;

PHAEDRA

HIPPOLYTUS

[*To huntsmen attending him*]
Go, surround the shady forests
and high mountain ridges of Cecrops' land!
Roam widely on swift feet, and range
the lands that lie below the crags
of Mt Parnethus
and the lands that the river in Thria's vale
buffets as it rushes with its whirling current;
climb the hills
always white with Riphaean snow.

    Other men, go here
where lofty alders weave a grove,
where meadows lie
caressed by the Zephyr's dewy breeze
inviting the growth of springtime grasses,
and where through thin-soiled
fields the slight Ilisos glides
sluggishly, and scrapes
the barren sands with its grudging stream.

    You men, go by the left-hand path
where Marathon opens its glades,
where in the company of their small brood
dams seek out forage at night;

20 vos qua tepidis subditus austris
frigora mollit durus Acharneus.
    Alius rupem dulcis Hymetti,
planas alius calcet Aphidnas.
pars illa diu vacat immunis,
25 qua curvati litora ponti
Sunion urget.
si quem tangit gloria silvae,
vocat hunc Phyle:
hic versatur, metus agricolis,
30 vulnere multo iam notus aper.

At vos laxas
canibus tacitis mittite habenas.
teneant acres lora Molossos,
et pugnaces tendant Cretes
fortia trito vincula collo.
at Spartanos
35 (genus est audax avidumque ferae)
nodo cautus propiore liga.
veniet tempus,
cum latratu cava saxa sonent;
nunc demissi nare sagaci
captent auras
40 lustraque presso quaerant rostro,
dum lux dubia est,
dum signa pedum roscida tellus
impressa tenet.

23 planas *Watt*: parvas *EA*
28 Phyle *Frenzel*: flius *E*: philippis *A*

you, where exposure to warm south winds
softens the frosts for the rugged Acharnian.
    Let one man tread the crags of sweet
Hymettus, another the plain of Aphidnae.
That region has long been lying untouched
where Sunion
pushes back the edge of the curving sea.
Phyle calls
to anyone roused by woodland glory:
here stirs the dread of farmers, a boar
famed by now for many a wound.

Now you men, give
free rein to the hounds that hunt in silence.
The keen Molossians should be kept on the leash,
and the quarrelsome Cretans should strain at the
    sturdy
chains abrading the coat on their necks.
But the Spartan hounds—
the breed is fearless and avid for the prey,
so fasten them carefully with a closer knot.
The time will come
when the circle of cliffs can ring with their barking;
now with heads lowered
they must sniff out the scent with their keen nostrils,
search the coverts with muzzles down,
while the light is dim,
while the dewy ground holds the marks of feet
imprinted on it.

    Alius raras
cervice gravi portare plagas,
45   alius teretes properet laqueos.
picta rubenti linea pinna
vano claudat terrore feras.
Tibi libretur missile telum,
tu grave dextra laevaque simul
50   robur lato derige ferro;
tu praecipites clamore feras
subsessor ages;
tu iam victor
curvo solves viscera cultro.

    Ades en comiti, diva virago,
55   cuius regno
pars terrarum secreta vacat,
cuius certis petitur telis
fera quae gelidum potat Araxen
et quae stanti ludit in Histro.
60   tua Gaetulos dextra leones,
tua Cretaeas sequitur cervas.
[nunc veloces figis dammas
leviore manu]
tibi dant variae pectora tigres,
tibi villosi terga bisontes
65   latisque feri cornibus uri.
quidquid solis pascitur arvis,
sive illud Arabs divite silva,
sive illud inops novit Garamans

62f. *deleted by Fitch*

Someone must quickly
bring the wide-meshed nets loaded on his neck,
someone else the fine-spun snares.
The line with its colourful crimson feathers
must pen the wild beasts with empty terror.
You must aim the throwing spear;
you, with both hands together, direct
the heavy shaft with its broad blade.[1]
You will drive the racing beasts with your shouts
after waiting by the nets;
at the moment of victory
you will loose the innards with the curving knife.

Come to your comrade here, virile goddess,
you for whose rule
the secluded parts of the earth are open,
whose unerring shafts seek out
the beast that drinks the cold Araxes,
the beast that frolics on the still Hister.[2]
Your hand hunts Gaetulian lions,
your hand, the deer of Crete.[3]
To you striped tigers present their chests,
to you shaggy bison show their backs,
so too wild oxen with their broad horns.
All creatures that feed in lonely lands—
whether known to the Arabs in their rich forests
or known to needy Garamantians

---

[1] The thrusting spear.

[2] I.e. on the river's frozen surface.

[3] Lines 62f. (deleted): "now you pierce swift fallow deer / with a lighter hand."

71	vacuisque vagus Sarmata campis,
69	sive ferocis iuga Pyrenes
70	sive Hyrcani celant saltus,
72	arcus metuit, Diana, tuos.
	Tua si gratus numina cultor
	tulit in saltus,
75	retia vinctas tenuere feras,
	nulli laqueum rupere pedes;
	fertur plaustro praeda gementi;
	tum rostra canes
	sanguine multo rubicunda gerunt,
	repetitque casas
80	rustica longo turba triumpho.
	En, diva, fave!
	signum arguti misere canes:
	vocor in silvas.
	hac, hac pergam
	qua via longum compensat iter.

PHAEDRA

85	O magna vasti Creta dominatrix freti,
	cuius per omne litus innumerae rates
	tenuere pontum, quidquid Assyria tenus
	tellure Nereus pervium rostris secat,
	cur me in penates obsidem invisos datam
90	hostique nuptam degere aetatem in malis
	lacrimisque cogis? profugus en coniunx abest
	praestatque nuptae quam solet Theseus fidem.

81 fave *EA*: faves *recc.*: favet *Delrius*

or to nomad Sarmatae on their empty plains,
whether the peaks of the wild Pyrenees
or the forests of Hyrcania conceal them—
all are afraid of your bow, Diana.

If a favoured worshipper takes your power
into the forests,
his nets hold the beasts fast-bound,
no creature's feet break the snares;
the prey is brought in on a groaning wagon;
then the hounds return
with muzzles reddened by plentiful blood,
and the rustic throng head for their cottages
in a long triumphal procession.

Ah! Favour me, goddess:
the clear-voiced hounds have sent the sign;
I am called to the woods.
I shall go this way,
where a path shortens the lengthy journey.

ACT 1

PHAEDRA

O Crete, great commandress of the vast sea, along whose
every coast countless vessels hold the deep, wherever
Nereus cuts a passageway for ships even as far as the land
of Assyria: why have you given me as hostage to a hated
house, married me to our enemy and forced me to spend
my life in pain and tears? See, my husband is playing truant
and runaway; Theseus shows his wife his usual faithful-

fortis per altas invii retro lacus
vadit tenebras miles audacis proci,
95   solio ut revulsam regis inferni abstrahat;
pergit furoris socius, haud illum timor
pudorque tenuit: stupra et illicitos toros
Acheronte in imo quaerit Hippolyti pater.
     Sed maior alius incubat maestae dolor.
100 non me quies nocturna, non altus sopor
solvere curis. alitur et crescit malum
et ardet intus, qualis Aetnaeo vapor
exundat antro. Palladis telae vacant
et inter ipsas pensa labuntur manus;
105 non colere donis templa votivis libet,
non inter aras, Atthidum mixtam choris,
iactare tacitis conscias sacris faces,
nec adire castis precibus aut ritu pio
adiudicatae praesidem terrae deam:
110 iuvat excitatas consequi cursu feras
et rigida molli gaesa iaculari manu.
     Quo tendis, anime? quid furens saltus amas?
fatale miserae matris agnosco malum;
peccare noster novit in silvis amor.
115 genetrix, tui me miseret. infando malo
correpta pecoris efferum saevi ducem
audax amasti. torvus, impatiens iugi
adulter ille ductor indomiti gregis—
sed amabat aliquid! quis meas miserae deus

---

4 Women to whom he was unfaithful included Ariadne and his wife Antiope.   5 A reference to Proserpine, whom the "suitor" Pirithous planned to kidnap.   6 Spinning and weaving wool

ness.[4] Bravely he travels through the deep darkness of the lake that none can recross, recruited by an audacious suitor to carry away one torn from the throne of the underworld's king![5] He presses on as the ally of madness, no fear or shame held him back; illicit, adulterous sex is sought in the depths of Acheron by Hippolytus' father.

But another, greater pain weighs on my distress. No nightly rest, no deep sleep releases me from my cares. My trouble feeds and grows and burns within me, like the heat that pours from Etna's cavern. Pallas' loom is idle, and the wool slips from between my hands.[6] I have no desire to honour the temples with votive offerings, nor to join the choruses of Athenian women amidst the altars and whirl torches in witness of the silent rites, nor to approach with chaste prayers and devout rituals the goddess who guards the land adjudicated as hers.[7] My pleasure lies in starting and pursuing beasts in the chase, and in hurling stiff javelins with my soft hand.

What course is this, my spirit? What is this crazy love of the woodland? I recognise my poor mother's fateful evil; our love is experienced at sinning in the forests. Mother, I pity you. You were seized by unspeakable evil, an audacious love for the wild leader of fierce cattle. A brute lecherer, impatient of the yoke, was that leader of the untamed herd—yet he loved *something*![8] What god or what

were standard domestic tasks for women, and under the patronage of Pallas as goddess of crafts.   [7] The silent rites are those of the Eleusinian Mysteries; the guardian goddess is Pallas.

[8] Namely the cow as which Pasiphae disguised herself with Daedalus' help. Daedalus also built the labyrinth to house the Minotaur (the "monster" of line 122).

120   aut quis iuvare Daedalus flammas queat?
     non si ille remeet, arte Mopsopia potens,
     qui nostra caeca monstra conclusit domo,
     promittet ullam casibus nostris opem.
     stirpem perosa Solis invisi Venus
125   per nos catenas vindicat Martis sui
     suasque, probris omne Phoebeum genus
     onerat nefandis: nulla Minois levi
     defuncta amore est, iungitur semper nefas.

NUTRIX

     Thesea coniunx, clara progenies Iovis,
130   nefanda casto pectore exturba ocius,
     extingue flammas, neve te dirae spei
     praebe obsequentem. quisquis in primo obstitit
     pepulitque amorem, tutus ac victor fuit;
     qui blandiendo dulce nutrivit malum,
135   sero recusat ferre quod subiit iugum.
       Nec me fugit, quam durus et veri insolens
     ad recta flecti regius nolit tumor.
     quemcumque dederit exitum casus feram:
     fortem facit vicina libertas senem.
140   Honesta primum est velle nec labi via;
     pudor est secundus nosse peccandi modum.
     quo, misera, pergis? quid domum infamem aggravas
     superasque matrem? maius est monstro nefas:
     nam monstra fato, moribus scelera imputes.
145   Si, quod maritus supera non cernit loca,
     tutum esse facinus credis et vacuum metu,
     erras; teneri crede Lethaeo abditum
     Thesea profundo et ferre perpetuam Styga:
     quid ille, lato maria qui regno premit

Daedalus could assist *my* unhappy flames of passion? Not even if that master of Mopsopian arts should return, who enclosed our monster in his blind house, could he promise any aid in my misfortune. Venus hates the offspring of her enemy the Sun; she is avenging through us the chains that bound her dear Mars and herself, burdening the whole tribe of Phoebus with unspeakable scandals. No daughter of Minos has got through a love affair lightly; always it is linked to infamy.

NURSE

Wife of Theseus, illustrious progeny of Jove: banish these unspeakable thoughts at once from your chaste heart, extinguish the flames, do not make yourself compliant to such an appalling hope. A person who resists and rejects love at the outset wins safety and victory; but one who nurtures the sweet evil by indulging it, protests too late at wearing the yoke he has put on.

I am well aware how obdurate and unused to the truth is royal pride, how unwilling to be corrected. But I shall bear any outcome that chance brings: the closeness of freedom makes the aged brave.

Best is an honorable purpose, with no going astray; second best is a sense of shame, to recognise some limit in sin. What path is this, poor woman? Why worsen the infamy of your house, and outdo your mother? This outrage is worse than monstrous, for the monstrous is attributable to fate, but crime to character. If you suppose that, because your husband cannot see the upper world, the deed is safe and free of danger, you are wrong. Suppose Theseus is held buried in Lethaean depths and endures the Stygian world forever: what of him who dominates the seas with his

150   populisque reddit iura centenis, pater?
      latere tantum facinus occultum sinet?
      sagax parentum est cura. Credamus tamen
      astu doloque tegere nos tantum nefas:
      quid ille rebus lumen infundens suum,
155   matris parens? quid ille, qui mundum quatit
      vibrans corusca fulmen Aetnaeum manu,
      sator deorum? credis hoc posse effici,
      inter videntes omnia ut lateas avos?
      Sed ut secundus numinum abscondat favor
160   coitus nefandos utque contingat stupro
      negata magnis sceleribus semper fides:
      quid poena praesens, conscius mentis pavor
      animusque culpa plenus et semet timens?
      scelus aliqua tutum, nulla securum tulit.
165   Compesce amoris impii flammas, precor,
      nefasque quod non ulla tellus barbara
      commisit umquam, non vagi campis Getae
      nec inhospitalis Taurus aut sparsus Scythes.
      expelle facinus mente castifica horridum,
170   memorque matris metue concubitus novos.
      miscere thalamos patris et nati apparas
      uteroque prolem capere confusam impio?
      perge et nefandis verte naturam ignibus!
      cur monstra cessant? aula cur fratris vacat?
175   prodigia totiens orbis insueta audiet,
      natura totiens legibus cedet suis,
      quotiens amabit Cressa?

broad sway and dispenses justice to a hundred communities[9]—your father? Will he let such a deed lie uncon-
cealed? Parents' care is shrewd. But suppose we conceal
such an outrage by cunning and deceit: what of him who
pours his light on the world, your mother's father? What of
him who shakes the heavens, brandishing the bolt from
Etna in his glittering hand, procreator of the gods? Do you
suppose it can be managed that between these all-seeing
grandfathers you will not be seen? But imagine this wicked
coupling is concealed by the gods' kindly support, imagine
your debauchery meets with the loyalty that is always with-
held from great crimes: what of the ever present punishment—the mind's fearful conscience, the spirit full of guilt
and afraid of itself? Some women have transgressed with
safety, but none with peace of mind.

Check these flames of unnatural love, I pray you, this
evil that no barbarian land has ever committed—not the
Getae wandering on their plains nor the inhospitable
Taurians nor the scattered Scythians. Banish this terrible
deed from your chaste mind; with memories of your
mother, shrink from unheard-of sexual union. Are you
planning to confound the beds of father and son, to hold a
progeny of confusion in an unnatural womb? Go on, overturn nature with your wicked fires! Why have monsters
ceased? Why is your brother's hall empty?[10] Shall the
world always hear of strange portents, shall nature always
abandon her laws, when a Cretan woman loves?

9 The "hundred cities" of Crete.
10 Her brother is the Minotaur, his hall the labyrinth.

PHAEDRA
       Quae memoras scio
vera esse, nutrix; sed furor cogit sequi
peiora. vadit animus in praeceps sciens
180 remeatque frustra sana consilia appetens.
sic, cum gravatam navita adversa ratem
propellit unda, cedit in vanum labor
et victa prono puppis aufertur vado.
quid ratio possit? vicit ac regnat furor,
185 potensque tota mente dominatur deus.
hic volucer omni pollet in terra impotens,
ipsumque flammis torret indomitis Iovem;
Gradivus istas belliger sensit faces,
opifex trisulci fulminis sensit deus,
190 et qui furentes semper Aetnaeis iugis
versat caminos igne tam parvo calet;
ipsumque Phoebum, tela qui nervo regit,
figit sagitta certior missa puer,
volitatque caelo pariter et terris gravis.

NUTRIX
195 Deum esse amorem turpis et vitio favens
finxit libido, quoque liberior foret
titulum furori numinis falsi addidit.
natum per omnes scilicet terras vagum
Erycina mittit, ille per caelum volans
200 proterva tenera tela molitur manu
regnumque tantum minimus e superis habet!
vana ista demens animus ascivit sibi
Venerisque numen finxit atque arcus dei.

---

[187] ipsumque *A*: laesumque* *E*

PHAEDRA

I know that what you say is true, nurse; but madness forces me to follow the worse path. My spirit goes knowingly into the abyss, and turns back ineffectively in search of sane judgement. So, when a sailor drives a laden vessel against the current, his efforts go to waste, and the overpowered ship is carried away by the headlong flow. What could reason do? Madness has conquered and rules me, and a mighty god controls my whole mind. This winged one has uncurbed power in every land, and with his unbridled flames he fires Jove himself. Warlike Gradivus has felt those firebrands; the craftsman god of the three-forked lightning[11] has felt them—the one who quickens the furnaces ever raging in Etna's peak grows hot with so small a fire. Even Phoebus, who aims arrows true from his bow, was shot more unerringly with a shaft fired by that boy, who flies about oppressing heaven and earth alike.

NURSE

The story that love is a god was invented by base lust, in the interests of its own depravity; to have greater scope, it gave its mad passion the pretext of a false divinity. Of *course* the goddess of Eryx sends her son wandering through the whole earth; he flies through the sky wielding wanton weapons in his tender hand, and holds such great sway as the smallest of the gods! It was a crazy spirit that adopted this fiction, and invented Venus' divinity and the god's bow.

11 Vulcan.

Quisquis secundis rebus exultat nimis
205 fluitque luxu, semper insolita appetit.
tunc illa magnae dira fortunae comes
subit libido; non placent suetae dapes,
non texta sani moris aut vilis scyphus.
cur in penates rarius tenues subit
210 haec delicatas eligens pestis domos?
cur sancta parvis habitat in tectis Venus
mediumque sanos vulgus affectus tenet
et se coercent modica, contra divites
regnoque fulti plura quam fas est petunt?
215 quod non potest vult posse qui nimium potest.
quid deceat alto praeditam solio vide:
metue ac verere sceptra remeantis viri.

PHAEDRA

Amoris in me maximum regnum puto
reditusque nullos metuo: non umquam amplius
220 convexa tetigit supera qui mersus semel
adiit silentem nocte perpetua domum.

NUTRIX

Ne crede Diti. clauserit regnum licet,
canisque diras Stygius observet fores,
solus negatas invenit Theseus vias.

PHAEDRA

225 Veniam ille amori forsitan nostro dabit.

NUTRIX

Immitis etiam coniugi castae fuit:

---

208 texta *Cornelissen*: tecta *EA*   scyphus *Jac. Gronovius*:
cibus *EA*

Those who grow too extravagant through prosperity, overflowing with luxury, are always seeking out the unusual. Then lust steals in, that dire companion of great good fortune. Ordinary meals are not satisfactory, nor fabrics of a sane style nor cheap drinking cups. Why does this infection choose pampered homes, and steal less often into humble families? Why is it that chaste love dwells beneath lowly roofs, that average folk have sane affections and modest status is self-controlled, while the rich and those bolstered by royal status seek more than what is right? Excessive power wants power beyond its power. Think what befits a woman endowed with a high throne: fear and respect the sceptre of your returning husband.

PHAEDRA

I hold the greatest sovereignty over me to be love's, and I have no fear of any return: nevermore does anyone gain heaven's vault, once he has descended and reached the silent halls of perpetual night.

NURSE

Do not place your trust in Dis. Though he has closed his kingdom and the Stygian hound watches the terrible doors, Theseus alone can find forbidden paths.[12]

PHAEDRA

Perhaps he will grant forgiveness to my love.

NURSE

He was implacable even to a chaste wife: barbarian An-

---

[12] An allusion to his escape from the labyrinth.

experta saevam est barbara Antiope manum.
sed posse flecti coniugem iratum puta:
quis huius animum flectet intractabilem?
230 exosus omne feminae nomen fugit,
immitis annos caelibi vitae dicat,
conubia vitat: genus Amazonium scias.

PHAEDRA

Hunc in nivosi collis haerentem iugis
et aspera agili saxa calcantem pede
235 sequi per alta nemora, per montes placet.

NUTRIX

Resistet ille seque mulcendum dabit
castosque ritus Venere non casta exuet?
tibi ponet odium, cuius odio forsitan
persequitur omnes?

PHAEDRA
Precibus at vinci potest.

NUTRIX

240 Ferus est.

PHAEDRA
Amore didicimus vinci feros.

NUTRIX

Fugiet.

PHAEDRA
Per ipsa maria si fugiat, sequar.

NUTRIX

Patris memento.

239 at *an anonymous scholiast*: haud E: aut A

466

tiope found his hand to be savage. But suppose your husband's anger can be softened: who will soften *this* one's intractable spirit? He hates and shuns all that is called woman, implacably devotes his youth to a celibate life, and avoids marriage: you would know his Amazon breeding.

PHAEDRA

Though he lingers on the ridges of snowy hills and treads jagged rocks with nimble feet, I intend to follow him across deep forests, across mountains.

NURSE

Will he stop and allow himself to be caressed, and throw off his chaste ways for an unchaste love affair? For you will he drop his hate, when hate of you perhaps makes him harry all women?

PHAEDRA

But he can be overcome by prayers.

NURSE

He is wild.

PHAEDRA

I have learnt that wild things are overcome by love.

NURSE

He will flee.

PHAEDRA

If he should flee across the very seas, I would follow.

NURSE

Remember your father!

PHAEDRA
Meminimus matris simul.

NUTRIX
Genus omne profugit.

PHAEDRA
Paelicis careo metu.

NUTRIX
Aderit maritus.

PHAEDRA
Nempe Pirithoi comes.

NUTRIX
245   Aderitque genitor.

PHAEDRA
Mitis Ariadnae pater.

NUTRIX
Per has senectae splendidas supplex comas
fessumque curis pectus et cara ubera
precor, furorem siste teque ipsa adiuva:
pars sanitatis velle sanari fuit.

PHAEDRA
250   Non omnis animo cessit ingenuo pudor.
paremus, altrix. qui regi non vult amor,
vincatur. haud te, fama, maculari sinam.
261   proin castitatis vindicem armemus manum.
haec sola ratio est, unicum effugium mali:
virum sequamur, morte praevertam nefas.

---

261 *transposed after* 252 *by Fitch, after* 266 *by Gronovius*

PHAEDRA

I remember my mother as well.

NURSE

He shuns our whole kind.

PHAEDRA

I have no fear of a rival.

NURSE

Your husband will be here.

PHAEDRA

You mean Pirithous' companion.[13]

NURSE

And your father will be here.

PHAEDRA

Ariadne's merciful father.[14]

NURSE

By these bright hairs of old age, by this care-worn heart and these dear breasts, I pray as a suppliant: check this madness and come to your own help. Part of health is the will to be healed.

PHAEDRA

My spirit has not lost all sense of shame and honour. I am ruled by you, nurse. The love that will not be governed must be vanquished. I will not allow my reputation to be stained. So I must arm my hands to defend my chastity. This is the only means, the one escape from evil. I must follow my man, and avert this enormity by death.

[13] As accomplice of a would-be adulterer, he can hardly condemn Phaedra.   [14] I.e. since Minos tolerated Ariadne's elopement with Theseus, he will show leniency to Phaedra.

NUTRIX

255 Moderare, alumna, mentis effrenae impetus,
animos coerce. dignam ob hoc vita reor
quod esse temet autumas dignam nece.

PHAEDRA

Decreta mors est: quaeritur fati genus.
laqueone vitam finiam an ferro incubem,
260 an missa praeceps arce Palladia cadam?

NUTRIX

262 Sic te senectus nostra praecipiti sinat
perire leto? siste furibundum impetum.

PHAEDRA

265 Prohibere nulla ratio periturum potest,
ubi qui mori constituit et debet mori.

NUTRIX

Solamen annis unicum fessis, era,
si tam protervus incubat menti furor,
contemne famam: fama vix vero favet,
270 peius merenti melior et peior bono.
temptemus animum tristem et intractabilem.
meus iste labor est aggredi iuvenem ferum
mentemque saevam flectere immitis viri.

CHORUS

Diva non miti generata ponto,
275 quam vocat matrem geminus Cupido
impotens flammis simul et sagittis:
iste lascivus puer ac renidens

---

264 haud quisquam ad vitam facile revocari potest *is unmetrical and found only in E*

PHAEDRA

NURSE

My child, restrain your mind's unbridled impulse, rein in your spirit. I think you deserving of life just because you judge yourself deserving of death.

PHAEDRA

Death is resolved; the question is how to die. Shall I end my life with a rope, or fall on a sword, or jump and fall headlong from Pallas' citadel?

NURSE

Shall my old age let you go headlong to your death like this? Check this frenzied impulse.

PHAEDRA

No consideration can prevent someone from dying, who has both the resolve and the duty to die.

NURSE

My mistress, only solace of my weary years: if such a reckless madness weighs on your mind, scorn reputation; reputation hardly favours the truth, better for the less worthy and worse for the good. Let us test his grim, intractable spirit. It is my task to tackle the wild youth, and soften the fierce mind of that implacable man.

CHORUS

Goddess born of the implacable sea,
called mother by Cupid the twinborn,
who is reckless with fires and arrows alike:
that wanton, smiling boy of yours

tela quam certo moderatur arcu!
[labitur totas furor in medullas
280   igne furtivo populante venas]
non habet latam data plaga frontem,
sed vorat tectas penitus medullas.
nulla pax isti puero: per orbem
spargit effusas agilis sagittas.
285   quaeque nascentem videt ora solem,
quaeque ad Hesperias iacet ora metas,
si qua ferventi subiecta Cancro est,
si qua Parrhasiae glacialis Ursae
semper errantes patitur colonos,
290   novit hos aestus. iuvenum feroces
concitat flammas senibusque fessis
rursus extinctos revocat calores,
virginum ignoto ferit igne pectus—
et iubet caelo superos relicto
295   vultibus falsis habitare terras.

    Thessali Phoebus pecoris magister
egit armentum, positoque plectro
impari tauros calamo vocavit.
Induit formas quotiens minores
300   ipse qui caelum nebulasque ducit!
candidas ales modo movit alas,
dulcior vocem moriente cygno;
fronte nunc torva petulans iuvencus
virginum stravit sua terga ludo,
305   perque fraternos, nova regna, fluctus
ungula lentos imitante remos
pectore adverso domuit profundum,

279–80 *found only in E, deleted by Bothe*

472

aims shafts from such an unerring bow![15]
The wound he gives has no broad surface,
but eats deep into the hidden marrow.
No peace for your boy: throughout the world
he spryly showers and scatters his arrows.
All regions that see the sun being born,
all regions that lie near his western goal,
any placed beneath the blazing Crab,
any frozen beneath the Parrhasian Bear
and enduring settlers who wander ever[16]—
all know these fires. He arouses youths'
ferocious flames, and in tired old men
he wakes again the extinguished warmth,
strikes maidens' hearts with unknown fire—
and bids the gods abandon heaven
and dwell with features disguised on earth.

Phoebus as master of a herd in Thessaly
drove cattle; setting aside his lyre
he called the bulls with a slanting reedpipe.
Even he who guides the clouds and heavens
so often put on humbler forms!
Now as a bird he moved white wings,
sweeter-voiced than the dying swan;
grim-faced now as a boisterous bull
he lowered his back for playful maidens,
and through a new realm, his brother's waves,
as his hooves played the role of pliant oars,
he breasted and overcame the deep,

---

15 Lines 279–80 (deleted): "The madness slides deep into the
marrow, / as the stealthy fire ravages the veins."

16 The nomads of the northern steppes.

pro sua vector timidus rapina.
Arsit obscuri dea clara mundi
310 nocte deserta nitidosque fratri
tradidit currus aliter regendos:
ille nocturnas agitare bigas
discit et gyro breviore flecti,
nec suum tempus tenuere noctes
315 et dies tardo remeavit ortu,
dum tremunt axes graviore curru.
   Natus Alcmena posuit pharetras
et minax vasti spolium leonis,
passus aptari digitis smaragdos
320 et dari legem rudibus capillis;
crura distincto religavit auro,
luteo plantas cohibente socco;
et manu, clavam modo qua gerebat,
fila deduxit properante fuso.
325   Vidit Persis
ditisque ferax Lydia harenae
deiecta feri terga leonis
‹sumptamque toris› umerisque, quibus
sederat alti regia caeli,
tenuem Tyrio stamine pallam.

---

326 ditisque *recc.*: ditique *EA*   harenae *Grotius*: regno *EP*:
regni *CS*   328 *lacuna recognised by Leo; supplement by
Fitch, based on Leo's* sumptamque armis.

---

17 These lines allude to Jove's wooing of Leda as swan and
Europa as bull; the following lines refer to the amours of Phoebe
with Endymion and of Hercules with Omphale. A lively anony-

fearing for the stolen cargo he carried.[17]
Fire touched the bright goddess of the darkened sky;
she forsook the night and entrusted her brother
with the different driving of her shining chariot.
He learnt to guide the two-horse team
of night, and wheel in a tighter circuit.
But the nights did not keep their proper hours,
and day returned in a tardy dawn
as the burdened chariot's axle trembled.

    Alcmene's son set aside his quiver
and the threatening spoil from the awesome lion,
allowing his fingers to be fitted with emeralds
and his rough hair to be brought to order.
He bound his legs with studded gold,
while yellow slippers confined his feet;
and the hand that had just now borne the club
drew out threads with the hurrying spindle.

    Persia was witness
    and Lydia fertile in rich sand
    as he cast aside the fierce lion's pelt,
    ⟨and took on those thews⟩ and shoulders, on
      which
    the palace of lofty heaven had rested,
    a delicate robe of Tyrian thread.

mous version of 300ff. appeared in 1557: "And oft eke him that
doth the heavens guide / Hath love transformed to shapes for him
too base. / Transmuted thus sometime a swan is he, / Leda [to en-
tice] and eft Europe to please; / A mild white bull, with wrinkled
front and face, / Suffereth her play till on his back leaps she, /
Whom in great care he ferryeth through the seas."

330   Sacer est ignis (credite laesis)
         nimiumque potens.
         qua terra salo cingitur alto
         quaque per ipsum candida mundum
         sidera currunt,
         hac regna tenet puer immitis,
335   spicula cuius sentit in imis
         caerulus undis grex Nereidum
         flammamque nequit relevare mari.
         Ignes sentit genus aligerum.
         Venere instinctus suscipit audax
340   grege pro toto bella iuvencus;
         si coniugio timuere suo,
         poscunt timidi proelia cervi,
         et mugitu
         dant concepti signa furoris.
345   tunc virgatas India tigres
         decolor horret;
         tunc vulnificos acuit dentes
         aper et toto est spumeus ore;
         Poeni quatiunt colla leones,
         cum movit amor;
350   tum silva gemit murmure saevo.
         amat insani belua ponti
         lucaeque boves.
            Vindicat omnes natura sibi,
         nihil immune est,
         odiumque perit, cum iussit amor;
355   veteres cedunt ignibus irae.
         quid plura canam?
         vincit saevas cura novercas.

Heaven-sent is that fire (believe its victims)
and all too powerful.
Where the earth is girdled by the deep salt sea
and where the bright stars run their courses
through the very heavens,
the implacable boy holds sovereignty.
In the watery depths his arrows are felt
by the sea-blue throng of Nereids,
who cannot allay those flames with the sea.
His fires are felt by winged creatures.
Roused by Venus, a bullock boldly
undertakes war for the whole herd.
If they fear the loss of their mates,
timid stags issue challenges to battle,
and with their roaring
they signal the madness engendered in them.
At that time banded tigers are dreaded
by swarthy India;
the boar sharpens his wounding tusks
at that time, with foam covering his muzzle;
Carthaginian lions shake their manes
when love has moved them;
then the woods echo with savage growls.
The leviathan of the maddened seas feels love,
the elephant too.
Nature asserts her power over all.
Nothing is immune,
and hatred vanishes when love commands;
inveterate anger yields to that fire.
To end my song:
love-cares conquer stepmothers' cruelty.

Altrix, profare quid feras; quonam in loco est
regina? saevis ecquis est flammis modus?

NUTRIX

360 Spes nulla tantum posse leniri malum,
finisque flammis nullus insanis erit.
torretur aestu tacito et inclusus quoque,
quamvis tegatur, proditur vultu furor;
erumpit oculis ignis et lassae genae
365 lucem recusant; nil idem dubiae placet,
artusque varie iactat incertus dolor:
nunc ut soluto labitur marcens gradu
et vix labante sustinet collo caput,
nunc se quieti reddit et, somni immemor,
370 noctem querelis ducit; attolli iubet
iterumque poni corpus et solvi comas
rursusque fingi; semper impatiens sui
mutatur habitus. nulla iam Cereris subit
cura aut salutis. vadit incerto pede,
375 iam viribus defecta: non idem vigor,
non ora tinguens nitida purpureus rubor;
[populatur artus cura, iam gressus tremunt,
tenerque nitidi corporis cecidit decor]
et qui ferebant signa Phoebeae facis
380 oculi nihil gentile nec patrium micant.
lacrimae cadunt per ora et assiduo genae
rore irrigantur, qualiter Tauri iugis
tepido madescunt imbre percussae nives.
    Sed en, patescunt regiae fastigia:

367 marcens *Axelson*: moriens *EA*
377–78 *deleted by Leo*

478

ACT 2

Nurse, tell us your news. What is the queen's situation? Is there any moderation of the cruel flames?

NURSE

No hope exists that such an affliction can be eased; there will be no end to the flames of insanity. The fever silently burns her, and her inner madness, however much concealed, is betrayed in her face. Fire bursts forth through her eyes; her weary sight cannot bear the daylight. Nothing pleases her fickle mind for long, and her restless pain disturbs her body in various ways: now she flags and collapses, with weakness in her step, and can hardly support her head on her drooping neck; now she prepares to rest, but forgets sleep and spends the night in laments. She bids them raise her body and lay it down again, unfasten her hair and arrange it once more; her condition is always impatient with itself and changing. No thought of food or health now occurs to her. Her feet falter as her strength fails; there is not that same vigour, not the ruddiness that coloured her glowing face,[18] and those eyes that once betokened Phoebus' torch have none of that inherited ancestral brilliance. Tears fall across her face, her eyes are flooded with constant moisture, as on the ridges of Taurus the snows melt when struck by warm rainshowers.

But see, the upper doors of the palace are opening;[19]

18 Lines 377–78 (deleted); "love-care ravages her body, her steps are trembling, and the delicate beauty of her bright body has faded."

19 Phaedra's chair is brought onto a balcony, so as to be visible to the audience while remaining indoors by theatrical convention.

385　reclinis ipsa sedis auratae toro
　　solitos amictus mente non sana abnuit.

PHAEDRA

　　Removete, famulae, purpura atque auro inlitas
　　vestes, procul sit muricis Tyrii rubor,
　　quae fila ramis ultimi Seres legunt:
390　brevis expeditos zona constringat sinus,
　　cervix monili vacua, nec niveus lapis
　　deducat aures, Indici donum maris;
　　odore crinis sparsus Assyrio vacet.
　　sic temere iactae colla perfundant comae
395　umerosque summos, cursibus motae citis
　　ventos sequantur. laeva se pharetrae dabit,
　　hastile vibret dextra Thessalicum manus.
　　talis severi mater Hippolyti fuit!
　　qualis relictis frigidi Ponti plagis
400　egit catervas Atticum pulsans solum
　　Tanaitis aut Maeotis et nodo comas
　　coegit emisitque, lunata latus
　　protecta pelta, talis in silvas ferar.

CHORUS

　　Sepone questus: non levat miseros dolor;
405　agreste placa virginis numen deae.

NUTRIX

　　Regina nemorum, sola quae montes colis
　　et una solis montibus coleris dea,

398 *deleted by Heinsius*

there she is, lying back on the cushions of her gilded chair, and refusing her usual clothes in her crazed frame of mind.

PHAEDRA

Slavewomen, take away those clothes bedaubed with purple and gold; let the scarlet of Tyrian die be banished, and the threads collected from branches by the remote Seres. My tunic must be free of restrictions, fastened with a short sash; my throat is to be without a necklace, my ears are not to be weighed down with snowwhite stones, gifts of the Indian Sea; my hair is to be loose, and free of Assyrian perfume. My locks shall be tossed just anyhow, sweeping over my neck and down to my shoulders; they shall stream on the winds as my racing moves them. My left hand will manage the quiver, my right shall wield a Thessalian spear. Such was the mother of stern Hyppolytus! As a woman from the Tanais and Maeotis, leaving the regions of chill Pontus, led her squadrons in pounding Attic soil,[21] with her hair knotted and then streaming, her flank guarded with a crescent shield: so I shall go to the woods.

CHORUS LEADER

(*To the distraught Nurse*) Set aside your sorrow: grieving does not help the troubled. Appease the virgin goddess who rules the countryside.[22]

NURSE

Queen of the forests, you who alone cherish the mountains, and alone are cherished as goddess in the lonely

[21] An allusion to the Amazons' raid on Attica following Theseus' capture of Antiope.
[22] There may be a scene break here, involving a lapse of time and possibly a scene change from the city to the country.

converte tristes ominum in melius minas.
o magna silvas inter et lucos dea,
410 clarumque caeli sidus et noctis decus,
cuius relucet mundus alterna face,
Hecate triformis, en ades coeptis favens.
animum rigentem tristis Hippolyti doma:
det facilis aures; mitiga pectus ferum:
415 amare discat, mutuos ignes ferat.
innecte mentem; torvus aversus ferox
in iura Veneris redeat. huc vires tuas
intende: sic te lucidi vultus ferant
et nube rupta cornibus puris eas,
420 sic te regentem frena nocturni aetheris
detrahere numquam Thessali cantus queant
nullusque de te gloriam pastor ferat.
    Ades invocata, iam fave votis, dea:
ipsum intuor sollemne venerantem sacrum
425 nullo latus comitante. quid dubitas? dedit
tempus locumque casus: utendum artibus.
trepidamus? haud est facile mandatum scelus
audere, verum iusta qui reges timet
deponat, omne pellat ex animo decus:
430 malus est minister regii imperii pudor.

HIPPOLYTUS

Quid huc seniles fessa moliris gradus,
o fida nutrix, turbidam frontem gerens
et maesta vultu? sospes est certe parens,
sospesque Phaedra, stirpis et geminae iugum?

411 face *A*: vice *E*
423 fave *E*: favet *A*: faves *recc.*

482

mountains: change these grim and threatening omens into good. O goddess, great amidst the woods and groves, bright orb of heaven and splendour of night, by whose alternating beams the world is lit, three-formed Hecate: come here, favour my undertaking. Tame grim Hippolytus' unbending spirit. Let him listen to me obligingly; soften his wild heart; let him learn to love, and feel shared flames of passion. Bind fast his mind; grim, hostile, fierce as he is, let him acknowledge Venus' laws. Direct your power here: so may you fare bright-faced, and travel through rifted clouds with horns undimmed; so, as you guide the reins of the nighttime sky, may Thessalian chants never have power to drag you down, and may no herdsman win glory over you.[23]

Come to my appeal, now favour my prayers, goddess. I see the very man worshipping at the customary shrine, no companion at his side. Why hesitate? Chance has provided time and place: I must use my skills. Trembling? It is not easy to venture on crime under orders; but one subject to royalty must put aside the right, and drive honour completely from the mind. Shame is a poor servant of royal authority.

HIPPOLYTUS

What makes you drag your weary old steps here, faithful Nurse, with a gloomy brow and sadness in your face? My father is unharmed, surely, and Phaedra unharmed, and their yoke of twin sons?

[23] "Herdsman" alludes to Endymion, with whom Phoebe fell hopelessly in love; for spells drawing down the moon cf. 791 with footnote.

NUTRIX

435 Metus remitte, prospero regnum in statu est
domusque florens sorte felici viget.
sed tu beatis mitior rebus veni!
namque anxiam me cura sollicitat tui,
quod te ipse poenis gravibus infestus domas.
440 quem fata cogunt, ille cum venia est miser;
at si quis ultro se malis offert volens
seque ipse torquet, perdere est dignus bona
quîs nescit uti. potius annorum memor
mentem relaxa: noctibus festis facem
445 attolle, curas Bacchus exoneret graves.
aetate fruere: mobili cursu fugit.
nunc facile pectus, grata nunc iuveni Venus:
exultet animus. cur toro viduo iaces?
tristem iuventam solve; nunc cursus rape,
450 effunde habenas, optimos vitae dies
effluere prohibe. propria descripsit deus
officia et aevum per suos ducit gradus:
laetitia iuvenem, frons decet tristis senem.
quid te coerces et necas rectam indolem?
455 seges illa magnum fenus agricolae dabit
quaecumque laetis tenera luxuriat satis,
arborque celso vertice evincet nemus
quam non maligna caedit aut resecat manus:
ingenia melius recta se in laudes ferunt,
460 si nobilem animum vegeta libertas alit.
truculentus et silvester ac vitae inscius
tristem iuventam Venere deserta coles?
hoc esse munus credis indictum viris,
ut dura tolerent, cursibus domitent equos
465 et saeva bella Marte sanguineo gerant?

NURSE

Have no fear, the kingdom prospers and the house is flourishing vigorously amidst good fortune. But you should meet your blessings with more geniality! I am troubled by anxious cares about you, because you subdue yourself like an enemy with heavy ordeals. A person coerced by fate may be forgiven for unhappiness; but if someone willingly volunteers for suffering and tortures himself, he deserves to lose the good things he is incapable of using. Instead, remember your years, and let your mind relax: raise a torch in nighttime celebrations, let Bacchus lighten your heavy cares. Enjoy your time of life: it runs swiftly away. Now your heart is free and easy, now your youth welcomes Venus. Let your spirit run riot! Why lie in a solitary bed? Unfetter your joyless youth. Now make all speed, let go the reins, and prevent the best days of life from slipping away. God has prescribed appropriate duties, and leads life through its proper stages: happiness suits the young, gloomy brows the old. Why inhibit yourself and strangle your natural disposition? That crop will pay the farmer great interest, whose plants when young grow lush and exultant; and that tree will overtop the grove with its towering crown, that is not cut or pruned back by a niggard hand: upright dispositions grow better to renown, if a lively freedom nourishes the noble spirit. As a truculent backwoodsman who knows nothing of life, will you pass your youth in gloom and abandon Venus? Do you think men have this obligation imposed on them, to endure hardships, tame horses by running them, and wage savage wars amid martial bloodshed?

---

452 ducit *recc.*: duxit *EA*

Providit ille maximus mundi parens,
cum tam rapaces cerneret Fati manus,
ut damna semper subole repararet nova.
excedat agedum rebus humanis Venus,
470 quae supplet ac restituit exhaustum genus:
orbis iacebit squalido turpis situ,
vacuum sine ullis piscibus stabit mare,
alesque caelo derit et silvis fera,
solis et aer pervius ventis erit.
475 quam varia leti genera mortalem trahunt
carpuntque turbam, pontus et ferrum et doli!
sed fata credas desse: sic atram Styga
iam petimus ultro. caelibem vitam probet
sterilis iuventus: hoc erit, quidquid vides,
480 unius aevi turba et in semet ruet.
proinde vitae sequere naturam ducem:
urbem frequenta, civium coetus cole.

HIPPOLYTUS

Non alia magis est libera et vitio carens
ritusque melius vita quae priscos colat,
485 quam quae relictis moenibus silvas amat.
non illum avarae mentis inflammat furor
qui se dicavit montium insontem iugis,
non aura populi et vulgus infidum bonis,
non pestilens invidia, non fragilis favor;
490 non ille regno servit aut regno imminens
vanos honores sequitur aut fluxas opes,
spei metusque liber, haud illum niger
edaxque livor dente degeneri pĕtit.
nec scelera populos inter atque urbes sata
495 novit nec omnes conscius strepitus pavet

486

PHAEDRA

That mighty father of the world made provision, when he saw that Fate's hands were so rapacious, to make good the losses always with new offspring. Come now, suppose our life should be deprived of Venus, who replaces and restores the depleted race: the world will lie rank in squalid neglect, the seas will stand empty of fish, the heavens will lack birds and the forests beasts, and the open air will be traversed by the winds alone. How varied are the kinds of death that ravage and erode the human throng—the sea, steel, treachery! But suppose such dooms did not exist: now by your way we head for black Styx of our own volition. Suppose our young people should adopt a celibate life without offspring: everything you see will be a population lasting one generation, and will collapse on itself. So then follow nature as your guide in life: frequent the city, cultivate the company of your fellow citizens.

HIPPOLYTUS

No other life is more free and blameless, or better cherishes the ancient ways, than that which abandons city walls and loves the forests. No madness of greed inflames the man who devotes himself innocently to the high hills; no breath of the crowd, no mob that betrays good men, no pestilential envy, no fickle favour. He does not serve a throne or strive for a throne, pursuing empty honours and fleeting wealth; he is free of hopes and fears; no black gnawing malice attacks him with its ignoble teeth. He is a stranger to the crimes spawned amidst crowded cities; he does not tremble with guilt at every clamour, or speak

472 piscibus *Bentley*: classibus *EA*

aut verba fingit; mille non quaerit tegi
dives columnis nec trabes multo insolens
suffigit auro; non cruor largus pias
inundat aras, fruge nec sparsi sacra
500 centena nivei colla summittunt boves:
sed rure vacuo potitur et aperto aethere
innocuus errat. callidas tantum feris
struxisse fraudes novit, et fessus gravi
labore niveo corpus Iliso fovet;
505 nunc ille ripam celeris Alphei legit,
nunc nemoris alti densa metatur loca,
ubi Lerna puro gelida perlucet vado
aestusque sedat. hinc aves querulae fremunt
ramique ventis lene percussi tremunt

     *   *   *   *   *

510 veteresque fagi. iuvat et aut amnis vagi
pressisse ripas, caespite aut nudo leves
duxisse somnos, sive fons largus citas
defundit undas, sive per flores novos
fugiente dulcis murmurat rivo sonus.
515 excussa silvis poma compescunt famem,
et fraga parvis vulsa dumetis cibos
faciles ministrant. regios luxus procul
est impetus fugisse: sollicito bibunt
auro superbi; quam iuvat nuda manu
520 captasse fontem! certior somnus premit
secura duro membra laxantem toro.

<hr />

508 aestusque sedat *exempli gratia Fitch*: sedes(-em *A*)que
mutat *EA*   509 *lacuna after* 509 *recognised by Peiper*
510 iuvat et *Peiper*: iuvat *EA*
521 laxantem *Axelson*: versantem *E*: versantur *A*

feigned words; he does not seek to hide amidst wealth behind a thousand columns, nor encase his roofbeams thickly
with gold amidst excess; no profusion of blood drenches
his pious altar, no snowy oxen in the hundreds bow their
necks when sprinkled with holy grain. But he is lord of the
empty countryside, and wanders guiltless under the open
sky. The cunning snares he knows how to devise are against
beasts only. Tired by hard toil, he refreshes his body in
snow-cold Ilisos. Now he follows the banks of the swift
Alpheus, now traverses the deep wood's thickets, where
cold Lerna's waters are crystal-clear and allay the heat. On
one side plaintive birds clamour, and branches tremble at
the winds' gentle buffeting . . .[24] and ancient beech trees.
He delights too to lie on the bank of a wandering river, or to
take a light sleep on the bare turf, whether a spring pours
out swift waters in profusion, or through fresh flowers a
sweet sound murmurs from a fleeting brook. Fruits shaken
from trees check his hunger, and wild strawberries
plucked from little bushes provide easy food. His impulse
is to flee from royal luxury. Uneasy the gold from which the
proud drink; what a pleasure it is to scoop up springwater
with one's bare hand! Surer sleep holds the man who rests
his carefree limbs on a hard bed.[25] He does not shamefully

[24] The lost line(s) probably began "on the other side . . ."

[25] A passage in Anon. *Arden of Feversham* (1591) is reminiscent of these lines: "Well fares the man, howe'er his cates do taste,
/ That tables not with foul suspicion; / And he but pines among his
delicates, / Whose troubled mind is stuffed with discontent. / My
golden time was when I had no gold; / Though then I wanted, then
I slept secure; / My daily toil begat me night's repose, / My night's
repose made daylight fresh to me."

non in recessu furta et obscuro improbus
quaerit cubili seque multiplici timens
domo recondit: aethera ac lucem petit
525   et teste caelo vivit.
                    Hoc equidem reor
vixisse ritu prima quos mixtos deis
profudit aetas. nullus his auri fuit
caecus cupido, nullus in campo sacer
divisit agros arbiter populis lapis;
530   nondum secabant credulae pontum rates:
sua quisque norat maria. non vasto aggere
crebraque turre cinxerant urbes latus;
non arma saeva miles aptabat manu
nec torta clausas fregerat saxo gravi
535   ballista portas, iussa nec dominum pati
iuncto ferebat terra servitium bove:
sed arva per se feta poscentes nihil
pavere gentes, silva nativas opes
et opaca dederant antra nativas domos.
540   Rupere foedus impius lucri furor
et ira praeceps, quaeque succensas agit
libido mentes. venit imperii sitis
cruenta, factus praeda maiori minor;
pro iure vires esse. tum primum manu
545   bellare nuda saxaque et ramos rudes
vertere in arma: non erat gracili levis
armata ferro cornus aut longo latus
mucrone cingens ensis aut crista procul
galeae micantes: tela faciebat dolor.
550   invenit artes bellicus Mavors novas
et mille formas mortis. hinc terras cruor
infecit omnes fusus et rubuit mare.

look to conceal his actions in seclusion on a dark couch, nor hide in fear in a labyrinthine house; he seeks open air and light, and lives life under the eye of heaven.

This was the way of life, I think, of those who burgeoned in the primal age and mingled with gods. No blind greed for gold touched them; no holy stone on the land divided up fields as arbiter between communities; not yet did overtrustful ships cut through the deep; the seas each man knew were his own. No cities flanked themselves with vast earthworks and serried towers; no soldier fitted cruel weapons to his hand; no wound-up catapult smashed closed gates with heavy rocks; nor was the earth, bidden to suffer a master, enduring servitude beneath teams of oxen. Rather the fields, fruitful of themselves, fed the peoples who made no demands; the woods provided natural resources, and shadowy caves provided natural homes.

This peaceful compact was broken by the unholy madness for gain, by hasty anger and by lust which goads inflamed minds. There followed the bloody thirst for power; the weaker fell prey to the stronger, and might was right. Then men first engaged in war with bare hands, and turned rocks and rough branches into weapons. There was no light javelin armed with slender iron, no long-bladed sword to gird one's side, no helmets with crests gleaming afar; wrath made its own weapons. The spirit of war created new arts, and a thousand forms of death. Hence bloodshed stained every land, and reddened the sea.

---

549 micantes *Axelson*: comantes *EA*

tum scelera dempto fine per cunctas domos
iere, nullum caruit exemplo nefas:
555 a fratre frater, dextera nati parens
cecidit, maritus coniugis ferro iacet
perimuntque fetus impiae matres suos.
taceo novercas: mitior nulla est feris.
Sed dux malorum femina: haec scelerum artifex
560 obsedit animos, huius incestae stupris
fumant tot urbes, bella tot gentes gerunt
et versa ab imo regna tot populos premunt.
sileantur aliae: sola coniunx Aegei,
Medea, reddet feminas dirum genus.

NUTRIX

565 Cur omnium fit culpa paucarum scelus?

HIPPOLYTUS

Detestor omnes, horreo fugio execror.
sit ratio, sit natura, sit dirus furor:
odisse placuit. ignibus iunges aquas
et amica ratibus ante promittet vada
570 incerta Syrtis, ante ab extremo sinu
Hesperia Tethys lucidum attollet diem
et ora dammis blanda praebebunt lupi,
quam victus animum feminae mitem geram.

NUTRIX

Saepe obstinatis induit frenos Amor
575 et odia mutat. regna materna aspice:
illae feroces sentiunt Veneris iugum;
testaris istud unicus gentis puer.

558 mitior nulla *Fitch*: mitius nihil* *EA*

Then, with restraints gone, crimes went through each home, and no outrage was unexampled: brothers fell to brothers, fathers at their sons' hands, husbands lie dead by their wives' swords, and unnatural mothers destroy their own offspring. I say nothing of stepmothers: not one of them is more merciful than wild beasts. But the leader in evil is woman. This artificer of crimes besets our minds; through this unchaste creature's adulteries so many cities smoulder, so many nations wage war, and so many peoples are crushed in the utter overthrow of kingdoms. To say nothing of others, Aegeus' wife Medea alone will reveal women as a monstrous tribe.

NURSE

Why are all blamed for the crimes of a few?

HIPPOLYTUS

I detest them all, dread them, flee them, loathe them. Be it reason or nature or dire madness, I am set on hating them. You will combine fire with water, and the doubtful Syrtes will sooner promise shoals friendly to ships, Tethys will lift the bright day from the farthest gulf in the west, and wolves will fawn with their muzzles on deer, before I am overborn and show a gentle spirit to a woman.

NURSE

Often Love puts a harness even on the stubborn, and changes their hatred. Look at your mother's kingdom: fierce as they are, those women feel Venus' yoke. You are testimony to that, as the sole boy of the race.[26]

[26] The Amazons were said by some to kill every male child born to them. Hippolytus was exempt from this fate as Theseus' son.

HIPPOLYTUS

Solamen unum matris amissae fero,
odisse quod iam feminas omnes licet.

NUTRIX

580 Ut dura cautes undique intractabilis
resistit undis et lacessentes aquas
longe remittit, verba sic spernit mea.
Sed Phaedra praeceps graditur, impatiens morae.
quo se dabit fortuna? quo verget furor?
585 terrae repente corpus exanimum accidit
et ora morti similis obduxit color.
attolle vultus, dimove vocis moras:
tuus en, alumna, temet Hippolytus tenet.

PHAEDRA

Quis me dolori reddit atque aestus graves
590 reponit animo? quam bene excideram mihi!

HIPPOLYTUS

Cur dulce munus redditae lucis fugis?

PHAEDRA

Aude, anime, tempta, perage mandatum tuum.
intrepida constent verba: qui timide rogat
docet negare. magna pars sceleris mei
595 olim peracta est; serus est nobis pudor:
iam movimus nefanda. si coepta exequor,
forsan iugali crimen abscondam face:
honesta quaedam scelera successus facit.
en, incipe, anime!—Commodes paulum, precor,
600 secretus aures. si quis est abeat comes.

596 iam movimus *Watt*: amavimus *EA*

494

HIPPOLYTUS

I think of it as the one consolation for my mother's loss, that
now I am allowed to hate all women.

NURSE

[*Aside*] Like a hard crag, intractable on every side, that resists the seas and flings the attacking waves far back, so he
rebuffs my words. But Phaedra approaches impetuously,
impatient with delay. What will befall? What will be the
upshot of her madness? Suddenly her body falls to the
ground in a faint, and a deathlike pallor has spread over her
face. [*To Phaedra*] Raise your head, find your voice again.
See, child, your own Hippolytus is holding you.

PHAEDRA

Who restores me to pain, and restarts these powerful tides
in my mind? How good it was to escape from myself!

HIPPOLYTUS

Why do you shun the sweet gift of light returned?

PHAEDRA

[*Aside*] Courage, my spirit! Make the attempt, carry out
your own command. Your words must be firm and fearless:
a timid request invites refusal. The greater part of my
crime was completed long ago; shame is too late for me: I
have already initiated the unspeakable. If I carry out what I
have begun, perhaps I shall conceal the crime behind the
torch of marriage. Some crimes are made honorable by
success. Come, begin, my spirit! [*To Hippolytus*] Lend me
your ears awhile in private, I pray you. Any companion
with you should leave.

HIPPOLYTUS

En locus ab omni liber arbitrio vacat.

PHAEDRA

Sed ora coeptis transitum verbis negant;
vis magna vocem mittit et maior tenet.
vos testor omnes, caelites, hoc quod volo
605 me nolle.

HIPPOLYTUS

Animusne cupiens aliquid effari nequit?

PHAEDRA

Curae leves loquuntur, ingentes stupent.

HIPPOLYTUS

Committe curas auribus, mater, meis.

PHAEDRA

Matris superbum est nomen et nimium potens;
610 nostros humilius nomen affectus decet:
me vel sororem, Hippolyte, vel famulam voca,
famulamque potius: omne servitium feram.
non me per altas ire si iubeas nives
pigeat gelatis ingredi Pindi iugis;
615 non, si per ignes ire et infesta agmina,
cuncter paratis ensibus pectus dare.
mandata recipe sceptra, me famulam accipe;
te imperia regere, me decet iussa exequi:
muliebre non est regna tutari urbium.
620 tu, qui iuventae flore primaevo viges,

---

[27] A *sententia* much quoted and adapted in Elizabethan drama, e.g. Chapman, *The Widow's Tears* (1605) IV.1: "These

HIPPOLYTUS

See, the place is clear and free of any observation.

PHAEDRA

Yet my lips refuse passage to the words I begin. A great
force impels my speech, a greater restrains it. I call all you
gods to witness that this thing I want—I do not want.

HIPPOLYTUS

Your spirit desires to utter something but cannot?

PHAEDRA

Light cares can speak, huge cares are dumfounded.[27]

HIPPOLYTUS

Entrust your cares to my ears, mother.

PHAEDRA

The name of mother is too grand and mighty. A humbler
name suits my feelings: call me sister, Hippolytus, or servant—yes, servant is better: I will bear any servitude. If
you bade me go through deep snows, I would not object to
travelling on Pindus' frozen heights; if you bade me go
through fire and enemy ranks, I would not hesitate to
breast drawn swords. Take the regent's sceptre, accept me
as your servant. It befits *you* to hold sway, me to carry out
commands. It is no woman's role to safeguard the thrones
of city-states. You, in the vigorous first flower of youth,

griefs that sound so loud, prove always light." Shakespeare develops it in *Macbeth* (1606) IV.3.209f.: "The grief that does not
speak/Whispers the o'erfraught heart and bids it break"; compare
Webster, *The White Devil* (1612) II.1.279: "Those are the killing
griefs which dare not speak," and Ford, *The Broken Heart* (1629)
V.2.2594: "Those are the silent griefs which cut the heartstrings."

cives paterno fortis imperio rege.
sinu receptam supplicem ac servam tege;
miserere viduae.

HIPPOLYTUS
Summus hoc omen deus
avertat! aderit sospes actutum parens.

PHAEDRA
625 Regni tenacis dominus et tacitae Stygis
nullam relictos fecit ad superos viam:
thalami remittet ille raptorem sui?
nisi forte amori placidus et Pluton sedet.

HIPPOLYTUS
Illum quidem aequi caelites reducem dabunt.
630 sed dum tenebit vota in incerto deus,
pietate caros debita fratres colam,
et te merebor esse ne viduam putes
ac tibi parentis ipse supplebo locum.

PHAEDRA
O spes amantum credula, o fallax Amor!
635 satisne dixi? precibus admotis agam.
Miserere, tacitae mentis exaudi preces—
libet loqui pigetque.

HIPPOLYTUS
Quodnam istud malum est?

PHAEDRA
Quod in novercam cadere vix credas malum.

---

28 Phaedra used *viduae* in the sense "husbandless" (she believes Theseus is not dead, but incapable of return); Hippolytus understands it in the strong sense "widowed."

should rule the citizens, strong in your father's power. Take me to your arms, protect your suppliant and slave; pity a husbandless woman.

HIPPOLYTUS

May the highest god turn aside that omen![28] Father will soon be here in safety.

PHAEDRA

The lord of that binding realm, the silent Styx, provides no passage to the upper world once it is left: will he release his own wife's ravisher? Unless perhaps Pluto's throne too is indulgent to love.[29]

HIPPOLYTUS

His return will be granted by the just deities. But as long as god keeps our prayers in uncertainty, I shall cherish my dear brothers with proper affection, and behave so that you shall not think yourself widowed, and fill my father's place for you myself.

PHAEDRA

[*Aside*] O gullible hope of lovers, o deceitful Love! Have I said enough? I shall use prayers to proceed. [*To Hippolytus*] Pity me, listen to my mind's covert prayers. I desire to speak and recoil from it.

HIPPOLYTUS

Whatever is this trouble?

PHAEDRA

A trouble you would hardly believe could fall on a step-mother.

[29] As in Orpheus' case; Pluto himself had carried off Proserpine. Phaedra calls Theseus "ravisher" as accomplice of Pirithous.

499

HIPPOLYTUS

Ambigua voce verba perplexa iacis:
640 effare aperte.

PHAEDRA

Pectus insanum vapor
amorque torret. intimis errat ferus
643 visceribus ignis mersus et venis latens,
ut agilis altas flamma percurrit trabes.

HIPPOLYTUS

645 Amore nempe Thesei casto furis?

PHAEDRA

Hippolyte, sic est: Thesei vultus amo
illos priores, quos tulit quondam puer,
cum prima puras barba signaret genas
monstrique caecam Cnosii vidit domum
650 et longa curva fila collegit via.
quis tum ille fulsit! presserant vittae comam
et ora flavus tenera tinguebat pudor;
inerant lacertis mollibus fortes tori,
tuaeve Phoebes vultus aut Phoebi mei,
655 tuusque potius—talis, en talis fuit
cum placuit hosti, sic tulit celsum caput.
in te magis refulget incomptus decor:
est genitor in te totus, et torvae tamen
pars aliqua matris miscet ex aequo decus;
660 in ore Graio Scythicus apparet rigor.
si cum parente Creticum intrasses fretum

---

641 intimis ferit ferus E^{ac} (errat *is Fitch's conjecture for* ferit):
intimas saevus* vorat A

642 penitus medullas atque per venas meat *found only in* A

HIPPOLYTUS

You throw out unclear words in cryptic speech: speak out openly.

PHAEDRA

My crazed breast is scorched by the heat of love. A fierce fire ranges deep in my body's core, hidden in my veins,[30] as swift flames run through tall timber.

HIPPOLYTUS

You mean you are crazed by a wife's love for Theseus?

PHAEDRA

Hippolytus, it is like this: I love the face of Theseus, that earlier face he had as a boy, when his first beard marked his smooth cheeks, and he set eyes on the unlit home of the Cnossian monster and gathered up the long thread on its winding path. How he shone then! Headbands fastened his hair, and a golden modesty coloured his tender face; there were strong muscles in his soft arms, and his looks were those of your Phoebe or my Phoebus, and actually more your own; like you, just like you he was when he attracted his enemy,[31] just so he carried his head high. In you there shines more brightly an unkempt beauty: all of your father is in you, and yet some part of your fierce mother contributes its glory equally; in your Greek face a Scythian sternness is evident. If you had entered Cretan seas with

---

[30] A's text, which includes line 642, runs: "A cruel fire eats deep into my inmost marrow and travels through my veins, buried in my body and hidden in my veins."

[31] Ariadne, daughter of Athens' enemy Minos.

tibi fila potius nostra nevisset soror.
Te te, soror, quacumque siderei poli
in parte fulges, invoco ad causam parem:
665 domus sorores una corripuit duas,
te genitor, at me natus.—en supplex iacet
allapsa genibus regiae proles domus.
respersa nulla labe et intacta, innocens
tibi mutor uni. certa descendi ad preces:
670 finem hic dolori faciet aut vitae dies.
miserere amantis.

HIPPOLYTUS

Magne regnator deum,
tam lentus audis scelera? tam lentus vides?
et quando saeva fulmen emittes manu,
si nunc serenum est? omnis impulsus ruat
675 aether et atris nubibus condat diem,
ac versa retro sidera obliquos agant
retorta cursus. tuque, sidereum caput,
radiate Titan, tu nefas stirpis tuae
speculare? lucem merge et in tenebras fuge.
680 cur dextra, divum rector atque hominum, vacat
tua, nec trisulca mundus ardescit face?
in me tona, me fige, me velox cremet
transactus ignis: sum nocens, merui mori:
placui novercae.—dignus en stupris ego?
685 scelerique tanto visus ego solus tibi
materia facilis? hoc meus meruit rigor?
o scelere vincens omne femineum genus,
o maius ausa matre monstrifera malum
genetrice peior! illa se tantum stupro
690 contaminavit, et tamen tacitum diu

your father, my sister would rather have spun the thread
for you. You, sister, wherever you shine in the starry heavens, I invoke you in a cause like yours. Two sisters have
been swept away by one family, you by the father, I by the
son. See, the daughter of a royal house lies fallen suppliant
at your knees. Stained by no dishonour, untouched, innocent, I am changed for you alone. I resolved to lower myself to prayers: this day will bring an end to my pain, or to
my life. Pity a lover.

HIPPOLYTUS

Great monarch of the gods, do you listen to crimes so
calmly, see them so calmly? And when will your fierce
hand launch the thunderbolt, if now the heavens are clear?
Let the whole sky collapse in ruin and bury the daylight in
black clouds, let the stars turn back and veering run their
courses awry. And you, celestial being, radiant Titan, do
you observe the outrage done by your grandchild? Drown
the light, flee into darkness! Why, ruler of gods and men, is
your hand empty? Why is the earth not catching fire from
the three-pronged brand? Hurl your thunder at me, transfix me, let the swift fire pierce and consume me. I am
guilty, I deserve to die: I have attracted my stepmother. [*To
Phaedra*] Look, am I suited to adulteries? Did I of all men
seem to you ready material for such a crime? Did my sternness earn this? Oh, you surpass all womankind in crime,
you have dared a mightier evil than your monster-bearing
mother, you are worse than your parent! She defiled only
herself with adultery, and yet her long-concealed guilt was

503

crimen biformi partus exhibuit nota,
scelusque matris arguit vultu truci
ambiguus infans. ille te venter tulit!
o ter quaterque prospero fato dati
695 quos hausit et peremit et leto dedit
odium dolusque! genitor, invideo tibi:
Colchide noverca maius hoc, maius malum est.

PHAEDRA

Et ipsa nostrae fata cognosco domus:
fugienda petimus. sed mei non sum potens.
700 te vel per ignes, per mare insanum sequar
rupesque et amnes, unda quos torrens rapit;
quacumque gressus tuleris hac amens agar.
iterum, superbe, genibus advolvor tuis.

HIPPOLYTUS

Procul impudicos corpore a casto amove
705 tactus! quid hoc est? etiam in amplexus ruit?
stringatur ensis, merita supplicia exigat.
en impudicum crine contorto caput
laeva reflexi: iustior numquam focis
datus tuis est sanguis, arcitenens dea.

PHAEDRA

710 Hippolyte, nunc me compotem voti facis;
sanas furentem. maius hoc voto meo est,
salvo ut pudore manibus immoriar tuis.

HIPPOLYTUS

Abscede, vive, ne quid exores, et hic
contactus ensis deserat castum latus.
715 quis eluet me Tanais aut quae barbaris

revealed by the damning evidence of her two-formed offspring; the mongrel infant with its bestial face proved the mother's iniquity. That was the womb that bore you! O thrice and four times blessed in their fate were those consumed, destroyed and done to death by hatred or treachery! Father, I envy you: this is an evil worse, worse than your Colchian stepmother.[32]

PHAEDRA

I too recognise the fate of my family: we seek what should be shunned. But I am powerless over myself. Even through fires, through the maddened sea I shall follow you, across crags and rivers whirling in torrent; wherever you turn your steps, there I shall madly run. Again, proud man, I throw myself down at your knees.

HIPPOLYTUS

Keep your wanton touch far from my chaste body! What is this? Even throwing herself into an embrace? Out, sword, exact the penalty she deserves. See, my left hand has twisted her hair and bent her wanton head back. Never was blood offered more justly at your altar, goddess of the bow.

PHAEDRA

Hippolytus, now you grant me fulfilment of my prayer, you heal my madness. To die at your hands with my honour safe—this is better than my prayer.

HIPPOLYTUS

Go, live, you will gain no boon from me. And this contaminated sword must leave my chaste side. What Tanais will

---

[32] Medea, who had attempted to kill Theseus by poison.

Maeotis undis Pontico incumbens mari?
non ipse toto magnus Oceano pater
tantum expiarit sceleris. o silvae, o ferae!

NUTRIX

Deprensa culpa est. anime, quid segnis stupes?
720   regeramus ipsi crimen atque ultro impiam
Venerem arguamus. scelere velandum est scelus;
tutissimum est inferre, cum timeas, gradum.
ausae priores simus an passae nefas,
secreta cum sit culpa, quis testis sciet?
725   Adeste, Athenae! fida famulorum manus,
fer opem! nefandi raptor Hippolytus stupri
instat premitque, mortis intentat metum,
ferro pudicam terret. en praeceps abît
ensemque trepida liquit attonitus fuga.
730   pignus tenemus sceleris. hanc maestam prius
recreate. crinis tractus et lacerae comae
ut sunt remaneant, facinoris tanti notae.
perferte in urbem!—Recipe iam sensus, era.
quid te ipsa lacerans omnium aspectus fugis?
735   mens impudicam facere, non casus, solet.

CHORUS

Fugit insanae similis procellae,
ocior nubes glomerante Coro,
ocior cursum rapiente flamma,
stella cum ventis agitata longos
740   porrigit ignes.

Conferat tecum decus omne priscum

₇₃₃ perferte *E*: referte *A*

506

wash me clean, what Maeotis, pouring its barbarous waters into the Pontic sea? Not even with the whole of Ocean could the great father himself cleanse so much guilt. O woods, o wild beasts! [*Exit*]

NURSE

Her guilt has been exposed. Why idle and dazed, my spirit? We must deflect the blame back on him, and actually accuse *him* of unnatural lust. Crime must be masked by crime. When afraid, it is safest to attack. What witness will know if we first dared the outrage or suffered it, since it happened in secret?

Here, Athens! Help, faithful band of servants! Hippolytus is intent on rape, on guilty sex; he is attacking, threatening death, menacing chastity with steel. [*Enter citizens and servants*] See, he has dashed away and left his sword here in the confusion of his panic flight. We have the proof of the crime. First comfort *her* in her distress. Let her hair stay pulled and torn as it is, as evidence of such wrongdoing. Take word to the city. Recover your senses, mistress! Why do you gash yourself and shun everyone's gaze? It is the mind that makes a woman unchaste, not what befalls her.

CHORUS

His flight was like a frenzied gale,
swifter than Corus massing clouds,
swifter than flame speeding on its path
when a wind-driven meteor lengthens out
     its trail of fire.

Let all former glory be compared to you

fama miratrix senioris aevi:
pulchrior tanto tua forma lucet,
clarior quanto micat orbe pleno
745   cum suos ignes coeunte cornu
iunxit et curru properante pernox
exerit vultus rubicunda Phoebe
nec tenent stellae faciem minores.
talis est, primas referens tenebras,
750   nuntius noctis, modo lotus undis
Hesperus, pulsis iterum tenebris
       Lucifer idem.
Et tu, thyrsigera Liber ab India,
intonsa iuvenis perpetuum coma,
755   tigres pampinea cuspide temperans
ac mitra cohibens cornigerum caput,
non vinces rigidas Hippolyti comas.
ne vultus nimium suspicias tuos,
omnes per populos fabula distulit,
760   Phaedrae quem Bromio praetulerit soror.

Anceps forma bonum mortalibus,
exigui donum breve temporis,
ut velox celeri pede laberis!
768   Languescunt folio lilia pallido
769   et gratae capiti deficiunt rosae;
764   non sic prata novo vere decentia
765   aestatis calidae despoliat vapor

755 temperans *Axelson*: territans *EA*
768–69 *transposed after* 763 *by Fitch*

508

by fame that admires an earlier age:
your beauty shines out fairer by far,
just as the moon gleams brighter at the full
when blushing Phoebe links her horns
to unite her fires, and shows her face
throughout the night from her hastening chariot,
and the lesser stars cannot keep their appearance.
Such, as he brings back the onset of darkness,
is the herald of night, who when newly sea-bathed
is Hesperus, but again after banishing darkness
  is Lucifer also.
And you, Liber from thyrsus-bearing India—
forever a youth with locks unshorn,
controlling your tigers with a vine-clad spear
and binding your horn-bearing head in a turban—
you cannot outdo Hippolytus' firm locks.
Lest you admire your own face too much,
the story has spread through every nation
whom Phaedra's sister preferred to Bromius.[33]

Beauty—a doubtful boon for mortals,
a brief and short-lived gift,
how fleeting, how swiftly passing!
Lilies with their pale petals wither
and roses fade that garland the head;
meadows lovely in early spring
are despoiled by the heat of scorching summer,

---

[33] This implies that Ariadne chose Theseus over Bacchus (here called Liber and Bromius) for his looks, which are now inherited by Hippolytus. In the more familiar version, Ariadne met Bacchus only after Theseus had abandoned her.

(saevit solstitio cum medius dies
et noctes brevibus praecipitant rotis),
770   ut fulgor teneris qui radiat genis
momento rapitur, nullaque non dies
formosi spolium corporis abstulit.
res est forma fugax: quis sapiens bono
confidat fragili? dum licet, utere.
775   tempus te tacitum subruit, horaque
semper praeterita deterior subit.

Quid deserta petis? tutior aviis
non est forma locis: te nemore abdito,
cum Titan medium constituit diem,
780   cingent, turba licens, Naïdes improbae,
formosos solitae claudere fontibus,
et somnis facient insidias tuis
     lascivae nemorum deae
     montivagive Panes.
785   Aut te stellifero despiciens polo
sidus post veteres Arcadas editum
currus non poterit flectere candidos.
et nuper rubuit, nullaque lucidis
nubes sordidior vultibus obstitit;
790   at nos solliciti numine turbido,
tractam Thessalicis carminibus rati,
tinnitus dedimus; tu fueras labor

767 praecipitant *Gronovius*: praecipitat *EA*

---

34 Samuel Johnson adapts these lines: "Not faster in the summer's ray / The spring's frail beauty fades away, / Than anguish and decay consume / The smiling virgin's rosy bloom. / Some beauty's

when at the solstice midday rages
and the nights speed on shortened courses.
More quickly is stolen the radiance that shines
in youthful cheeks; there is no day
that does not plunder a beautiful body.
Beauty is fugitive: can a wise man trust
so fragile a boon? Use it while you may.
Silently time subverts you, and the hour
stealing up is always worse than the last.[34]

Why seek the wilds? Beauty is no safer
in pathless places. In the woods' seclusion,
when the Titan has brought midday, a brazen
throng will surround you, the shameless Naiads,
apt to catch handsome boys in springs;[35]
and an ambush will be set for your siesta
    by the wanton woodland goddesses
        or mountain-roving Pans.
Or gazing on you from the starry heavens
the orb born after the old Arcadians
will be helpless to guide her shining chariot.
Just lately she blushed, and there was no dingy
cloud obstructing her bright face.
We, alarmed at the deity's gloom,
thinking her tugged by Thessalian spells,
made jangling noises;[36] but *you* had caused

snatched each day, each hour; / For beauty is a fleeting flower: /
Then how can wisdom e'er confide / In beauty's momentary
pride?" [35] The allusion is to Hylas. [36] Lunar eclipses
were attributed in folklore to witchcraft drawing down the moon;
the countermagic involved clashing brass vessels.

et tu causa morae, te dea noctium
dum spectat celeres sustinuit vias.

795   Vexent hanc faciem frigora parcius,
haec solem facies rarius appetat:
lucebit Pario marmore clarius.
quam grata est facies torva viriliter
et pondus veteris triste supercili!
800   Phoebo colla licet splendida compares:
illum caesaries nescia colligi
perfundens umeros ornat et integit;
te frons hirta decet, te brevior coma
nulla lege iacens. tu licet asperos
805   pugnacesque deos viribus audeas
et vasti spatio vincere corporis;
aequas Herculeos nam iuvenis toros,
Martis belligeri pectore latior.
si dorso libeat cornipedis vehi,
810   frenis Castorea mobilior manu
Spartanum poteris flectere Cyllaron.
Ammentum digitis tende prioribus
et totis iaculum derige viribus:
tam longe, dociles spicula figere,
815   non mittent gracilem Cretes harundinem.
aut si tela modo spargere Parthico
in caelum placeat, nulla sine alite
descendent, tepido viscere condita
praedam de mediis nubibus afferent.

her lingering, her pining; while gazing at you
the goddess of night had checked her swift course.

Let frosts more seldom harm this face,
let this face more rarely seek the sun:
it will shine purer than Parian marble.
How attractive a face of flinty manhood
and the sombre frown of an older sternness!
Your gleaming neck could vie with Phoebus'.
A full head of hair shades and adorns him,
never confined, overflowing the shoulders;
shorter hair that covers the brow suits you,
lying at random. You could dare
to vanquish rough, aggressive gods
with the power and span of your burly body,
for in youthful muscle you are Hercules' match
and broader of chest than warlike Mars.
If you choose to ride astride a racehorse,
your hand on the reins will be able to guide
the Spartan Cyllaros swifter than Castor.
Stretch the thong with your forefingers
and aim the spear with all your strength:[37]
Cretans, trained in firing arrows,
will not shoot the slender reed as far.
Or if you decide to shower your arrows
into the sky in Parthian style,
each will fall buried in a bird's warm body
and bring you prey from the very clouds.

---

[37] The thong was used to put spin on the spear as it was
thrown, thus improving aim and distance.

820 Raris forma viris (saecula perspice)
impunita fuit. te melior deus
tutum praetereat, formaque nobilis
deformis senii monstret imaginem.

Quid sinat inausum feminae praeceps furor?
825 nefanda iuveni crimina insonti apparat.
en scelera! quaerit crine lacerato fidem,
decus omne turbat capitis, umectat genas:
instruitur omni fraude feminea dolus.
    Sed iste quisnam est regium in vultu decus
830 gerens et alto vertice attollens caput?
ut ora iuveni paria Theseo gerit,
ni languido pallore canderent genae
staretque recta squalor incultus coma!
en ipse Theseus redditus terris adest.

835 Tandem profugi noctis aeternae plagam
vastoque manes carcere umbrantem polum,
et vix cupitum sufferunt oculi diem.
iam quarta Eleusin dona Triptolemi secat
paremque totiens Libra composuit diem,
840 ambiguus ut me sortis ignotae labor
detinuit inter mortis et vitae mala.
pars una vitae mansit extincto mihi,
sensus malorum. finis Alcides fuit,
qui cum revulsum Tartaro abstraheret canem,
845 me quoque supernas pariter ad sedes tulit.
sed fessa virtus robore antiquo caret

---

831 Theseo *Fitch*: Pittheo *Damsté*: piritho o *E*: perithoi *A*

PHAEDRA

Beauty in men is rarely unpunished:
scan the ages. May a kindlier god
leave you in safety, and your famous beauty
show the stamp of unbeautiful old age.

ACT 3

What would the woman's reckless madness leave undared?
She is preparing wicked charges against the innocent
youth. Such crimes! She seeks credence with her torn hair,
she mars all the beauty of her head, she wets her cheeks.
The plot is marshalled with every female trick.

But who is this, that bears a royal grace in his countenance and carries his head so high? How similar his face to
Theseus' son!—except that his cheeks are white with the
pallor of exhaustion, and unkempt squalor stands in his
bristling hair. See, it is Theseus himself, restored to earth.

THESEUS

At last I have escaped the region of eternal night, the world
that darkens the dead in their vast prison; and my eyes
can scarcely endure the longed-for daylight. Now for the
fourth time Eleusis is reaping Triptolemus' bounty, and
Libra has balanced day and night four times, while the un-
resolved torment of an unknown lot kept me between the
evils of death and life. Dead as I was, one part of life stayed
with me: awareness of evils. An end was given by Alcides,
who, when dragging off the hound[38] stolen from Tartarus,
brought me at the same time to the world above. But my
manhood is exhausted, lacks its ancient strength, and my

[38] Cerberus, brought into the upper world by Hercules (=
Alcides).

trepidantque gressus. heu, labor quantus fuit
Phlegethonte ab imo petere longinquum aethera
pariterque mortem fugere et Alciden sequi!
850   Quis fremitus aures flebilis pepulit meas?
expromat aliquis. luctus et lacrimae et dolor,
in limine ipso maesta lamentatio—
hospitia digna prorsus inferno hospite.

NUTRIX

Tenet obstinatum Phaedra consilium necis
855 fletusque nostros spernit ac morti imminet.

THESEUS

Quae causa leti? reduce cur moritur viro?

NUTRIX

Haec ipsa letum causa maturum attulit.

THESEUS

Perplexa magnum verba nescioquid tegunt.
effare aperte, quis gravet mentem dolor.

NUTRIX

860 Haud pandit ulli; maesta secretum occulit
statuitque secum ferre quo moritur malum.
iam perge, quaeso, perge: properato est opus.

THESEUS

Reserate clausos regii postes laris.
O socia thalami, sicine adventum viri
865 et expetiti coniugis vultum excipis?
quin ense viduas dexteram atque animum mihi
restituis et te quidquid e vita fugat
expromis?

steps falter. Ah, what a toil it was to head from deepest
Phlegethon to the distant heavens, both to escape death
and to follow Alcides!

What sounds of weeping strike my ears? Explain, someone. Mourning and tears and grief, sad laments on the very
threshold: a fitting reception indeed for a guest from the
underworld.

NURSE

Phaedra is stubbornly resolved on suicide; she disregards
our tears and is bent on death.

THESEUS

What reason does she have for dying? Why die now as her
man returns?

NURSE

That very reason has brought about her imminent death.

THESEUS

These cryptic words conceal some great issue. Speak out
openly: what pain is burdening her mind?

NURSE

She tells no one; in her grief she hides the secret, and is determined to take the fatal trouble with her. Come now,
come, I beg you: you must be quick.

THESEUS

[*To slaves*] Unbar the closed doors of the royal house. [*The
interior scene is revealed, with Phaedra holding Hippolytus' sword*] O consort of my marriage bed, is this how you
respond to your man's arrival, the face of your long-missed
spouse? Why not uncouple your hand from the sword, restore my spirit to me, and explain whatever it is that drives
you from life?

PHAEDRA

Eheu, per tui sceptrum imperi,
magnanime Theseu, perque natorum indolem
870 tuosque reditus perque iam cineres meos,
permitte mortem.

THESEUS

Causa quae cogit mori?

PHAEDRA

Si causa leti dicitur, fructus perit.

THESEUS

Nemo istud alius, me quidem excepto, audiet.

PHAEDRA

Aures pudica coniugis solas timet.

THESEUS

875 Effare: fido pectore arcana occulam.

PHAEDRA

Alium silere quod voles, primus sile.

THESEUS

Leti facultas nulla continget tibi.

PHAEDRA

Mori volenti desse mors numquam potest.

THESEUS

Quod sit luendum morte delictum indica.

PHAEDRA

880 Quod vivo.

THESEUS

Lacrimae nonne te nostrae movent?

PHAEDRA

PHAEDRA

Alas! By your sceptred power, great-souled Theseus, by the promise of our sons, by your own return, and by my ashes soon to be, let me decide on death.

THESEUS

What cause compels your death?

PHAEDRA

If the cause is told, the profit of my death is lost.

THESEUS

No one else will hear it but me.

PHAEDRA

A chaste woman fears her husband's ears above all.

THESEUS

Speak out: I shall hide your secret in my faithful heart.

PHAEDRA

If you want another to keep a secret, first keep it yourself.

THESEUS

You will be given no opportunity for death.

PHAEDRA

If someone wants to die, death is always in reach.

THESEUS

Let me know the offence that needs to be punished by death.

PHAEDRA

The fact that I live.

THESEUS

Do my tears not move you?

SENECA

PHAEDRA
Mors optima est perire lacrimandum suis.

THESEUS
Silere pergit.—verbere ac vinclis anus
altrixque prodet quidquid haec fari abnuit.
Vincite ferro. verberum vis extrahat
885   secreta mentis.

PHAEDRA
Ipsa iam fabor, mane.

THESEUS
Quidnam ora maesta avertis et lacrimas genis
subito coortas veste praetenta obtegis?

PHAEDRA
Te te, creator caelitum, testem invoco,
et te, coruscum lucis aetheriae iubar,
890   ex cuius ortu nostra dependet domus:
temptata precibus restiti; ferro ac minis
non cessit animus: vim tamen corpus tulit.
labem hanc pudoris eluet noster cruor.

THESEUS
Quis, ede, nostri decoris eversor fuit?

PHAEDRA
895   Quem rere minime.

THESEUS
Quis sit audire expeto.

PHAEDRA
Hic dicet ensis, quem tumultu territus
liquit stuprator civium accursum timens.

PHAEDRA

To die mourned by loved ones is the best of deaths.

THESEUS

[*Aside*] She continues to keep silence. Blows and chains
will make the old nurse reveal what this one refuses to tell.
[*To attendants*] Bind her with iron. Violent blows must
root out her mind's secrets.

PHAEDRA

Wait, I shall tell you myself.

THESEUS

Why do you turn your sad face aside, pull your cloak over
it, and hide the tears that suddenly sprang into your eyes?

PHAEDRA

Begetter of the gods, I call on you as witness, and on you,
gleaming rays of heaven's light, from whose rising my family traces its lineage: though beset by his prayers, I resisted;
my spirit did not yield to threats or the sword; but my body
suffered his violence. My blood will wash away this stain on
my chastity.

THESEUS

Tell me, who was the destroyer of my honour?

PHAEDRA

One you would least expect.

THESEUS

I demand to hear who he is.

PHAEDRA

This sword will tell you: frightened by the outcry the rapist
left it, fearing that citizens would gather.

THESEUS

Quod facinus, heu me, cerno? quod monstrum intuor?
regale parvis asperum signis ebur
900 capulo refulget, gentis Aegeae decus.
sed ipse quonam evasit?

PHAEDRA

       Hi trepidum fuga
videre famuli concitum celeri pede.

THESEUS

Pro sancta Pietas, pro gubernator poli
et qui secundum fluctibus regnum moves,
905 unde ista venit generis infandi lues?
hunc Graia tellus aluit an Taurus Scythes
Colchusque Phasis? redit ad auctores genus
stirpemque primam degener sanguis refert.
est prorsus iste gentis armiferae furor,
910 odisse Veneris foedera et castum diu
vulgare populis corpus. o taetrum genus
nullaque victum lege melioris soli!
ferae quoque ipsae Veneris evitant nefas,
generisque leges inscius servat pudor.
915   Ubi vultus ille et ficta maiestas viri
atque habitus horrens, prisca et antiqua appetens,
morumque senium triste et affectus graves?
o vita fallax, abditos sensus geris
animisque pulchram turpibus faciem induis!
920 pudor impudentem celat, audacem quies,
pietas nefandum; vera fallaces probant
simulantque molles dura. silvarum incola

---

900 Aegeae (*spelt* Aegaeae) *Axelson*: Actaeae* *EA*

that wild backwoodsman, chaste, untouched, inexperienced, were you saving yourself for me? Did you decide to
inaugurate your manhood with my bed, with such a crime?
Now I give thanks to the powers above that Antiope fell
by my hand, and that when I descended to the Stygian
caverns I did not leave you your mother.

Run in your flight through unknown, far-off nations!
Though some remote land at the ends of the earth separate
you from me by expanses of Ocean, though you dwell in
the world opposite our feet,[40] though hidden in the furthest retreat after crossing the shuddering realms beneath
the high pole, though placed beyond winter and white
snow after leaving the howling threats of chill Boreas raging behind you: you will be punished for your crimes. I
shall hound you tenaciously in your flight through every
refuge; I shall traverse lands that are distant, closed, inaccessible, remote, trackless; no place will stop me: you know
where I return from. Where weapons cannot be aimed,
there I shall aim prayers. My father the seagod granted
that I could make three wishes he would comply with, and
he invoked the Styx to ratify this gift.

Come, fulfil this grim gift, ruler of the sea! Let Hippolytus not look on the bright daylight any longer; in youth
let him meet the spirits his father angered. Now, my sire,
give your son this abhorrent aid. I would never use up your
divinity's final gift, if great evils were not pressing. Faced
with deep Tartarus and fearsome Dis and the menacing
threats of the infernal king, I held back from using a
prayer. Now keep the promise you pledged. Do you delay,

---

[40] This line alludes to the Antipodes, the following lines to the
land of the Hyperboreans.

genitor, moraris? cur adhuc undae silent?
955 nunc atra ventis nubila impellentibus
subtexe noctem, sidera et caelum eripe,
effunde pontum, vulgus aequoreum cie
fluctusque ab ipso tumidus Oceano voca.

CHORUS

O magna parens, Natura, deum
960 tuque igniferi rector Olympi,
qui sparsa cito sidera mundo
cursusque vagos rapis astrorum
celerique polos cardine versas,
cur tanta tibi cura perennes
965 agitare vias aetheris alti,
ut nunc canae frigora brumae
nudent silvas,
nunc arbustis redeant umbrae,
nunc aestivi colla Leonis
970 Cererem magno fervore coquant
viresque suas temperet annus?
sed cur idem qui tanta regis,
sub quo vasti pondera mundi
librata suos ducunt orbes,
975 hominum nimium securus abes,
non sollicitus prodesse bonis,
nocuisse malis?
Res humanas ordine nullo
Fortuna regit
sparsitque manu munera caeca
980 peiora fovens:

965 vias *EA*: vices *Peiper*

vile lust prevails against the pure,
treachery reigns in the lofty palace;
the commons delight to hand the fasces[41]
to shameful men that they court and hate.
Stern virtue gains
contrary rewards for following the right:
the chaste are plagued with harsh privation,
while adulterers reign, raised up by vice.
How futile is modesty, how false is honour!

ACT 4

But what news does the messenger bring with hurried
steps, his tearful eyes drenching his sorrowful face?

MESSENGER
O hard and bitter lot, o heavy service, why do you call me
to announce an unspeakable fate?

THESEUS
Do not fear to tell boldly of harsh calamities. I have a heart
not unprepared for distress.

MESSENGER
My tongue refuses this sorrow its harrowing utterance.

THESEUS
Disclose the fortune that burdens my shaken house.

MESSENGER
Hippolytus, to my sorrow, lies pitifully dead.

---

[41] This language has strong overtones of a Roman election; the
fasces were the rods symbolising the power of an elected official at
Rome.

THESEUS

Natum parens obisse iam pridem scio;
nunc raptor obiit. mortis effare ordinem.

NUNTIUS

1000 Ut profugus urbem liquit infesto gradu
celerem citatis passibus cursum explicans,
celso sonipedes ocius subigit iugo
et ora frenis domita substrictis ligat.
tum multa secum effatus et patrium solum
1005 abominatus saepe genitorem ciet,
acerque habenis lora permissis quatit:
cum subito vastum tonuit ex alto mare
crevitque in astra. nullus inspirat salo
ventus, quieti nulla pars caeli strepit
1010 placidumque pelagus propria tempestas agit.
non tantus Auster Sicula disturbat freta
nec tam furens Ionius exsurgit sinus
regnante Coro, saxa cum fluctu tremunt
et cana summum spuma Leucaten ferit.
1015 consurgit ingens pontus in vastum aggerem:
1022 latuere rupes numine Epidauri dei
1023 et scelere petrae nobiles Scironides
1024 et quae duobus terra comprimitur fretis.
1017 nec ista ratibus tanta construitur lues:
terris minatur: fluctus haud cursu levi
provolvitur; nescioquid onerato sinu
1020 gravis unda portat. quae novum tellus caput
ostendet astris? Cyclas exoritur nova?
1025 haec dum stupentes quaerimus, totum en mare

1022–24 *transposed after* 1015 *by Fitch*
1025 quaerimus *E*: querimur *A*   totum en *Peiper*: en
totum *EA*

THESEUS

As father, I know my son died long ago; now the rapist has died. Tell the course of his death.

MESSENGER

After he forsook the city with fury in his steps, unfurling a swift course on flying feet, he quickly set his steeds beneath the high yoke, and fastened and curbed their mouths with tightened bridle. Then, talking much to himself and cursing the soil of his fatherland, he invoked his father many times. Wielding the whip vigorously, he gave the horses their head. Then suddenly the sea thundered mightily from its depths and swelled towards the stars. No wind was sweeping the saltwater, and the sky was peaceful, nowhere in uproar; the sea's calm was stirred by a storm all its own. Not so powerfully does the south wind disturb the Straits of Sicily, nor so madly does the Ionian Gulf well up beneath a tyrannous northwester, when rocks shudder under waves, and white foam strikes Leucate's summit. The vast sea rises into a huge mound; it hides the cliffs famed for the power of the Epidaurian god, and the rocks famed for Sciron's crimes, and the land hemmed in by two gulfs.[42] Yet this towering cataclysm is not for ships—it threatens the land: the wave rolls forward apace, a heavy surge bearing something in its burdened womb. What land will show its new face to the stars? Is some Cycladic island rising? While we ask such questions in amazement, behold the

---

[42] The places mentioned lie on the Saronic Gulf. The god is Aesculapius, who had a healing shrine at Epidaurus, on the southwestern coast of the Gulf; Sciron's rocks are on its northern coast; and the land between two gulfs (Saronic and Corinthian) is the Isthmus.

immugit, omnes undique scopuli astrepunt,
1016 tumidumque monstro pelagus in terras ruit.
1027 summum cacumen rorat expulso sale,
spumat vomitque vicibus alternis aquas,
qualis per alta vehitur Oceani freta
1030 fluctum refundens ore physeter capax.
inhorruit concussus undarum globus
solvitque sese et litori invexit malum
maius timore; pontus in terras ruit
suumque monstrum sequitur.

                           Os quassat tremor.
1035 quis habitus ille corporis vasti fuit!
caerulea taurus colla sublimis gerens
erexit altam fronte viridanti iubam.
stant hispidae aures, orbibus varius color,
et quem feri dominator habuisset gregis
1040 et quem sub undis natus: hinc flammam vomunt
oculi, hinc relucent caerula insignes nota.
opima cervix arduos tollit toros
naresque hiulcis haustibus patulae fremunt.
musco tenaci pectus ac palear viret,
1045 longum rubenti spargitur fuco latus;
tum pone tergus ultima in monstrum coit
facies et ingens belua immensam trahit
squamosa partem. talis extremo mari
pistrix citatas sorbet aut frangit rates.
1050   Tremuere terrae, fugit attonitum pecus
passim per agros, nec suos pastor sequi
meminit iuvencos; omnis e saltu fera
diffugit, omnis frigido exsanguis metu
venator horret. solus immunis metus
1055 Hippolytus artis continet frenis equos

whole sea bellows, and all the surrounding cliffs roar back; swelling with a monster, the flood rushes towards the land. Its crest showers a fountain of brine, it foams and spews out water at intervals, just as a whale, journeying through Ocean's deeps, pours out of its mouth the stream it has swallowed. The ball of water shakes, trembles, breaks open, and brings to shore an evil that outdoes fear; the sea rushes onto the land, chasing its own monster.

My lips tremble with fear. What an impression was given by that vast body! A bull, carrying high its dark-blue neck, with a tall crest rising above its greenish brow; ears erect and shaggy; eyes of varying colour, both such as the overlord of a wild herd might have, and such as a seaborn creature: in part the eyes spew flame, in part they gleam with a striking sea-blue quality. The neck full, raising its muscles aloft; the nostrils broad and distended, snorting as he breathes. Chest and dewlap are green with clinging moss, the long flanks daubed with red seaweed. Then the hindparts merge into a monstrous shape—a huge creature trailing an immense scaly appendage. Such is the leviathan in remote seas that swallows or smashes boats under sail.

The earth trembled, everywhere frenzied cattle fled through the fields, and the herdsman took no thought to chase his stock; every wild beast fled from the woodland, every huntsman shuddered, pale with chill fear. Alone undaunted, Hippolytus held the horses on tight reins, and

---

1016 *transposed after* 1026 *by Damsté*

pavidosque notae vocis hortatu ciet.
Est alta ad Argos collibus ruptis via,
vicina tangens spatia suppositi maris;
hic se illa moles acuit atque iras parat.
1060 ut cepit animos seque praetemptans satis
prolusit irae, praepeti cursu evolat,
summam citato vix gradu tangens humum,
et torva currus ante trepidantes stetit.
contra feroci natus insurgens minax
1065 vultu nec ora mutat et magnum intonat:
"Haud frangit animum vanus hic terror meum:
nam mihi paternus vincere est tauros labor."
    Inobsequentes protinus frenis equi
rapuere currum, iamque derrantes via,
1070 quacumque rabidos pavidus evexit furor,
hac ire pergunt seque per scopulos agunt.
at ille, qualis turbido rector mari
ratem retentat, ne det obliquum latus,
et arte fluctum fallit, haud aliter citos
1075 currus gubernat: ora nunc pressis trahit
constricta frenis, terga nunc torto frequens
verbere coercet. sequitur assiduus comes,
nunc aequa carpens spatia, nunc contra obvius
oberrat, omni parte terrorem movens.
1080 non licuit ultra fugere: nam toto obvius
incurrit ore corniger ponti horridus.
tum vero pavida sonipedes mente exciti
imperia solvunt seque luctantur iugo
eripere rectique in pedes iactant onus.
1085   Praeceps in ora fusus implicuit cadens
laqueo tenaci corpus, et quanto magis
pugnat, sequaces hoc magis nodos ligat.

rallied their panic with his encouraging, familiar voice. There is a steep road towards Argos along the broken hills, running close to the reaches of the sea below. Here that colossus whets its anger in preparation. After rousing its mettle and testing itself fully in rehearsal for wrath, it flies forth, fast and direct, scarcely touching the ground's surface with its galloping feet, and halts truculently in front of the panicked team. In response your son rises up with a threatening glare, not changing countenance, and thunders loudly: "This empty terror does not break my spirit, for conquering bulls is a task I inherit from my father."

But straightway the horses, disobedient to the reins, sweep the chariot away. Now, swerving off the road, they head wherever frenzied panic carries their rampage, propelling themselves across the cliffs. But as a helmsman holds a ship steady in turbulent seas, lest it turn broadside, and cheats the waves with his skill, just so he steers the speeding team: now he curbs and drags on their mouths with reins tight, now he controls their backs with repeated use of the coiling whip. He is followed by a constant companion, now keeping equal pace, now whirling around to meet them head-on, bringing terror from every side. Further flight is impossible, for head-on, full in their path, there charges the terrible horned sea-creature. Then indeed the steeds, crazed with fear, reject control and struggle to tear themselves from the yoke; as they rear up, they jettison their burden.

Flung headlong on his face, he catches his body as he falls in a tangling snare. The more he fights, the more he tightens the clinging knots. The beasts sense their mis-

---

1069 currum *EA*: cursum *recc.*

sensere pecudes facinus, et curru levi,
dominante nullo, qua timor iussit ruunt.
1090 talis per auras non suum agnoscens onus
Solique falso creditum indignans diem
Phaethonta currus devium excussit polo.
Late cruentat arva, et inlisum caput
scopulis resultat; auferunt dumi comas
1095 et ora durus pulchra populatur lapis,
peritque multo vulnere infelix decor.
moribunda celeres membra pervolvunt rotae;
tandemque raptum truncus ambusta sude
medium per inguen stipite eiecto tenet;
1100 paulumque domino currus affixo stetit,
haesere biiuges vulnere—et pariter moram
dominumque rumpunt. inde semianimem secant
virgulta, acutis asperi vepres rubis,
omnisque truncus corporis partem tulit.
1105   Errant per agros funebris famuli manus,
[per illa qua distractus Hippolytus loca
longum cruenta tramitem signat nota]
maestaeque domini membra vestigant canes.
necdum dolentum sedulus potuit labor
1110 explere corpus. hocine est formae decus?
qui modo paterni clarus imperii comes
et certus heres siderum fulsit modo,
passim ad supremos ille colligitur rogos
et funeri confertur.

THESEUS
O nimium potens
1115 quanto parentes sanguinis vinclo tenes

deed, and with the chariot lightened and no one ruling them, they rush wherever fear bids. Just so in the sky a team, not recognising its proper burden and indignant that daylight was entrusted to a false Sun, tossed the straying Phaethon out of the heavens. Far and wide he bloodies the countryside; his head smashes against boulders and snaps back; brambles tear away his hair; hard stones ravage his handsome face, and his ill-fated beauty is destroyed by many wounds. The swift wheels roll his dying limbs over and over. At last, as he is dragged along, a tree trunk, charred into a stake, grips him with its stock thrust out, right through his groin. The team stops a moment, with its master impaled; the wound halts the yoked pair. Then they break the delay and with it their master. Now, barely alive, he is cut by the undergrowth of thornbushes bristling with sharp brambles, and every treetrunk takes part of his body.

A funereal band of his servants is wandering through the fields;[43] the sorrowful hounds are tracking their master's limbs. Not yet has the mourners' diligent toil been able to complete his body. Is this the glory of his beauty? He who just now shone starlike, as resplendent companion of his father's power and its certain heir, is now gathered from everywhere for the final pyre and brought together for funeral.

THESEUS

O Nature, all too powerful: how strong the bond of blood with which you hold parents! How we give you allegiance

---

[43] Lines 1106–07 (deleted): "Through those places where the broken Hippolytus marked a long trail with bloody traces."

1092 devium *Axelson*: devio *EA*   1099 eiecto *A*: iecto *E*: erecto *τ*   1106–07 *deleted by Fitch*

Natura! quam te colimus inviti quoque!
occidere volui noxium, amissum fleo.

NUNTIUS
Haud flere honeste quisque quod voluit potest.

THESEUS
Equidem malorum maximum hunc cumulum reor,
1120   si abominanda casus optanda efficit.

NUNTIUS
Et si odia servas, cur madent fletu genae?

THESEUS
Quod interemi, non quod amisi, fleo.

CHORUS
    Quanti casus, heu, magna rotant!
    minor in parvis Fortuna furit
1125   leviusque ferit leviora deus;
    servat placidos obscura quies
    praebetque senes casa securos.
Admota aetheriis culmina sedibus
Euros excipiunt, excipiunt Notos,
1130   insani Boreae minas
      imbriferumque Corum.
Raros patitur fulminis ictus
umida vallis;

1123 heu magna *Axelson*: humana *EA*

538

even against our will! For his guilt I desired to kill him, but now he is lost, I weep.

MESSENGER

A person may not rightfully weep for what he himself desired.

THESEUS

For me, this is the pinnacle of evils, that fortune should make us desire what we detest.

MESSENGER

And if you retain your hatred, why are your cheeks wet with tears?

THESEUS

I weep for destroying him, not for losing him.[44]

CHORUS

What mighty disasters toss the mighty!
Fortune rages less against lesser targets,
god's blows are weak against the weak.
Humble retirement brings peace and safety,
and a cottage bestows old age and calm.
Peaks lifted close to heaven's seat
catch easterly winds and southerly winds,
the crazy norther's threats
and the northwester's storms.
Rarely are the blows of lightning felt
by the misty valley;

---

[44] The messenger's criticisms force Theseus to define his grief more accurately than in 1117: it is not for the death of his son, whom he regards as lost some time ago (998), but for his own role as father in destroying him.

tremuit telo Iovis altisoni
Caucasus ingens
1135 Phrygiumque nemus matris Cybeles.
metuens caelo Iuppiter alto
vicina petit.
non capit umquam magnos motus
humilis tecti plebeia domus;
1140 circa regna tonat.

Volat ambiguis mobilis alis
hora, nec ulli
praestat velox Fortuna fidem.
hic qui clari sidera mundi
1145 nitidumque diem ⟨tandem repetît⟩
morte relicta
luget maestos tristis reditus
ipsoque magis flebile Averno
sedis patriae videt hospitium.

Pallas Actaeae veneranda genti,
1150 quod tuus caelum superosque Theseus
spectat et fugit Stygias paludes,
casta nil debes patruo rapaci:
constat inferno numerus tyranno.

1145 *lacuna located after* 1145ᵃ *by Zwierlein (after* 1144ᵃ *by Leo); supplement by Fitch*

but the bolt of Jove high-thundering staggers
the mighty Caucasus
and Mother Cybele's Phrygian grove.
Jove in fear for the lofty heaven
attacks its neighbours.
Great upheavals are never felt
by a commoner's house with its lowly roof;
    but around thrones it thunders.

The shifting hour flies on inconstant
wings, and hasty
Fortune pledges her faith to none.
This man, with the stars of shining heaven
and the radiant day ⟨at last regained⟩
and death behind him,
mourns in sorrow his sad return;
more full of tears than Avernus itself
is the welcome he sees from the house of his
    fathers.

Pallas, to whom belongs worship from the people of
    Athens,
chaste goddess, you owe your rapacious uncle no debt
for the fact that your Theseus beholds the sight of the
    heavens
and the upper world, and escaped the Stygian marshes:
for the tyrant below the sum total remains unchanged.[45]

45 Theseus has been replaced by Hippolytus.

Quae vox ab altis flebilis tectis sonat
1155 strictoque vecors Phaedra quid ferro parat?

THESEUS

Quis te dolore percitam instigat furor?
quid ensis iste quidve vociferatio
planctusque supra corpus invisum volunt?

PHAEDRA

Me me, profundi saeve dominator freti,
1160 invade, et in me monstra caerulei maris
emitte, quidquid intimo Tethys sinu
extrema gestat, quidquid Oceanus vagis
complexus undis ultimo fluctu tegit.
O dure Theseu semper, o numquam tuis
1165 tuto reverse! natus et genitor nece
reditus tuos luere; pervertis domum
amore semper coniugum aut odio nocens.
    Hippolyte, tales intuor vultus tuos
talesque feci? membra quis saevus Sinis
1170 aut quis Procrustes sparsit aut quis Cresius,
Daedalea vasto claustra mugitu replens,
taurus biformis ore cornigero ferox
divulsit? heu me, quo tuus fugit decor
oculique nostrum sidus? exanimis iaces?
1175 ades parumper verbaque exaudi mea—
nil turpe loquimur. hac manu poenas tibi
solvam et nefando pectori ferrum inseram,
animaque Phaedram pariter ac scelere exuam—
et te per undas perque Tartareos lacus,

---

[46] The father was Aegeus, who killed himself for grief because

PHAEDRA

ACT 5

What voice of sorrow sounds from the lofty palace? What is
Phaedra's insane purpose with the drawn sword?

THESEUS

What madness goads you in this frenzy of grief? What is
the meaning of this sword, this outcry, this self-bruising
over a body you hate?

PHAEDRA

Me, assault me, you cruel overlord of ocean's depths, send
out against me the dark-blue sea's monsters, all that remot-
est Tethys bears in her inmost recess, all that ocean enfolds
in its wandering waters and hides in its furthest flood. O
ever brutal Theseus, never returning to your family without harm! Your son and father have paid with death for
your returns; you ruin your home, destructive always,
whether through love or hatred of your wives.[46]

Hippolytus, is this how I see your face—how I have
made it? What savage Sinis, what Procrustes has scattered
your limbs? What Cretan bull, filling his Daedalean prison
with tremendous bellowing, ferocious biformed creature
with horned face, has torn you apart? Ah me, where has
your beauty fled, and your eyes, my stars? Do you lie lifeless? Be with me just briefly, hear out my words: I speak no
dishonour. With this hand I shall make you amends, thrust
the sword into my evil breast, and release Phaedra from
life and crime at one moment—and shall follow you madly
through the waters and lakes of Tartarus, through Styx and

Theseus' ship displayed black sails as it returned from Crete; the
wife whom Theseus hated, and executed, was Antiope.

543

1180 per Styga, per amnes igneos amens sequar.
placemus umbras: capitis exuvias cape
laceraeque frontis accipe abscisam comam.
non licuit animos iungere, at certe licet
iunxisse fata.

              Morere, si casta es, viro;
1185 si incesta, amori. coniugis thalamos petam
tanto impiatos facinore? hoc derat nefas,
ut vindicato sancta fruereris toro.
o mors amoris una sedamen mali,
o mors pudoris maximum laesi decus,
1190 confugimus ad te: pande placatos sinus.

    Audite, Athenae, tuque, funesta pater
peior noverca: falsa memoravi et nefas,
quod ipsa demens pectore insano hauseram,
mentita finxi. vana punisti pater,
1195 iuvenisque castus crimine incesto iacet,
pudicus, insons—recipe iam mores tuos.
mucrone pectus impium iusto patet
cruorque sancto solvit inferias viro.

    Quid facere rapto debeas nato parens,
1200 disce a noverca: condere Acherontis plagis.

THESEUS

Pallidi fauces Averni vosque, Taenarii specus,
unda miseris grata Lethes vosque, torpentes lacus,
impium rapite atque mersum premite perpetuis malis.
nunc adeste, saeva ponti monstra, nunc vasti maris,

1199–1200 *attributed to Phaedra by A, to Theseus by E*
1204 vasti maris *Axelson*: vastum mare *EA*

rivers of fire. I must pacify your shade; take from my head
these spoils, accept this hair cut from my wounded brow.
We could not unite our spirits, but at least we can unite our
deaths.

[*To herself*] Die—if you are chaste, for your husband; if
unchaste, for your love. Shall I seek my husband's marriage
chamber, which is defiled by such an unnatural crime?
This outrage was missing, for you to enjoy his bed as if it
were avenged and you blameless. O death, sole relief from
evil love, o death, greatest glory for blighted honour, I flee
to you: open wide your merciful arms.

Listen, Athens, and you, father worse than a murderous
stepmother: I told a false story, and alleged with lies the
outrage that I myself had madly dwelt on in my own crazed
breast. As father you have punished in vain, and a chaste
young man lies dead on an unchaste charge, though pure
and innocent—[*to Hippolytus*] now receive back your true
character. My unnatural breast is justly opened by the
sword, and my blood pays funeral offerings to a righteous
man.

What you as father must do now your son is stolen,
learn from his stepmother: hide in the regions of Acheron.

THESEUS

Gaping jaws of pale Avernus, and you Taenarian caves,
waters of Lethe that soothe distress, and you lethargic
    pools,
drag this unnatural man below, crush him with endless
    pain!
Now, you cruel sea monsters, come, come from the
    mighty main,

1205 ultimo quodcumque Proteus aequorum abscondit sinu,
meque ovantem scelere tanto rapite in altos gurgites.
Tuque semper, genitor, irae facilis assensor meae:
morte facili dignus haud sum qui nova natum nece
segregem sparsi per agros quique, dum falsum nefas
1210 exequor vindex severus, incidi in verum scelus.
sidera et manes et undas scelere complevi meo:
amplius sors nulla restat; regna me norunt tria.

In hoc redîmus? patuit ad caelum via,
bina ut viderem funera et geminam necem,
1215 caelebs et orbus funebres una face
ut concremarem prolis ac thalami rogos?
donator atrae lucis, Alcide, tuum
Diti remitte munus; ereptos mihi
restitue manes.—impius frustra invoco
1220 mortem relictam. crudus et leti artifex,
exitia machinatus insolita effera,
nunc tibimet ipse iusta supplicia irroga.
pinus coacto vertice attingens humum
caelo remissum findat in geminas trabes,
1225 mittarve praeceps saxa per Scironia?
graviora vidi, quae pati clausos iubet

---

47 A reference to the three lots by which Jupiter, Neptune, and
Dis divided the cosmos among themselves.

48 "Your gift" is Theseus himself, released as a gift from Dis to
Hercules (*Herc* 806).   49 Chiefly as his son's killer: *impius*
denotes transgression against family members ("unnatural") and
gods.   50 The method of murder employed by Sinis, and
used on its perpetrator by Theseus. Theseus also served Sciron as
he had served others.

every creature that Proteus hides in ocean's farthest
gulfs,
and drag me down to your swirling depths, who triumph
in such a crime.
And you my father, who always comply so easily with my
wrath:
I do not deserve an easy death, who caused my son's
strange killing
scattered in pieces throughout the fields, and who, while
I pursued
a fictitious wrong with vengeance stern, fell into genuine
crime.
My crimes have now pervaded stars and underworld and
sea.
No other allotted portion remains;[47] I am known in all
three realms.

Did I return for this? Was a path opened to the upper
world so that I could see two deaths, a double slaughter—
so that I, bereaved and widowed, could ignite with one
torch the funeral pyres of child and spouse? Giver of light
that is darkness, Alcides, return your gift to Dis;[48] restore
to me the world of shades you have stolen from me. But as
a godless man[49] I pray in vain for death, which I abandoned. You man of blood, you craftsman of death, who
contrived bizarre, barbaric destructions, now inflict just
punishments on yourself. Shall pine trees, forced down to
touch the ground with their tips, split me between their
two trunks when released to the sky,[50] or shall I hurl myself
over the Scironian cliffs? I have seen more grievous things,

Phlegethon nocentes igneo cingens vado.
quae poena memet maneat et sedes, scio.
umbrae nocentes, cedite et cervicibus
1230 his, his repositum degravet fessas manus
saxum, seni perennis Aeolio labor;
me ludat amnis ora vicina alluens;
vultur relicto transvolet Tityo ferus
meumque poenae semper accrescat iecur.
1235 et tu mei requiesce Pirithoi pater:
haec incitatis membra turbinibus ferat
nusquam resistens orbe revoluto rota.
Dehisce tellus, recipe me dirum chaos,
recipe, haec ad umbras iustior nobis via est:
1240 natum sequor. ne metue qui manes regis:
casti venimus. recipe me aeterna domo
non exiturum.—non movent divos preces;
at, si rogarem scelera, quam proni forent!

CHORUS
Theseu, querelis tempus aeternum manet:
1245 nunc iusta nato solve et absconde ocius
dispersa foede membra laniatu effero.

THESEUS
Huc, huc, reliquias vehite cari corporis
pondusque et artus temere congestos date.
Hippolytus hic est? crimen agnosco meum:
1250 ego te peremi. neu nocens tantum semel
solusve fierem, facinus ausurus parens
patrem advocavi. munere en patrio fruor.
o triste fractis orbitas annis malum!

that Phlegethon forces the guilty to suffer, confining and encircling them with its stream of fire. What punishment and what abode awaits me, I know. You guilty shades, make way. Let the rock be repositioned on *this* neck and burden my weary hands, the ancient Aeolid's perennial task. Let *me* be mocked by the river that flows close to one's lips.[51] Let the savage vulture fly over to me, abandoning Tityos, and let my liver grow constantly for torment. And you take rest, father of my own Pirithous;[52] let *these* limbs be carried in a whirling gyre on the revolving orbit of the never ceasing wheel. Gape open, earth; take me in, dread Chaos, take me, this time my journey to the shades is more righteous: it is my son I follow. Fear not, you lord of the ghosts: I come with chaste purpose. Take me into that everlasting home, never to leave.

My prayers do not move the gods. But if I were asking for crimes, how eager they would be!

CHORUS LEADER

For laments, Theseus, infinite time remains; now pay your son due rites, and quickly bury his limbs, so foully scattered and savagely torn.

THESEUS

Here, carry here the remains of that dear body; that mass of limbs heaped randomly together, give me them. Is this Hippolytus? I recognise my crime: it was I that killed you. And lest I should incur guilt just once or just for myself, as a parent embarking on crime I invoked my father. See, I enjoy a father's boon. How bitter an evil is bereavement in

---

[51] The rock is Sisyphus' punishment, the elusive water Tantalus'.   [52] His father is Ixion.

complectere artus, quodque de nato est super,
1255   miserande, maesto pectore incumbens fove.
     Disiecta, genitor, membra laceri corporis
in ordinem dispone, et errantes loco
restitue partes. fortis hic dextrae locus,
hic laeva frenis docta moderandis manus
1260   ponenda: laevi lateris agnosco notas.
quam magna lacrimis pars adhuc nostris abest!
durate trepidae lugubri officio manus,
fletusque largos sistite arentes genae,
dum membra nato genitor adnumerat suo
1265   corpusque fingit. hoc quid est forma carens
et turpe, multo vulnere abruptum undique?
quae pars tui sit dubito, sed pars est tui:
hic, hic repone, non suo, at vacuo loco.
haecne illa facies igne sidereo nitens,
1270   animosa flectens lumina? huc cecidit decor?
o dira fata, numinum o saevus favor!
sic ad parentem natus ex voto redit?
En haec suprema dona genitoris cape,
saepe efferendus; interim haec ignes ferant.
1275   Patefacite acerbam caede funesta domum;
Mopsopia claris tota lamentis sonet.
vos apparate regii flammam rogi;
at vos per agros corporis partes vagas
inquirite.—istam terra defossam premat,
1280   gravisque tellus impio capiti incubet.

    1270 animosa *Watt*: inimica *EA*

my broken years! Embrace his limbs, pitiable man, kneel over him and enfold in your sad bosom all that remains of your son.

Arrange in order, father, his torn body's sundered limbs, put back in place the straying parts. This is the place for his strong right hand; here must be set his left hand, skilled in controlling the reins— I recognise the signs of his left side. How great the part still lacking for my tears! Trembling hands, be firm for this sad service; eyes, be dry, check your copious tears, while the father is portioning out limbs to his son and fashioning his body. What is this ugly formless thing, that multiple wounds have severed on every side? What part it may be I am uncertain, but it is part of you. Here, set it down here, not in its proper place, but in an empty place. Is this the face that shone with star-like fire, and directed a spirited gaze? Has his beauty fallen to this? O dire fate, o cruel favour of the gods! Is this how son comes back to father in answer to his prayer?

See, receive these final gifts from your father. Repeated burial will be needed; meanwhile let the fire take these things.

[*To groups of attendants*] Throw open the house, soured with death's gore; let the whole of Mopsopus' land resound with clear laments. You, make ready the royal pyre's flames; but you, search through the fields for parts of his body astray.

As for her, may earth crush her after burial, and soil lie heavy on that unnatural being.